GUN-RUNNERS

Jackson Cole

GUNSMOKE

First published in the US by Pyramid Books

This hardback edition 2013
by AudioGO Ltd
by arrangement with
Golden West Literary Agency

ISBN 978 1 471 32131 3

British Library Cataloguing in Publication Data available.

Printed and bound in Great Britain by
MPG Books Group Limited

Prologue

THREE men dreamed of wealth and power. Two, seated in a dimly lighted room in the border town of San Rosita, conversed earnestly in low tones. The third, lithe, sinewy, dark of face, with glittering black eyes and lank black hair, furtively forded the shallow Rio Grande and rode northward under the bright stars of Texas.

He glanced repeatedly to right and left and scanned the trail ahead. Riding slowly, ever watchful, he still did not see the silent figure that slipped along in the shadow just out of sight of the trail, a tireless figure that easily paced the steadily jogging horse.

In the dusky cabin room, lighted by but a single low-turned lamp, the two men spoke in guarded tones, despite shuttered windows and closed doors. One was tall and broad of shoulder. The other hunched grotesquely in his chair, the smoking lamp, behind and slightly to one side of him, casting his distorted shadow across the warped board floor.

From time to time the tall man glanced impatiently toward the door which he faced.

"He'd oughta be here any minute now," he growled. "Late now. Wonder if anythin's happened to him? He knows we're takin' a big chance, gettin' t'gether this way. Hadn't oughta keep us waitin'."

The other nodded, and raised his head suddenly at a slight sound outside the cabin. The other tensed, his eyes fastened on the door. The hands of both dropped out of sight beneath the table. Then both grunted with relief as the door swung outward on silent hinges and a dark, lithe man stepped carefully into the room lifting his booted feet high and setting them down gently before he turned to draw the door shut behind him.

"Bolt it!" the tall man shot at him. The newcomer nodded and slipped the rusty bolt under its rusty hasp. Drawing a third chair to the table, he sat down.

Young Dick Webb, Texas Ranger, slept lightly in his little room over the livery stable. Hardly had the echoes of a knock at the door died away before he was on his feet and slipping quietly across the room. As his hand reached for the knob, the knock was repeated. Webb's eyes snapped with excitement as he slipped the bolt and swung the door wide.

A sinewy, dark-faced little man slipped into the room and spoke in liquid Spanish—

"*He* crossed the river tonight."

"Cartina, you mean? Cartina, the bandit?" exclaimed Webb. "Where'd he go?"

"He is here," replied the other imperturbably.

"Here in San Rosita!"

"*Si!* He entered the old cabin that sits in the shadow of the bluff. A light burned within the cabin, and there were men inside. I saw before the door closed."

Dick Webb was hurriedly drawing on his clothes. He buckled his heavy cartridge belt into place with a snap, drew his Colt from its holster and slipped it back again, assuring himself that the action was smooth and free. The little man watched with beady eyes. Webb's face worked with eagerness.

"The chance I've been waiting for!" he exulted. "The chance to catch Cartina on this side the Line. Pancho, you're making no mistake about this, I hope."

The little Yaqui tracker grunted.

"Meestake the man who slew father and mother?" he asked in broken English. "*Señor,* that ees not likely. Pancho knows! Pancho himself would have slain thees night, had not Pancho promised the tall *señor,* his friend. Pancho forgets not the great favor, the kindness."

"You've more than paid back the little thing I was able to do for you, Pancho," Webb declared earnestly. "This means one helluva lot to me, who's just got into the Rangers. Any

6

man in the outfit would give his right arm to bag Cartina; and here's where I get him!"

He slapped his wide-brimmed hat onto his head and strode to the door.

"I go also?" questioned Pancho. "There is more than one?"

Webb shook his head. "No Pancho," he said, "I think I can make out alone. You keep out of sight. The fact that nobody knows you're tied up with me is what makes you so valuable. If you went with me, it would tip your hand. You wait here for me."

Pancho said no more, but his dark countenance voiced silent disapproval. However, as the door closed, he squatted on his heels and rolled a cigarette with slender, nimble fingers.

It was less than three minutes' fast walk from the livery stable to the ramshackle old cabin by the bluff. The cabin, originally built by a wandering prospector, had long been deserted. It was seldom visited, even by children, and never at night. Crouched in the shadow of the steep bluff that overhung the trail, young Dick Webb surveyed it with eager eyes.

As he had said, Webb was new to the Rangers, and he was anxious to distinguish himself. He had been sent to San Rosita because of the raidings and killings of this very Pedro Cartina, the Mexican bandit, leader of a powerful and utterly merciless outfit. Cartina had defied the local authorities on both sides of the Line and even had routed a detachment of *El Presidente's rurales,* the efficient Mexican mounted police, which had been sent against him. The capture, lone-handed, of Cartina would be a feather in the cap of the oldest veteran of the Rangers. It would be a priceless boon to a recruit, the ink on whose commission was hardly dry.

Cautiously, Webb circled the cabin. He noted a front and rear door. It would not do to wait for Cartina to leave the shelter of the shack, for it was impossible to watch both doors at once and the Ranger had no way of knowing which the bandit would use. Cartina's horse was nowhere in sight, or Webb would have waited beside it. There was but one thing to do—tackle the cabin itself. Loosening his gun in its holster,

Webb glided toward the front door. It opened outward, he saw, and doubtless was bolted on the inside.

Dick Webb was a big man and extraordinarily powerful. He had huge shoulders and muscle-packed arms. He saw that it was possible to slip his thick fingers between the warped door and the jamb, which it fitted imperfectly.

To do so was the work of an instant. With a mighty wrench he ripped the bolt screws from the wood and flung the door wide open. Gun in hand he leaped forward, and sprawled with a crash on the cabin floor, the Colt clattering across the room. A rope had been stretched across the doorway, ankle-high.

Webb rolled over on his side as the cabin seemed to fairly explode with the roar of six-shooters. He never had a chance. He died sprawled on the floor, his body battered and broken by bullets.

The bandit Cartina hissed words through the smoke.

"Out, *pronto!* Someone will have heard! Out, and away! We are agreed! Each knows what he is to do! Out!"

Boots clattered over the boards. The tall man and the Mexican vanished amid the shadows. The third man whisked the ponderous table from the floor as if it were made of straw and hurled it at the guttering bracket lamp. There was a crashing of glass and hot oil spattered the floor. Flame flickered for an instant, then snuffed out in a cloud of evil smelling smoke. The man, seeing the failure of his plan for burning the cabin and thereby destroying all evidence of the killing, growled a curse and stumbled after his companions. A moment later fast hoofs drummed southward toward the Rio Grande.

Sheriff Branch Horton shipped the body of Dick Webb to Ranger headquarters at Presidio.

". . . . and can't tell how it happened," the sheriff concluded his report. "Folks up the trail heard the shooting and reported it. All I could find was some cigarette butts the kind a Mex smokes—and horse tracks leading toward the river."

8

Stern old Captain Brooks had notions of his own, however. He made bitter exclamation and chalked up another murder against Pedro Cartina or some one of his outfit. He noted a peculiarity of the wounds in Webb's bullet riddled body.

"Not much to go on," he muttered to himself, "but it might mean something."

And the sardonic Gods of the Hills, looking down at the ant-like activities beneath their mountain tops, chuckled to themselves and warped another thread into the grim web that Death and Destiny were weaving back and forth across the silvery river.

Night over the Tamarra Valley, with the bright stars of Texas flaming like beacon lights on the towering crests of the gaunt Tamarra Hills. A lonely wind whispering through the blue grasses, and the Rio Grande a lovely silver mystery in the moonlight.

All the banks of the silver river were the purple pools of ragged-edged shadow, which marked the dense clusters of black willow, interlaced with scraggly button-bush. The hardy button-bush ventered even into the shallow water and seemed to reach tentative branches toward the dim Mexican shore. Welcoming branches, perhaps, extending an invitation to the moving shadows that flowed almost soundlessly into the murmuring water, and forged steadily toward the inquisitive button-bush and the willow screen.

The moonlight showed swarthy faces, lean sinewy bodies and the blue-gray glint of rifle barrels. Under the men and their guns were the blurry forms of tough little mountain mustangs with shaggy heads and dainty goat-hoofs. Five minutes later, the soft rustling and crackling among the willows ceased and those swift little hoofs drummed over the rolling rangeland of the Tamarra.

The gibbous moon swung low over the Tamarra Hills, faltered, seemed to hesitate and then slowly sank behind the glowering crags. For a moment the hill crests were outlined, grim and forbidding, against the wan afterglow. Then they

9

softened to nebulous tracings on the star-flecked velvet of the sky.

Under that velvety, silver-jeweled sky, the great Slash K trail herd drowsed peacefully. The two night hawks riding herd silently blessed the docility of their long-horned charges. There was not a faint flicker of lightning along the horizon or a far distant mutter of thunder to disturb the tranquillity of the cattle. Stomachs full of sun-sweet grasses of the great valley, the great beasts chewed ruminative cuds and allowed cattle-dreams to move sluggishly through their furry-edged minds.

The two cowboys, *their* stomachs full of steak, hot biscuits, sugary molasses, and other things equally delectable to puncher appetites, also drowsed comfortably in their saddles, their even-paced ponies moving slowly around the herd.

Beside the chuck wagon, the other Slash K punchers slept soundly, with nothing to disturb their slumbers. Nothing while the golden stars turned silver with the first faint kiss of the dawn.

And then—"lightning" flashed, "thunder" rolled and shrieking "rain" spattered the sleeping camp. But the lightning was the spurting fire from the black muzzles of unseen rifles, the thunder was the crash of the reports and the rain was a leaden rain of death.

The Slash K punchers by the chuck wagon died in their blood-sodden blankets—died without awakening from their sleep.

The two night hawks also went down under that first withering blast of fire, one drilled dead center with only a single spasmodic twitch left in his long body after it thudded to the ground. The other, crashing through a tangled clump of brush, came to rest with his bleeding head jammed against the gnarled roots, the low growing branches completely hiding him from view.

Silent and motionless he lay, while the band of swarthy-faced, yelling fiends got the great herd into motion and sent it thundering toward the Rio Grande. Dizzy, shaking, he crawled forth as the clamor dimmed into the distance. A stumbling run to the bloody shambles that had been the camp quickly showed

10

that he was the sole survivor of the raid. As the first light of dawn glowed softly over the crest of the eastern peaks, he caught a horse that had been overlooked, managed to crawl onto its bare back and set out for Presidio, where he knew there was a Ranger post. The sun was hardly an hour high before a compact body of Rangers was riding with loose rein and busy spur toward the spot where the silver band of the river marked the Texas Border.

"What are we going to do if we don't catch up with 'em before we reach the river?" a fresh-faced young Ranger asked of the tall, silent man who rode a splendid golden sorrel and led the troop. "Did Cap'n Brooks say anything about us crossing the river, Hatfield?" he added.

The tall leader turned slightly in his saddle and favored the young Ranger with a level glance from his gray eyes. His lean, bronzed face was stern but there was a slight twinkle of humor in the strangely colored eyes.

"Well," he drawled, "he didn't say anything about us *not* crossing."

A murmur of approbation greeted the reply. The Rangers straightened in their saddle.

"Cap'n McDowell did it in the old days," exclaimed one. "Brought his man back, too. We're with you, Jim. Whatever you say goes."

The man whom a taciturn old Lieutenant of Rangers had named the Lone Wolf, smiled at their enthusiasm, and that smile wrought a singular change in his stern face. His wide mouth quirked at the corners, his even teeth flashed white against his bronzed cheeks and his eyes grew sunny. The smile was fleeting as a shadow at sunset, however, and an instant later the mouth was a hard line and the eyes were as coldly gray as a snow-burdened wind sweeping under a leaden sky. Directly ahead was the silver shimmer of the Rio Grande, and beyond the wide river a rolling dust cloud fogged the clear crystal of the morning.

A buzz of exultation arose.

"It's them" exclaimed the young Ranger, "and they're on the other side of the river!"

11

Hatfield glanced to right and left.

"I understand there's a ford right over by those cottonwoods," he remarked casually, swerving his tall sorrel.

The Rangers followed. In another moment they were surging through the shallow waters of the ford.

Once across the river, they gained rapidly on the scurrying dust cloud. Soon they were able to make out the undulating line of the herd. To right and left were riders who urged the tired cattle to greater effort. Hatfield's dark brows drew together as he estimated their number.

"Must be nearly a hundred of them," he muttered. "This is a pretty ambitious outfit. It must be Cartina, himself."

An angry hum arose at mention of the bandit-revolutionary's name. There was not a man of the outfit but who had his feud with the snaky-eyed, swarthy Cartina whose ruthless cruelty was a byword along the Border. Time after time the Mexican raider had swooped down onto Texas soil, left a line of robbery, arson and murder in his wake and dashed back across the river and into the mountains before organized pursuit could catch up with him and mete out the justice of the frontier.

The bandit was uncannily skillful in timing his raids and picking spots unguarded at the moment. The Tamarra Valley lived in terror of the clatter of his horses' hoofs and the thunder of his guns. Usually he operated toward the west end of the valley—seldom indeed did he come so far east as the scene of his present raid: it was too near the temporary Ranger post at Presidio. Doubtless the temptation of the great Slash K trail herd had proven too great.

"The devil's got brains," was the general verdict of the valley —"Brains and nerve, and no heart."

Jim Hatfield had caused silent old Captain Brooks to knit his white brows thoughtfully just a few days before.

"Uh-huh," Hatfield remarked, "he's got nerve—that's sure and certain, but brains? Maybe, and then again, maybe the brains belong to *somebody else!*"

Swiftly the Ranger troop closed the distance. Puffs of smoke from the dark figures riding beside the herd, and the whine of bullets, told them they were observed. Hatfield eyed the dust cloud thoughtfully.

"Thre's too many of them for us to tackle head on, boys," was his verdict. "Hold back a bit and let's see what a little fancy shooting will do."

It did plenty! Saddles began to empty once the Rangers opened fire. The shrewd Hatfield gave another order—

"Hold back a bit more. I think our guns have got a longer range than theirs."

The order was obeyed and the results were immediate and salutary. Several more raiders were hit and return bullets kicked up puffs of dust yards in front of the troops. There was a wild milling among the Mexicans, a frantic waving of arms and a general disposition to seek shelter behind the terrified herd. Then order came out of chaos.

Hatfield saw a tall figure ride forward, another slighter one following closely; then the Mexicans stormed forward in a straggling body. They closed the distance quickly and bullets began whining about the Rangers. Hatfield immediately gave orders for retreat. The Rangers, on fresher horses, outdistanced the raiders, who finally halted and appeared to hold a conference. A moment later the two tall leaders detached themselves from the main body and rode away at a sharp angle. Hatfield watched them go, his eyes narrowing.

"That won't do," he told his men. "Those two are going for help. If they get it, they'll cut in behind us and get us between two fires; and that's liable to be uncomfortable.

"Haskins," he told a lean, grizzled Ranger, "you take charge of things. Keep after the herd and drive those horned toads off, if you can. If you get them on the run, turn the herd and head it back toward the river. I'll light out after those other two. Old Goldy won't have any trouble running them down. So long."

He spoke to the sorrel and crashed away in pursuit of the fleeing pair. As he had predicted, the tall golden horse gained steadily.

The pair were well mounted, however, and the bellowing

13

herd was out of sight before he got in rifle range of the quarry. He could still hear the battle that was sweeping south, faintly crackling like dry sticks breaking or a winter fire popping.

"The boys are sure keeping them occupied," he chuckled, loosening his heavy Winchester in its scabbard.

Another ten minutes of hard riding and he was within shooting distance of the fleeing pair. His face set in grim lines, he reached for the rifle.

And then, the malignant Hill Gods decided to take a hand in this grim game whose stake was death. The flying sorrel put a foot into a badger hole, and got it out just in time to save himself a broken leg.

Not in time, however, to escape a prodigious tumble. Down he went, turned a complete somersault, rolled over and staggered to his feet, blowing and snorting. His rider lay where he had been thrown, silent, motionless, arms widespread, face to the sky.

The fleeing bandits, glancing over their shoulders from time to time, saw the mishap. They pulled their horses to a halt, conferred a moment and then raced back to the fallen man. The sorrel saw them coming and trotted away, pausing at the edge of a grove. One flung a rifle and slapped a shot at the golden horse. The slug came close and Goldy, who had been shot at before and knew what to do, went away from there. The grove swallowed him up before the outlaw could fire again.

"Leave him be," growled the taller of the two. "We ain't got no time to fool with a stray cayuse."

Tense, watchful, guns ready for instant use, they approached the fallen Ranger. The slighter of the two, a sinewy, swarthy-faced man with snaky black eyes, slowly raised his rifle until his dark cheek snugged against the stock. His evil eyes glanced along the sights and drew a bead on the Ranger's breast. His companion reached out a big hand and shoved the rifle barrel aside.

"Wait," he rasped, "that's too easy! I got a better notion. Those meddlin' Rangers need a real lesson. We'll give 'em somethin' to think about when they come lookin' for this guy. Lay holt of him and help me get him up in front of me. I

14

know this section and a little ways ahead there's jest what we need. Wait. I ain't takin' no chances."

Drawing a black handkerchief from his pocket, he bound it about the lower portion of his face. When his broad-brimmed hat was pulled low, little could be seen but the glint of eyes in the hat brim's shadow.

Together they got the Ranger's limp form across the horse's back. For another mile they rode swiftly, paralleling the grove. Neither saw the golden sorrel pacing them in the shadow of the trees. When they halted at a sandy open space, the sorrel halted also, still under cover, and watching with great liquid wondering eyes all that went on.

He saw one of the outlaws cut four pegs from a stunted piñon pine that grew near the edge of the grove. He watched the pegs driven deep into the earth about a low mound. Then he saw the motionless form of his master stretched over the mound, his wrists and ankles firmly bound to the pegs with rawhide thongs taken from a saddlebag. Goldy did not know what it was all about, but he felt that something was very much wrong.

Jim Hatfield *knew* something was very much wrong when, a few minutes later, he regained consciousness from the shock of water being dashed into his face. He opened his eyes and blinked at the sun washed blue sky into which he was staring. His head ached and his whole body felt sore. About his wrists and neck was an unpleasant crawling sensation. He tried to jerk his hands down from their strained position and realized that they were firmly bound. He turned his head at the sound of a rasping chuckle.

Standing nearby, staring down at him were two men. One was slim and sinewy, swarthy of face, black of eye. The other, taller and broader than the first, was so masked by a black handkerchief and low drawn hat, the Ranger could make nothing of his face.

The tall man spoke, in a muffled, unnatural voice.

"Hope you and the ants have a nice time t'gether, feller," he said. "Mebbe yore Ranger pals will get here while they's still a little left of yuh, but it's sorta uncertain. The ants seem kinda hungry and they'd oughta get busy 'fore long. Yeah, yuh oughta have a nice time, pertickler when a ant runs in one empty eye socket and out the other, and yuh're still alive and kickin'. I've seed it happen 'fore now. Well, *adios*. Fellers that mess in Pedro Cartina's affairs usually wish they hadn't. Yuh won't be the fust."

The dark-faced man chuckled and turned to his horse, which was standing nearby. The other did not chuckle. He glared down at the Ranger with burning, hate-filled eyes for a moment. Then his glance faltered, turned aside from the Ranger's answering stare, came back, and wavered away once more. Growling curses back of the mask, he strode forward, kicked the prostrate man viciously and then whirled to join his companion. A moment later hoofs clicked away into the distance.

High in the sun-golden sky, a black shape whirled and hovered. Another joined it, and another, and another. They planed lower, staring with telescopic eyes that could see the ants streaming from the disrupted hill. Stared, and croaked dismally. The vultures knew that when the ants had finished, little would be left for them, and even their cold courage shrank away from the vicious little killers of the dark tunnels and passages underground.

For long moments Jim Hatfield lay staring into the hot sky. Despite the sunlight he felt cold, cold with a horror that left his body clammily moist and the hair prickling at the back of his neck. There are many ways in which a man may die, but few so frightful as being slowly eaten alive by the voracious ants. Hatfield had seen what was left of victims who had endured the torture of the ants and died screaming an agonized welcome to death.

With all his strength he tugged at the unyielding rawhide, cutting his wrists cruelly. Already he could feel the slow crawl of the questing insects, as yet merely curious as to what was this monster who had crushed their hill. Soon, he knew, they would scent blood and begin their carnage. Panting with effort he relaxed his straining muscles, his mind racing at top speed,

16

seeking for the avenue of escape that did not exist. He writhed at the first stinging bite. His wrists were bleeding and the scent of the fresh blood was maddening the ants.

He strained his ears to a sound that came to him along the ground and for a moment a wild thrill of joy coursed through his veins. The sound was the beat of hoofs. Perhaps his companions, sensing his danger, were hurrying to the rescue. Then a plaintive whinny sounded and he realized the source of the hoof beats. It was the sorrel, coming to his master, perplexed at his strange position.

For a moment the pang of destroyed hope left the Ranger sick and weak. With an iron effort of the will he shook the feeling off, pursed his lips and whistled to the sorrel. Goldy answered with another whinny, padded up to the hill and thrust his damp muzzle into his master's hand. Hatfield managed to touch the friendly, inquiring nose with his fingers, and found comfort in the contact. The horse might be of no help, but his very presence was something.

Goldy nuzzled the hand, blowing softly, nipping Hatfield's fingers with gentle teeth.

"God, Goldy, if you could only chew that rawhide!" the Lone Wolf breathed. "It's no use, though—that's too much to expect of any hoss."

Goldy snorted questioningly and nuzzled again at the Ranger's hand. Again he nipped, with velvety lips, champing his bit, slobbering over the constraining steel. Hatfield's hand and wrist were wet. So was the peg against which it was bound, and so was the rawhide thong. Goldy continued to nuzzle.

The ants were biting freely now. Hatfield writhed despite his iron control and cursed softly through his set teeth. Again he tugged with all his strength, arching his body with effort, slicing the flesh of his wrists.

With a mad thrill of joy, he felt that his right hand moved the merest trifle. Yes, he was sure of it! It was not so close against the peg now. He redoubled his efforts, and the hand moved a little more.

Suddenly, the solution of the mystery burst upon him. The

nuzzling, slobbering horse was wetting the rawhide thong—*and rawhide stretches when wet!*

Hatfield began talking to the horse, softly, persistently, using all the endearing terms he had ever employed toward the intelligent animal. Goldy blew his appreciation and continued to nuzzle the hand whose fingertips caressed his nose. Abruptly he started back with an explosive snort. An ant had crawled into his nostril, and had bitten him. He blew prodigiously and backed away a pace.

Hatfield's voice rose, urgent, insistent. The dubious horse hesitated, fidgeted on restless feet, and thrust his muzzle back into the caressing hand. Hatfield strained with every atom of his magnificent strength. Goldy nipped at his hand.

Again the sorrel reared away, snorting with indignation. A score of ants had crawled upon his nose. He shook them off and eyed his prostrate master reproachfully. Hatfield put forth his strength in one final terrific effort. The planing vultures dropped lower. The black shadow of one rested on the Ranger's face for a fleeting instant—rested like the cold shade of Death's reaching hand. Hatfield gave one last desperate lunge.

The stubborn rawhide, yielded, held, yielded a trifle more as the moisture reached the inmost fibre, yielded again, and the loosened loop flipped over the head of the stake!

Hatfield twisted over on his side, gripped the stake that held his left hand and tore it from the ground. He sat up, ripped free the thongs that held his ankles and staggered to his feet. Instantly he fell headlong, so numbed were his limbs. On hands and knees he crawled away from the terrible hill. Again he got to his feet, beating the ants from his clothing. The vultures croaked their disappointment, spiralled high into the sky and drifted away in search of easier prey. Hatfield shed the last of the ants, freed his wrists and ankles from the thongs and shambled to his horse.

"Thanks, Goldy," he said quietly, and the golden horse seemed to understand.

Swinging into the saddle, the Ranger galloped back toward where he had left his troop. Before he reached the spot, he saw the dust cloud boiling against the sky. But this time it was rolling north. A little later he could make out the toiling herd. The Rangers were driving it toward the Rio Grande, meanwhile fighting a rear guard action with the disheartened Mexicans.

Three of their number were wounded when Hatfield reached them, none seriously. His deadly rifle was an added inducement for the Mexicans to give up the fight. Soon the silver river shimmered in the sunlight and the pursuit fell back. A score or more cowboys were riding along the northern bank. Others were urging their horses into the water. That night the Slash K trail herd, heavily guarded by watchful punchers, was again on its way to market.

"Fine work, son," white-haired old Captain Brooks told the Lone Wolf, "as fine a piece of Ranger work as I've seen in many a day. Captain McDowell is going to be prouder than ever of you when I write him about it."

He stroked his snowy beard with a hand whose thinness and pallor still bespoke the ravages of recent illness. He did not appear over-pleased with what he had to say next, and his voice held a regretful note when he spoke.

"Got news for you," he said. "You'll probably be glad to hear it—gladder than I am to tell you. You're transferred back to McDowell, effective today. I'm over my sick spell and strong enough to take charge of things at this post again, and Cap. Bill is anxious to have you back with him, particularly since he's at the new post in El Paso county, 'way over west. I hear there's trouble brewing over on the Salt Flats, and along that new railroad they're building. McDowell probably has plenty for you to do; but I'll hate to lose you, son. You certainly have handled things first rate since you took over here while I was on the sick list. Yes sir, I hate to lose you."

Hatfield nodded, staring somberly out of the window toward the grim Tamarra Hills.

"I'm not so glad as I thought I'd be, sir," he said. "Of course I like getting back with my own outfit—that's just natural—but I sort of hate to be leaving here right now. I'd like to have another crack at those two men who turned me over to the ants. And it seems, sir, that there are some funny things going on in this valley these days."

Old Captain Brooks was slow in replying.

"Yes," he said at length, "yes, there is—almighty funny. There's some mighty sinister influences at work hereabouts, son. Powerful influences that have to be reckoned with. The sort of thing that doesn't belong in Texas, or anywhere else in America, for that matter. Mark my word, son, there are bitter days in store for this state if certain folks get where they can have the whole say. What's goin' on in the Tamarra Valley will spread all over the state. It's got to be stopped."

"Maybe the Rangers can take a little hand in the stopping," suggested Hatfield.

Brooks slowly shook his white head.

"It's the Rangers who are liable to be stopped," he predicted soberly. "Mark my words—this post at Presidio isn't going to last. It'll be abandoned before the year is out."

"But, sir," exclaimed the surprised Ranger, "there isn't a district where a post is needed worse, what with Cartina and those other outlaws down below, and the Comanches to the north. Why—"

"Those things won't be allowed to count," Brooks interrupted. "The Rangers are the one organization certain folks are scared of. The Rangers can't be bought, and they can't be scared. The only thing is to get them out of the way. That'll be the move, see if it isn't. And if *he* gets to be governor, like he's planning on, in a mighty short time there won't be any Rangers—the outfit will be disbanded and a mighty different sort of outfit will be riding over this state."

"*He* ought to be stopped, sir."

"Uh-huh. But so far as anybody can see, he doesn't ever do anything that is a real law violation, and that's the only thing the Rangers can act on. John Chadwick's a law-abiding citizen if there ever was one. It's just that in this valley he comes mighty close to *being* the Law!"

20

"And that kind of Law has no place in Texas, or America, sir."

"No, it hasn't, son. It certainly hasn't. Well, I guess it's something for wiser heads than you and I to worry about. We have our own work to do. So, you head back to McDowell in the morning. Somebody else'll do the job of runnin' those rustlers down. They won't last much longer. You think one was Cartina, all right?"

"Pretty sure the smaller one was Cartina," the Ranger replied.

"And the other one?"

"Can't say *who* he was—had his face covered up—but I've got a good notion of *what* he was."

"Huh? *What* he was?" repeated the surprised Captain. "Well, what?"

Hatfield fixed him with his level gray eyes, his voice was soft and steady.

"The brains!" he replied.

CHAPTER 1

Westward across the Tamarra Valley from the desert's edge, a range of gaunt hills shouldered the brassy-blue Texas sky. There was nothing beautiful about them. Scantily clothed with sparse, dry vegetation, their slopes, fanged with boulders, and seamed by watercourses, straggled upward toward a sheer wall of craggy cliffs that formed their crest. In the shadow of those towering cliffs the slopes were darkly blue and somberly mysterious, and there seemed to be a concealed threat in the deep gorges with their shadows.

Farther down the slopes, the rocks and earth were splashed with gold and the gnarled trees burned pale amber in the hot shimmer of the afternoon sunshine. Water sounded in the gorges, water that leaped over black rocks or hissed smoothly against canyon walls.

Very silent were the hills, save for the sound of the water and the restless whimper of the wind in the burr oaks and pinon pines.

21

It was a crouching sort of silence. It was the silence of watching eyes and listening ears, and a poised threat.

"Threatening" described it best of all. The gaunt hills wore the silence as an executioner wears his black robe, wrapping it about their shadowy shoulders, with the tattered fringe trailing away toward the sun-drenched plain.

Ed Shafter, trudging across the gold and emerald sweep of the Tamarra, his gray old burro following him, sensed the ominous silence even as he crossed the sun spangled rangeland toward the hills.

His eyes narrowed as they swept the gray loom of the hills and the big muscles of back and arms swelled under his patched coat. For a moment his whole long, lean body was tense. Then he shrugged his wide shoulders, laughed a little in his beard and lengthened his stride. He hoped to camp in some sheltered draw at the base of the hills, where wood and water would be plentiful.

"Ought to be able to knock over a rabbit or a couple blue grouse," he told the burro. "That'll sort of change my diet off from bacon and beans. Oh, I know, *you* don't care, you scraggle-tailed old grass burner, but *I* crave chuck that's a little different now and then. C'mon, 'fore I leave you out here to grow roots and turn into a loco weed!"

The burro wagged a contemplative ear and did not appear particularly impressed; but he quickened his pace a bit to keep at the heels of his tall master.

Ed Shafter was forty years old and looked sixty. Gray streaked the brown beard that hung over his arching chest and spread out almost to his wide shoulders. There was gray in the hair that escaped from beneath his ragged hat, and what could be seen of his face was deeply lined. His blue eyes were clear and bright. He was long of limb, stringy of muscle and his every movement was assured.

The clothes he wore were a weird patchwork, the original base of which had been faded blue overalls, blue woolen shirt, coat of some nondescript dark color and black slouch hat. Now there were more patches than base, even patch upon patch,

22

running the gauntlet from rawhide to rabbit skin. His boots were also carefully patched and sound of sole. A heavy sixgun sagged on his right hip and the rough handle of a Bowie knife protruded from one boot top. Crooked in his arm was a Winchester.

The sun was still peering over the hill tops when Ed Shafter left the prairie and began toiling up a long dry wash whose sides were green with grama grass and splashed and starred with flowering weeds. The floor of the wash was studded with water-rounded boulders and littered with fragments casually, but his chief interest seemed centered on the ragged rim of the wash, and on the marbled ledges that flung up at its head. He appeared to be a prospector with a definite goal in view, with no time to waste on dubious surface indications.

That he was a wandering prospector, a typical desert rat, it seemed there could be little doubt. Pick and shovel peeped from the burro's pack. A chipping hammer was also in evidence.

As Shafter neared the head of the wash, he proceeded more slowly. Several times he paused, as though listening for something and his gaze roved backward and forward along the irregular ledges ahead. He could see now that the wash turned sharply and was really but the entrance to a deeper gorge that slashed the hills. His dark brows drew together at the discovery and he muttered something back of his bearded lips. He began to examine the ground carefully.

Suddenly he paused. His eye had caught the gleam of deep mineral stains on a bit of float. He picked up the stone and examined it with growing excitement. Beard and moustache pursed together in a soundless whistle. Shafter raised his eyes to stare incredulously at the beetling breast of the hills. He shook his head in a dazed unbelief. Again he glanced at the stone, read its story with a trained mining man's practiced glance. The evidence in his bronzed hand was indubitable.

Again he raised his eyes to the unpromising battlements of those forbidding hills. Still shaking his head, he strode onward, and a moment later picked up another piece of float, and in another moment a third. Shafter halted, and stared at

23

the mineral fragments, his face working. Again his glance sought the hill crest, and again he incredulously shook his head.

Silver in the Tamarra Hills! Silver of a richness vouched for by the bits of float borne down the draw by turbulent storm water! It just couldn't be! Spanish Conquistadore, scout, emigrant, cattleman, wandering prospector—all had passed the forbidding range, giving the grim crags and battlements a wide berth. Only the marauding Apache, the fleeing outlaw, the furtive smuggler sought sanctuary amid the cliffs and canyons and gloomy caves.

"Somebody might have dropped them rocks out of a pack or somethin'," Shafter declared to his burro. But his voice held no conviction. The miner in him knew that the mineral-packed float had been torn loose from some ledge farther up the draw.

Sunset was flaming in all its scarlet and gold and shimmering bronze glory when Ed Shafter made his camp near the head of the draw. And as he boiled his coffee and fried his bacon, Destiny shuffled through the prairie grasses to the East and Death drifted silently across the purple-silver ribbon far to the south that was the stately Rio Grande.

Shafter could not hear those dragging footsteps through the grasses nor the muffled plod of hoofs up the muddy river bank, but a cold wind fanned his face and he hunched closer to his little fire, his mind brooding over twin problems. From time to time he drew a crumbling fragment of float from an inner pocket and stared at the blue threads that were silver. After each examination he would raise his eyes and gaze toward that shadowy river far to the south, and the muscles of his lean jaw would quiver beneath the beard. Finally he fumbled within his shirt, touching something there with his bronzed, sinewy fingers. As if by magic, the indecision left his steady eyes and with a shrug of his broad shoulders he dropped the bit of float back into his pocket, nodded purposefully toward the unseen river and prepared his bed.

And Destiny and Death drew nearer.

24

CHAPTER 2

MORNING came and Shafter, tired out by a long and hard trudge across the rangeland, slept late. The sun was high behind a sullen veil of clouds as he cooked his breakfast and ate it leisurely. He was washing his few dishes when his keen ears caught the sound that drifted up the draw.

There was a patient clicking of little hoofs on stone, and another sound, a dragging shuffle that kept laborious time with the first.

"Burro comin' t'other side that brush, and a man," Shafter deduced. "Man walks like he's hurt," he added, listening to the hesitant shuffle.

Picking up his rifle he cradled it negligently in his arm, where it could be swung into instant action should occasion warrant. Then he lounged carelessly in the shadow of a gnarled burr oak, where he could see better than he could be seen. There was something menacing about that indecisive shuffle. Shafter felt it, but was at a loss to explain why.

Abruptly he relaxed, an exclamation on his lips.

Through the final fringe of the growth, a man had appeared, a man and a burro. The burro was a sturdy little animal, loaded with a well arranged pack. The man was the strangest individual Shafter had ever seen.

Wide, thick shoulders hunched high about the massive neck, powerful, simian arms dangling loosely, ending in finely shaped hands with slim, tapering fingers that hung well below his knees. He was not over five feet tall. His legs were bowed and crooked and worked stiffly from the hips, giving him a peculiar shuffling gait that dragged feet singularly small for the rest of him. His body was unutterably grotesque, utterly misshapen, vibrating crude physical power.

"Those arms could crack a hoss's ribs, and he could come darn near gettin' 'em around a hoss, too," muttered Shafter, staring amazedly at the face, so out of place on that distorted form.

As grotesque as the stranger was in body, he was beautiful of

25

face. The pushed-back *sombrero* revealed crisply curling hair golden as the evening sunlight, a broad, finely shaped forehead, delicately curved dark brows that shaded eyes as clearly blue as a summer sky. The nose was straight with sensitive nostrils. The mouth was wide but with perfectly formed lips above a prominent, determined chin. It was a proud, sensitive, intelligent face.

The hunchback carried no rifle, but twin holsters swung from his heavy double cartridge belts, one holster worn slightly higher than the other. He paused a dozen paces distant from the tall bearded man, bowed courteously and spoke.

"Buenas dias, señor," he said in a voice that was like the music of the waters echoing from the soundboard of the hills.

"Mawnin'," replied Shafter, concealing his surprise at the other's Spanish greeting. The man certainly did not look Mexican.

The hunchback spoke again, in unaccented English that was free of the soft drawl and slurred word-endings that characterize the Southwest.

"I smelled your coffee," he said. "Been out myself for two days," he added with a flash of white, even teeth.

Shafter chuckled his understanding.

"It shore is tough, especially if you're sorta used to havin' it reg'lar," he admitted. "Amble up here and set. Pot's still nigh onto half full. I made plenty this mawnin'."

He stopped to stir the embers together as he spoke. He straightened with his back to the other and stood, lithe and tall as a young pine of the forest.

Into the hunchback's blue eyes suddenly came a murky light of intense bitterness. His unbelievably handsome face contorted and for a moment its marvellous beauty dimmed as does the bright loveliness of the prairie under the shadow of a storm cloud. Then, as Shafter turned, the light died, the cameo-perfect features smoothed and the eyes became clear again.

"Thanks," he accepted the offer.

Before he squatted beside the fire, however, steaming tincup in hand, he slipped the pack from the burro's back and dropped it to the ground. Shafter liked him for that little act of thoughtfulness. His shrewd eyes ran over the outfit.

"Prospector?" he asked.

The hunchback nodded.

"No luck," he volunteered in answer to the unspoken question in the other's eyes. "Thought I'd work up through the Tamarra Hills and over to the Huecos, maybe. I've a notion there ought to be something worth while up there."

"Know the country?" Shafter asked.

"Fairly well," the other replied. "My ancestors owned most of it at one time. They lost title when the courts invalidated the old Spanish grants in this section."

His blue eyes hardened slightly as he spoke. In Shafter's was a light of understanding.

"You come down from one of the old Spanish families, then?"

The question was really a statement. The other nodded.

"Yes," he replied quietly, "I'm a Capistrano—Amado Capistrano is my name."

"And I callate you're entitled to write *Don* 'fore the Amado, if you take a notion," observed Shafter.

Amado Capistrano shrugged with Latin eloquence.

"It would be rather out of place before a desert rat's name, don't you think?" he replied.

"Not necessarily," answered Shafter, gazing thoughtfully at the proud sensitive face. With instinctive tact he changed the subject.

"Yore folks used to own the rangeland down there?" with a wave of his hand toward the lovely Tamarra Valley.

"Yes," the other replied. "John Chadwick owns it now. Know him?"

"Heard of him," Shafter replied.

That was not very definite. Almost everyone in that section of Texas had heard of John Chadwick, the cattle king. Chadwick was reputedly very wealthy, had served a term as State Senator and was spoken of as a possible candidate for governor.

Capistrano finished his coffee and stood up.

"Thanks," he said again, lifting the pack to the burro's back. "Guess I'll head on up the draw."

A little later Shafter watched the other man's grotesque form shuffle toward the wide mouth of the gorge. At the end of the wash he hesitated, apparently doubtful whether to turn to the right or the left, and as he paused, Destiny cast the dice. There was a flutter of grayish white, a skittering among the stones as a cottontail rabbit darted from a covert, weaved erratically for a moment and then sped away to the right. Shafter could almost hear the hunchback's amused chuckle as he too turned to the right and vanished up the gorge.

Late afternoon found Shafter on the move. He entered the gorge, drove straight ahead for a mile or two and then veered slightly to the left. Suddenly he paused, his eyes narrowing.

Directly ahead a ledge of grayish rock, marbled with black and yellowish blotches, undulated along the dark side of an abrupt rise. Shafter eyed it, breathing deeply. He strode forward with long strides, paused, loosened his prospector's pick from the burro's pack and sank it into the rock. It came crumbling down in brittle lumps.

With a trembling hand, Shafter picked up one of the fragments. It was streaked and veined with silver. He examined another, and another. Each was as the first—unbelievably rich in silver ore.

Shafter straightened up, his eyes blazing. Clenching the stones in sweat-moistened hands he stared at the ledge, turned abruptly and gazed toward the south. Lips tight, he dropped the bits of ore into his pocket, carefully scuffed dirt over the remaining fragments, smeared dust on the fresh scar his pick had left and resolutely turned his back on the ledge. He turned sharply to the left and strode southward with long strides.

And several miles to the north, the hunchback descendant of the Conquistadores paused before the face of a sheer cliff, sighed wearily and, turning, retraced his steps, veering more and more to the left as the shadows lengthened.

As the blue dusk was descending on the hill tops, Shafter made a fireless camp less than half a mile from the precipitous slope that was the south wall of the gorge. In the shadow of an overhanging rock he sat silent, motionless, rifle across his knees, eyes fixed on a wide notch that cut the gorge wall. From this notch flowed a ribbon of trail, or what passed for a trail. Shafter, who, like Amado Capistrano, was fairly familiar with the country, knew that it was the sinister Huachuca Trail that writhed its blood-splotched way northward from the purple mountains of Mexico.

Silently he watched the gloomy notch, while a great white moon soared up over the eastern rim of the world and edged the black velvet of the hills with silver.

The moon climbed higher, bathing the gorge in ghostly light, and still the bearded Shafter sat motionless, alert.

Suddenly he stiffened, his lean hands gripping the rifle. Eyes eager, he leaned forward.

There was motion in the notch—furtive, indistinct motion that quickly became clearcut and real. Shadowy forms bulked large and grotesque in the wan moonlight.

Tense, quivering with excitement, Shafter watched them jolt down the trail—the mounted men, the loaded mules. Even at that distance he could recognize the long, deadly looking cases and the chunky boxes that seemed to swell with lethal power. His breath came quick and fast.

"I was right!" he muttered. "It wasn't a loco yarn of a drunken Mex! Nobody but me b'lieved it, but I was right! They're doin' it! They're gettin' ready! This is big! And nobody but me caught on to what was happenin'!"

His whole attention riveted on the stream of men and beasts flowing down the distant trail, he failed to see his gray old burro shuffle up a little rise and stand outlined clear and distinct in the moonlight.

For long minutes Shafter watched the ghostly caravan slide through the notch and vanish amid the shadows of the gorge. When the last outrider disappeared, he straightened his cramped limbs, stood up and strode out of the shadow. He turned quickly, gripping his rifle, at a slight sound behind him. Not ten paces distant stood a form blending into the shadows. A shaft of moonlight bathed the face, outlining every feature.

For a paralyzed second Shafter stared, his face that of a man whose judgment and trust has been shattered. Then he read the message in the eyes glaring into his, he flung his rifle to his shoulder. The other's hands moved with blinding speed.

Ed Shafter died with his finger squeezing the trigger of his rifle—died under the blast of lead-belching from two blazing guns, black holes blotching his broad forehead. He crumpled back in the shadow of the overhanging rock, a shapeless bundle of patched clothes, almost hidden from view. The killer deliberately fired twice more. He was taking no chances. A moment later he shot the old burro.

The white moon slid down behind the western crags. The stars dwindled to pin points of pale flame before they vanished in the whitening vault of the sky. The silent dawn spread its red mantle over the lonely mountains. The sun rose in gold and scarlet splendor and it was day.

Other days came, gray days and golden days, and moon bright nights and nights of lashing rain and wailing winds. Summer gave way to Autumn. And still the huddled bones of Ed Shafter lay in their moldering rags under the overhanging rock.

Strange sounds came to the hill country—unwonted thunders, mysterious boomings that puzzled the coyotes and sent the owls winging away. Also a low growl and mutter that swelled and lessened, rose and fell, but never ceased.

Two wandering miners discovered Shafter's skeleton. They stared at the grisly remains, bent over them gingerly. One pointed to the holes in the fleshless skull. The other nodded, bending closer as a gleam of metal caught his eye. With a hesitant hand he fumbled the tattered shirt, jerking loose the shining object pinned to the rotten undershirt beneath. He held the bit of silver in his horny palm and he and his companion stared at it with dilated eyes.

"Bill," he said, mouthing the words nervously, "this ain't no ord'nary killin'. Yuh know what *this thing* stands for. We'd better hustle down to town and report this. Sheriff's purty apt

30

to be there—spends more time in Helidoro now than at San Rosita, the county seat."

The other shifted uncomfortably.

"Curt," he objected, "we hadn't oughta be havin' no truck with that sheriff, not after that run-in we had with him last week. I don't hanker to go reportin' no killin' to him. Can't tell what might be liable to happen."

The first speaker considered.

"Mebbe yuh're right," he admitted, "but jest the same this'd oughta be reported—I won't feel right if it ain't. Them fellers is square shooters and they ain't nobody got no bus'ness pluggin' 'em. Tell yuh what. Franklin ain't sich a turrible ja'nt fer fellers like you and me—hardly a hundred miles. S'posin' we jest amble over there and report to the post?"

"Now yuh're talkin', feller," his companion agreed heartily. "That's jest what we'll do."

He glanced about with keen eyes, calculating distances, noting landmarks. He nodded toward the Huachuca Trail sliding furtively through the notch.

"Got the place all easy marked for the tellin'," he said with satisfaction. "I can lay 'er out so a blind man with the shakin' palsy can find 'er. C'mon, podner, stretch yore laigs."

CHAPTER 3

RARELY does rain fall upon the Tamarra Desert, that grim waste of alkali, scrub and dust powdered sage which stretches from the Huecos to the Tamarra Hills. But when it does rain, it is as if the floodgates of the heavens were opened. And always, before the first hissing lances spatter the gray leaves of the sage, a roaring wind swirls the choking alkali dust in blinding clouds that blot out the sun and fill the air with a rasping grit.

Nothing lives in the Tamarra Desert, not even a callous snake or hardened lizard. The wolf and the coyote give it a wide berth and seldom do even the vultures sail over the dreary expanse. Only when some ill-advised wanderer gets caught in a storm do they appear.

How do they know the lost one is there? Perhaps they hear the Hill Gods chuckle, even above the roar of the storm. Doubtless they were whetting their beaks in anticipation as they peered down with telescopic eyes, that could perhaps pierce the dust clouds, at the man who struggled blindly across the dismal waste, gasping, choking, bending his head to the beat of the winds, reeling drunkenly from time to time.

He was a little man, dark of face, scrawny of body, clad in a greasy shirt and pantaloons, rope sandals, tattered *separe* and floppy straw *sombrero*.

Hugged to his breast, a rag wrapped around the lock to protect it from the dust, he held a shiny new rifle.

Through all his bitter battle against the storm he grimly clutched the heavy weapon, even when he tripped over some unseen straggle of sage or scrub and fell, which was often. He still held onto it when for the last time he crashed to the earth, writhed feebly for a moment and was still, while the dust drifted and settled upon his unconscious form.

Farther south and to the west another man fought the storm, a tall man mounted on a splendid sorrel horse. The sorrel's glorious golden coat was streaked and smeared with the gray dust, his ears and his mane were furred with it, but he held his head high and snorted defiance to the stinging clouds. With rare instinct he avoided the snarls of sage and scrub, planting his hoofs daintily on the yielding silt. North by east he forged ahead, the wind blasts ruffling his tail and tossing his mane, apparently untired despite the hundred miles he had put behind him in the past two days.

The rider was as noteworthy as the horse he rode. Tall, broad of shoulder and lean of waist and hip, he rode with the easy grace of one born to the saddle. His hair, where it was not dusted with the gray alkali, was crisp and black. His face was lean and bronzed with a wide mouth and level gray eyes.

Those eyes were the most striking feature of the man's face. To oldtimers they called to mind other eyes, the eyes of men

32

who had walked through the smoke-misted West with courage
—unafraid, in whose presence other men were wont to speak
softly and move their hands with care.

"All steel and hickory and coiled-up chain lightnin'," a
critical observer would have said, "and when he goes after
those two guns, there's nothing for the other fellow to do but
die gracefully!"

The two guns hung low in carefully worked hand-made
holsters, their long barrels tapping against the rider's muscular
thighs, the black butts flaring away from his lean hips. A
heavy Winchester swung in the saddle boot.

Through the clouds of dust there suddenly came the hissing
deluge of icy rain. The sorrel snorted explosively at the sting
of the water, but the rider grunted relief.

"Don't be kicking, oldtimer," he admonished, "it'll lay this
dust, and that's something to be thankful for. My lips are
cracked open and my eyes feel as though I'd been rubbing sand
in them. And I guess you're in about the same fix. This'll
wash us off and make us feel a big sight better—you see if it
doesn't!"

The sorrel snorted again, and shook his head as if in dis-
agreement. Abruptly he shied, jolting his rider by his unexpected sideways leap.

"Easy, Goldy," growled the man. "What's eating you?"

The sorrel snorted again, capering nervously and rolling his
eyes toward a low mound which appeared to be just another
dust-covered clump of sage.

Jim Hatfield had long ago learned to trust the instinct of
his big mount. Anything that appeared out of the ordinary to
Goldy, he had learned, would bear investigation. The tall
Ranger Lieutenant halted the sorrel, quieted him with a sooth-
ing word and gazed at the silent mound with speculative eyes.
He could just distinguish its outlines through the rain, which
was now descending in wind-whipped sheets.

Lithely he swung to the ground, shaking the water from the
brim of his hat. A long stride and he reached the motionless
form. Another instant and he was kneeling beside it, brushing

33

away the sodden dust, to reveal a dark-faced little man who lay limp, something clutched to his scrawny chest. It was a task to break his grip on the heavy rifle with its rag wrapped lock.

For an instant the gun drew Hatfield's attention from the man. He examined it with growing curiosity, recognizing it as a latest model United States Army rifle. His gaze shifted back to the man.

"Now where in blazes did a little half-starved Mex get hold of a gun like *this?*" he wondered. "Got about as much business with it as a hog with a hip pocket!"

He felt of the unconscious man's heart, found that it beat with fair strength.

"Just knocked out by the dust and heat," he decided. "He ought to snap out of it before long. The rain'll help. I'd better get him to some place where I can make a fire. Hot coffee will be just the thing when he comes to."

He picked up man and rifle with no apparent effort. Just as easily he mounted, cradling the limp form in front of him. He spoke to the sorrel and the big horse moved on, evidently as little affected by the burden as was his master. Another hour of battling the rain and the wind and they struck the first slopes of the Tamarra Hills.

In a sheltered canyon, beneath the overhang of a tall cliff which formed a perfect protection from the rain, Hatfield built a fire. The little Mexican still lay silent, but his breathing had become regular and his pulse beat stronger.

"Just tuckered out," Hatfield diagnosed the case. "Sleeping now. He'll wake up in a little and be okay."

The Mexican was, in fact, stirring before the coffee had boiled. Abruptly he opened wide, bewildered eyes and stared about him. Stark terror filmed the eyes as they rested on the tall form of the Ranger. Hatfield's quick glance caught the expression of fear, and he smiled.

"Take it easy, *amigo*," he said, "you're all right now. Just a minute and I'll have something hot for you to get inside you. That'll fix you up pronto."

34

The little man stared at him dazedly and Hatfield repeated the words in fluent Spanish. The Mexican found his tongue.

"Gracias, señor, gracias!" he exclaimed. "The English I understand eet," he added, a trifle proudly. "Eet I speak also, but not well."

"Fine!" Hatfield nodded, "but don't try any talking in either lingo just yet. Here, surround this cup of coffee while I cook us up some supper. I've got some ham and eggs in this saddlebag, if the eggs aren't smashed up. No, they're still in one piece. The hen that laid 'em did a good job on the shells. Hope the insides are as good. Uh-huh, they look fine," he added as he broke the eggs into the frying pan.

Jim Hatfield, usually a very silent individual, knew that nothing was more effective in putting a frightened man at his ease than just such rambling small talk. A few minutes later the little Mexican was sitting up, eating hungrily.

"Now, I wonder," the Ranger mused, studying the other while he ate. "I wonder just what he was doing out there in the desert, carrying a Government rifle? I'd better find out about that rifle, if I can."

He had already found that the gun was unloaded and that the Mexican had no ammunition in his possession.

He rolled a cigarette with the slim fingers of one hand, passed it to the Mexican and rolled another for himself. The smokes were almost consumed when Hatfield offered a casual comment and an equally casual question.

"Nice looking gun you have there, *amigo.* Where'd you happen to get it?"

Again the beady eyes filmed over. The dark face contorted. "I—I f-found it, señor."

The voice that mumbled the words was a thick stutter. The little man's thin fingers balled into nervous fists, straightened, worked convulsively.

Hatfield, whose steady gaze missed nothing, spoke again in the same casual manner.

"You're lucky. I've always wanted a gun like that. What say you sell it to me? How much?"

Sweat beaded the Mexican's haggard cheeks and Hatfield could see the palms of his hands grow moist.

"I—I would rather not sell it, señor." He spoke little above a whisper.

"Aw, come on," Hatfield replied jovially, apparently taking no note of the other's agitation, "I'll give you a good price. More than you'll get from anybody else."

He poised a gold piece temptingly on his forefinger as he spoke.

The Mexican shook his head vehemently, although his eyes glowed at the sight of the gold.

"I—I can—I—I will not sell, señor. I too have long wished for an *escopeta* like this one."

Hatfield nodded with well-feigned regret.

"Okay. If you won't, you won't," he resigned himself. "Well, I'd better take these pans down to the creek and scrub 'em up a bit. Back in a minute."

He picked up the tin plates and the cups and sauntered to the bank of the little stream which flowed through the canyon. It was just within the range of the firelight, less than a dozen paces distant. As he scoured the plates with sand, he pondered the Mexican's reaction to his questioning.

"Started to say *'cannot'* instead of *'will not* sell,'" he mused as he bent over the water. "That *is* funny. Seems like that gun doesn't belong to him, even from the *finding's keeping's* angle. Looks like he's scared of letting it get away from him. He wanted that twenty dollars, and wanted it bad. I could see it in his eyes. More money than the poor devil ever saw before, chances are. Something that looked bigger than the twenty dollars kept him from taking it, and the only thing what would look bigger is something he's scared to death of. Now what could *that* be? Nice combination—scared Mex and a brand-new Government rifle. There isn't an army post within fifty miles of here, and I can't figure where else a gun like that one would come from. I suppose I ought to hang onto this fellow, but how am I going to do it and do the job I come up here to do? I'd be a dead give-away. I—"

A sudden clatter of loose stones brought his head around with a jerk. He caught a fleeting glimpse of a dark figure vanishing from the circle of firelight. By the time he had straightened up, not even the whisper of the rope sandals could be heard above the beat of the rain. A glance told him that the rifle also had vanished.

Hatfield grinned a trifle ruefully, but with a distinct sense of relief.

"Running like a scared rabbit," he chuckled, "and there's no chance of catching him in the rain and the dark. There won't be any tracks to follow by dawn, the way the water's coming down.

"Well, that solves the problem. I didn't want to let him go without finding out something about where he got that gun, but doing that was liable to ball things up for me. We'll just forget him for a while."

He would never forget the little Mexican's face, however, nor the mysterious rifle. The big Ranger was just putting both into the back of his mind, to make room for more pressing matters.

Back beside the fire, in the shelter of the cliff, he smoked thoughtfully. The rain ceased as abruptly as it had begun and the wind died down. Soon a watery moon peeped through the clouds and cast a wan light over the wild landscape. Hatfield glanced about speculatively, nodded and got to his feet.

The sorrel horse came at his whistle and Hatfield saddled up.

"We'll just mosey on a spell," he told the horse. "According to directions, three or four more hours ought to bring us to where we're heading for. Then we'll take a good rest after we look things over and find out what's what. Okay by you?"

Goldy nodded his head and sneezed. Hatfield chuckled as he slipped the bit between the sorrel's teeth.

"Don't go trying to tell me you're catching cold," he bantered. "Fact is, I believe you're too darn slow to even catch that, you spavined old mud turtle."

Goldy's answer to this outrageous slander was an indignant snort and an apparently vicious snap at his tall master's high

37

bridged nose. Hatfield swore at him affectionately and swung into the saddle.

East by north he rode in the pale moonlight. Less than four hours later the sorrel was daintily picking his way along the crest of a long ridge. The southern slope of the ridge was gentle, but the northern side dropped sharply toward the floor of what appeared to be a wide box canyon cutting the hills from east to west.

"This ought to be it," Hatfield mused, glancing keenly about him. "The Huachuca Trail cuts this hogback somewhere ahead, according to what those two fellows said, and right across from the notch is where *he* is. Huh! that looks like the notch down past those white rocks."

A few minutes later he reached the lip of the notch and glanced into the shadowy depths. The sides of the gash were almost sheer, the trail a score or more feet below the crest of the ridge. Where it dipped sharply down the northern slope of the ridge, it was bathed in the pale moonlight. Hatfield stiffened as he glanced in that direction.

Down the winding trail moved a long string of loaded pack mules, with mounted men beside and behind them. Just in time the Ranger caught the warning glint of quickly shifted metal. He was going out of the saddle when the rifle cracked. He heard the bullet scream through the space his body had occupied a second before. The rifle blazed a second time.

An instant later Jim Hatfield's limp body was sliding and rolling down the steep side of the notch. It thudded onto the hard surface of the trail, quivered convulsively for a moment and lay still. In the dark depths of the canyon, fast hoofs thudded, swiftly dying to a mere whisper of sound and ceasing altogether.

The moon slid farther toward the west, poured questing beams into the notch. They crept along inch by inch until they rested upon the Ranger's blood-streaked face, crept on and left the motionless form to the silent dark.

On the lip of the notch, the tall sorrel horse whinnied de-

38

jectedly, pawed the earth with a dainty hoof and stared downward with great, questioning eyes.

CHAPTER 4

THE sun was rising in the east and the western peaks were crowned with pale light when Jim Hatfield groaned, groped about him with uncertain hands and opened his eyes. A white stab of pain caused him to close them quickly and for some minutes he lay fighting a deadly nausea before he dared try it again. The light had strengthened greatly by then and he could make out the crumbling sides of the notch.

A small stone tumbled down and thumped in the dust beside him. He glanced up and saw Goldy outlined hugely against the brightening sky. Painfully he sat up, raised a trembling hand to his head and felt the lump he found there. There also was a slight cut just above one cheek bone and his face was stiff with crusted blood. Somewhat shakily he got to his feet and stood swaying uncertainly for a moment.

As strength returned, he recalled the events of the night before.

His last conscious recollection had been of his boot heels skidding on a smooth stone as he had hurled himself from the saddle.

"Hit my head on the rock as I came down. Knocked myself out and rolled over the edge of the notch," he growled. "Lucky I didn't break my neck on the way down! Gosh, I feel as though I'd been pulled through a knot hole and hung up to dry!"

He was stiff and sore in every joint and his head ached abominably, but he had apparently suffered no serious injury. A few minutes later he scrambled up the side of the notch and reached his worried horse.

"This is turning out to be some trip!" he told the sorrel. "Who do you suppose those men were who started throwing lead the minute they set eyes on us? Smugglers, the chances are—those mules were all loaded and they were heading up the Huachuca from the south, like they might have come from the other side the Line.

"Funny looking loads they were carrying—long wooden boxes. Certainly weren't rawhide *aparejos*, the kind of pack sacks the Mexicans generally use. Couldn't have been silver *dobe* dollars they were packin'."

He considered a moment before he made an impatient gesture with one hand.

"I've got to put them off until later, too," he said. "Right now I've got other things to look after. But I'd like to even up for this busted head with that gun slinging gent, but it'll have to wait."

His head felt better as he turned the sorrel's nose to the north and rode down the steep slope. Soon he reached the floor of the canyon, glanced about keenly and rode slowly toward a low cliff with a decided overhang. In the shadow of the rock he dismounted, and approached the cliff.

The ground at its base was thickly grown with grass and prickly pear. High on a single stem, a cluster of drooping white yucca blossoms swayed in the breeze. To right and left, tall tree trunks, widely spaced, soared up like the columns of some great cathedral.

And here indeed was Death's cathedral. Something shone whitely beneath the green of the prickly pear. It was a skull, topping a skeleton which lay among the tatters of rotting clothes.

For long minutes Jim Hatfield stood staring down at the skeleton. Silently he removed his wide hat and bared his dark head.

The gray eyes were somber now, and as he stared at the holes in the bullet battered skull, they turned cold as the shimmer of snow-dusted ice under a gray and wintry sky. The lean face grew bleak and the good-humored mouth tightened to a thin, merciless line.

Jim Hatfield was looking down at the pitiful remains of a Ranger slain—slain in the performance of his duty.

He recalled the day, less than a week before, when two weather-beaten miners had walked into Ranger headquarters at Franklin and handed a silver star set on a silver circle to Captain McDowell. Patiently, they had answered the Captain's questions, describing in painstaking detail the location of the skeleton they had stumbled upon at the base of the cliff.

"Haid was shot fulla holes," Bill, the taller one, had said. "Rifle right beside him, bones of one hand still over it. Nope, we didn't touch nothin'—didn't see nothin' of his outfit if he had one. Shine of his badge caught Curt's eye and that's how we knowed what he was.

"Callated we'd oughta mosey over here and tell you fellers 'bout it. Somethin' oughta be done, we figgered. Decent fellers like us don't favor Rangers gettin' blowed out from under their hats that-a-way. Nope, we didn't go tell the sheriff. We had a ruckus with him over to Helidoro, the new minin' town, and he told us to get out and not come back. Curt and me was scairt he might do somethin' to make trouble for us if we come tellin' him 'bout findin' a murdered Ranger, so we decided to come over here."

Captain McDowell thanked the miners warmly and shook hands with both. Bill and Curt had partially cleared up a mystery which had puzzled two Ranger posts for many months.

When the stern old commander, the man who "would charge hell with a bucket of water," turned to Jim Hatfield, there were tears in his eyes. Cap'n Bill loved his "boys" as a father loves his sons.

"It can't be anybody but Ed Shafter," the Captain said. "Poor Ed! He was with me for a couple of years when I was stationed in the panhandle. I brought him up in the Rangers. Later he was transferred to Brooks' company. You recollect Brooks sent him to San Rosita about a year back to look into the killing of young Dick Webb by Cartina, the bandit. Was there about a week and talked to a lot of fellows; then all of a sudden he disappeared.

"Nobody knew what had become of him and nobody has seen hide nor hair of him since. Last seen of him he was in a saloon one night, talking with a little fellow who might have been an Indian. Barkeep happened to remember it, but didn't recall much what the Indian looked like. All Indians look alike to him, he said. Now these two men drop in and bring a Ranger's star they took off a skeleton, 'way up by the Huachuca Trail. Couldn't be anybody but Shafter. But what in blazes was he doing in the Tamarra Hills?"

"Must have had reasons to be there," Jim Hatfield replied quietly, as he stood up. "That territory is in our district now, isn't it?"

"Uh-huh," the Captain replied, "now that we're over here at this new post. Used to be in Brooks', but it isn't any more."

"Any assignment for me, sir?" Hatfield asked. He had just arrived at the post after satisfactorily completing a difficult and dangerous mission.

"Nothing particular right now, Jim," the Captain answered.

Hatfield stretched his long arms above his head and the powerful muscles caused the seams of his coat sleeve to start. The tips of his fingers nearly reached the ceiling.

"Well, sir, guess I'd better be riding over to the Tamarra Hills for a spell, then," he stated.

"But good gosh, Jim!" the Captain remonstrated, "it's nearly a hundred miles over there and you've just come in from a mighty hard trip."

Jim Hatfield smiled down at the old Captain from his great height.

"Ed Shafter went on a longer trip, and he didn't come back," he said softly. "Ed won't rest over easy up there in the hills so long as the man that killed him is running around loose. You see, sir, I knew Shafter, too. I met him while I was running Brooks' company last year when Brooks was sick. I've got a personal interest in this business, too. Besides, the fellow who got young Dick Webb hasn't been brought in. Brooks figured it to be Cartina, and Cartina is still operating in that section, according to last reports. I've a notion that he's likely to hang around that new mining town, Helidoro. Ought to be some fat pickings for his kind there. I'll just ride up and

42

look the situation over, if it's agreeable with you, sir."

For several minutes Captain McDowell sat staring straight ahead, his blue eyes frostier than usual.

"Jim," he said softly at length, "Rangers aren't over welcome in the Tamarra Valley, it appears. You know the Presidio post was abandoned a few months back and Brooks' outfit moved back east."

"You mean to say I can't go up there, sir?"

"I mean to say I can't *order* you up there. The Big Boss of that district seems to think local authorities can take care of things there without any outside help, and he's got enough drag at the Capital to make folks *there* think his way."

"Folks in the Tamarra Valley think that way, too?"

McDowell shook his head.

"No," he replied, "they don't. There's been more than one letter sent to headquarters asking for Ranger help to wipe out Cartina and his kind, but headquarters replied that reports of conditions were exaggerated and that the local authorities were able to cope with the situation, leaving the Rangers free for duty in districts where they were needed more. It appears John Chadwick has organized a vigilante committee to help look after things. Chadwick's paying the expenses of the organization and everything's under control, according to reports—from Chadwick."

"And Chadwick's going to run for governor."

"Uh-huh, and it looks like he'll get the nomination, and that means election, of course."

"And that means he'll run the whole state like he runs the Tamarra Valley and the county and all the counties surrounding Tamarra. Why, sir, he's running a big section of the state now! And he isn't running it the Texas way, either. It isn't right!"

"No, it isn't," Captain Bill agreed, "but it doesn't look like there's much anybody can do about it. Chadwick is honest, everybody agrees on that. He just wants things run his way. He plans on being governor, all right, and United States senator after that, I reckon, and that'll put him before the whole country, and nobody knows where he'll stop! Well, I don't suppose there's anything *we* can do about it. Fellows like Cartina are more our style."

Hatfield nodded. "Guess that's right, sir. Well, so long as you don't tell me *not* to, I guess I'll take a little ride. Maybe I'll be lucky."

The rugged old Captain said nothing, but he thrust a gnarled hand across the table to meet Hatfield's steely grip.

"Lucky!" Captain Bill growled to himself when the door had closed on his tall Lieutenant. "Lucky! Some folks may call it luck, but I have another name for it. I have a notion it's going to be almighty *un*lucky for the men that did for Shafter and Webb, now they have the Lone Wolf on their trail.

"Uh-huh, old Carney surely named that big fellow right. He's one fine Ranger when he's with a troop, but when he's by himself, he's a holy terror. Has never failed to outsmart or outshoot any tough, clever man he's been sent after, and he always brings his man in—or buries him! The Lone Wolf!"

CHAPTER 5

JIM HATFIELD was thinking of that parting handshake as he stared at the bleached bones of Ranger Ed Shafter. Stern old Captain Bill's confidence meant a great deal to the Lone Wolf. He was thinking of that when he knelt beside the skeleton and began to painstakingly examine the bones and the rags of clothing which covered them.

The bullet-riddled skull received his first attention and as he gazed at the holes in the forehead, the concentration furrow between his level black brows deepened. He recalled a paragraph in the report relative to the killing of young Dick Webb, a paragraph dealing with the bullet wounds in the Ranger's body.

"Begins to look as though the man who killed Shafter was the same one that got Webb," he muttered. "Well, that's something to go on—not much, but something. Fellows who carry guns that way aren't so common. I don't recall ever knowing

44

more than one or two who did, and they were both lefthanded. Seems lefthanded fellows handle guns better that way; some of them, anyhow. And *that's* something to remember."

Hatfield next turned to the remnants of clothing. From the pockets he turned out a miscellany of articles—a knife, a stoppered bottle filled with matches, a pencil stub, and other trinkets. There was a notebook, but the writing on the mouldy pages was smeared and illegible.

A heavy Colt was rusted in its mildewed sheath, each chamber loaded with unfired shells. The cartridges in the belt loops were green with verdegris. Finally, from the side pocket of the coat, the one which remained entire, he drew forth three fragments of stone. With narrowed eyes he stared at them and his lips pursed in a soundless whistle. Jim Hatfield knew silver ore when he saw it and the richness of the specimens astounded him.

"I don't know what Ed was doing, 'way up here, but he sure hit on *something* worth while, judging from the looks of these rocks," he told himself.

Sitting back on his heels, he stared about him, and his keen eyes saw what the two miners, Bill and Curt, had missed.

Snugged down under the overhang of the rock, almost obscured from view by the trailing prickly pear, was a bulky object. A moment later he hauled Ed Shafter's pack into the sunlight. A quick survey of its contents deepened the line between his brows.

"Prospector's outfit!" he muttered. "Now why *that?* Was Ed on the trail of something and using this outfit to cover up with, or was he really on a prospecting trip? Funny thing for a Ranger on assignment to be doing, but you never can tell. Ed was a mining man before he joined up with the Rangers, and when a mining man gets a lead to something like the story these rocks tell, he's pretty hard to hold.

"Brooks figured it was Cartina who got Webb, and figuring that way, Ed's only job was to drop his loop on Cartina. Maybe he had a tip about when Cartina would come back on this side the Line and while he was waiting, he might have heard of something good up here in the hills. That would account for him mavericking up here with a prospecting outfit.

"And if Brooks figured right on Webb's killing, and it was Cartina did the job, Ed must have tangled with Cartina up here. Cartina might have come up here over the Huachuca Trail for some reason or other and met up with Ed. Then again Ed might have got a tip on him and was up here on that tip. All of which doesn't tie up very satisfactorily, I'll admit."

Hatfield was, in fact, evolving another theory. He was still working on it when he left the skeleton and the pack and began ranging the neighborhood of the cliff. Working away from it in widening circles he discovered, more than a hundred yards distant from its foot and on the crest of a little rise, the skeleton of a burro. The skull was drilled with a clean hole. Hatfield stood over it thoughtfully.

"Uh-huh, killed the burro, too," he immediately understood. "Didn't want it straying around and attracting attention. Begins to look more and more like the fellow who did the shooting was planning to come back to this neighborhood."

Hatfield dug a grave with Shafter's pick and shovel. He wrapped the bones in a blanket which had been protected by the waterproofed covering of the pack and gave them decent burial. Later, they could be disinterred and taken to a cemetery. He hid the pack. Then he moved off a little way, built a fire and cooked the last of his food. After breakfasting and allowing the sorrel ample time to graze, he saddled up and rode away, leaving Ed Shafter to sleep in his lonely grave.

As he left the neighborhood of the overhanging rock, he heard, faint with distance, a deep and sullen rumble, and another and another. He nodded understanding and headed almost due east along the slightly sloping floor of the wide gorge.

More than one angle of the mystery was puzzling Hatfield. He knew that Shafter had been a dead shot with his old single-action Colt, and could draw with blinding speed. That he had been killed by revolver shots at comparatively short range was obvious. Why had his sixgun remained unfired in its sheath, while his rifle lay beneath the clutching bones of his dead hand? And, *the rifle had been cocked when Shafter fell!* The hammer was rusted into position.

Undoubtedly Shafter had been holding the rifle when killed. Ordinarily, a man making camp would not be holding a rifle in his hands. Hatfield had no way of knowing for sure that Shafter had been making camp when killed, but the evidence pointed that way. The pack had not yet been opened, and the Ranger had searched in vain for traces of a fire. There was no smudge against the face of the rock, the logical place for the blaze to have been kindled. A smudge there would not have been washed away, even during a period of months. Little or no rain would strike the face of the rock, no matter from what direction it came.

"Looks like he might have been watching for something, and somebody crept up on him," Hatfield deduced shrewdly. "It's funny. If he'd been shot in the back it wouldn't be so queer, but for Ed to get drilled between the eyes while facing somebody was unusual, considering the way that boy could handle a gun. Looks almost as though he knew the fellow who did it and wasn't expecting trouble from him and let him get the drop."

A mile or so distant from the rock, Hatfield became conscious of a peculiar sound drifting through the quiet of the canyon. It was a strange hissing and clicking that steadily increased in volume. It grew as he threaded his way through a grove of burr oaks and slanted around the curve of a low ridge. He passed a jutting cliff and the sound became much louder. From out the shadows rushed something huge and menacing.

Goldy gave a bound as the dark mass hurtled toward him. Hatfield was jolted sideways in the saddle and for a moment he had all he could do to control the frightened horse. The dark mass whizzed by, high overhead, and almost instantly another burst from the shadows cast by the cliff. Goldy immediately had another tantrum.

"Hold it, you darned jughead!" Hatfield roared. "Those things won't hurt you!"

Goldy subsided, sweating and shivering, and still snorting his apprehension each time one of the great missiles hurtled past. The Ranger eyed them with a speculative glance that held much of approval.

"Somebody surely knows their business," he declared.

High overhead stretched two heavy wire cables. From post to post they marched up and down the gorge. From the east, where the gorge dwindled to a wide dry wash, which in turn opened upon the level rangeland, clicked an endless succession of ponderous iron buckets, empty buckets that were drawn toward the head of the gorge. But those which whizzed downward toward the rangeland were loaded to the rim with crushed stone.

"Yes, somebody surely knows their business," the Ranger repeated. "Sending the ore down from the mines by conveyor buckets. Down below are the stamp mills, where there's plenty of water and fuel. Makes all the difference in the world. The mines in this district ought to be coining money. No wonder folks say that Helidoro town is a whizzer. Things must be booming down there."

Jim Hatfield had studied engineering in the course of his two years in college, before the death of his father, subsequent to the loss of the elder Hatfield's ranch, had cut short his scholastic career. He could understand and appreciate the worth of the conveyor system working before his eyes, and admire the man who had the foresight to replace pack mules or wagons with the efficient mechanical device.

Undoubtedly the Helidoro mines were making money and making it fast. He felt surer than ever that his surmise had been correct and that the mining town would represent opportunities hard for a bandit leader like Pedro Cartina to resist. Sooner or later, he was confident, Cartina would show up in the town, either leading a raid of some sort or scouting the ground preparatory to one.

Hatfield knew that the Tamarra Valley had been Cartina's favorite hunting ground even before the mining strike. In the year and more that had passed since that sunny day when

48

the bandit and his mysterious companion had delivered the Ranger to death by torture, Cartina had continued his depredations. For a while after Hatfield's troop had killed a number of his men and brought the Slash K trail herd back from Mexico, little had been heard of him. Later, however, Ranger reports on the district showed his renewed activity.

Hatfield, posted far to the east, had followed these reports with unflagging interest. He had looked forward to the time when he might possibly be assigned to a post that would take in the territory over which Cartina operated. The Lone Wolf had never forgotten that terrible experience on the ant hill. Later, the news of the death of young Dick Webb, apparently at the hands of the Cartina outfit, had strengthened his resolve to even the score with the snaky-eyed Mexican. The blood of a slain Ranger cried out for vengeance and Hatfield, intense in his loyalty to the outfit, would never rest easy so long as Webb's killer was not brought to justice. Now the death of Ed Shafter, Webb's successor in the district, was a further incentive to solve the mystery that brooded over the Tamarra Valley.

As to whether Cartina was responsible for Shafter's death, Hatfield was not sure. The clear-headed Ranger was not one to jump to conclusions. Many a man of the West had been killed because of his discovery of a rich mining claim. Perhaps Shafter had gone to swell their number. That he had struck it rich in the district seemed certain, to judge from the specimens in his pocket. Rich mines had been developed in the section during the past year. It looked like there might be a tie-up between those unexpected discoveries and Shafter's murder. Perhaps Cartina and his outfit must be absolved of this particular killing.

Ranger headquarters had received a number of bitter complaints from John Chadwick, the cattle king of the valley, and others. Young Dick Webb had been posted at Santa Rosita because of Cartina's continued depredations, and there had been talk of sending a troop after his death.

However, the serious outlaw trouble on the Oklahoma Border,

the Cuevas County cattle war and the Comanche Raids had made it impossible to spare such a number of men. Ed Shafter, the ace man of Brooks' command, had been sent to investigate Webb's death and, if possible, snare Cartina. It was all too evident now that Shafter had failed.

"Maybe he sowed the seed, though," mused the Lone Wolf as he rode along the line of the overhead conveyor. "Maybe what I've learned will be what it takes to clean up this mess."

As he turned into the shallow wash that led to where the smoke haze of Helidoro stained the clear blue of the eastern sky, Hatfield began to hear a low throb and mutter that swelled and swelled, never ceasing, never changing the steady beat of its monotonous tempo. He knew it meant stamp mills, not one but several, where the silver ore was ground to powder by the thundering dance of the ponderous steel pestles, preparatory to separating the silver from the stone.

"Sounds like big ones, too," he nodded. "Yes, this is going to be a salty town. Most anything's liable to happen, I guess."

He was not, however, prepared for what did happen as he cantered up the dusty main street just as the blue mystery of the dusk was whispering down from the hill crests.

The Ranger had already passed the gaunt buildings that housed the stamp mills before he turned into the main street of the town, which ran from north to south. Bars of light from windows and open doors were slashing the dusk with gold and in the dust of the street lay golden rectangles with misty purple edges. Men who paused before the doorways were clothed in blue and gold as light and shadow merged.

But those who suddenly came thundering down the street were not pausing anywhere. They were quirting their horses furiously, bending low in their saddles, close behind the necks of their mounts. Behind them sounded a stutter of shots and a chorus of yells.

Straight at the Ranger crashed the group of six or seven riders. Hatfield caught a glimpse of dark, savage faces and glinting black eyes. Then guns blazed and bullets stormed about him.

What it was all about, Jim Hatfield did not know, but he

had a decided aversion to being shot at. A twitch of the reins and Goldy went across the street in a weaving series of jumps that made him as elusive a mark as a scared rabbit. Hatfield, knowing his trained horse would do what was expected of him, dropped the reins on the sorrel's neck and went for his guns.

With a rattling crash, both Colts let go. Fire streamed from their black muzzles, smoke wisped up before the Ranger's grim face. He swayed and weaved in the saddle, a deceptive, uncertain figure in the deepening dusk. A bullet flicked a bit of skin from his neck. Another plucked at his shirt sleeve like a ghostly hand. Again his big single-actions roared.

Yells of rage and pain answered the boom of the Lone Wolf's guns. A man reeled in the saddle, gripping his smashed shoulder with reddened fingers. Another toppled sideways and thudded in the dust of the road, where he lay without sound or movement. Still another pitched forward onto his horse's neck and slithered to the ground as the group crashed past Hatfield. As they passed he saw that one was clutching the pommel to stay on his horse.

Hatfield jammed his empty guns into their sheaths and slid his rifle from the saddle boot. He flung the heavy Winchester to his shoulder and his finger crooked on the trigger. Then he hesitated, the sights of the long gun lining on the back of the rearmost rider. Without pulling the trigger, he lowered the rifle.

After all, he was not sure just what was going on. He had come out very much ahead in the encounter and it took a good deal of justification to shoot a man in the back. The whole business might be a case of the defeated contingent in some sort of a personal row fleeing the scene and mistaking the Ranger for an obstacle in their path.

A moment later, he was sorry he had held his fire.

Down the street came a group of men on foot, shouting, yelling, brandishing rifles and revolvers. In their lead was a tall, handsome man with iron-gray hair and flashing dark eyes. Beside him lumbered a squat individual with a tremendous spread of shoulders, a beefy face and a hard mouth. A silver star gleamed on the front of his sagging vest. In his hands he carried a heavy rifle. An instant later the muzzle of the rifle lined with Hatfield's broad breast.

"Drap that shootin' iron 'fore I plug yuh!" bellowed the sheriff. "Drap it, I say!"

Jim had no desire to argue with the forces of law and order. He did not drop the rifle, but with a slow gesture that could not be misunderstood, he shoved the weapon into the saddle boot.

"Guess that'll do just as well," he drawled, "and it won't get all full of dirt that way. Anything else you'd like me to do?"

"Yeah, get yore hands up!" snarled the sheriff. "Get his belt guns, Chadwick."

An amused light in his eyes, the Lone Wolf raised his slim hands to the height of his shoulders. The tall man moved toward him somewhat uncertainly.

"Maybe this fellow wasn't one of them, after all, Horton," he said.

"What's he doin' here with a gun in his hand, then?" growled the sheriff. "We can't take any chances, John."

"Here's two of 'em, stone dead!" a voice suddenly shouted.

Men were bending over the two riders Hatfield had downed.

"And here's nearly all of the money from the bank," another voice shouted. "Where's Elder? Let him check it and see."

The tall man had hesitated at the shouts. Now, however, he moved forward again and reached up for Hatfield's guns. As he did so a clear voice cut through the babel of whirling words like a silver knife blade of sound.

"Those guns are empty, Chadwick. You will find the bullets in the bodies of those two dead bandits there in the dust. I see our estimable sheriff is running true to form. The chances are that if he started out to arrest a card shark, he'd bring in the village padre."

Sheriff Horton whirled to face the far side of the street.

"Listen, Capistrano," he cried, "you'll horn into my affairs once too often sometime! I ain't takin' yore word for nothin'."

"It isn't necessary for you to do so," replied the silvery voice. "*Señor* Walsh here saw the whole thing also. Surely you will not contradict the president of the bank."

A thin little man came hurrying from between a couple of shacks. In his hands he carried a rifle.

"Amado's right," he said. "I was at his place when a boy ran in and yelled that the bank was being held up. We hurried over here hoping to intercept the outlaws as they rode out of town. We were too late, but we saw this man shoot it out with them and get two of them. I think he wounded one or two others. You should be thanking him, Sheriff, instead of thinking of arresting him."

The sheriff sputtered and rumbled in his throat.

"Well, if that's the way of it, Walsh," he said, "we made a mistake. Yuh can't hardly blame us, though. Runnin' onto this man with a saddle gun in his hand right while we was chasin' them bandits did look sorta suspicious."

Hatfield nodded briefly, accepting the sheriff's gruff apology. He already had catalogued Horton as being a slow thinking individual with a one-track mind. Clever enough in some ways, doubtless, but liable to mistakes where quick decisions were required. And excited men, the smartest of them, are apt to jump to wrong conclusions.

In fact, he hardly heard Horton's rumbled words. His whole attention was riveted on the extraordinary individual who had shuffled from the shadows with the banker Walsh. He was hatless and a bar of light from a lighted window revealed hair like crisply curling gold. Beneath the golden hair was the most astonishing handsome face Jim Hatfield had ever looked upon. The shapely head was set on a columnar neck that might have graced a heroic Greek statue.

But below the classic neck was pitiful distortion. There was a hump on the twisted back, another on the broad but mis-shapen breast. The mighty shoulders of the dwarf—he was not over five feet in height—were hunched, the arms amazingly long and powerful, ending in finely formed hands. The legs were crooked and bowed and dragged from the hips.

"Looks like God and the Devil both had a hand in making him!" the Lone Wolf exclaimed under his breath.

He was suddenly aware that the tall Chadwick was reaching up to shake his hand.

"You sure did a fine job, stranger," the big rancher congratulated. "Any time you feel like riding out to my place, I'd be mighty pleased to have a talk with you."

Hatfield had heard of the cattle baron, but had never before seen him. Chadwick was a fine figure of a man and his appearance justified the stories told about him. A light seemed to burn in the depths of his gray eyes. His jaw was heavy and powerful, his mouth firm. His nose was hooked like the beak of a hawk and more than hinted of strength and ability.

"A real fighting man who gets things done," was Hatfield's decision.

He shook hands with Chadwick and thanked him for his invitation. Walsh's voice broke in on their conversation.

"It looks like most of the money must be here," said the banker. "I can't say for sure. Where's Elder? He can tell in a minute."

"You mean the cashier?" asked a gangling cowboy. "Huh! he's daid. That tall man who rode in front shot him plumb 'tween the eyes!"

CHAPTER 6

MORE men were arriving on the scene. Among them was Long John Dyson, the sheriff's deputy. Horton immediately gave him instructions as to the disposal of the dead outlaws.

"I'll be expectin' yuh to show up at the coroner's inquest t'morrer, stranger," the sheriff told Hatfield. "Don't yuh be leavin' town till I give yuh permission."

Then he hurried back to the bank. Chadwick and Walsh went with him.

"Drop into the bank in the morning, I'd appreciate it," were the banker's last words to the Ranger.

Hatfield glanced down at a movement beside his horse. The

54

hunchback was standing there, an amused gleam in his clear blue eyes.

"Invitations appear to be in order," he observed in his musical voice, "so I'll just add another one. After you have stabled your horse—Flintlock Horner runs a good stable a little ways down the next street you cross—come over to my place, *Una Golondrina*. It's on this street a little ways further on. You can't miss it. You can eat there, if you're hungry."

"I could do with about ten pounds of steak," Hatfield admitted. "I'll be there as soon as I look after old Goldy."

The hunchback nodded and vanished in the shadows. Hatfield stared after him thoughtfully. Glancing around he met the eye of a smiling young Mexican.

"Know that fellow?" he asked, jerking his thumb in the direction the hunchback had taken.

"*Si*," replied the Mexican pleasantly. "Eet ees *Don* Amado Capistrano. He ees the very rich man. He owns the Cibola mine."

"A mining man, eh?" nodded Hatfield. "I had a notion he might be a cattleman. Legs look that way."

"*Si*," the Mexican agreed. "*Don* Amado ees descended from those who once owned much land and many cattle. It was he who first discovered the silver in the hills. He staked the first claim and built thees town. *Si*."

Hatfield was very thoughtful as he rode slowly toward the livery stable.

"Staked the first claim," he repeated the young Mexican's words. "That's interesting. Wonder if the ore out of the Cibola is full of funny zigzag threads of silver that sort of follow the same pattern?"

The sinewy fingers of one hand dropped into a side pocket and touched the fragment of stone which rested there.

He chuckled a little later, as he passed a building whose sign proclaimed it to be "Una Golondrina."

"*Una Golondrina!*" said Hatfield. "That means 'one swallow' in Spanish. Must be a saloon!"

It was, and a big one. Hatfield returned to it after turning

Goldy over to the care of Flintlock Horner, a six foot six individual with a pessimistic outlook on life.

"Almighty fine hoss," said Flintlock sadly, looking Goldy over with an appreciative eye. "Too fine. Chances are he'll get stole or somethin' 'fore long. That's the way things us'ally work out. He sorta reminds me of my fourth wife—no it was my fifth. She was a sorrel, too. She only had two feet, though, which made her sorta dif'rent from this cayuse. Does he kick and bite? Nope? Well, he ain't much like her after all. Yeah, I'll look after him good, don'tcha worry. I like hosses and wimmen, and they sorta take to me, too. That's how I come to lose my sixth—wife, I mean, not hoss. Never had six hosses, 'ceptin' at one time onct."

It was early in the evening when Hatfield pushed through the swinging doors, but already the *Una Golondrina* was doing a roaring business. There was a long bar running the entire length of the room on one side. Across from the bar was a lunch counter with stools and tables. There was a dance floor, two roulette wheels, a faro bank and a number of poker tables. Threading his way through the crowd, Hatfield saw the hunchback seated by himself at a corner table. He saw the Ranger and nodded an invitation.

Hatfield sat down and the hunchback ordered a meal. The Ranger, who appreciated good food when it came his way, did ample justice to the spread. After the dishes were removed, they rolled cigarettes and sat smoking in silence. Finally the hunchback asked:

"Are you just passing through, or figuring on stopping in this district a while?"

Hatfield smoked contemplatively a moment before replying.

"Depends on whether I can find a job in this section," he said. "I'm not particular, one way or another. I've got to stay around for the coroner's inquest tomorrow. After that I'm sort of uncertain about just what I'll do. I'll have to drop my loop on a job of some kind before long. There ought to be something for a hand on one of these big spreads hereabouts. This is just about the finest stretch of rangeland I've seen for a long

56

time. Folks are mighty lucky to own land in this section."

A cloud seemed to drift across the hunchback's clear eyes; the deep blue turned to a smoky gray. His delicately formed lips straightened to a hard line and the strong chin thrust out grimly. Hatfield saw the slim powerful hands ball into iron-hard fists. But when he spoke, his voice was unchanged in its bell-like quality and as softly modulated as before.

"Yes," he said, "it is a wonderful country and people living here are indeed fortunate. The very best of the land is owned by John Chadwick, but there are other fine ranches. I own a small one myself, adjoining Chadwick's property and bordering on the river. I acquired it recently from the widow of a man who died."

He was silent for a moment, and gradually his eyes changed color again and the hard lines of his mouth straightened out. He smiled suddenly at the tall Ranger and his teeth flashed. Again he spoke, almost diffidently.

"I was planning on offering you a job," he said. "I can use a hand or two on my little ranch, but that is not what I really had in mind. Would you consider a job other than cow punching?"

Hatfield considered a moment, his mind working swiftly.

"Depends on what it happens to be," he said at length. "I'm not much on working indoors if I can get out of it, but I'll take anything if I have to, particularly if the pay happens to be good."

"What I have to offer will pay you better than range riding, and it is not apt to keep you inside much," replied Amado Capistrano earnestly. "Ranching is but a side issue with me—as yet. My chief interest lies in my silver mine, the Cibola."

"Looks to me like you've got a *gold* mine right here," interpolated Hatfield, nodding toward the crowded bar and busy tables.

Amado Capistrano shrugged with Latin expressiveness.

"Yes, the place makes money," he admitted. "I set it up after I saw the kind of dens the silver strike brought to life. I decided there should be at least one place in the town where my workers would not be robbed. The drinks sold here are good and the games are straight."

Hatfield's keen gaze had been studying the crowd for some time.

"Some of those fellows don't look exactly like miners or waddies to me," he remarked. The hunchback smiled a somewhat wry smile.

"No," he admitted, "they don't. In fact, they are neither one nor the other. It may seem strange, but the worst element was also attracted to a place where they could get good liquor and depend on a straight game. I think I am safe in hazarding the guess that a good many of the shady characters from the Tamarra Hills and from the other side of the river are here tonight, and most every other night."

"It's likely," Hatfield replied. "You see, those fellows risk their lives, as a rule, for the pesos they manage to get their hands on. Naturally, they don't want to have it taken away from them by a crooked wheel or an extra smooth dealer, or to shell it out for drinks that are a mixture of cactus juice, rattlesnake poison and barbed wire."

"Their choice has caused me more than a little embarrassment," Capistrano said. "But to get back to the matter we were discussing. As I stated, my chief interest is my mine. The Cibola is a rich claim and much of the ore is high-grade stuff. Not only is it rich in silver but the gold content is high. It doesn't take much of that high-grade to mount into real money. Which brings me to the point, *Señor*—" He glanced at the Ranger questioningly.

Hatfield supplied his name, giving his real one, as he did not have much fear of it being recognized. It was not an uncommon one throughout the Southwest, and he was comparatively new to the district.

"*Señor* Hatfield," Capistrano continued, "I am being robbed; steadily, systematically and successfully robbed. High-grade ore is vanishing from my mine at an alarming rate. The veins are as rich as ever, but the cleanup at the mills has been steadily falling off. In some manner the rich ore is being pilfered from the mine and almost worthless rock put in its place."

"What makes you think the stealing is going on at the mine?" Hatfield asked. "Maybe somebody is taking it out of the conveyor buckets on the way to the mills."

Capistrano shook his head in a decided manner.

"It isn't possible," he explained. "The number of buckets that leave the mine must check with the number received at the mill. The buckets do not pause on their trip from the mine to the mill. If they did so, it would be instantly known. Once they leave the mine they must keep on moving until they reach the mill. Even were it possible to empty them on the way down, the arrival of empty buckets at the mill would at once be noticed. No, the conveyor system is practically proof against theft. The robbing is done either at the mine or at the mill. The mill seems out of the question, so it must be the mine."

Hatfield nodded, gazing expectantly at the other. He offered no further comment. Capistrano rolled a cigarette with his tapering fingers, lighted it and inhaled a lungful of smoke. Hatfield waited patiently.

"I've tried in various ways to run the thieves down," the hunchback continued, "but as yet with no success. Complaints to the sheriff are useless—he is not overly fond of me—and my foremen and superintendents are thoroughly baffled. I watched you have that brush with Cartina and his men tonight, and I—"

"Just a minute," Hatfield interrupted. "How do you know that was the Cartina outfit?"

"The tall, black-eyed man with the lank hair, the one who rode in front, was Pedro Cartina," the hunchback replied quietly.

Hatfield nodded. Capistrano spoke again.

"Before I offer you a job," he said, "I am going to proffer some good advice—leave this district, now, tonight. Get on your horse and ride—any direction, just so it is away from the Tamarra Valley. Cartina never forgives, and he never forgets. He will avenge the killing of his men, and his vengeance is something to make the bravest shudder. You will not be safe a moment while you are here. He has followers everywhere. I would not be the least surprised if some are in this room at the moment. Cartina has power."

Again Hatfield nodded.

"He sort of wobbled in his saddle when I was cutting down on the gang," he remarked irrelevantly.

"He's hard to kill," replied Capistrano with instant understanding. "If you wounded him, that will just make his vengeance the more certain and the more terrible. I repeat, *señor*, ride, and at once."

"Thanks for the advice," Hatfield said quietly, "I'm not taking it."

The hunchback smiled.

"I did not think you would," he admitted, "but I felt it my duty to warn you. Well, if you are going to stay in the district, I'll make my offer. As I said, when I saw you in action tonight it came to me that I was watching the man who could handle the situation here if anybody could. If you'll take the job, I'll hire you to run down the thieves who are robbing me. I'll pay double what you could get on a ranch, and if you are successful, there'll be a substantial bonus for you."

"And what do I get if I'm not successful?" Hatfield asked with the suspicion of a smile quirking the corners of his stern mouth.

Amado Capistrano did not smile and there was no jest in his voice when he replied:

"The chances are, a six-foot pine box!"

"That would be rather close quarters," Hatfield grinned. "I'm six-foot-four. I'll take the job!"

CHAPTER 7

CAPISTRANO summoned a waiter and the latter brought him pen, ink and paper. He wrote steadily for a moment or two, and as he wrote, the Lone Wolf watched him with slightly

60

narrowed eyes and a deepening of the concentration furrow between his black brows.

"Here," Capistrano said, handing him the note, "this will introduce you to Bowers, my superintendent at the mine, and to Fuentes at the mill. They will cooperate with you to the fullest extent. You have freedom to act as you see fit."

"Let me be the one to tell these two fellows about our agreement," suggested Hatfield.

Capistrano nodded.

"I have the fullest confidence in Bowers and Fuentes," he replied, "but I will follow your suggestion. Now let's have a drink to seal the bargain."

The glasses were filled and they were just raising them to their lips when the swinging doors crashed open and a man strode into the room. It was John Chadwick and he was in a furious temper.

The uproar hushed as the tall cattle king glared about the room, his flashing eyes finally fixing on Amado Capistrano. Lips drawn back from his teeth, he headed for the table at which the hunchback sat. Men and women made way for him, but Chadwick did not appear to notice them. At the table he halted, his face working with anger.

"Capistrano," he barked, "there was another raid on my ranch this afternoon. Two of my men killed and a couple of hundred head of cattle widelooped. And they went across your spread!"

The hunchback gazed calmly into Chadwick's blazing eyes. In his silvery voice he spoke one word.

"Well?"

Chadwick fairly choked with rage.

"Well!" he mimicked, his voice hoarse with passion. "Well, I've stood about all I'm going to stand, that's what. Those thieving killers cut across your spread and into greaserland. Then when my men started after them, your paid cutthroats held them up at your fence and wouldn't let them go through!"

"What proof have you that the rustlers went across my land?" Capistrano asked calmly.

"Proof!" sputtered Chadwick, "Proof! What other way could they go? What other way *would* they go except by Huachuca Trail? And it runs across your spread, doesn't it?"

"Then you are just surmising they crossed my land? You really do not know?"

"I know this much!" raged Chadwick. "I know one greaser always stands up for another!"

Even Jim Hatfield was not prepared for the speed with which the apparently awkward hunchback moved. Capistrano's amazingly long arms shot across the table, his slim hands gripped Chadwick's elbows. One mighty heave of his great shoulders and the ranch owner hurtled through the air. He landed on his back with a crash a dozen feet distant, rolled over, writhed for an instant and surged erect, right hand flashing to his left armpit.

"Hold it!"

John Chadwick tensed rigid, the butt of the half-drawn gun gripped in his hand, the long barrel still in the shoulder holster. Face working with anger, he glared at the tall Ranger.

Jim Hatfield's hands had moved with blinding speed, sliding his big Colts from their carefully worked and oiled cut-out holsters in a blurred flicker of motion. The black muzzles yawned toward Chadwick. The Lone Wolf's voice smashed at him.

"Cut your wolf loose in the right way, Chadwick, and it's okay, but this fellow isn't heeled—you can see that. It isn't just the correct thing to throw down on a man who isn't carrying a gun."

Slowly Chadwick let the gun slide back into its sheath. His contorted features smoothed out. He nodded agreement.

"Right," he said. "You've got a head on your shoulders, stranger, but maybe if you'd just been pitched clean through yourself and out the other side, you'd be sort of off balance, too. As for you, Capistrano—"

Crash!

Just in time Jim Hatfield had caught the flicker of steel across the room. He fired over his right arm with his left-hand gun and a man reeled back against the bar, clutching a blood-spouting shoulder. The gun he had furtively drawn clattered to the floor. Hatfield peered through the wisping smoke, sweeping the crowd with his cold eyes.

Outside sounded the thud of running feet. The swinging doors crashed open and men boiled into the room—lean, capable-appearing men, a half dozen of them. Hatfield tensed, the big Colts clamped rigidly against his sinewy thighs. The tight group paused just inside the door, hands hovering over their gun butts, eyes sweeping the room.

One, a rangy, rawboned individual with a drooping moustache, took a long stride forward, his eyes fixed on John Chadwick.

"Yuh all right, Boss?" he called. "We heerd shootin'."

"All right, Edwards," Chadwick called back. "Just a little misunderstanding."

The lanky Edwards, Chadwick's foreman, glanced suspiciously at Jim Hatfield, who had holstered his guns and was lounging easily against the table.

"That big feller shot Bill Thompson, Ed," a voice shouted.

Edwards stiffened, but Chadwick's voice cut at him.

"Bill had it coming," the ranch owner said, "he's always going off half-cocked. He meant all right but he used bad judgment."

"Shore 'pears he did," grunted Edwards, turning and striding toward the group that had laid the wounded man on a table and were attending to his injury.

"He ain't hurt bad," somebody offered. "High up through the shoulder. Didn't bust the bone."

Chadwick addressed the hunchback.

"I apologize for calling you a greaser, Capistrano," he said in a level tone. "That was out of turn and I shouldn't have done it. But that's the only thing I'm taking back," he added, his voice hardening, "and I'm warning you—the next time my men start across your spread they're *going* across. They're not going to be stopped!"

"When they have a legitimate reason for crossing, they are

welcome to do so," the hunchback replied quietly, "but I don't intend to have another barn burned nor another water hole poisoned."

Chadwick glared at him, his gray eyes flashing. Then he strode straight across the room and out the door. His men, two of them supporting the wounded Thompson, followed.

Hatfield and the hunchback sat down to their unfinished drink. Business in the saloon went on as usual. The roulette wheels spun merrily, cards slithered, dice rattled. The bartenders sloshed drinks into glasses. The orchestra blared out a rollicking tune; boots thumped and dainty French heels clicked. Somebody began bellowing a song.

Capistrano leaned forward and smiled into the Ranger's eyes.

"Relative to what I said a few moments ago about your leaving this section," he said, "I now repeat the warning, more earnestly than ever. Leave Helidoro at once, tonight!"

Hatfield stared at him in astonishment.

"I thought we'd settled that," he remarked.

Capistrano smiled again.

"That was before the little incident which just occurred," he said. "That was before you made an enemy a thousand times more dangerous than Pedro Cartina could ever be. You bitterly offended the most powerful man in the Tamarra Valley, one of the most powerful in the entire state, in fact. John Chadwick will never forget what you did tonight."

"Chadwick doesn't strike me as the sort who would play the game the Cartina way," Hatfield remarked.

"Oh, no, nothing so crude as that," Capistrano shrugged with Latin expressiveness. "Chadwick's methods are more subtle, but just as deadly. It is strange, but men who offend or thwart him seem to have much bad luck. Some suffer unexplainable accidents, due, apparently, to natural causes. Others are convicted of surprising crimes and are now serving long terms in the state prison. Others, wealthy and influential, suffer disastrous business reverses and become ruined men. Strange, but true."

"Chadwick has always had a good reputation, as far as I ever heard," the Ranger said.

Capistrano shrugged again.

"Excellent," he admitted. "He always stays within the law. But a smart man with great wealth and great influence can sometimes find the law remarkably elastic. Oh, yes, John Chadwick is a good citizen. No one could be more industrious in the running down of such petty outlaws as Alfredo Zorrilla and El Zopilote and others of their ilk. Crooked gamblers, gunmen, robbers and such on this side the Line have also felt the weight of his hand. John Chadwick upholds the Law. John Chadwick, in fact, *is* the Law!"

"You don't seem in awe of him," Hatfield commented dryly.

Capistrano shrugged deprecatingly.

"Chadwick hates me," he replied. "I do not agree with his notions as to how a district, or a state, should be governed. That is enough to earn his dislike. Then not long ago I managed to acquire a piece of property he had his heart set on. Also, I am a candidate for the office of sheriff, on a platform somewhat opposed to that on which his friend, Sheriff Branch Horton, is running. The election is but a short time off and Chadwick is using every means available to insure my defeat. He considers me an outlander with no right to hold office.

"Really, Señor Hatfield," he added, smiling his charming, melancholy smile, "I am forced to believe that at the bottom John Chadwick is an honest man. He truly believes what he believes. He feels that he is divinely appointed to control the destinies of his fellowmen and that anyone who opposes him should be ruthlessly crushed. It is an attitude developed and fostered by the great landowners. My ancestors, some of them at least, held much the same attitude. If they considered a thing right, it, of necessity, *must* be right because they believed it was. John Chadwick is of the same breed."

Hatfield nodded his understanding. He too had encountered this attitude on the part of the barons of the open range. Accustomed to ruling with an iron hand, they were intolerant of any interference and willing to go to desperate lengths to maintain the prerogatives they honestly believed should be theirs.

Chadwick, one of the really large owners of the state, doubtless was subject to his feeling in a marked degree and would bitterly resent anything that might be construed as an encroachment upon what he considered his rights and privileges. He surrounded himself with men of his own kind, who saw eye to eye with him and were ready at all times to uphold him.

"Those rannies of his who barged in here are a salty lot," Hatfield mused as he sipped his drink. "They're not the kind to take water from anybody and they're all set to back their boss up in anything he says. Maybe Chadwick isn't altogether a bad fellow, but he belongs to the breed that has to be taken down a peg every now and then. Can't get it through their heads that this country is for everybody and not just for a few big toads who're liable to slop all the water out of the puddle if they keep on swelling themselves up."

Flintlock Horner had a spare room over the livery stable and he rented it to Hatfield for the night. Before lying down, the Ranger sat on the edge of the little built-in bunk and smoked a final cigarette. His face was very thoughtful and there was a speculative light in his gray eyes.

He was thinking, in fact, not of the stirring events of the past twenty-four hours, but of a commonplace incident that, ordinarily, would have been of little interest. He was visioning Amado Capistrano writing that note of introduction to his mine superintendent—*writing with his left hand!*

Then he dismissed the matter with a shrug and stretched out to relax in slumber, resolutely putting puzzles out of his mind. In a moment he was asleep.

CHAPTER 8

In men who for long periods of time ride stirrup to stirrup with deadly danger, there develops an eerie sixth sense that ofttimes warns of approaching peril. Many a time during his adventurous years as a Ranger, Jim Hatfield had felt death's stealthy approach. Many a time this strange premonition of evil had saved him. He had learned to respect the seemingly inexplicable and to accept the warnings when they came.

Thus, when he suddenly awoke with every nerve tingling and every muscle tense, he did not dismiss the alarming manifestations as figments of an overwrought imagination. Silent, motionless he lay, ready for instant action, listening with keen ears, endeavoring to pierce the quiet dark of the little room.

From the other side of town came the monotonous rumble of the stamp mills. In the livery stable below a horse pawed impatiently Another stamped in his stall. A strain of music drifted faintly from some still active dance hall. Otherwise the night was silent.

And yet—the thick dark was acrawl with menace. Hatfield could feel it, a stealthy, furtive, deadly thing that drew closer and closer. Waiting there in the black shadow, the palms of his hands grew moist, his muscles ached with strain. The weird premonition fairly screamed its warning in his ears. Hollow-eyed murder was abroad in the night; was approaching the cot in the little room.

Slowly, quietly, the Ranger stretched his hands toward the heavy Colts always within easy reach. He gripped the black butts, drew the big guns from their sheaths and lithely slipped over the foot of the cot. Crouched against the end wall of the room, he watched the opaque blot that was the door.

A crack split the intense dark, a dimly luminous crack that widened by almost imperceptible degrees. A tiny creaking filtered through the silence; the glowing crack remained stationary for a long moment. Then again it began to widen, slowly, steadily as the door opened and the feeble beams from the lantern hanging in the stable below seeped through the dark.

The clean edges of the widening crack of light abruptly blurred as a grotesque shadow absorbed the glow. Jim Hatfield, tense against the wall, saw a man slip into the room. Another followed him, and another. They merged with the shadows thronging the room.

The crack of light now stretched across the room and faintly illumined the bunk built against the wall. It fell on the tumbled blankets from under which the Ranger had slipped, and in the illusive gleam the bedding took on the shape of a huddled human form. The indistinct shape was suddenly blotted out by the shadow of a man who leaned over the cot.

There was a flashing glitter, then the sodden ripping blows of a knife that slashed the blankets to ribbons. Instantly there followed a startled curse.

"Hell's fire! There ain't nobody here! He's—look out!"

With a rattling crash, both the Ranger's guns let go. The knife wielder screamed shrilly, whirled sideways and thudded to the floor. The walls of the little room seemed to reel and bulge to the roar of six-shooters.

Hatfield, pouring lead at the two shadowy figures, ducked and weaved, sliding back and forth along the wall as bullets hammered the boards. He heard another yell, snapped a shot at a fleeing shadow and hurled his body to the floor as fire streamed through the dark.

Feet were thudding on the stairs. They hit the landing just as the two remaining killers hurtled through the door. With a terrific roar, a shotgun let go. Then there was another deafening crash as a cursing, clawing, fighting knot of men whirled end-over-end down the narrow stairs.

Hatfield reached the door just as the shotgun bellowed a second time. He saw a slight, dark man literally blown across the stable, his face a bloody smear of buckshot-riddled flesh. He saw the grim, rage-distorted face of lanky Flintlock Horner glaring through the shotgun smoke, and for the briefest instant he glimpsed another face as a tall, broad-shouldered man bounded across the stable toward the outer door—just a fleeting glimpse of a weatherbeaten face with flashing black eyes and a lean, hard jaw.

For an instant he thought the fleeing man might be Pedro Cartina, but as instantly discarded the thought. The man was taller, broader, and his skin was tanned, not swarthy.

All this Hatfield noted in the split second before he lined

68

sights on the fleeing man and pulled trigger. The hammers of his guns fell with a chilly double-click on empty cartridges.

Ejecting the empties and jamming loaded shells into one gun, he bounded down the stairs. Flintlock flung up the reloaded shotgun, but Hatfield roared a warning in the nick of time. Getting the gun down threw Horner off-balance, however, and he barged smack into the racing Ranger. The two hit the floor in a wild tangle. By the time they scrambled to their feet and shot out the door, the fleeing man was nowhere in sight.

"I told you somebody'd try to steal that yaller hoss!" bawled Flintlock. "A yaller hoss and a red-haided woman! They means trouble all the time! The only thing what's wuss'n either of 'em is both!"

The stable keeper was a sight. One eye was rapidly closing, a bleeding nose had already swelled to twice its normal proportions, and his face was otherwise scratched and battered. He held the ten-gauge shotgun at full cock and brandished it wildly. Hatfield looked into the yawning black muzzles and hastily stepped aside. Horner hammered the butt of the gun on the floor to lend emphasis to his shouts and both barrels went off with a roar like the crack of doom.

The blast reeled and startled Flintlock into a stall, and a mule promptly kicked him out again. He scrambled to his feet, rubbing the seat of his trousers, and resumed his yelling where he had left off. Hatfield got the shotgun and shoved it out of sight behind a feed barrel.

Men were pouring into the stable, aroused by the terrific tumult. They bellowed questions which nobody could answer, and for a few minutes a fair imitation of bedlam ensued. Hatfield finally restored some semblance of order, and the two bodies were hauled forth and examined.

Both wore the garb of Mexicans. The face of the man who had received the shotgun charge was little more than a bloody smear. That of the one Hatfield had shot was swarthy, slit-mouthed, high of cheekbones and nose bridge.

"Pure-blood Yaqui," was the verdict of members of the crowd. "Coupla hoss lifters from t'other side the river, that's what."

Flintlock Horner's contention that Hatfield's splendid sorrel had been the object of the raid was accepted without argument. The Ranger expressed no opinion to the contrary.

Sheriff Horton bustled in a little later and glared at Hatfield.

" 'Pears yuh been mixed up in plenty of trouble since yuh hit town," he growled accusingly.

"Meaning?" the Lone Wolf drawled.

"Meanin' nothin', 'cept watch yore step!" Horton snorted. "This is a law-abidin' section and we don't favor quick-draw men hangin' out here. But don't yuh be pullin' out 'fore the coroner's inquest this mornin'."

He stamped out, grumbling under his breath. Flintlock Horner tentatively fingered his swelling nose and grunted.

"Some day, plumb by accident, Horton's gonna have a sensible thought—and it'll bust his head wide open!" said Flintlock.

After the room was put in order, Hatfield went to bed again. He could hear Horner swearing about the stable, searching for his shotgun. Hatfield chuckled as he closed his eyes, but the chuckle died and his mouth set in stern lines as he recalled the face and form of the tall man racing across the stable floor.

"Uh-huh, and it was a big, tall, broad-shouldered fellow who pegged me down on that anthill down in Mexico. I wonder, now? Could that be the brains behind Pedro Cartina?"

CHAPTER 9

Jim Hatfield decided to ride to Capistrano's A Bar C ranch the following afternoon.

"It'll be better to have it look like I'm just taking a job of riding with you," he told the hunchback. "If I go spreading around as a sort of special detective you've hired to run down the men making away with your ore, they'll have the same line on me as they have on the sheriff and his deputies. There's some mighty shrewd people back of this business, and it wouldn't be wise to give them any more headway on us than we have to."

Capistrano agreed with the wisdom of this course.

"I'll ride to the ranch with you," he told the Lone Wolf. "I'll introduce you to Felipe, my foreman, and tell him that you are going to ride the west range and plan winter shelters and get a line on waterholes and feed in the canyons. Then you can cut into the hills whenever you take a notion. My spread covers all that section.

"The Huachuca Trail cuts through the hills within a few miles of the conveyor lines and not a great way west of the mines. My conveyor line is the one farthest west, incidentally, On the east are the lines of the Root Hog, the Lucky Turn, the Humboldt, and others. Yes, it is a big working. Those hills are bursting with silver, something no one ever suspected and which I discovered by merest chance. I'll tell you about it sometime."

"I'd be interested in hearing it," Hatfield admitted.

Sheriff Horton's office was also the office of the coroner, a bewhiskered and cantankerous individual known as Ol' Doc Draper. Doc was a typical cow country physician, shrewd, irascible, efficient. He was close to seventy years of age but had the energy of a man forty years younger. Hatfield immediately placed him as a character, and a likeable and dependable one. His questions were brief and to the point.

"Murdered in performance of his duty by Pedro Cartina or some other outlaw like him," was his verdict on the death of the bank cashier Elder.

"Cashed in when they had it comin'," he ruled relative to the bandits Hatfield had shot.

"Yuh shore must have almighty good eyesight to pick out that leadin' rider as Cartina," he told Amado Capistrano, a point Jim Hatfield had already noted.

That finished the inquest. Sheriff Horton, however, had a word with Jim Hatfield on his own account.

"Yuh 'pear to be the right sort," he told the Ranger, "but yuh seem to be gettin' into the wrong comp'ny. I've been told yuh've signed up to ride for Capistrano. I ain't got nothin' personal 'gainst Amado, but he don't strike me as bein' jest the

71

right sort. The worst characters in this here district hang out in his place, and he hires mostly greasers for his mine and his spread.

"He hadn't oughta had that spread in the fust place. Lots of folks figger it was some of his outfit what did for Walt Bloodsoe, who owned A Bar C 'fore Capistrano got holt of it. He shore was all-fired quick to hustle over and buy the spread offa Walt's widdy after Walt was cashed in. John Chadwick was gonna take over the outfit, but Amado got there fust. Seems almost like he knowed to make his plans in advance. I'm jest tellin' *yuh*."

Hatfield mentioned the matter to Walsh, the bank president, to whom he had taken a strong liking.

"I don't know about that," Walsh said, "but I do know that Amado paid the Widow Bloodsoe more than the ranch was worth; more, I believe, than she could have gotten from anybody else."

Which gave the Lone Wolf something more to ponder over as he cinched Goldy and rode out to meet his new employer.

Capistrano wore regulation cow country garb, his only concession to his Spanish blood being an ornate *sombrero* heavy with silver. He wore heavy, double cartridge belts and two guns. One holster, the left, swung much lower than the other. The sheaths were cut high and only the black butts of the guns showed.

"Both regulation .45 frames, or I'm mistaken," Hatfield decided, after a quick glance. "He's not a real two-gun man but the sort of fellow who draws one gun first and then draws the other one to back it up. Pulls the left one most of the time and always first. Yes, there's no doubt about it, he's really left-handed—doesn't just write that way."

They rode in silence for the most part. Capistrano seemed busy with thoughts of his own, and the Ranger, too, had plenty to think about. The hunchback, likeable though he seemed, was occupying a peculiar position in the Ranger's mind. He was the first man to benefit by the silver strike, a strike that had taken place, as near at Hatfield could ascertain, at about the same time Ed Shafter had vanished into the Tamarra Hills.

The Cibola mine, while located some distance from where the slain Ranger's body had been found, was in the same general section—in the same wide gorge, to be exact, only farther east and to the north, a district it was quite logical to believe Shafter had passed over to reach the Huachuca Trail.

And Capistrano was left-handed—and the Ranger's experience had been that it was usually a left-handed man who carried guns of the type that had inflicted the death wounds of both Shafter and young Dick Webb.

Then there was the poor opinion of Capistrano held by Sheriff Horton, who, to all appearances, was an honest if somewhat stupid officer; and by John Chadwick, easily the foremost citizen of the valley, a man who had held positions of trust and was spoken of for positions of still greater honor.

"Well," mused the Lone Wolf, "a man is innocent till he's proved guilty. But," he added, the corners of his firm mouth quirking a trifle, "that doesn't mean a man can't keep his eyes open."

The A Bar C was a comparatively small ranch, but a good one, Hatfield quickly decided. It was well wooded and a little stream flowed through it from northwest to southeast. There were also quite a number of waterholes, while to the south, the silver sheen of the Rio Grande formed its boundary. Curved about the spread, east and north, like a lion around a crouching lamb, was John Chadwick's great Circle C, the finest and by far the largest outfit in the valley. Still farther east was the Rocking Chair, the Lazy V, the Bowtie, and others.

Capistrano's half-dozen riders were young Mexican *vaqueros* with dark faces and white grins. They were courteous and pleasant. Felipe, the foreman, was jolly and moon-faced and he had an infectious chuckle. They conversed with Hatfield in broken English and many gestures. The Lone Wolf spoke Spanish fluently and understood it equally well but he did not always allow the fact to become common knowledge.

The riders treated Capistrano with great respect, addressing him as *Don* Amado.

"Their fathers and their fathers' fathers before them were retainers of my family," the hunchback explained. "The time was when more than twice a hundred men rode the great *hacienda* of the Capistranos, which included this entire valley."

He was silent for a moment gazing with eyes that seemed to dream across the wide expanse of beautiful rangeland to the far distant edge of the grim Tamarra Desert that stretched eastward from the Hueco Mountains, curving north around the Tamarra Hills and then rolling southward to the Rio Grande. The heat-tortured waste of gray alkali and sand enclosed the rich valley and the barren silver hills. The desert was sinister, but here on the green range was sunshine and peace.

"A mighty pretty country," said the Lone Wolf.

"Yes," said Amado Capistrano.

Jim Hatfield rode the range the following morning.

"I can find my way about," he told Felipe, when the foreman courteously offered to place a guide at his disposal.

"Sometimes a fellow just looking around can see what a fellow who knows the country misses," he added by way of explanation.

Felipe agreed and answered questions relative to general directions. He also offered a word of warning.

"The Huachuca Trail crosses our land near the foot of the hills," he said. "The señor will do well to beware that trail. The men who use eet are all too often, what you call eet, not nice. They are *muy malo,* very bad."

Hatfield thanked the foreman and rode away. All day he probed the canyons and gorges, drifting far to the south, until he reached the shimmering band of the river. Then he turned north by west and rode into the red eye of the setting sun. Dusk was misting over the range before he reached the foothills of the Tamarra.

It was a weird night! A cold, dead moon soared up over the dim crags beyond the desert, shining fitfully through scurrying clouds. A wailing wind swept restlessly through the burr oaks and the sage. There were patches of desert bordering the gaunt slopes of the hills and on them giant chola cactuses brandished grotesque arms that twisted and writhed like malignant devils tortured with pain. The wan moonlight cast strange shadows and all things were distorted and unreal.

Just as distorted and just as unreal was the writhing gray ribbon of the Huachuca Trail. Jim Hatfield had often sensed an intangible something about the trail that differentiated it from others.

There was something brazen about the Huachuca, something sinister, something definitely evil. It did not slip furtively, nor did it march boldly. It writhed—writhed like a bad-tempered snake that knew its power for evil and its ability to destroy.

The Huachuca slid into gloomy canyons as if it belonged there, slid out again, seeming to carry some grim secret that would be well worth the telling but which wouldn't be told, unless bleached bones could talk.

In the shadow of a grove of burr oaks, Hatfield pulled his big sorrel to a halt. For long minutes he sat gazing at the trail. Suddenly he tensed in the saddle and eyes narrowed.

Sound was drifting up from the south, from the direction of that broad, shallow river that shimmered in the furtive moonlight. At first it was but a whisper, but it grew steadily to a mutter, a faint drumming, a low thunder.

Out of the gray-cloaked dark burst shadowy figures, sweeping north with steady swiftness. Hatfield identified them as mounted men. Leaning forward he clamped his hand gently over the sorrel's nose. Goldy was usually a silent horse, but he might feel an urge to call out a comradely greeting to one of the horses passing up the trail. And Hatfield much preferred his presence in the grove to remain unnoted. Instinctively he counted the riders as they passed.

He missed some, but more than a hundred had flashed by the grove before the last hoofbeat dimmed away into the distance.

"And every one carrying a rifle!" the Ranger muttered as he urged Goldy onto the trail.

Silent, watchful, he rode up the gray track in the wake of the speeding band. Intent on what was ahead, he did not see the shadowy forms that rode half a mile to his rear. Nor did

75

this second group of riders, apparently hurrying to overtake the first, realize that the Ranger rode between them and their objective. They were a compact body, many less in number than those ahead, and their leader was a tall man whose broad-brimmed hat was drawn low over his eyes.

On through the gloomy gorge burrowed the Huachuca Trail, dipping and rising, snaking along in the shadow of overhanging cliffs, turning sharply to the left at length and climbing along the face of a beetling wall of rock. To the right was a sheer drop into black darkness where water boiled and murmured. A swift stream ran along the base of the cliff, a deep little river that gushed from under a towering cliff at the head of the gorge and thundered into a yawning chasm beneath another cliff a few miles farther to the south. It was a "lost river" of mystery that held its course from darkness to darkness and hugged the canyon wall as if shrinking away from the light.

Jim Hatfield, however, paid scant attention to the bluster of the water as he rode swiftly up the Huachuca Trail. His mind, set at trigger edge, concentrated fully on the grim band of armed men who rode the trail ahead. He was certain that he had, partly by lucky accident, intercepted Pedro Cartina and his raiders as they rode north to rob and murder.

"Maybe I can get a line on what they're up to and figure out some way to crack down on them before they can get back across the Line," he muttered, peering through the gray darkness and straining his ears for signs of the quarry.

He knew that the valley was up in arms against the outlaws and that he could swiftly organize a force competent to deal with even a large and well armed band. The recollection of the rear guard fight he and his Rangers had waged against the Cartina outfit came to his mind and he chuckled.

"If I can get a dozen men together, armed with good Winchesters, we'll hang onto them and head them off from the river," he declared. "It'll work out just like it did that time in Mexico, only we'll round up a different kind of cattle this time."

The sky was clearing and the moon casting more light.

The trail ahead shimmered wanly as it straightened out and mounted a long rise. Hatfield rode warily, his eyes fixed on the distant crest where the trail seemed to end abruptly. The men he followed were not in sight and he could no longer hear the sound of their horses, but there was the danger that they might be just the other side of the dip. Anxious to catch up with them, but not daring to risk topping the rise and finding himself in their midst, he slowed the sorrel to a walk and halted him a score of paces distant from the crest. He swung to the ground and crept forward on foot, bending low and hugging the cliff wall. A moment later he could see over the rise.

A half mile or so ahead was the band, riding slowly along the winding trail. They were bunched together and it seemed to the Ranger that an air of anticipation hung over the group.

"Looks like they were expecting something or somebody," he told himself.

He shifted his position slightly, moved away from the cliff in order to get a clearer view.

Cr-r-r-rack! Wham! Whe-e-e-e!

A bullet screamed past, scant inches from his head, slammed against the cliff, screeched off on a wild ricochet and whined away into the darkness. Hatfield ducked instinctively and whirled, guns coming out. The slug had come from *behind him!*

One swift glance and he was racing for his horse. Down the trail, only a few hundred yards distant, rode a body of men, thundering toward him, yelling and shooting. Hatfield reached Goldy amid a rain of bullets, swung into the saddle and yelled to the sorrel. Goldy shot forward in a racing gallop, topped the rise and thundered down grade. A few seconds later the pursuing band swooped over the rise and bullets began to whine past the Ranger.

The group ahead had halted. Hatfield, swiftly estimating the distance, felt safe from their guns for a few minutes longer. He was astounded when a bullet from their direction fanned his face and another plucked at his sleeve.

"They've got guns that can *carry!*" he growled.

His predicament was truly desperate. Between two hostile

forces, bullets storming about him, one of which would surely find its mark, to his left was an insurmountable wall of rock, to his right a sheer drop into the river. How far it was to the canyon floor Hatfield had no way of knowing. The questing beams of the moonlight did not penetrate the gloom of the gorge and the elusive murmur of the water told him little.

"Have to chance it, though," he grunted as a slug grazed his cheek. He swerved the sorrel sideways, gripped the reins with steely fingers and braced himself in the saddle.

Goldy did not want to take the jump, and wildly snorted his protest. But he took it, bunching his dainty hoofs and tensing his big body, as he shot over the lip of the cliff.

Down he rushed—down—down, the wind shrieking past in a hurricane, black fangs of rock soaring up to meet him. He grazed a reaching hand of jagged stone, struck the water with a splash and vanished under the inky surface. Hatfield swung from the saddle, gripped the sorrel's mane and held tight as they slowly rose from the dark depths. Instantly a mighty current seized horse and man and hurled them down-stream— toward the point where the river roared ominously as it dashed into the bottomless chasm beneath the cliff.

On the trail above sounded the angry yells of the raiders and the crackle of their guns as they spattered the unseen water with bullets.

Hatfield paid scant attention to the whining lead. His entire effort was put forth in a desperate struggle to reach the shore before the current hurled him and his horse to certain destruction in the depths under the black cliff. It seemed to him, strong swimmer that he was, that he did not gain an inch toward the bank as they shot downstream.

A questing beam of moonlight lighted the surface ahead, and rested on what looked like an undulating snake that stretched from the cliff wall to the far bank of the river. Hatfield knew it to be the curve of the stream as it took the last terrible plunge into the underground depths. The current seemed to drag at him with hungry fingers, the river seemed to shimmer exultantly in the moonlight.

There was a scraping sound of iron on stone. Goldy snorted explosively and gave a wild scramble. The sorrel's hoofs had touched bottom. He lunged for the shore. Hatfield, gripping the horse's mane with iron fingers, was dragged after him. An instant later his own boots were scraping on the rocks. Together they floundered through the shoaling water and scrambled up the shelving bank, less than a score of feet distant from the curving plunge of the river.

For a long time the Ranger lay on the coarse grass of the canyon floor. Goldy stood over him with hanging head. Both were exhausted. Finally, the Ranger summoned strength to wring the water from his clothes, empty his boots and at length swing into the saddle. He rode slowly down the gorge, cutting diagonally to the east. He chuckled grimly as he rode.

"Well, boy," he told the sorrel, "about the only thing we found out tonight is that those fellows have got guns that carry as far as ours. There won't be any more hanging back and picking them off from now on. It'll be straight fighting, man to man, and there are plenty of them to match up with the vigilante committees being rounded up in this valley. I reckon it's about time to see what brains will do."

His mind drifted back to that dark night on the Tamarra Desert, the stricken little Mexican and the new model rifle.

"That's the answer," he growled. "But how in blazes did they get Government rifles? Well, when I find out how, and who engineered the deal, I'll have a line on whoever's back of that outfit. I certainly don't believe it's Cartina."

And the chuckling Hill Gods warped still another thread into Death and Destiny's tangled web as Jim Hatfield, all unknowing, rode to meet with the man who was the "brains" of Pedro Cartina's outfit.

CHAPTER 10

HATFIELD rode parallel to the trail until it poured through the notch. There he left it, striking across the canyon to the spot where Ed Shafter lay buried. He paused beside the lonely grave, glanced down and bared his head. High in the tops of the pines, the wind mourned and whispered. The moonlight seeped through the rents in the scurrying clouds and the whole scene was shadowy and unreal. The notch through which the Huachuca Trail entered the canyon took on the semblance of grinning fleshless jaws and the misty trail itself seemed to writhe slowly with torpid life.

The Ranger rode away from the grave and to the overhanging rock in whose shade the two miners had found the body. For long minutes he sat gazing into the gloom beneath the gnarled overhang. As he gazed he seemed to see a crouching figure there, a figure that fixed eager eyes on the gloomy notch that knifed the canyon wall, a figure tense with waiting, in its pose an expectancy. And instinctively he knew that figure to be Ed Shafter as he had crouched in the shadow of the rock nearly a year before—crouched and waited for something to take form in the dark notch which cramped the Huachuca Trail.

"Yes, that's what he was doing up here," muttered the Lone Wolf. "Ed was on the trail of something—that prospector outfit was a blind."

His eyes narrowed as he stared toward the notch and the concentration furrow between his dark brows deepened in perplexity.

"But how in blazes did he come to have a pocket full of rich silver ore?" he added.

Back and forth across the moonlit terrain his keen gaze wandered, probing, analyzing, and all the while his fertile brain grouped and catalogued the meager facts as he knew them.

"That's why he had his rifle," he deduced. "He was watching the notch and prepared for long-range shooting. But how did the killer, whoever he was, slip up behind Ed and get the drop on him? Did he know Ed was here? Was it somebody Ed trusted and maybe had working with him? I don't think anybody could see Ed down there in the dark under the overhang, particularly from the trail. Let's see, now—"

Suddenly his glance paused on the little hilltop where lay the bones of the slain burro. It shifted to the trail and back again. The gray eyes blazed with excitement.

"That's it!" he exclaimed. "That's it, certainly! The burro wandered up onto that hill and was standing there in plain sight. Somebody spotted the burro and come slipping around looking for the man who owned him. He spotted Ed, maybe when he stepped out of the shadow. Spotted him and drilled him dead center."

But the perplexity had not left his eyes as he built a tiny fire in a sheltered hollow some distance from the hanging rock and cooked a meal. He was still convinced that the man who had faced Ed Shafter that fatal night was someone the Ranger knew—knew and trusted, or at least someone he credited with no hostile intent, until too late. The cocked rifle was mute evidence that Shafter had realized his error before he died.

Still pondering, Jim Hatfield rolled into his blankets. In a few moments he was asleep.

He was up again at dawn and saddling Goldy after a scanty breakfast.

"Let's go take a look at the mine," he said as he swung himself into the saddle.

The buckets were crashing past when he reached the conveyors, and Goldy did not favor them any more than formerly. He snorted disgustedly as the Ranger turned his nose parallel with the marching line of cables.

"If we follow this, we can't help but fetch up at the mine," Hatfield assured the horse. "I know this isn't much of a trail, but you've made it over worse ones. Stop your kickin'!"

Deeper and deeper into the hills bored the twin lines of cables. Twice within the hour, Hatfield heard the dull boom and rumble of distant blasts, proof that he was approaching the mines, which were still a considerable distance off, judging from the sound.

The conveyor line was running past towering cliffs that formed the eastern wall of the gorge. The cliffs, seamed with fissures, mottled with mineral stains, shut out the sun and cast an unnatural gloom over the canyon floor. Goldy shivered in the dank shadow and snorted disapproval. He snorted again as his hoofs crunched on a litter of loose stone.

Hatfield glancing down, abruptly pulled the sorrel to a halt. The stones were not boulders worn by water and weather. Their edges were sharp and their sides showed a clean line of cleavage from some parent body.

The Ranger glanced up at the conveyor line. From time to time the loaded and empty buckets clicked past, sliding evenly past the dark loom of the cliffs. There was a curve in the line here, quite slight, but enough to cause the pulleys to whine a bit.

"Looks like some of the ore gets jostled off here," he mused as he swung down from the saddle! He watched each loaded bucket as it approached lest there be a recurrence of the spillage—some of the bits of ore were large enough to inflict a painful injury, falling from such a height—but the career of the loaded conveyors was slight and no fresh stones swelled the scattering at the base of the cliff.

"Must have been an extra heavy load in one of them," the Ranger decided as he picked up several fragments of the fallen ore. Stepping back from the line of the cables, he carefully examined the bits of stone, and as he did so, his eyes turned coldly gray and his bronzed face grew bleak. Pulling a small chunk of stone from a side pocket, he compared it with the fragments he had picked up.

The peculiar zigzag pattern of the blue threads of silver was identical. Without a doubt, the Cibola ore came from the same ledge as had the bits of weather-stained rock he had found in the pocket of Ed Shafter's mouldering coat!

For many minutes, Jim Hatfield stood beside the scattered fragments of ore. Overhead the conveyor buckets whined past on their humming cables. A gloomy rift in the cliff face, directly opposite, seemed to leer at him like an eyeless socket. Everything in these grim hills seemed to smack of death and decay and sly treachery. Eyes stern and brooding, the Lone Wolf mounted his golden horse and rode up the dark gorge.

Two miles farther and the hum and clatter of the mine was apparent. Abruptly the cliffs fell back and revealed a wide space flooded with sunshine as golden as the sorrel's coat. The spot appeared singularly wholesome after the sombrous gorge— like a flower garden reached by way of a narrow passage through a thick wall.

Here were the mine buildings, the mouth of the shaft which burrowed into the bowels of the earth and the cheerful voices of the workers.

Not all the voices were carefree and peaceful, however. In front of a building marked "Office" a loud altercation was taking place. Hatfield was surprised to see that one of the disputants was Sheriff Branch Horton. The other was a tall, broadshouldered man with a weatherbeaten face and flashing eyes. His mouth was hard, his jaw lean and prominent.

The sheriff, whose clothes were powdered with gray dust and who showed other evidence of a long, hard ride, was redfaced and angry. A little to one side, a group of men were watering their horses and glancing from time to time toward the bickering pair. John Chadwick, the tall cattle king, was one of the group and Hatfield recognized Edwards, his foreman, and other men who had entered the *Una Golondrina* on the night of Amado Capistrano's argument with Chadwick. Bill Thompson was there, his shoulder bandaged, but apparently little the worse for his encounter with the Ranger. All were grinning and apparently amused.

They glanced up at the sound of Goldy's hoofs and their faces hardened. Horton and his adversary were too intent on each other to notice the new arrival.

"Yuh'd do better spendin' a little time runnin' down the men who are robbin' this mine right and left 'stead of scootin' 'round in the hills chasin' a bandit who, the chances are, is south of the Rio Grande, all the time," the tall man boomed as Hatfield came within hearing.

Sheriff Horton swore a crackling oath.

"I ain't a detective, Bowers," he shouted. "I'm a peace officer and I arrest people I know has committed a crime. I'm plumb shore and sartain it's some of yore own outfit that's doin' the stealin' up here. *You* get a line on 'em—that'd oughta be part of yore bus'ness—and I'll drap a loop on 'em quick enough. I *know* what Cartina and his outfit has done and whenever I get a line on *him,* I'm gonna foller it."

"Yeah, foller, and never ketch up!" snorted the tall Bowers. "Yuh couldn't ketch cold on a rainy day!"

Horton opened his mouth to roar an answer, when he caught sight of Jim Hatfield lounging easily in his saddle. He waved a hand in greeting. The Ranger shrewdly surmised he was glad of an opportunity to change the subject and get away from the irate mine superintendent.

"Strays must be sproutin' wings, if they've took to amblin' up this high," he observed jocularly.

"I had to ride to the west range and took a notion I'd amble up and look the Boss's mine over before I rode back," Hatfield explained easily. "Nice section up this way."

"Nice for them that likes it!" grunted Horton. "I shore have had enough of it since yest'day aft'noon. Been up in these hills ever since then. Heerd tell Pedro Cartina was snoopin' 'round up here and started out with a posse to ride herd on him. Spent mosta the night freezin' under a cliff way over toward the nawtheast of Chadwick's range. John's been losin' a sight of steers of late and he's gettin' almighty tired of it."

"Been in the hills all night?" Hatfield asked in sympathetic tones, his glance running over the sheriff's posse and back to the stocky peace officer.

"Uh-huh," Horton grunted, "all night. Well, reckon we'd better be headin' back for town, now the bronks has filled up. Yuh ridin' back thataway?"

"Not just yet," Hatfield replied. The sheriff nodded.

"I'll head up this way in a day or two and see if I can do anythin' for you, Bowers," Horton flung at the mine superintendent. Bowers grunted something unintelligible and glanced inquiringly at Hatfield.

The possemen swung into their saddles. John Chadwick favored the Ranger with a curt nod.

"That invitation to ride over to my place still holds," he said, "even though I don't think much of your choice of outfits to sign up with."

"Nobody else offered to sign me up, sir," Hatfield responded quietly, "and I haven't seen anything wrong with the one I'm with."

"You will, if you stay around long enough," the cattle king replied. "Come on, Horton," he called to the sheriff. "Let's be heading home."

From the direction of the gorge suddenly sounded fast hoofs. An instant later a man rode into view. His horse was lathered with sweat and flecked with foam.

"Hey, sheriff!" he shouted at sight of Horton, "Cartina held up the San Rosita stage this mawnin'. Killed the driver and creased yore deputy. They got away with the Humboldt's payroll money!"

CHAPTER 11

AFTER the posse had departed at a gallop, Hatfield dismounted at Bowers' invitation.

"Callate yuh're the feller what went to work for the Boss," he commented, running his keen gaze over the Ranger's tall form. "One of the boys from the ranch rode up here yest'day afternoon and mentioned yuh," he added by way of explanation. "Figgered it couldn't be anybody else when I set eyes on yuh, from the way he d'scribed yuh. C'mon inter my shack. I was jest gettin' ready to have a bit of chuck when that jughaid of a sheriff happened along."

The "shack" was a comfortable one-story house. It had two large rooms and a kitchen. An ancient Mexican was laying a cloth on a table in the main room. While Hatfield was washing up in the kitchen, Bowers talked in low tones with the old Mexican cook in the main room. Hatfield could hear the rumble of voices but could not make out what was said. After placing food on the table, the Mexican drifted silently out the back door and vanished in the direction of the mine. A little later, the Ranger heard hoofs click away toward the lower gorge mouth.

The meal was good and both did ample justice to it. For some minutes there was eloquent silence. Over a final cup of coffee, Bowers became more communicative.

"That blankety-blank sheriff!" he growled. "He means well, I reckon, but he's got one of them single-cinch minds and when he gets what he callates is a idea, there ain't room for nothin' else till it's plumb worked out."

"He's been chasin' Pedro Cartina for more'n a year now and ain't never come within shootin' distance of him. I callate Cartina is really responsible for 'bout one third of what Horton blames him for. If a rooster gets lifted outa a coop or a greaser goes to sleep and wakes up 'thout his pants, Horton yells 'Cartina!' and c'lects a posse and goes ridin'. When Cartina really does figger on pullin' somethin', like he did this mawnin', he arranges for Horton to be gallivantin' 'round somewhere else on a tip that's all made to order.

"The only time Horton was anyways close to him was t'other evenin' when the bank was robbed, and then he was as far behind as a cow's tail. I don't see what John Chadwick sees in the potbellied galoot. Reckon he figgers 'cause Horton can get them shoulders of his under a hoss and lift it off the ground, he's got the makin's of a peace officer. Anyhow, he got Horton elected and is figgerin' on runnin' him for 'nother term."

"Lift a horse off the ground?" repeated the Ranger.

"Uh-huh, he can do that. Horton's a bull when it comes to bein' strong. There ain't a man in the district can give him a good go in a rassle, 'less it's the Boss, Amado Capistrano. There ain't anythin' much Capistrano can't do with them arms of his. Jest the same, bein' able to straighten hoss shoes, and lift kegs of spikes with yore teeth ain't all what's nec'sary to make a good peace officer. Brains sorta comes in handy at times, and Horton was down in the cellar when they was

86

handin' *them* out. Oh, well, what can yuh 'spect of sich a tailend of Creation as this section is!"

"You don't like this country?"

"Who would like it?" growled Bowers, a bitter light in his stormy eyes. "The only reason I'm here, runnin' a blankety-blank silver mine is 'cause I got to be."

Hatfield was glancing at the titles of the books that rested on shelves built against the walls.

"You're an engineer," he stated rather than asked.

The bitter light in Bowers' eyes grew intense.

"Was," he corrected. "Ever hear of the Talmapaso River bridge?"

Hatfield nodded.

"Well," continued Bowers, "you'll recollect the span went into the river the day after it was completed. Three men were killed. That finished me as an engineer in this country. Was gettin' ready to starve or go back to punchin' cows at forty per when Amado Capistrano give me this job."

Hatfield was much interested.

"I remember there was quicksand under the center pier of the Talmapaso Bridge and it shifted," he commented.

Bowers gave him a shrewd glance in which was something of an element of surprise, and perhaps some other emotion.

"Yes, that's right," he said, and as he spoke his voice underwent a subtle change, the careless slurring of the cow country sluffing off and final endings taking their proper places.

"Yes, that's right," he repeated. "The consensus of opinion and the verdict of the investigating board was that I did not sink my caissons deep enough, and I was judged accordingly. The truth of the matter was that springs opened up through fissures in the bed rock and changed a perfect foundation of hard packed sand to quicksand. Perhaps you can understand what that means?"

"I get the idea," Hatfield replied in his easy drawl.

Bowers shrugged.

"But that's water over the dam," he added, his tones changing again. "Callate I'm lucky to have this job. It pays well and the work's sorta int'restin', partickler since some galoot's figger'd out a scheme to rustle highgrade ore outa the diggin's."

"You installed the conveyor system, didn't you?" Hatfield remarked.

"Uh-huh. Puttin' up a mill here in the hills was mighty near outa the question, and packin' ore down by mules is slow and costly. The conveyors are a sight faster and cheaper. The other mines have 'em, too."

After that they smoked in silence. Bowers appeared to be brooding over the past and his clever, bad-tempered face grew more and more morose. Finally he pinched out his cigarette and rose to his feet.

"Gotta be lookin' things over," he said, "wanta come along?"

Hatfield hesitated a moment.

"I guess I've got time," he admitted at length.

Together they entered the shaft cage and were dropped plummet-like into the depths of the mine. Here they walked along endless gloomy galleries. High overhead, for hundreds of feet, stretched the intricate cribbing of heavy timbers that held apart the sides of the gutted lode. It was like the picked bones of the giant skeleton of some prehistoric monster, with lights that were the lamps of the miners flickering about among the bleached ribs and vertebrae. Most of the workers, Hatfield noted, were Mexicans. As was his custom, he scanned closely each face that came into view under the dim lights. Most were of the humble *peon* type, with scant intelligence showing in the dark eyes.

Rounding an abrupt turn, they came upon a group of pick-men bringing down a face of rock previously shattered by dynamite. A scrawny little fellow glanced up from his work and Hatfield caught a flicker of stark terror in the beady eyes. Without comment he passed on, apparently lending an attentive ear to Bowers' comments but in reality hearing little of what was said.

For in the scrawny little pickman he had recognized the man he had rescued from the grip of the Tamarra Desert, the man who had vanished into the rainy night, hugging to his breast a new government-model rifle. He had also noticed that Joseph Bowers, the mine superintendent, had nodded to the little laborer in a familiar fashion and had received a nod in return.

This, and certain peculiarities he had noted about the mysterious rifle, were occupying the Lone Wolf's mind as the shaft cage rose to the surface. He was still thinking about them when he bade Bowers good day and rode slowly toward the lower gorge. The bitter-eyed superintendent stared after him speculatively.

"And *what* are *you?*" Bowers muttered as the tall form vanished around a bend. "Funny thing, a wandering cowboy who knows about the Talmapaso Bridge disaster and understands how quicksand could form under a pier. The boss and me had better have a little gabfest. And there won't be any slip-up this time!"

At the same instant Jim Hatfield's mind was going back to that hot day not so long ago when he had stared up at the masked face of a tall, broad-shouldered man while the hot jaws of the ants nipped his flesh; a man whose eyes had been bright and burning in the shadow of his wide hat.

He had conclusively recognized Bowers as the tall man who had fled from Flintlock Horner's livery stable as the Ranger's gun hammers clicked on empty shells. He wondered if Bowers suspected that his identity was known.

Hatfield was inclined to doubt it, feeling that his own dissimulation had been too real. But either way, Jim Hatfield knew that truly he rode in the very shadow of Death's wing.

For the Lone Wolf's keen eyes had noted something else—something that vastly complicated the whole matter; something that opened up such possibilities that his breath caught at thought of them. And that "something" was nothing more startling than the film of gray dust on Sheriff Horton's hat!

CHAPTER 12

HATFIELD rode swiftly down the gorge, for the sun was already slanting low toward the west. He followed the conveyor line most of the way, but veered away from it as the track entered the narrow gut where the canyon opened onto the dry wash.

For nearly half a mile the trail ran under a steep slope that extended for a thousand yards or more upward toward the splintered faces of towering cliffs. This slope, of loose shale and crumbling earth, was strewn with boulders, many of them weighing tons. The far side of the gut was a sheer granite wall, at the base of which was a dry watercourse which would be a raging torrent in time of rain. The gut itself was not much over a hundred yards in width, its floor uneven, broken by ridges and hummocks and littered with boulders and float.

Carefully Goldy picked his way amid the treacherous rocks. It would be easy to turn a hoof here and the sorrel knew it. Hatfield eyed the ominous slope thoughtfully, wary of rocks loosened by vibrations of the blasting at the mine.

"Wouldn't take much to set the whole mess rolling down," he mused. He was almost a quarter of the distance through the gut.

Without warning, smoke mushroomed from the base of the cliff that crowned the slope. There was a yellowish flash and a shattering roar. A huge section of the cliff bulged outward, seemed to hang for an instant and then toppled forward with a deafening crash. Down the slope rushed the splintered mass, gathering an increment of shale and loose boulders. In a few seconds, the entire surface of the slope was in motion.

One swift glance and Hatfield yelled to his horse. The big sorrel shot forward, heedless of the treacherous footing beneath his hoofs. The terrible rumbling roar and the billowing dust clouds up the slope lent frantic speed to the racing mount. Hugging his long body to the ground, he fairly poured himself over the shifting rubble, and with every breathless second, the thundering avalanche rolled closer to the doomed pair.

90

Ahead, far ahead, was the widening mouth of the gut, and safety, but Hatfield knew the straining horse could never make it. Already boulders and fragments of shale that had outstripped the main body of the avalanche were whizzing past, striking the floor of the gut with terrific force and bounding on to shatter against the cliffs on the far side. He knew that in another few seconds the thundering mass would pour into the gut, destroying all that lay in its path.

Hatfield veered Goldy toward the cliff wall, as far away from the moving slope as possible, but there was no hope of safety there. The main body of the avalanche undoubtedly would roll to the foot of the cliffs, shattering them with a barrage of stones as deadly as an artillery bombardment. There was not one chance in a million for horse or rider to escape the rain of bounding missiles.

All this flashed through the Ranger's mind as the horse sped forward. He glanced up at the billowing dust clouds, through which the boulders whizzed and leaped, at the cliff on his right and then down the gut.

Ahead, a hundred yards or so distant, was a low hillock, a rocky uprearing that swelled from the floor of the gut almost equidistant from the slope and the cliff wall. Its sides were precipitous, its summit a wind-smoothed knob of granite.

Hatfield turned the sorrel slightly. Straight at the almost perpendicular side of the hillock he sent the flying horse. Goldy snorted explosively and it seemed that certainly he would crash in red ruin against the craggy base.

But like a mountain goat he took the dizzy rise. Scratching, clinging, the muscles of his powerful haunches swelling in mighty bands, he went up the slope, carried forward by the impetus of his mad gallop. The instant he began to falter, Hatfield left the saddle in a lithe movement of consummate grace. Together, man and horse strained and scrambled up the rise. Not until they reached the base of the rounded knob did they pause. Facing about, his back against the smooth stone that towered many feet above his head, the Ranger watched the roaring rush of the avalanche as it thundered onto

91

the floor of the gut and rolled onward toward the cliff wall.

It reached the hillock, coiled about it, splitting like a wave of water on a rugged reef. Up and up piled the mass of stone and earth, reaching with splintered fingers toward the crouching man and horse. Nearer and nearer, straining to flow over the resisting granite and engulf the hillock. A mighty blast of air flattened them against the knob and threatened to whirl them from their refuge like leaves in an autumn gale. It shrieked and howled about the knob, adding its clamor to the booming voices of the avalanche. Up and up piled the flowing earth and shale.

In the wake of the main body of the avalanche came great boulders loosened from their beds of centuries. Faster and faster they rolled, whirling, bounding, leaping high into the air. They battered the hillock, tearing away tons of stone from its rugged sides, filling the air full of flying splinters that were deadly as rifle bullets. One hurtled through the air and struck squarely on the crest of the knob. It shattered the knob and burst into a thousand fragments which went whizzing away, each singing its own wild song. Stone from the splintered knob rained about Hatfield and the sorrel and some small fragments struck them stinging blows.

That was the last supreme effort of the avalanche. Gradually the clamor died. The dust clouds settled. Occasional boulders still whizzed down, bursting like meteors through the dust fog, but they grew less frequent. The air cleared and Hatfield, watching intently, could see the cliffs above the slope. He had drawn his rifle from the saddle boot and abruptly he flung it to his shoulder. He had sensed movement in the shadow at the base of the cliff.

The rifle muzzle held level with rock-like steadiness. Hatfield's eyes, coldly gray, glanced along the sights. Goldy snorted as the clanging, metallic crash of the report echoed back and forth among the crags.

Again the rifle spoke, and again appeared the flashes, palely golden in the dying sunshine, the smoke wisping up from the muzzle in blue spirals.

High against the cliff face a puff of dust sprang into the air, and another as Hatfield's slugs struck the rock wall. Then there was an answering flash from a gun and a blue spiral of smoke wavered against the white surface of the cliff.

Before the crack of the report reached Hatfield's ears, a bullet spattered viciously against the knob less than a foot above his head. An instant later a second slug fanned his face with its deadly breath.

"The fellow can shoot," he muttered, changing his position slightly, "almost as good as he can blow down rocks. *Now* where is he?"

Outlined against the sun-drenched knob, he was at a distinct disadvantage, the unknown rifleman being in the shadow. Suddenly he saw the bright flicker of flame in the pool of shadow and with a quick glance along the sights he fired in reply.

A slug whined past and whanged against the knob, but Jim Hatfield hardly noticed it. His whole attention was centered on the dark figure that was bounding and rolling down the steep slope.

"I guess that will hold him!" grated the Lone Wolf, lowering his smoking rifle.

Down and down bounded the limp body, setting shale and loose boulders rolling as it came. The body was the nucleus of a miniature avalanche when it finally came to rest amid the heaped rubble on the gorge floor.

Picking his way carefully over the wild jumble the avalanche had left in its wake, Hatfield led his horse down the hillock which had provided a haven of refuge and reached the spot where the body lay half-buried in rock rubbish. He hauled it forth and stared at what had once been a small man.

So battered and mangled was it by its fall down the slope, that it was impossible to do little more than imagine what the man had looked like in life. The features were a raw smear of bloody flesh and every bone in the man's body seemed to have been shattered. The dark skin of one wrinkled hand

93

pointed to Mexican or Indian blood; the black hair was plentifully shot with gray.

"An oldish fellow, I reckon," the Ranger mused, "and. he was a Mexican, all right. Wonder if there's anything in his clothes that'll tell something about him?"

A careful search revealed little. The rifle, of course, was missing and an empty holster was evidence that a sixgun had fallen out on the way down the slope. One cartridge belt was still in place and Hatfield examined the shells with intense interest. They were the type of cartridges designed for just such a rifle as the wizened little Mexican had hugged to his breast that wild night on the Tamarra Desert, but Hatfield was convinced that the broken body before him was not that of the mysterious little man.

"Looks like there's an arsenal of those long guns loose hereabouts," he mused, dropping the cartridge into his pocket.

He glanced about the gut, noting that the conveyor lines were down in a wild jumble of tangled cables, battered buckets and splintered poles. Hatfield knew that crews would soon be hurrying from the mills and the mines to repair the damage. He did not wish the body of the dead dynamiter to be found at this spot.

To carry the mangled form in his arms would mean blood smears on both himself and his horse, so he flipped the loop of his lariat about the crumpled shoulders and drew the body after him as he rode up the gut and beyond the havoc wrought by the avalanche. He buried the body in a crack between two rocks and weighted it down with boulders. Then he rode up the slope toward the base of the cliffs which overhung the scene of the avalanche. The grade was steep, but here it was grown with brush and grass and Goldy had little trouble keeping his footing.

In a hollow, a few hundred yards from where the cliff had been dynamited, Hatfield found what he sought—the dynamiter's horse. For long minutes he studied the brand which marked the animal and his eyes were cold as the winter wind in the tops of the pines.

"It's beginning to tie up," he muttered at last. "Yes, it's beginning to tie up. Ed Shafter sowed the seed, and there's going to be a mighty surprising reaping hereabouts before long!"

He relieved the horse of saddle and bridle and left it to shift for itself. After concealing the equipment, he rode through the hills until he could descend into the dry wash. A little later he met the first group of repairmen from the mills. He gave them directions to the seat of the trouble and rode on, not mentioning his own hair-raising experience. The first stars of evening were glowing in the quiet sky as he rode along the main street of Helidoro.

And from the *Una Golondrina* saloon, startled, incredulous eyes watched him swing from the saddle and hitch his horse. Before he entered the saloon, hurrying feet padded away through the dark.

Jim Hatfield was not thinking of furtive footsteps or watching eyes as he entered the One Swallow saloon. He was thinking of *the dust on Sheriff Horton's black hat!*

CHAPTER 13

AMADO CAPISTRANO was not present. Hatfield had something to eat, and then went in search of Walsh, the banker. He found him working in his little office in the front of the bank.

"Capistrano has always lived in this section," the banker replied to Hatfield's question. "His family once owned the entire valley. They lost it through court decisions relating to the old Spanish grants. Amado was only a child then. That was during John Chadwick's first term in the legislature. I have heard that Chadwick was instrumental in instigating the judicial action.

"Anyway, there is no love lost between him and the Capistranos. Chadwick bought up all the land he was able to at the time. Since then he has acquired other slices of the valley. I believe his ambition is to acquire the whole of it. Capistrano has some such ambition himself, in my opinion. Chadwick was furious when Capistrano got the jump on him and bought the Widow Bloodsoe's property right from under his nose. John's a good man, but he has the failing of men who have always got what they wanted—he feels that it is actually wrong for anybody to oppose him in anything.

"Nobody ever paid much attention to Amado Capistrano until he made his silver strike in the hills. He's a rich man now, but it doesn't seem to have changed him any. His saloon is the hangout of a lot of questionable characters, but Amado doesn't seem to mix with them much. Horton has more than once intimated that he has a connection with Pedro Cartina. It has never been proven."

"Does Chadwick own mining property?" Hatfield asked.

"He has a controlling interest in the Lucky Turn and the Humboldt," Walsh replied. "They're good mines, but not so rich as the Cibola. That's the ace of the district. The Humboldt has been doing well of late, I understand."

In answer to another question, Walsh stated:

"Yes, there's a telegraph station at San Rosita. It's about eighteen miles southeast of here, right on the river. Take the San Simon Trail, the one the stage follows. By the way, the stage was held up this morning by Cartina, they say. Long John Dyson says he recognized Cartina, said he had his shoulder bandaged and shot with his left hand. They knocked Long John off the box before he could use his shotgun, split his scalp but didn't do him much damage. Killed the driver and escaped with the Humboldt payroll money.

"I'm thankful it wasn't in the bank's hands yet. The express company is responsible. That's twice the Humboldt has lost money. They got the Lucky Turn payroll about six weeks ago. Cartina shows uncanny skill in picking times when the stage is carrying money—and that information is not given out for general consumption."

"I imagine not," Hatfield agreed. "Express company lose in those other holdups, too?"

"Yes. The company is responsible for the money while it is in transport. It has suffered heavy loss, due to these robberies. I

96

have expected they would assign one of their operatives to this district, but—"

He broke off suddenly, regarding the tall Ranger with newly-aroused interest. Hatfield read the question in the little man's honest eyes. He smiled down at Walsh from his great height and slowly shook his head.

"No, I'm not working for the express company," he said softly.

He eyed the banker speculatively for a moment and arrived at a swift decision. He needed someone upon whom he could rely, who could be depended upon to supply needed information freely and accurately. His slim hand fumbled inside his shirt for a moment and laid a shining object on the banker's desk.

Walsh stared at the familiar silver star on a silver circle, that badge of courage and efficiency. He drew a long breath.

"A Ranger!" he exclaimed, almost to himself. "I might have known it the first time I clapped eyes on you. Now we'll get somewhere!"

He immediately gave Hatfield a letter to the bank in San Rosita.

"Now you will be able to use their private wire to send your telegrams," he explained. "Information is much less liable to leak out that way. Men of Cartina's ilk appear to have an uncanny ability to ferret out what's going on. I can't understand how they do it. This ought to help you keep things secret. Hardy, president of the San Rosita bank, is absolutely dependable—I'll stake my life on that. He'll do all he can to help you."

Hatfield was still unable to locate Amado Capistrano. The barkeepers at the saloon knew nothing of his whereabouts. Long John Dyson, Sheriff Horton's gangling deputy, who happened in a little later with a bandaged head, could supply no information as to the hunchback's whereabouts. Hatfield liked Long John, who had a weary face, a cast in one eye and a discouraged-looking moustache. An habitual twinkle made one forget the cast, however, and the moustache could not hide the grin wrinkles about his mouth.

Not until Doc Draper bustled in for a double slug of his "fav'rite pizen," did Hatfield get a line on Capistrano.

"Shore, I know where he is," grunted Ol' Doc. "Come along and I'll take yuh to him."

He led the way to where the humble cabins of the Mexican laborers crouched in the shadow of the great mills. He entered a dimly lighted hut. Hatfield, bending his tall head, followed.

At first he could make out little of the interior. Then he saw that a man and a woman stood near the table on which a lamp burned. They were young and the woman's face was beautiful, though tear-stained and tired. Doc nodded briefly and they replied with courteous bows. Hatfield followed the old man's gaze and saw, in one corner, a blanket spread on the earthen floor. On the blanket lay a wasted little form and beside the blanket crouched Amado Capistrano, his face lined with weariness, but with a light in his blue eyes. He smiled fleetingly at Hatfield and raised his right hand to his lips in a gesture for silence.

His other hand, Hatfield saw, lay on the worn blanket and in it rested the tiny, almost transparent fingers of the little girl who slept so silently on the earthen floor. The fragile fingers clung tightly to the hunchback's thumb, as if that were their sole hold on the life spirit that threatened momentarily to take wing.

"He's been settin' there for nigh onto eighteen hours now," breathed Doc. "If he moves he's afraid the kid'll wake up, and sleep means life to her. She's been hangin' in the balance for a week, now, but yest'day she drifted into a nacherel sleep while Amado was holdin' her hand. That sleep's gonna make her all right, or I'm much mistaken."

He nodded to Capistrano and led the Ranger from the cabin. A little distance from the door they paused and glanced back.

"Folks down here think sorta well of *Don* Amado," Doc remarked.

Jim Hatfield bared his dark head and looked up at the glowing Texas stars.

"And I guess the folks up *there* think right well of him, too," he replied softly.

"Who?" asked Doc, in surprise.

"Those grand old ancestors of his," Hatfield said. "Those salty old hombres they called the Conquistadores, who came from across the Atlantic and fought the Indians and the deserts and the mountains and did their part to make this country worth living in. Yes, I have a notion *they* think mighty well of *Don* Amado, too. Doc, I reckon that when God Almighty sets out to make a *man,* He concentrates on what He puts inside and doesn't waste too much time on what He covers it up with!"

CHAPTER 14

HATFIELD slept at the A Bar C bunkhouse that night and mid morning found him riding the range again. As previously, he headed southwest, but once he was well away from the home range, he turned Goldy's head sharply. An hour later he struck the San Simon Trail, that ran southeast to the county seat, San Rosita.

Arriving at San Rosita, he found the bank president, Hardy, and showed him Burton Walsh's letter. Hardy cooperated gladly and Hatfield sent several long telegrams in the name of the Rangers. One, directed to an eastern firearms manufacturer, was answered promptly, Hatfield receiving the information he desired before nightfall. It caused him to knit his dark brows and stare long and earnestly across the gleaming river that separated Texas from Mexico. The others were briefly acknowledged and cooperation promised.

Following Hardy's directions, he strolled about the little town, finally arriving at the poorer quarter, occupied chiefly by Mexicans and a few Indians. Here he had a drink in a dingy little *cantina* whose dark-faced bartender grinned jovially and was inclined to be loquacious.

"I've been looking for a bunky of mine," Hatfield told him over a glass of fiery *tequila*. "He headed down this way about a year or so back and I heard he was seen in this town. He was a mining man, a big fellow with brown whiskers sort of dappled. There was gray in his hair, too. Wasn't very old, though. Name was Shafter, Ed Shafter."

The bartender listened courteously, nodding his sleek black head from time to time.

"Me, I know not for sure," he replied when Hatfield had finished. "Many men come thees way and many men drink here. I will ask of others, however, and if the señor should pass this way tomorrow—"

"Yes, I reckon I'll be hanging around this section another day or two," Hatfield told him. "Let's have another drink. Then I'm goin' to bed."

The bartender had learned nothing the following afternoon and Hatfield left town, assuring the drink mixer that he would return in a few days. The young Mexican pocketed the shining gold piece the Ranger had left and redoubled his inquiries.

Hatfield reached the A Bar C bunkhouse after dark. An animated discussion was under way, the subject being a raid on the Bowtie ranch by rustlers. It appeared a herd of several hundred head had been widelooped.

"They figger it was Pedro Cartina did it?" asked the Ranger.

There was a sudden silence and an uncomfortable shuffling of feet. Hatfield glanced inquiringly from one *vaquero* to another. The jolly Felipe at length broke the silence.

"Eet ees, what you call, sometimes not healthy to speak of certain ones," he said gravely. Hatfield nodded his understanding.

"Yes, you never know who you can trust and who you can't," he agreed.

The next day Hatfield rode across Chadwick's great Circle C and far east. Everywhere he was struck by the richness of the valley. The ranches were exceptionally fine, with splendid buildings, and fat herds in abundance.

"Yes, it sure is one fine section," he mused as he rode slowly

100

home under the glowing stars. "No wonder Chadwick and Capistrano both have a hankering to own the whole business. Plenty of room for both of them, too, and no real need for trouble. Seems that when a man has about everything in the world he needs, he should be satisfied and not be taking chances with what he's got to get something more that he doesn't really need. Funny folks in this world!"

In the beginning, just prior to the death of a young Ranger by the name of Dick Webb, three men had dreamed of an empire. That is, at least one of them had dreamed of an empire, while the other two had envisioned wealth and power in the Tamarra Hills country.

This dream, this will o' the wisp which has beckoned men down through the ages to their doom, was now by way of becoming a concrete fact. At the same moment that Ranger Jim Hatfield, the pernicious fly in this particular ointment, was riding east of the Circle C and deliberating on the intricate pieces of this puzzle which were gradually falling into place for him, two of these three men were closeted with a third man in the back room of a saloon in the mining town of Helidoro. The third member of this infamous trio was absent.

The saloon in which this meeting occurred was not the *Una Golondrina* of Amado Capistrano. Further, not one of the three men in conference was masked. One of them walked the streets of Helidoro whenever he was in town, a respected citizen and officer of the law. Sheriff Branch Horton was cradled in false security, little dreaming that Jim Hatfield had already penetrated that mask of respectability.

The second member was, oddly enough, the very man that Sheriff Horton could never lay an official hand upon—Pedro Cartina. He had ridden into town under cover of darkness the previous night for a conference. He sat in his chair now, a vicious scowl on his swarthy face, wincing now and then from pain as he shifted his bandaged right shoulder.

The third man in the room, the one making a worried report, was Jefferson Bowers, superintendent of the Cibola mine.

"I can't understand how he come outa it in one piece,"

101

Bowers stated in perplexity. "I examined that cut myself, and it's piled fulla rock and dirt enough to wipe out a regiment. When yuh sent me word, Horton, that he had showed up in town as if nothin' had happened, I couldn't believe it."

"*I* couldn't believe it," snarled the sheriff, and there was nothing slow about his bearing now. "Yuh said yuh could tend to him, before I left for town with my posse, so I didn't worry any more about him till he showed up life-size. Mebbe your dynamite man can explain things. What did he say?"

"That's the queerest part of it," frowned Bowers. "Just before supper I gave Juan definite instructions and sent him on ahead of Amado's new man. There ain't no doubt that Juan did the job—nothin' short of dynamite would of caused that avalanche, and Juan was the best powder man I had at the mine. But Juan has disappeared. Nobody's seen hair or hide of him since that job."

"Perhaps Juan failed," shrugged Cartina, and then cursed at the quick little pain which gnawed at his shoulder. "When he saw he had failed, he vamoosed to Mexico."

"Juan knew better than to do that," said Bowers. "He knew yuh'd get him for that, Cartina. It begins to look to me like, somehow, that big fellow got Juan."

Pedro Cartina smiled, a swarthy grin that split his face wolfishly to expose gleaming white teeth.

"Then, *señores,*" he said, "it seems that the job must be done by Cartina himself. Do you still think he is a detective from the express company?"

"Must be," grunted Horton. "He don't fit in as a driftin' range tramp like he claimed to be. I wish yuh'd shot him out of his saddle, Pedro, when yuh raided Walsh's bank that night."

"It was dark," said Cartina, "and we just took him for a rider who was in our way."

"He proved to be that, all right," said Horton sourly. "The boss was sore over that bobble."

"He's not an express detective," said Bowers positively. "I think he's a Cattlemen's Association man. Sancho swears he's the feller who pulled him out of the desert the night of the storm, but he said that feller could talk Spanish like a Mex, and this man don't seem to know the lingo. He looked familiar to me, and—"

"He asked Sancho questions about his gun?" demanded Horton quickly.

"Shore," nodded Bowers. "And I'm beginnin' to think that gun-runnin' idea you fellers had was a mistake. They're mighty fine shootin' irons all right, but they might be traced. If they are, we'll have the U. S. Army in this section."

"Not so," said Cartina smoothly. "The guns were shipped to my friend, the captain of the *Rurales,* and the ordair was from the Department of War, or State, or so it seemed. There is nothing to fear from that source."

"Well, there's a lot to fear from this man we can't kill," said Bowers in an ugly tone. "Cartina, I tell yuh I recognized—"

"Everythin' else is workin' out fine," cut in the sheriff, relieved. "The boys are learnin' to shoot straighter. They know their business. There's more'n a hundred of 'em now. They have their orders, and they know what to do. Another week, and we'll be ready for big clean-ups. As soon as this election is out of the way, we'll get goin' right. There might be a few men we ain't shore of—"

He paused and glanced at Cartina, who smiled again—like the unsheathing of a knife.

"*I* am sure of all," the Mexican said thinly. "Men think twice before they hand to Pedro Cartina the, what you say— doublecross."

"Yeah," nodded Sheriff Horton in satisfaction, "I guess they do."

"Now, for this detective," went on Cartina, "I, Pedro Cartina, will attend to him without more ado. Me, I am able to dispose of men so they do not come back to life."

"Yeah!" said Bowers dryly. "Mebbe yuh are. But I'm tryin' to tell yuh that yuh already had one whack at this man, and yuh made a mess of it."

"What?" hissed Cartina, his black eyes flashing. "That, *amigo,* is one damn lie!"

Bowers laughed shortly.

"I told yuh I recognized that Hatfield feller, didn't I? That's why I'm shore he's a cattle detective. Do yuh remember that little raid on the Slash K trail herd down on the Rio Grande which didn't work out because of that tall feller leadin' them cow hands?"

"You mean the hombre we staked out over the ant hill?" demanded Cartina.

"Him," nodded Bowers laconically. "This man is him!"

"But—but—" stuttered the bandit in astonishment, "that is not possible. The ants never fail."

"They fell down on that job!" said Bowers grimly. "I don't know how he got loose. Yuh drove them stakes, and I pigged him with the rawhide myself. If he ever finds out it was me with yuh that day, I won't live till sundown. We ain't safe a minute while that man runs free. Think he'll forget that ant hill?"

"That, as I recall it, was your idea, *Señor* Bowers," said Cartina in silky politeness. "I preferred to end his career with a rifle then. Now, I must do so. What did you say his name is?"

"Hatfield!" snapped Bowers angrily. "Jim Hatfield, so he says."

Pedro Cartina forgot his wounded shoulder as he leaped to his feet, his face livid, his eyes almost starting from his head.

"Hatfield?" he ejaculated. "Jeem Hatfield! He ees tall, most tall? And broad? And his eyes, they are gray? *Madre de dios! Sangre de cristo! Maldito!*"

"Yes, yes," nodded Bowers, paling slightly in unreasoning panic. "Why?"

"Mother of God!" groaned Cartina. "And to think that I had him under the sights of my rifle and let him get away."

"What are yuh talkin' about?" demanded Sheriff Horton savagely.

"Hatfield!" gasped the bandit. "Of all the men in the world I, Pedro Cartina, most hate and fear, it is this man. You wish to know who he is? You think he is express detective, or cattle detective? Ha, ha, I laugh! *Señores,* this man is called

104

the Lone Wolf. He is a devil. He is a Texas Ranger!"

"Holy smoke!" exclaimed Bowers, utterly startled.

"Hell!" snarled Sheriff Horton. "Ain't we already killed one Ranger last year—that Webb feller? John Chadwick thinks he can run this country without Texas Rangers nosin' around here. He depends on me, don't he? Ain't he already exerted influence to keep Rangers officially out of Tamarra country? This Hatfield ain't got no official standin' here. We'll treat him like we do everybody who gets in our way."

"Do yuh think Amado knows he hired a Ranger?" asked Bowers keenly.

"'Course not!" snorted Horton. "Think he's crazy? His feud is personal with Chadwick."

"I guess I'd better tell him," said Bowers. "Yuh're shore of yore information, Cartina?"

"Am I?" shuddered the bandit. "Hatfield is the one man I have dreaded having set on my trail."

Sheriff Horton pulled his six-shooter and laid it on the table. His eyes were full of meaning as he looked at both of his companions.

"It wasn't Lincoln who made men equal," he chuckled evilly. "It was Sam Colt! Here's the difference between this Ranger Hatfield and the smallest man who ever forked a hoss."

Pedro Cartina shook his head dubiously.

"Perhaps," he hissed. "But my thought of *el infierno* is this Jeem Hatfield with a pair of guns!"

"He's human, ain't he?" Horton snapped viciously. "This Hatfield feller can die, like anybody else. And he's got to die—sudden!"

CHAPTER 15

"I WARNED you," Amado Capistrano told Hatfield. "Not for a moment is your life safe. Twice they have failed, partly by luck, chiefly because of your own vigilance and skill. But it can't go on this way. The next time they're liable not to fail. I still think you should leave this district."

"I think things are going to get interesting around here during the next few days," the Ranger countered.

Capistrano nodded gravely.

"Yes, the election campaign is drawing to a close," he said. "Monday night both Horton and I will make speeches here in Helidoro. Then next day is election day.

"Those speeches are important," he added, "Helidoro will just about swing the election. Chadwick is doing everything he can to defeat me, but there is a large element throughout the valley who will vote for anybody who is against Horton, and I believe most of the mining element is favorable to me. Also I count heavily on the river towns. Most of the voters there are of Mexican extraction, although Texas citizens, and naturally favor one of their blood."

"Why does Chadwick set such store on this county election?" Hatfield asked. "It doesn't look so important to me."

"It's a test of strength," Capistrano replied. "This is, and always has been, an independent county. If Chadwick can show the surrounding counties that he can swing Tamarra, it will add tremendously to his prestige. Enough, I feel sure, to gain him the nomination for governor next year."

Hatfield nodded. He was very thoughtful as he sought his little room over the livery stable.

"And if Chadwick gets to be governor, he'll run the state like he runs this valley," the Lone Wolf mused, "and that means goodby to the Rangers, among other things. Goodby to the Rangers, and Chadwick's riders will be all over the state. Such things just don't seem possible; but it doesn't seem possible that a little sore can grow into a cancer that'll kill a man. Just the same, it happens.

"The way to cure a sore is to treat it before it gets too big to *be* cured, even if it doesn't seem worth noticing at first. Wait till it gets big enough to notice, and it's liable to be too big to handle. I'm afraid Chadwick is a sore. Well, the Rangers have cured 'sores' before now. I reckon we can handle this one."

Things were gay in the river town of Zapata. The *cantinas* were decorated with flowers and colored cloth. Svelte señoritas, their dark eyes flashing like jewels, multicolored skirts billowing out from slim silken legs, danced with lithe young *vaqueros* in velvet and silver.

Gay *serapes,* elaborate *sombreros,* and fluttering *mantillas* lent color to the scene. Everywhere was music, and laughter. In the sun-drenched plaza a crowd had gathered to hear the words of the *alcalde.* The mayor, his dark face wreathed with smiles, spoke from a raised platform—warmly lauding his friend, *Don* Amado Capistrano, who soon would be sheriff of the county.

"It is the great honor to help elect our friend and patron," the *alcalde* said. "Zapata will do her part, as will her sister towns. I ordain this a day of *fiesta.* Tomorrow—"

He paused at a sudden drumming of hoofs growing steadily louder. Persons glanced inquiringly one to another.

"El bandidos?" ran a nervous whisper.

Into the plaza thundered a veritable army of mounted men. There were fully fourscore riders. Each carried a heavy rifle of a pattern unusual along the Border. They crashed to a halt and their leader, a rangy, rawboned man with a low-drawn hat brim, rode through the crowd that made way for him. At his back rode two dark-faced, sinewy men. The grim trio halted beside the platform. The tall leader leaned forward in his saddle and addressed the apprehensive mayor.

"Mister," he said harshly, "yuh been barkin' on the wrong side of the fence. Yuh need a lesson."

He gestured to his two dark followers, who instantly swung to the platform and seized the mayor.

An angry mutter ran through the crowd, rising to a sullen growl. Instantly there was a thunderous crash of rifles. Lead squalled over the heads of the crowd. Acrid smoke swirled about the plaza.

Demoralized, panic-stricken, the people huddled together. In the *cantinas* the music was stilled. Shutters closed hastily.

The two men who had seized the mayor ripped the gay silk shirt from his back, baring his shoulders. The tall leader dismounted and vaulted upon the platform, running muscular fingers along the lash of his heavy quirt.

Then the quirt rose, and fell. A red welt leaped across the mayor's dark shoulders. Again the lash whistled through the air, and again. The mayor writhed. An agonized groan burst from his lips. Then a shriek as blood spurted under the lash. The shrieks merged in a gabbling crescendo of screams as the quirt rose and fell.

Finally the rawboned man turned from his moaning victim, flicked drops of blood from his lash and faced the crowd.

"Jest in case yuh folks don't know it," he said harshly, "I'm here to tell yuh we got the right kind of a sheriff in this county right now, and we aim to keep him. Bear that in mind t'morrer."

He swung into the saddle, running his fingers along the blood-soaked quirt.

"All right," he told his followers, glancing at the sun, "get goin'. We got three more towns to visit, then we ride north. Got to be in Helidoro before dark."

In a cloud of dust the grim band thundered away. The stricken people of Zapata crept into their homes, casting many a fearful glance in the direction of that diminishing dust cloud. Shaking men succored the quivering mayor. The *fiesta* had become a tragedy.

Helidoro was also gay as the sun sank in scarlet and gold and the western peaks were ringed about with saffron flame. Crowds jostled in the streets. Other crowds thronged the bars. Roulette wheels whirred busily. Cards slithered and dice galloped across the green cloth. Boots thumped and high heels clicked.

Lithe cowboys from the valley ranches rubbed shoulders with brawny miners. Gamblers in somber black raked hard-earned gold across their tables. Bartenders were too busy to make change; the drinkers too busy to ask for it. Fiddles squeaked and guitars thrummed.

In the streets hastily organized bands blared forth weird discords that were enthusiastically received as music. Everywhere there was a holiday air, for the mines and the ranches had paid off that evening in anticipation of election day on the morrow.

At either end of town was a final political rally. At one end Sheriff Horton, candidate for re-election, held forth. At the opposite end, Amado Capistrano, who was seeking the office of sheriff, planned to address a huge crowd made up chiefly of mill and mine workers. Dark faces were predominant in that crowd and there were more *"vivas"* heard than "hurrahs!"

Jim Hatfield, lounging on the outskirts of the crowd, chuckled to himself.

"Amado's got four times the turnout Horton has," he grinned. "If this is the way things are going in the river towns, he'll win hands down. Looks like *Señor* Chadwick might find a tangle in his rope before he's finished."

Excited cheering broke forth, and a moment later Amado Capistrano mounted the low platform and stood smiling his melancholy smile. He began speaking in his musical voice and the crowd hushed expectantly. The western peaks were wreathed in shadow now and the dusk was purply thick.

Hatfield was suddenly conscious of a low drumming filtering out of the deepening dusk. He turned in surprise, his eyes narrowing.

"Horses," he muttered, "lots of them, and coming fast."

Others had heard the sound and were glancing in the direction of the San Simon Trail. The sound swiftly grew louder. Something huge and menacing loomed against the gray surface of the trail.

What happened next did so with paralyzing suddenness. Out of the night burst a compact band of mounted men. Straight for the crowd about the platform they rode, quirting their horses, shouting loudly.

Panic was immediate and universal. Men fought madly to escape the churning hoofs of the horses and the slashing quirts of the riders. Many fell and were trampled by their frenzied companions or ridden down by the horses. The platform went to pieces with a crash and in the glare of the falling flares, Hatfield saw a rope snake through the air, the loop settling about Amado Capistrano's shoulders. The hunchback was hurled to the ground and jerked along it as the rope tightened.

Jim Hatfield streaked across the intervening space like a flickering shadow. He seized the rope with both sinewy hands and surged backward with all his iron strength. The horse which drew it, just getting under way, faltered in his stride.

Again the Ranger put forth every ounce of his strength. The muscles of his splendid back and shoulders stood out like writhing snakes. The veins of his forehead were big as cords. One final mighty effort. The saddle girth burst and rider and saddle hurtled to the ground.

The man lit on his head, flopped over on his side and lay with twitching limbs, his neck twisted to a horrid, unnatural angle. Capistrano and the Ranger sprawled together, the coils of the loosened rope tangled about them.

Rifles crashed a volley and lead stormed over the prostrate pair. Yells of agony arose from the milling crowd. Again the rifles crashed, and again cries of pain followed the blast of lead. Hatfield, rolling over on his side, jerked both his guns and emptied them after the fleeing horsemen. Other shots sounded, but the mysterious band was already out of range. The rope wielder, a sinewy young Mexican, appeared to have been their only casualty.

Men from the other end of town were running down the street. As Hatfield helped the badly shaken Capistrano to his feet, Sheriff Horton pounded up.

"It's too bad that you fellers can't hold a political meetin' without turnin' it into a riot!" he bellowed. "What *is* goin' on here, anyhow?"

Jim Hatfield glanced down at him from his great height.

"Horton," he drawled, "some day you're going to head in the wrong direction so fast you'll meet yourself coming back!"

That night it rained, and all the next day. Toward evening, Amado Capistrano's election headquarters were as gloomy as the day. The river towns had registered a mere trickle of votes, and the turnout of miners in Helidoro was negligible.

"Horton wins, hands down," the hunchback conceded with

a wry smile. "I imagine they're having quite a celebration over at the town hall."

Jim Hatfield dropped into the hall a little later. Sheriff Horton, his mouth stretched in a grin of triumph, was speaking from the stage.

"That's all I got to say, boys," he concluded, "I jest say, 'much obliged,' and yuh done yoreselves proud. Now I want yuh to listen to somebody else for a spell. I want yuh to listen to the Honorable John Chadwick, *our next governor!*"

As Chadwick arose from his chair and cheers rocked the building, the Lone Wolf smiled thinly with his lips—his eyes were icy cold—and left the room.

CHAPTER 16

Two DAYS later, Hatfield rode back to San Rosita. He found his friend the bartender in the little *cantina* all smiles. Instead of serving Hatfield's drink at the bar, he hurried him to a table in a corner.

"Be pleased to sit, *señor*," he bobbed. "I will return with the much speed."

Summoning an assistant to take over the bar, he hurried from the room. Hatfield sipped his drink reflectively and waited. Soon the bartender returned. He brought with him a sinewy, dark little man with lank black hair, high cheekbones and glittering black eyes.

"Thees ees Pancho," he introduced. "He would speak with the *señor*."

Pancho, whom Hatfield placed as an almost pure Yaqui Indian, sat down diffidently and accepted a drink. He stared steadily at the tall Ranger, his black eyes inscrutable. After his first greeting, Hatfield said nothing. He was content to let Pancho begin the conversation. He did so in a surprising manner.

"*Señor*," he said softly, "the *Señor* Shafter whom you seek was of the Rangers?"

Hatfield returned the Yaqui's steady gaze.

"What makes you think so?" he parried. Pancho's eyes did not waver.

"The *Señor* Webb, he too was of the Rangers and," the Yaqui added, "the *Señor* Webb was my friend. He saved my little daughter from the river. *Si,* he was my *amigo.*"

"I begin to understand," replied Hatfield.

Pancho leaned close.

"You, too, tall *señor,* are of the Rangers," he whispered. "Pancho has eyes that see much. Pancho knows! You come to avenge your brothers. *Si,* it is so?"

Hatfield made a quick decision. He decided the little man was trustworthy and his affection for the slain Ranger, Dick Webb, was undoubtedly real. The hatred that burned in his black eyes when he spoke of avenging Webb's murder was too vibrantly real to be simulated.

"Yes, I come to avenge," he replied simply, employing the terms Pancho would understand and appreciate. "I have to find the men that did it."

"Pancho knows," said the Yaqui. "Pancho told the *Señor* Shafter. He departed and returned not. Perhaps the tall *señor* knows where he may be found?"

"Yes, I know where he can be found," Hatfield replied briefly. "It's the men who killed him and Webb I'm interested in, Pancho."

The little Yaqui leaned forward, his eyes glowing.

"Listen, *Señor,*" he whispered. "Listen closely—"

Under cover of darkness, Hatfield and the Yaqui left town. Hatfield rode his tall sorrel horse, but the little tracker trotted easily at his stirrup, scorning the mount Hatfield offered to obtain for him.

"When the *caballo* falls with rolling eyes and heaving sides, Pancho runs on and is not tired," he declared proudly in Spanish.

"I believe you," Hatfield nodded, glancing at the coiling ropes

112

of muscle that showed plainly through the thin pantaloons the Yaqui wore.

North by west they travelled, under the golden stars that studded the purple-blue vault of the sky; until the stars faded in the dawn of a new day. They were among the gaunt Tamarra Hills now, and as the east brightened Pancho stealthily led the way to the lip of a great hollow brimful with purple shadows.

At Pancho's advice, Hatfield tethered Goldy in a dense thicket. Then he crouched on the lip of the hollow beside the Yaqui and waited while daylight brightened, revealing the hollow to be grass grown and dense with undergrowth. Through the undergrowth ran a trail, twisting up the far slope and vanishing into a dark opening beneath a huge over-hang of reddish stone.

"It is there they meet and plan," whispered the Yaqui. "There their stores are kept. It is from there that they ride forth to do evil."

"Regular hole-in-the-wall outfit," muttered Hatfield. "They— say, there's something coming out of there now!"

Tense, eager, the Ranger and the Yaqui tracker watched the long line of loaded pack mules wind from the dark cavern opening. Each mule was half hidden beneath a great rawhide *aparejo,* or kyack, as cowboys often called the unwieldy pack sacks.

More than a score of the sturdy animals emerged from the cave, trotted across the hollow and vanished over its lip. Beside and behind the mules rode dark-faced, watchful men. When the last had dipped over the lip of the hollow, Pancho turned a be-wildered face to the Ranger.

"*Señor*, I know not what *that* may mean," he said.

"I have a notion, Pancho, and a good hunch," Hatfield re-plied, his eyes glowing with excitement. "We've got to see inside that cave. I wonder if anybody is left behind on guard."

"No, *señor*, I would say," replied the Yaqui, "but Pancho will soon learn. Wait here!"

Like a stealthy snake he was gone, worming through the

113

undergrowth, vanishing from sight almost instantly. It was half an hour or more before he reappeared.

"*Señor,* there is no one," he reported. "I am sure."

Taking advantage of all possible cover, Hatfield followed him to the cave mouth. It was dark and silent. Pancho pointed out a heap of torches stacked in a cleft beside the entrance. They lighted one and stole along the comparatively narrow tunnel. The tunnel abruptly opened into a wide room with a lofty ceiling. The floor was level and smooth from the action of water in years gone by. Hatfield glanced about with increasing interest. Pancho exclaimed sharply as they approached a wall.

Row on row stood scores of shiny new rifles of the same model as provided for United States Army use but lacking the army stamp and serial numbers.

"They're made in this country, shipped into Mexico to a captain of *rurales,* the manufacturers thinking they're for Mexican Government service," Hatfield explained. "Then they're smuggled back across the Line and used to equip this outlaw gang. That way, they don't attract any attention, as they would if they were shipped to somebody this side the Line. I guess each member of the gang is responsible for the gun issued to him and catches plenty if anything happens to it. That's why that little Mex I found with one in the desert was so scared about it getting away from him."

Pancho nodded his understanding. He pointed to a stack of heavy square boxes.

"Cartridges," Hatfield replied. "That's the kind of box I saw on the mules the night I was shot at there on the Huachuca Trail. I stumbled on part of this outfit and they let drive at me."

They were working their way toward the back of the great room. A moment later Hatfield gave an exclamation of satisfaction. He indicated two heavy cables stretching from a narrow gallery that opened onto the main room.

"That's just what I suspected," he exulted. "Pancho, those mules we saw were loaded with ore from the Cibola mine. It comes in over those cables, somehow. Let's go see how it's done."

They lighted another torch and entered the gallery. For

114

nearly a mile they followed it, the cables stretching on overhead. Pancho suddenly uttered a sharp grunt. Both halted instinctively.

Almost at their feet yawned a dark gulf that seemed to be bottomless. Hatfield kicked a stone over the edge and, long moments later, a faint, muffled splash hissed up to them from the black depths.

"Lord, what a hole!" growled the Ranger, "and look at the trail that leads past it."

Hugging the sheer wall was a narrow track over which the cables passed on supporting piles sunk into the crumbling stone.

Gingerly, they edged out onto the ledge. For nearly a hundred yards it skirted the gulf. Then the unbroken floor of the gallery began once more. A slight distance further on the natural tunnel widened and the torch light revealed the simple but ingenious method utilized for robbing the Cibola mine of high-grade ore.

Twin lines of cables similar to the conveyor lines stretching down the canyon and the wash to Helidoro ran toward the graying opening which was the cleft Hatfield had noted when examining the spilled ore beneath the conveyor line. There was a simple switch and cutback which could easily splice into the main conveyor lines. Along this cutback, loaded buckets of ore could be detoured from the conveyor line and other buckets loaded with base rock switched onto the line in their place. The buckets of rich ore were routed along the cables to the great room where the guns and ammunition were kept. There they were rifled of their precious contents and worthless rock substituted. The scheme was disarmingly simple, once it was understood.

"But it took a mighty smart engineer to figure that out," declared Hatfield. "I suppose this tunnel through the hills was taken into consideration when the conveyor lines were run. I wondered, the first time I saw them, why they swung over here by the cliffs. It would have been a more direct route to have run them further south."

The torch was burning low and they hurried back toward the main cave. Hatfield took time, however, to closely examine the crumbling ledge which skirted the gulf. The huge overhang of stone at the cavern mouth also excited his interest. He stared at it with calculating eyes and studied the trail that dipped across the hollow.

"When they're all here, it means nearly a hundred fighting men, well armed and ready for anything," he mused. "Routing them out and putting them under arrest would be a mighty bloody business and peace officers' blood isn't to be wasted. Maybe a little brains will take the place of it."

Again he studied the overhang and at the same time visualized the crumbling ledge. He chuckled as the plan unfolded; then explained it to Pancho.

The little Yaqui's eyes snapped.

"It will be simple, *señor*," he declared. "You, *señor*, and I will do the work in the dark hours, both here and within the cave. Fear not of chance discovery, *Capitan*. None may approach without Pancho knowing."

This doubtless explained the trip Jim Hatfield and the Yaqui made to the gloomy hollow the following night. They carried mysterious packages with them, which they handled gingerly, and during the space between a sun and a sun they worked at the cavern mouth and on the crumbling ledge.

"It's all ready," the Ranger said at length, straightening his weary back and setting aside drill and sledge. "You'll handle this end when the time comes and I'll take care of the ledge. You're sure you can find out when they'll ride this way again?"

"Pancho will know," the Yaqui replied tersely. "Even now he hurries beyond the river, there to listen and watch. He will warn *El Capitan* in time."

"And after that things will be a lot better in this district," the Ranger commented.

"*Si, Capitan*, and my friend the young *Señor* Webb, will sleep more soundly, doubtless."

Jim Hatfield nodded, his eyes grayly cold. He was thinking of a lonely grave beneath the whispering pines close by the bloody Huachuca Trail.

CHAPTER 17

THREE nights later Jim Hatfield sat in the *Una Golondrina* and talked with Amado Capistrano. The hunchback was recounting his discovery of the silver lode which became the Cibola mine.

"It was the merest chance," he said. "Had the rabbit darted the other way, I would have cut straight across the canyon toward the Huachuca Trail and never have approached the ledge. I owe much to that rabbit, and I feel, somehow, that I also owe much to a strange and likeable character I met with that same day.

"He was a tall man, nearly as tall as yourself, with a great brown beard shot with gray and fine eyes. He gave me coffee and appeared not to notice my misshapen body. I have often wondered what became of him.

"Strange, on the ledge which was the outcropping of the Cibola lode, I found the marks of a pick, very fresh marks, and I have often wondered did not that kindly stranger stumble upon the rich find before I? If so, why did he not return to claim what was rightly his? There were no notices posted, and no location filed. I searched the records and could find none. Nor could I learn anything of whom the man might be."

"You'll never see him again, *Don* Amado," Hatfield replied softly, "and I guess you were right in thinking he hit on your ledge, too. I happen to know," he added, "that fellow, whose name was Shafter, left an old mother without much to live on."

Amado Capistrano glanced up at the tall Ranger, a warm light in his clear eyes. He smiled his charming, melancholy smile.

"You make me very happy, my friend," he said. "That old mother will never know want, nor lack with the material things to make happy the declining years. Now tell me—"

The talk was suddenly interrupted by a man who came striding across the dance floor. It was John Chadwick, wearing a jovial smile. He stopped at the table occupied by Hatfield and the hunchback.

"Amado," he said, "I've been doing some thinking. There

isn't one bit of sense in you and I being on the prod against each other the way we have been. Supposing we call it quits and try and get along together?"

Capistrano smiled his reply.

"Nothing would appeal to me more," he declared heartily.

"Fine!" exclaimed Chadwick. "Tell you what—supposing you come over to my place tomorrow, about noon. It isn't but about three hours' ride, you know. We'll have a little talk and thrash things out proper. You come along, too, Hatfield. I've got a bottle or two of the right stuff and my Mex cook puts up a mighty fine meal. What do you say? Is it a go?"

He rested his broad hands on the table top and leaned forward as he spoke. His coat swung open and Hatfield could see the guns in his carefully adjusted shoulder holsters. His gaze rested for a long moment on Chadwick's heavy double cartridge belt, and on the brass rims of the shells snugged in the loop. He raised his eyes to the cattle king's and the look in them was inscrutable.

"Yes, I'll come," he said quietly. "I think we ought to have an interesting session."

Amado Capistrano had already accepted the rancher's invitation.

Glancing toward the door, Hatfield saw a lithe, dark little man enter the saloon. A moment later he left the table with a word of excuse and sauntered through the swinging doors. Outside he waited until Pancho, the Yaqui tracker, joined him.

"They ride tonight, *Capitan*," Pancho whispered, his eyes snapping with excitement. "All will be there tonight, or nearly all. Cartina himself will be there, and perhaps the other of whom you spoke. We strike, *Capitan*?"

Jim Hatfield glanced toward the distant hilltops, and Pancho, eagerly reading his expression, gazed upon the face of the Lone Wolf, a bleak, terrible face in which were set eyes that glittered coldly as frosted dagger points under a winter sun.

Again the Ranger and the tracker rode into the hills. On the crest of a long ridge they separated, Pancho making his way to the cavern mouth in the hollow. Hatfield rode to where the conveyor buckets clicked past the gloomy cleft in the cliff. He

118

concealed Goldy in a thicket on the banks of a little stream, where he could have grass and water, and entered the cleft. On the lip of the ghastly pit he crouched, listening to the murmur of the far-off water, which came up from the vast depths.

Hatfield was listening for another sound—a sound that would tell him Pancho had successfully completed his dangerous task. He could visualize the little tracker, creeping silently as a lizard toward the mighty mass of rock which overhung the cave mouth. He could see him, in his mind's eye, counting the evil-faced riders who passed beneath the gloomy arch to enter the cave. He could see the Yaqui tense as the last one vanished in the dark depths—see him strike a light and fire the end of the long fuse that led to the hidden dynamite. His palms grew clammily moist as he thought of the mighty mass of stone thundering down to block the entrance to the cavern and make of it a living tomb.

"They've got it coming," he muttered as he fingered the length of fuse which was attached to the dynamite planted along the surface of the crumbling ledge. "It'll be good for them to think for a spell that they really *are* buried alive without any water or food."

Suddenly he tensed and his muscles swelled like iron bands. Down the gloomy aisle of the corridor drifted a sullen boom followed by a rumbling thunder. Hatfield could almost hear the cries of terror and see the sudden rush toward the narrow corridor which led past the pit and to the cleft in the cliff by the conveyor line. Grimly he stooped and set fire to the end of the fuse. It sputtered, smoked, and then burned steadily.

Hatfield stood up, and instantly hurled himself sideways and down. He had sensed rather than seen or heard the menace creeping toward him through the clammy dark. He was flat on the ground when the gun flashed fire and a bullet whistled through the space his body had occupied the instant before. He shot forward in a streaking dive and crashed into the man who had fired the shot.

He heard the gun clatter to the stone floor. Then arms like

119

bands of steel wrapped about his body and he was lifted off his feet.

With all his strength he lashed out viciously. His fist crunched against flesh and bone with a shock that jarred his arm to the shoulder. The other's hold loosened slightly and the Ranger regained his feet.

Mightily, the two powerful men wrestled, reeling, swaying, their breath coming in panting gasps. Never in his life had the Lone Wolf encountered such superhuman strength. The abnormally long, gnarled arms crushed his chest until it was as if a red hot clasp of iron encircled it. He bowed his back and resisted to the last atom.

Backward the other forced him. Suddenly, with a terrible chill of horror, he felt a foot slip over the edge of the pit. Another instant and he would be hurled into the awful depths. With a final mighty effort he sent his opponent reeling away from the lip of the gulf. Then, utterly unexpectedly, he hurled himself down upon his back, gripping the other's forearms at the same instant and kicking upward with all the strength of his sinewy legs.

Caught by the mighty thrust of those pistoning legs, the other man shot into the air. Hatfield jerked down on the forearms at the same instant and then let go.

The squat, powerful body of Hatfield's assailant shot through the air, cleared the edge of the pit and hurtled downward with an awful scream of terror and despair. Up from the depths came the cry, growing thin with distance—then the faint whisper of a splash. Then silence.

Gasping and panting, Hatfield scrambled to his feet. Numbly he remembered the dynamite and the burning fuse. He staggered away from the edge of the pit, shambling toward the outer air and safety.

With a clap of thunder and a lurid reddish glare, the dynamite let go. Down into the pit crashed yard after yard of the ledge, making the way past the gulf unpassable, imprisoning the men who came yelling down the long corridor from the great central cavern.

But Jim Hatfield did not hear the thudding feet nor the howls of despair. Near the mouth of the cleft he lay, silent and motionless, with the acrid fumes of the burned powder wisping about his white face.

CHAPTER 18

JIM HATFIELD regained consciousness to feel the drip of cold water on his face. Opening his reluctant lids, he glanced up into the dark, anxious face of Pancho, the little tracker. The Yaqui's black eyes, glowed warmly as Hatfield struggled to a sitting position.

"*Capitan!* you live!" he exclaimed.

"I'm not so sure of it," the Ranger replied. "Feel as though I ought to be dead. What happened?"

"I know not," replied the Yaqui. "After making sure that the entrance to the cavern was blocked securely, I hurried across the ridge as you directed. I found you here, pale and still. I thought you to be dead."

The whinny of a horse brought Hatfield's head up around. Tied to a tree was a sturdy roan, Sheriff Branch Horton's horse. Sunlight was shimmering on his black coat.

The sight of that sunlight, pouring almost straight down from the brassy-blue sky, sent remembrance crashing through the Ranger's mind. He struggled to his feet and headed, somewhat shakily, for the thicket in which he had left his tall golden sorrel.

"Unhitch that black horse and ride him," he called to Pancho. "You and I have got some riding to do, Pancho! If we're not a long way the other side of these hills by noon, a mighty fine man is going to die!"

Together they rode across the hills, the Yaqui clinging like a burr to the unaccustomed saddle. They drummed on as the blazing sun arched upward into the sky toward the misty blue west. It was well past noon when the white buildings of John Chadwick's Circle C came into view.

Hatfield and Pancho circled the apparently deserted ranch

buildings, approaching them from the rear by way of a thick grove of burr oaks. No sound greeted them as they crept stealthily through the close-set tree trunks.

At the edge of the grove, several feet from the ranchhouse, they paused. Then the Yaqui crept on, a drifting shadow that seemed to lack real substance. He flattened himself against the wall as footsteps sounded inside the house. A door opened and Edwards, Chadwick's foreman, stepped into view, a rifle in his hands. His quick eye caught the loom of Hatfield's tall form amid the trees and he flung a rifle to his shoulder.

For a tense instant, disaster hovered in the balance. The crash of the report, no matter who fired first, would warn any other inmates of the house. Hatfield's hands had moved with blurring speed and the muzzles of his Colts yawned hungrily at Edwards, but he hesitated to pull trigger.

In that split instant, Pancho drifted along the side of the ranchhouse like a swirl of dusky smoke. His sinewy arm rose and fell. Something gleamed brightly in the sunlight, and was dimmed by a reddish stain.

Edwards' body fell forward as Pancho wrenched his knife from between the foreman's shoulder blades. The Yaqui caught the limp body in his wiry arms and eased it silently to the ground, preventing the rifle from clattering at the same instant. Hatfield reached him in three giant strides. He motioned to the door which Edwards had left ajar. They slipped through and moved silently along the shadowy hall toward the front of the house, from which came voices. Crouched just outside a second door, they peered through a crack.

Seated on one side of the room was Amado Capistrano. His arms were bound and he was tied to his chair. On his handsome face was an expression of faint amusement as he stared into the flashing eyes of John Chadwick, who stood facing him. His glance strayed across the room to Joseph Bowers, his mine superintendent, and his clear eyes mirrored contempt.

"Yes, you're not going to live long, you wriggle-backed greaser sidewinder," Chadwick was saying. "You crossed me once too often. I'm doing for you as soon as your Ranger friend gets here, and for him, too. Folks are going to think you killed each other. It won't be hard to fix it that way."

For the first time Capistrano's face showed concern.

"Let the Ranger alone, Chadwick," he said in his musical voice. "Murdering him won't get you anything."

Chadwick snarled an oath.

"He's in my way," he grated. "The time will come," he boasted, "when his kind will come eating out of my hand, when I get things going right in this state. Right now when they get in my way, I squash them like I would a horned toad."

He shouted over his shoulder:

"Hey, Ed, aren't the boys riding in yet?"

"I don't think the boys will ever come riding in again, Chadwick," drawled a quiet voice from the doorway.

Chadwick whirled in amazement to face the doorway. The Lone Wolf stood there, towering in his great height. His face was as cold as wind-beaten granite, his eyes like icy water torturing under frozen snow. The eyes shifted suddenly and his slim hands moved with blinding speed. From the muzzle of one black Colt wisped a spiral of blue smoke. The room echoed to the roar of the explosion.

Joseph Bowers reeled sideways, his half-drawn gun clattering to the floor. Retching and choking, he writhed on the woven rug, his face ghastly, blood pouring from the gaping wound in his chest. Hatfield holstered his smoking gun and turned his terrible eyes on Chadwick once more.

"I'm giving you a full chance, Chadwick, you murdering skunk," he said, his voice deadly in its softness. "More than you gave Dick Webb or Ed Shafter. Get going, Chadwick! Reach for those mismated guns of yours—the forty-five and the thirty two-twenty. Those guns gave you away, Chadwick. Dick and Ed had holes in their heads made by different caliber bullets. Reach for them, Chadwick—or come along peaceably and be hanged!"

For an instant John Chadwick seemed to hesitate. Then blind, ungovernable fury blackened his face and his guns came roaring from their shoulder holsters.

Through a haze of powder smoke he saw Jim Hatfield standing straight and tall, blood trickling down one bronzed cheek. Blood was welling in Chadwick's mouth. His breast was crushed and shattered by the heavy slugs that had hammered the bone to bits. Forward he fell, toppling slowly, to lie silent and motionless at the Lone Wolf's feet.

"Dyson can get a posse together and get into that cave to haul out that nest of snakes we've got penned up there," Hatfield told Amado Capistrano after the other had been released.

"Dyson's honest—dumb, but honest. He didn't know Horton was in cahoots with Chadwick. He didn't know Chadwick was the prize crook of the district. Yes, I know Chadwick planned to kill us both when he got us here. I was coming prepared for him, but things worked out to make me late."

He smiled briefly.

"Well, it all ended okay so that's that," he said. "Now you can go on back to your business of sending sick kids to hospitals and planning schools for the well ones, and helping folks who are in trouble. Things will be better in this district now, and here's hoping you end up owning all of the old Capistrano home ranch before you get through!"

Several days later, Jim Hatfield reported in full to grim old Captain McDowell at Ranger headquarters.

"A lie Horton and Chadwick told gave me my first real line on them," he told Captain Bill. "That day I met them at the Cibola mine, they said they'd been in the hills all night. They were mighty anxious to have me believe they *had* been in the hills. They hadn't!"

"How'd you know they hadn't?" Cap. Bill asked. Hatfield chuckled.

"They were all covered with dust, sir, and it wasn't the red dust of the hills," he explained. "It was the gray alkali dust of the desert. They'd been around the hills to meet the rest of their outfit from down Mexico way.

"Then when I sent telegrams and traced down Bowers' activities since the time he got fired for being drunk and miscalculating that bridge job, I found out he'd been associating with Chadwick for a long time. Bowers had a penitentiary record for crooked work. Chadwick got him pardoned because he could use him. Bowers was a smart engineer, but he couldn't keep straight."

He paused a moment, rolling a cigarette with the slim, bronzed fingers of one hand.

"Chadwick's scheme was a lulu!" he exclaimed. "He wasn't going in for the plain ordinary brand of banditry. He was planning to clean out the whole Tamarra Valley.

"He drilled those men of his like they were an army. Pedro Cartina was his front man, who took all the blame and did the strutting. Chadwick was the brains. Horton was another blockhead he'd raised up from nothing."

He lit the cigarette and exhaled a long ribbon of smoke.

"The ore stealing idea was Bowers', and it was a smart one," he continued. "Chadwick was sending the ore to his Humboldt mine and slipping it into his stamp mill. No wonder the Humboldt was doing well. Holding up the stage and stealing his own insured payroll wasn't so bad, either, and they even took a whack at the bank, and nearly got away with a fat haul.

"Some of the gang," he continued, "were real bad men, and those that weren't Cartina scared into doing whatever was wanted, like that poor little devil I picked up in the desert. He was a spy in the Cibola mine, sending reports when high-grade ore was coming out. Giving him one of those Government model rifles was a mistake.

"Webb and Shafter caught on to what was going on, particularly Shafter, and Chadwick wiped them out. It was seeing those different sized loops on Chadwick's cartridge belt that cinched my case on him. Well, sir, I guess that about clears up everything, doesn't it?'"

"Uh-huh," agreed Cap. Bill, "excepting what you're going to do with that little saddle-colored Indian you brought along with you."

"Oh, Pancho," grinned Hatfield. "Pancho's the best tracker to ever come out of Mexico, and he sure is dependable."

"Better take him with you where I'm sending you next, then," remarked Captain Bill drily. "From what I hear, there isn't much dependable in that district, and you've got a tough job ahead of you, if you ever had one!"

"Yes, sir!" replied the Lone Wolf, his eyes sunny with pleasurable anticipation. Then the Ranger's eyes turned somber, but with a quiet satisfaction in their depths.

Jim Hatfield was thinking of a lonely grave on a hillside overlooking the Huachuca Trail where the winds whispered softly through the cathedral aisles of the pines and a tall yucca lifted high on its single stem a great cluster of drooping lily-white blossoms that swayed gently in the breeze like a swung censer.

He knew that Ed Shafter could sleep peacefully now.

THE END

Leslie Scott was born in Lewisburg, West Virginia. During the Great War, he joined the French Foreign Legion and spent four years in the trenches. In the 1920s he worked as a mining engineer and bridge builder in the western American states and in China before settling in New York. A bar-room discussion in 1934 with Leo Margulies, who was managing editor for Standard Magazines, prompted Scott to try writing fiction. He went on to create two of the most notable series characters in Western pulp magazines. In 1936, Standard Magazines launched, and in *Texas Rangers*, Scott under the house name of **Jackson Cole** created Jim Hatfield, Texas Ranger, a character whose popularity was so great with readers that this magazine featuring his adventures lasted until 1958. When others eventually began contributing Jim Hatfield stories, Scott created another Texas Ranger hero, Walt Slade, better known as *El Halcon*, the Hawk, whose exploits were regularly featured in *Thrilling Western*. In the 1950s Scott moved quickly into writing book-length adventures about both Jim Hatfield and Walt Slade in long series of original paperback Westerns. At the same time, however, Scott was also doing some of his best work in hardcover Westerns published by Arcadia House; thoughtful, well-constructed stories, with engaging characters and authentic settings and situations. Among the best of these, surely, are *Silver City* (1953), *Longhorn Empire* (1954), *The Trail Builders* (1956), and *Blood on the Rio Grande* (1959). In these hardcover Westerns, many of which have never been reprinted, Scott proved himself highly capable of writing traditional Western stories with characters who have sufficient depth to change in the course of the narrative and with a degree of authenticity and historical accuracy absent from many of his series stories.

ACADEMIC PRESS LIMITED
24-28 Oval Road
LONDON NW1 7DX,UK

U.S. Edition Published by
ACADEMIC PRESS INC.
San Diego, CA 92101, USA

This book is printed on acid-free paper

Originally published in Dutch under the title *Multimedia Begrippengids*.
Copyright © 1994, Data Scripta, Gorredijk

A catalogue record for this book is available from the British Library

ISBN 0 12 648720 0

Printed and bound by in Great Britain by Hartnolls Ltd, Bodmin, Cornwall

The
Multimedia
dictionary

Edited by

H. Sleurink

ACADEMIC PRESS
Harcourt Brace & Company, Publishers
London San Diego New York Sydney Tokyo Toronto

The
Multimedia
dictionary

FOREWORD

The purpose of the Multimedia Dictionary is to provide clear explanations and definitions of the most important multimedia terms in the areas of concepts, equipment and technology. An attempt is made to explain all the jargon used in the texts. Such terms are printed in italics. In some cases, terms which are indirectly related to the subject have also been referred to. In such cases, a 'See also' reference is used. This creates a complete reference system, whereby access is given to information on separate sections of the subject field.

The contribution of a number of companies and individuals was crucial in the making of this publication. We are particularly indebted to Apple, IBM, Microsoft, Philips and PTT Telecom. The knowledge, dedication and efforts of André Schuurman, Gea Vellinga, Ester Verheul and Irma de Witt also played an essential role. All of the above valued colleagues work for Data Scripta, which consistently gave constructive criticism in the best possible manner. Dark Mooy, systems analyst, and Karin Kincaide, who makes teaching aids for the graphic industry, also made significant contributions to the final product through their critical questions and suggestions, during the translation.

Nothing made by people is perfect. This must be equally true of this book, which strives to explain the terminology of an area undergoing explosive growth. New ideas, concepts, technologies and terms are constantly arising. Not all of these are crucially important, but nevertheless, should you come across terms you think should be included, please let me know. The same applies if you have any additions for the terms which are included, I would be pleased to hear them.

Hans Sleurink
datascrp@knoware.nl

Data Scripta
Postbox 175
8400 AD Gorredijk
The Netherlands

Figure words

1.22
See: floppy disk.

1.44
See: floppy disk.

10Base-2
See: thin Ethernet.

10Base-5
See: thick Ethernet.

10Base-T
A common used *IEEE* standard for *Ethernet*. The standard describes, amongst others, the cabling, the connection between cable and network card and the *network topology*. 10Base-T uses *unshielded twisted pair* cables. The connector is a *RJ-45 jack* and it uses the *star* topology. The speed is 10 megabits per second.

100Base-T
A *network protocol*, developed by 3COM, with speeds up to 100 *Mbit/s*. It is derived from *100VG-AnyLAN*. A difference is that it uses the *CSMA/CD* protocol.100Base-T is also called *Fast Ethernet*. Expectations are that the protocol will become a standard as *IEEE* 802.3.

100VG-AnyLAN
A *network protocol* developed by Hewlett-Packard in cooperation with IBM and AT&T which can operate at a speed of 100 *Mbit/s*. 100VG-AnyLAN's advantage (and an important difference from its rival *100Base-T*) is the access method. The access method—called *demand priority*—guarantees *bandwidth*. This makes it more suitable for *multimedia* applications. 100VG-AnyLAN is known as *IEEE* standard 802.12. See also: guaranteed bandwith.

16 bit
A computer systems and software description that processes information as 2-byte words (16 bits). The more bytes that can be processed

simultaneously, the faster the system. The Intel 8086/8088 and 80286 are 16-bit processors.
See also: 80x8; 80x86; 32 bit; 64 bit.

16450 UART

A *chip* for *serial* communication in a computer. Like its predecessor, the *8250 UART*, it still has a one *byte memory* buffer. The chip does, however, support higher communication speed.
See also: 16550 UART; universal asynchronous receiver/transmitter.

16550 UART

A *chip* for *serial* communication in a computer. This chip is the successor of the *16450 UART*. It has two 16 *byte memory* buffers (one for incoming and one for outgoing traffic). The speed of communication is therefore higher than with the 16450 UART.
See also: 8250 UART; universal asynchronous receiver/transmitter.

2.88

See: floppy disk.

3-chip module

A type of 1-megabyte SIMM module, which contains two 4-megabit chips and one 1-megabit *chip*, instead of nine 1-megabit chips. This type of chip can only be used on newer motherboards because their timing differs slightly from the *9-chip module*.
See also: single in-line memory module.

3.5-inch

1. Description for a *floppy disk* with a 3.5-inch diameter.
2. A standard for internal devices and housings which are 3.5 inches wide.

32 bit

A computer systems and software description that processes information as 4-byte words (32 bits). The more bytes that can be processed simultaneously, the faster the system. The Intel 80386 and 80486 and the Motorola *680x0* are 32-bit processors.
See also: 80x86DX; 680x0; 16 bit; 64 bit.

340x0

A *graphic coprocessor* by Texas Instruments. The 34010 and 34020 models are controlled using the so-called TIGA-interface (Texas Instruments Graphics Architecture).

360K
See: floppy disk.

3D
Description of an object that is spatial and therefore has height, width and depth.

3D digitizer
A device for scanning three-dimensional objects and saving the *image* in a *digital* format. There are two kinds. Most commonly used is the surface *scanner* that scans an object with *laser* rays or uses a *camera* and a beam of light to make an exposure. This results in a frame model of the original. Some scanners can also record the colors of the object. This is stored separately as a *bitmap*. When the image is displayed the colors are painted over the frame model.

The second kind is used frequently in the medical world. It scans the content of an object and stores this *data* as so-called *voxels*. These devices often use electromagnetic radiation to accomplish this.

3DO
The name for a *multimedia* format as well as a multimedia system designed by the 3DO company. 3DO is used to create and playback *interactive* multimedia productions (including *full-motion* and *full-screen video*). A double-speed *CD-ROM* is used for storage.

A complete system consists of: development software, prescribed compression and decompression methods and a *compact disc* drive. 3DO can be compared with CD-i and therefore a potential competitor.
See also: Compact Disc Interactive.

4:2:2
Indication for the quality of digital *component video* and a specification for video signal storage.

The first digit (4) indicates the number of bytes used for recording the brightness. The next two digits indicate the number of bytes used for the color system. Sometimes a fourth digit is added (for example: 4:2:2:4). This digit indicates the number of bytes used for the *key-signal*.

Quality indications in use are: 4:2:2 (professional quality), 4:1:1 (consumer quality) and 4:4:4 (high-end professional quality). The 4:2:2 ratio is described among others in the *CCIR 601/656* standard for video.
See also: YCrCb.

5.25 inch

1. A *floppy disk* with a 5.25-inch diameter.
2. A standard for internal devices and housings that are 5.25 inches wide.

64 bit

A computer systems and software description that processes information as 8-byte words (64 bits). The more bytes that can be processed simultaneously, the faster the system. The Intel *Pentium* and the DEC *Alpha AXP* are 64-bit microprocessors.
See also: 16 bit; 32 bit.

680x0

The microprocessor family manufactured by Motorola used in Apple *Macintosh* computers and others. The first 68000 is a 32-bit processor with a 16-bit wide *bus* connection with the motherboard and an addressable *memory* of 16 megabytes. The successors are the 68020 (32-bit wide bus and 4 gigabytes addressable memory), the 68030 (a faster version of 68020 with a built-in cache) and 68040 (three times faster than the 68030 with a built-in numeric *coprocessor*).
See also: central processing unit; 32 bit; 64 bit.

720K

See: floppy disk.

80486DXx

A type of microprocessor manufactured by Intel used in PC-compatible computers. The last 'x' is replaced by a digit (for example 80486DX2) which indicates that *clock* frequency in the processor is higher than the frequency used in the motherboard. 'DX2' means that the frequency is doubled; 'DX4' means (inconsistently) that the frequency is tripled.
See also: central processing unit; bus; 80x86DX.

80x86DX

A type of microprocessor manufactured by Intel used in PC-compatible computers. The 'x' is replaced by a digit (for example 80386DX or 80486DX) which indicates the processor generation. 'DX' means that the processor has a complete (32-bit wide) connection with the motherboard and that the *clock* frequency in the processor is equal to the frequency used in the motherboard.
See also: central processing unit; 80x86SX; 80x86SL; 80x87.

80x86SL

A type of microprocessor manufactured by Intel used in PC-compatible computers. The 'x' is replaced by a digit (for example 80386SL or 80486SL) which indicates the processor generation. 'SL' means that the processor has lower power consumption than *80x86DX* or *80x86SX*, while it is functionally identical. This makes it suitable for portable computers.
See also: central processing unit; 80x86DX; 80x86SX; 80x87.

80x86SX

A type of *microprocessor* manufactured by Intel used in PC-compatible computers. The 'x' is replaced by a digit (for example 80386DX or 80486DX) which indicates the processor generation. 'SX' means that the processor lacks some of the features present in *80x86DX* processors. The 80386SX, for instance, has a 16-bit connection to the motherboard and a 32-bit internal architecture. The 80486SX has no numerical coprocessor while the 80486DX does.
See also: central processing unit; 80x86DX; 80x86SL; 80x87.

80x87

A type of coprocessor manufactured by Intel used in PC-compatible computers. The 'x' is replaced by a digit (for example 80287, 80387 or 80487) which indicates the processor generation. The '7' indicates that it is the numerical *coprocessor* to the matching 'DX' or 'SX' series.
See also: 80x86DX; 80x86SX; 80x86SL.

8250 UART

A *chip* for *serial* communication in a computer. The maximum transmission speed for this chip is 9600 bits per second with an internal data *buffer* of (only) one *byte*. This chip is outdated when its speed is compared to the capabilities of newer modems and devices.
See also: 16450 UART; 16550 UART.

8514/A

An IBM display adapter. Possible screen resolutions are 1024 * 768 pixels (*interlaced*) with 256 colors and 640 * 480 pixels with 256 colors. It contains an on-board *coprocessor* for performing 2-D graphics and it is designed to coexist with VGA for dual *monitor* capability.
See also: video adapter; video mode.

9-chip module

A type of 1-megabyte SIMM containing a total of 9-megabit *memory* divided into nine 1-megabit chips.
See also: single in-line memory module; 3-chip module.

A

A/B-roll

An installation with two video sources (video recorders or videodiscs) and one video recorder. With this installation, clips from the sources are mixed to create *transition* effects between *scenes.* This is done through a *digital video effects generator.* The result is recorded on the third machine.
See also: editing.

A/UX

A *Unix* emulation by Apple corporation. A/UX makes it possible to run Unix applications on a *Macintosh* computer.
See also: Apple Macintosh system.

A4-display

A *monitor* for displaying an A4 size (21 cm * 29.7 cm) page in *portrait* orientation in a 1:1 ratio to the printed page. This requires a screen diagonal of at least 16 inches. To display two A4 pages side by side, a screen diagonal of at least 21 inches is required.

ablation

A technique used to write *data* on an optical medium. A *laser* beam is used to burn tiny holes (*pits*) into a reflective layer of aluminum.
See also: optical disc.

accelerando

Music term describing a gradual acceleration of *tempo.*

access time

The time needed to access *data* on storage medium. A *hard disk*, for instance, can access data in less than 20 milliseconds, whereas the access time for a *floppy disk* is many times higher. Reading and writing files on a hard disk is therefore faster.
The storage medium with the highest access time is *flash memory* with access times between 150 and 250 nanoseconds.
See also: PCMCIA.

accidentals

A music term for two symbols in staff-notation which indicate that a note must be raised a semitone (sharp) or lowered a semitone (flat). The accidental applies only to the bar it appears in.

acknowledge

ACK - The name for the character used in some network *protocols* to confirm that a message is received correctly. When the sender receives the ACK character it can send the next message, otherwise it retransmits the current message.
See also: carrier sense multiple access/collision detection.

acknowledgment

An audible or visible signal indicating the user has succesfully activated a certain element on the screen.
See also: active.

Acrobat

Application made by Adobe Systems for electronic document exchange. A document processed with Acrobat can contain a special *hypertext link* called an article. This is an invisible path through a document. With it the reader navigates automatically through related material. Standard hypertext links relate topics within an individual document or between separate documents. It is possible even to run other *Windows* programs with them or play sound or *video clips.* To locate *information* fast full-text indexes can be created.
Acrobat is composed of several independent programs:
- The Reader is for viewing the documents and searching through the indexes.
- The Exchange package allows a user, besides viewing the document, to add notes and links, to crop or rotate images and to add or remove pages. Also included is a printer driver that stores *PostScript* output of a program as an Acrobat document.
- The Distiller is used to create documents with all the features described above.
- The Catalog package creates the full-text indexes.
Acrobat creates documents in Portable Document Format (PDF) from PostScript files. This format allows document exchange between computer platforms (these are currently: Microsoft Windows, Apple *MacIntosh*, Microsoft DOS and *Unix*). A document created on one platform has the same appearance when read on an other computer platform. All page *formatting* and fonts are preserved.
See also: full-text index.

active
In a multiwindow environment, the *window* or document that is operative and can receive commands from the user.
See also: select (to).

active page
A video adapter displays on the screen the *data* it reads from *video memory*. Video memory can be divided into several parts, called pages, each with a different *content*. Only one page can be shown at a time. The visible page is called the *active* page.
See also: frame buffer.

active play
Videodiscs recorded using the *constant angular velocity* principle (CAV).

adapter
Component that connects a computer with a peripheral *device*, for example a network card connects the computer to the network *server*.
See also: add-on card.

adaptive differential pulse code modulation
ADPCM - A speech-coding method that calculates the difference between two consecutive speech samples in standard *Pulse Code Modulation* (PCM) coded voice signals. This calculation is encoded using an adaptive filter and is therefore transmitted at a lower rate than the standard 64-Kbps technique. A sample is taken 8000 times per second and contains three or four bits, which represent the difference between two adjacent samples. PCM uses 8 bits for a sample. Therefore ADPCM encodes voice in half the space PCM needs.

add noise filter
This is a tool used in an image editing program to make an image look like a coarse-grained photograph.
See also: filters.

normal   add noise

additive color synthesis
See: color synthesis.

address
Identification for a location in computer *memory*, on a *hard disk* or for a *workstation*. With this identification *data* can be stored or retrieved at the location.

address bus

Internal *channel* from the CPU to *memory* across which the addresses of *data* (not the data itself) are transmitted. The number of lines (wires) in the address bus determines the amount of memory that can be directly addressed as each line carries one *bit* of the address. For example, the 8088 CPU has 20 address lines and can address 1,048,576 bytes. The 68020 has 32 address lines and can address 4 gigabytes.

See also: addressing; bus.

addressing

Addressing is how a computer accesses *data* at a *memory* location. Each location has an *address* that identifies it. With the address the data can be reached by sending the address over the *address bus*.

Adobe type manager

ATM - Adobe type manager makes fonts available for use by *Windows* and *Macintosh* programs. ATM makes a *font* in any desired size. A font looks the same whether it is displayed on the screen or printed on the *printer*. This makes it possible to see on the screen what a font will look like when it is printed.

ATM makes fonts on demand from *outline fonts*. This saves much space compared to *bitmap fonts* that have to be present in advance in every conceivable size. ATM also manages the downloading of fonts to the printer when a requested font is not available in the printer. On printers that do not support font downloading, the font is converted into a bitmap and printed as such. With ATM the font usage is no longer limited to fonts present in the printer.

Many fonts are available electronically from the public domain.

See also: SuperATM.

Advanced Communications Technologies and Services

A European program (1994-1998) to stimulate development of communication technology and services. ACTS is a continuation of earlier Research and development in Advanced Communication technologies in Europe (RACE program). ACTS is divided in six subjects:

1. interactive digital multimedia services;
2. photonic technologies;
3. high speed networking;
4. mobility and personal communication networks;
5. intelligence in networks and service engineering;
6. quality, security and safety of communication services and systems.

The ACTS program was established to develop applications for Integrated Broadband Communications Network (IBCN).
See also: Research and development in Advanced Communications Technologies in Europe.

AES/EBU
A standard for the electric connection of stereo, *digital* and *audio* signals through a shielded three-wire cable. The *jack* is an XLR (microphone) which is used in most digital/audio equipment. The *ANSI* standard is S.4.40-1985.
See also: Audio Engineering Society; European Broadcast Union; American National Standards Institute; Sony/Philips Digital Interface.

agent
1. An animated figure on the screen that explains how to use a program.
2. A program that can be taught to execute repetitive tasks. This is comparable to macros. Agents are also called 'softbots'. This is a contraction of 'software robot'.

AIP kubus
See: virtual reality.

air brush
A tool used in a drawing, painting or image editing program. It creates an effect similar to an actual air brush. The edges of the sprayed colors are blurred. The longer one sprays on the same spot the darker the color becomes. The color shade of the air brush is usually adjustable.
See also: gradient.

AIX
A *Unix* variant made by IBM. It is available on the RS/6000 *RISC workstation*, on IBM mainframes and on the PS/2.

alerting
A signal from the system (usually a small message on the screen) that informs the user that *electronic mail* has arrived.

algorithm
Set of ordered, sequential steps for solving a problem, such as a mathematical formula or the instructions in a program.
An example is the algorithm E (for Euclid): Given two positive integers n and m, find the greatest common denominator (GCD).

E1: Divide m by n and compute remainder r.

E2: If r = 0 then n = GCD, the process stops; else

E3: Let m be n and let n be r. Return to step E1.

alias

An alias is an abbreviated name for a *file*. On a *Unix* system file /pub/ethc/educational/source/oberon can be given an alias of /usr/oberon. When the content of *directory* /usr is listed, the file oberon will appear. The file is not moved however. The directory /usr now holds an entry oberon and in it is the original name of the file.

On a *Macintosh* one can also create an alias by adding the *icon* from one *folder* to another folder. This can save a user the time of having to wade through a large folder hierarchy.

align (to)

A program command which aligns objects.

To a *desktop publishing* program it means that text in adjacent columns must be aligned at the same height.

With a drawing program, figures can be aligned horizontally or vertically.

With a wordprocessor, text can be aligned with the left or right margin.

align left

See: left justification.

align right

See: right justification.

alignment

In a wordprocessor one can specify the alignment of text lines. Possibilities are: align to the left margin, the right margin or *center* text between left and right margins, or justify between the left and right margin.

See also: justification; left justification; right justification.

All Points Addressable graphics

APA graphics - Refers to an array (bitmapped screen, matrix, etc.) in which all *bits* or *cells* can be individually manipulated, because each *pixel* has an *address*.

See also: bitmap.

Alpha AXP
A microprocessor manufactured by the Digital Equipment Corporation (DEC). The Alpha AXP is a *RISC* processor connected to a 64-bit *bus*. The Alpha AXP is designed to execute machine instructions used in other microprocessors. This makes it possible to run programs from other computer platforms unaltered. The Alpha AXP does this through using the PAL-code (Privileged Architecture Library) which can translate a foreign machine code into its native equivalent.
See also: central processing unit; 64 bit.

alpha channel
The alpha channel is the group of eight leftmost bits in a sequence of 32 *bits* used by some graphics adapters to represent a *pixel*. In image editing these eight bits can be used as an additional layer to mask an image or parts of it. When two images are overlaid, the eight bits specify how much of the bottom layer shines through the top layer. The eight bits consist of a percentage. Zero per cent means that the top layer is completely visible; 100 per cent means the bottom layer is completely visible. With this technique can be created gradual transitions between images.
See also: pixeldepth; overlay; genlock.

alphanumeric character
Any of the characters that can be represented in a computer. Characters are classified in several groups. These are:
- alphabetic (all letters);
- numeric (all digits);
- digits, punctuations;
- special symbols (i.e. + - =).

ambient light
A light source used to illuminate the environment of a *scene*.
See also: spotlight.

American National Standards Institute
ANSI - An organization for normalization and standardization. It develops standards for technology, including computer applications such as *programming languages*, for example COBOL and C.
See also: Institute of Electrical and Electronic Engineers; International Standards Organization.

American Standard Code for Information Interchange

ASCII - pronounced 'askee'.

1. This is a code table describing how characters are represented in a computer. A computer can only work with zeroes and ones. ASCII defines, in hexadecimal 'shorthand' (code) the series of zeroes and ones (*binary*) which represent a particular *character*. That is why letters etc. are coded as numbers. ASCII defines which series of zeroes and ones encodes a certain character. There are 128 different characters defined which means that a code occupies 7 bits. The first 32 characters are control characters. The remaining codes are digits, lower and *upper case* letters, punctuation and other symbols. In a *personal computer* data is stored in units of eight bits (a byte). This allows the ASCII code to be extended by 1 bit making 256 different characters possible. This is called the Extended ASCII character set. It also includes *diacritical marks*, Greek symbols and line drawing characters, etc. The definition of the 128 extra characters is not clearly standardized. Several definitions exist mainly to accommodate the diacritical marks needed in different European languages.

2. A *file* containing only ASCII characters. Nearly all computer applications across platforms can handle a file in ASCII format. Mostly the applications translate the file to their internal format for processing.

ampersand

& - A symbol meaning 'and'. It is a *ligature* of the letters 'e' and 't' that form the word 'et' which means 'and' in Latin.

amplitude

The maximum value of a periodically varying quantity, for example the vibrating string of a guitar. The amplitude of the string vibration determines the volume of sound. A large amplitude produces a loud sound. See also: analog; frequency; waveform.

analog

Analog electric signals are signals with varying *frequency* and *amplitude*. They are called analog because the electrical signal mimics the original signal, for instance sound. The frequency and amplitude of a signal varies on a sliding scale. This means that an infinite number of values can be recorded between two points.

Examples of analog signals are sound and temperature. Electric light can be analog (dimmer switch) or *digital* (on/off switch).

See also: digital-to-analog converter.

analog display

A video monitor that accepts *analog* signals from the computer (digital-to-analog *conversion* is done in the video *adapter*). A variant is the *red, green, blue* (RGB) monitor that has a screen that requires separate red, green and blue signals from the computer. It generates a better *image* than composite signals, which merge the colors together. The color combinations are infinite but in practice the number of combinations is limited by the video adapter.

analog loopback

A method for testing a *modem*. The transmit side of the modem is connected to its receive side. A signal is transmitted and compared to the received signal. The signals must be exactly the same.

analog sound

Sound in its audible form.
See also: analog.

analog video

Signals represented by an infinite number of sliding-scale transitions between video levels, for example TV signals. In computers, *analog* video is often used because the quality is better than *digital video*. However, when analog video is copied too often, the quality decreases. Digital video can be copied infinitely without quality loss.

analog-to-digital converter

ADC - A device for converting *analog* signals to *digital* signals. It takes samples of the analog signal many times per second. The sample is translated into a number (= a digital value) representing the measured *frequency* and *amplitude*. ADC devices are used in *audio, video* and *scanner* equipment. Analog-to-digital conversion is often used to store images or sounds in a computer.
See also: digital-to-analog converter.

anchor

A code one uses in a *desktop publishing* program for instance to keep an illustration and a *paragraph* attached to each other. When the paragraph is relocated in the document, the illustration will move along with it.

anchor point

Beginning and end of a *Bézier curve.* In a drawing program, the anchor point can be moved with the *mouse*. The program then changes the size, location and form of the curve accordingly.

angle

The angle a *camera* uses to photograph a *scene*. The focal distance determines the angle. The smaller the focal distance, the greater the angle.

See also: wide angle.

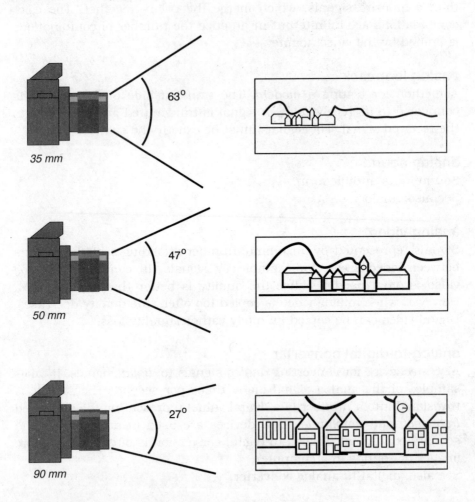

35 mm   63°

50 mm   47°

90 mm   27°

animated screen capture

An application that records everything that happens on a computer screen. This includes *mouse* and *cursor* movement. This recording is played later, for instance to give a user an animated instruction on how to use a program. Often the recorder allows the addition of a narrative voice.

animating on fields

A way to smooth motion in animation clips on video. The animation is recorded in frames. A *frame* consists of two parts called fields. These are stored separately in *field* animation. When the recording is played, the viewer sees 50 half frames instead of the usual 25 whole *frames per second*, making the movements look smoother.
See also: persistence of vision.

animation

Technique to create the illusion that stationary objects are moving. This is done by recording *frame* by frame small changes in a *scene*. This recording is played at full speed thus creating the illusion that objects are moving. The term comes from the Latin word 'animare', which means to bring to life.
See also: in-betweens; key-frames.

animator

The designer of animated figures. This person (usually an artist) often only draws the *key-frames*.
See also: in-betweens.

ANSI

See: American National Standards Institute.

ANSI-lumen

Unit for measuring the effective light output of, for instance, LCD-projectors. The ANSI-lumen is determined by taking the average *lumen* value of nine predefined areas of a projection surface. The result is multiplied by the total area of the projection surface.
See also: candela; lux.

anti-aliasing

A correction technique used for monitors and printers. It is applied to smooth sharp contrasts and to remove ragged edges between two colors.

See also: interpolation; dithering.

anti-reflection surface panel

A special (and rather expensive) anti-glare coating for screen surfaces that reduces the reflection of light.

anti-static coating

A coating that prevents a screen from getting an electrostatic charge. Such a screen attracts much less dust.

Apple Macintosh system

Operating system for *Macintosh* computers. Remarkably, part of the system is located in the ROM. The other part (simply called the System) is located on the *hard disk*. This part adds features like fonts, keyboard, drivers, the *Finder* and other utilities to the system. The Finder is the *graphical user interface* used to control the system.

See also: read only memory (ROM).

AppleTalk

The name for a network *protocol* developed by Apple. All *Macintosh* computers have an AppleTalk connector. It is primarily intended for connecting a *printer* (the LaserWriter). AppleTalk is slow (230.4 kilobits per second) and is not compatible with other networks. In 1989, version 2 of AppleTalk was released. This version supports *Ethernet* and *Token Ring*. AppleTalk is based on the OSI model for communication.

See also: Open System Interconnection (OSI).

application programming interface

API - Documentation describing how operating systems and other service programs are controlled by an application program.

application specific integrated circuits

ASIC - This is a *chip* built for a specific application. Often the chip consolidates many chips into a single package, reducing system board size and power consumption.

archive bit

A *bit* used by DOS for file *backup* purposes. The archive bit is located in the directory entry for a file. The archive bit is activated by DOS when an application program modifies or creates a file. A backup program can use this bit to make a partial backup that copies only the modified (or created) files. Depending on the backup scheme (incremental or differential) the archive bit is cleared or left unchanged after backup.

See also: Microsoft disk operating system; differential backup; incremental backup.

ARCnet

Attached Resource Computer network - One of the first and most popular *LAN* architectures. It was introduced in 1968. It uses the *Token*

Ring protocol. For cabling optical *fiber*, *unshielded twisted pair* and *coax* cables can be used. The transmission speed is 2.5 megabits per second. In 1990, a 20-megabit version was introduced. This was too late for ARCnet to regain the market share it had lost to the faster *Ethernet*.
See also: protocol.

arrow key
The keys identified with arrows. They move the *cursor* or the selection bar in a *menu*. They can also serve as an alternative to the *mouse* in graphic applications.

artifact
Small distortions visible when playing back compressed *digital video*. The distortions are not present in the original but are introduced by the compression program.
See also: compress; video errors.

ascender height
The upright stroke of the letters b, d, f, h, k and l. The length of the ascender is often equal to the height of *upper case* letters. Sometimes, however, the ascender exceeds the capital height, for example in the Bembo *font*.
See also: cap height; x-height; base line.

ascending letter
The *lower case* letters b, d, f, h, k and l whose vertical stroke exceeds the *x-height*.

ASCII
See: American Standard Code for Information Interchange.

aspect ratio
The ratio between the height and width of the picture element used to display an image on screen. Only with a 1:1 ratio is a circle displayed as perfectly round. Old systems which worked with low *resolutions* had considerably distorted aspect ratios.

assemble edit
A form of video editing where clips are placed in sequel without any *transition* or smoothing effects. It's a simple and fast way to edit a tape. This term is also used to describe video material that is added to the end of a tape.

assets

Data blocks (*audio*, *video*, text and so on) processed by a *multimedia* program.

asymmetrical compression

Compression is called asymmetrical when the result of decompression does not reproduce the source of the compression. This occurs with the compression of *digital video*. There is so much data in an *analog video* that not all of it can be saved to obtain a reasonably sized compressed *file*.

This technique is also called *lossy compression*. After decompression the video will not be exactly the same as the original version.

See also: compress; decompress.

asynchronous transfer mode

ATM - A *broadband*, high speed, *data communication* technique suitable for transmitting *analog* data (*audio*, *video*) and *digital* data. ATM combines the advantages of *circuit switching* (guaranteed transmission capacity) and *packet switching* (very efficient because of the high occupation of the connection). This combination is called *cell switching*. ATM divides the traffic into small packets called cells. A *cell* contains an *address* and data. The fixed length (53 bytes) makes it possible to bring a cell to its destination quickly. The small size of a cell makes it possible to process so many cells that even audio and video can be transmitted.

ATM is chosen by the *CCITT* as the transmission technique for broadband ISDN. In the near future ATM will be applied in LANs.

See also: Integrated Services Digital Network (ISDN).

asynchronous transmission

A kind of *serial* transmission in which a message contains just one *character*. Each character is preceded by a start bit (0) and is followed by a stop bit (1). This way the receiver can tell where a character starts

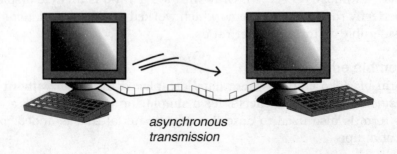

*asynchronous
transmission*

and ends. The transmission is called asynchronous because no negotiating takes place between sender and receiver regarding the time of transmission.

See also: synchronous transmission.

AT compatible
An Advanced Technology-compatible computer is compatible with the IBM AT computer, a machine with an Intel 80286 processor.

ATM
See: asynchronous transfer mode.

attachment unit interface
AUI - A 15-pin connector for connecting computers to an *Ethernet* network.

attenuation
The diminishing of light intensity or the strength of an electrical signal.

attributes
1. The characteristics of an object stored in a computer. For a *3D* object the attributes can be color, transparency, smoothness, location, scale and angle of rotation.
2. The characteristics of a *file* maintained by the *MS-DOS* operating system, for example hidden, read-only and system file.

See also: Microsoft disk operating system (MS-DOS).

audible cue
A sound a computer uses to warn the user that his/her attention is required. This occurs when an error is detected (like forgetting to put a *floppy disk* in a *drive*) or for signaling the end of a lengthy operation.

audio
Sound in electronic form.

audio CD
See: Compact Disc Digital Audio.

audio dubbing
The addition of sound to existing *film* or *video* material. This can be done when video and audio are recorded on separate *tracks*. It is used to add a narrative or music to a production.

See also: post production.

Audio Engineering Society

AES - American Association of Audio Professionals. The association has branches worldwide and organizes seminars, makes recommendations and assists in the development of audio standards.

audio frequencies

AF - Frequencies between 20 and 20,000 Hz. This is the range that is audible to human hearing.

audio mixer

An electronic board (panel) connected to and controlling several sound sources. Sources are: microphones, instruments, playback devices, etc. The volume of each source can be controlled and mixed to create the final sound track that is sent to the recording device.

audio processing

The processing of *analog* or *digital* sound by, for example, adding special effects or mixing soundtracks.
See also: audio mixer; sound effects.

audio segment

A part of a *digital* soundtrack.
See also: audio track.

audio stream

The compression of *digital* sounds. When compression is applied significantly more data can be stored.
See also: compress.

audio synthesis

The *conversion* as well as *simulation* of digitally stored sound to its *analog* equivalent. In some sound cards this is done by looking up the sounds in a wave table of prerecorded musical instruments or even human voices and then playing that sound.
See also: analog sound; analog; Frequency Modulation synthesis.

audio track

The *track* that contains the audio signals. An audio track can be combined with video tracks.

audio video interleaved

AVI - A *file format* developed by Microsoft for storing *digital video* on a PC. Audio and video data are interleaved to ensure that they are

synchronized. Without (hardware) decompression a *resolution* of only 160 * 120 pixels at 15 *frames per second* is possible (on computers with an 80486 processor and a clock frequency of 33 MHz).
With hardware compression, higher resolution and frame rates are possible.

audit trail

A *file* containing *data* on *network* usage, which includes network user activities as well as the modifications made to files.

author profile

A *file* with information on the author of a *multimedia* title and the computer system the author used.

authoring

The process of creating a *multimedia* product. The supporting software is called *authorware*.

authoring language

A script language for developing a *multimedia* production. The script contains instructions on what is displayed and how to respond to user interaction. It is a high-level language. This means that the author specifies what must be done, but not how to do it. To accomplish the same in a lower-level language would involve much more programming.
See also: authoring system.

authoring system

Software for developing multimedia applications. In one authoring system an application is designed by drawing a flow diagram, where icons are placed to represent movie clips, audio clips, graphics, etc. These items are created using separate software tools, such as a drawing program or a sound recorder. With this visual developing method no knowledge of programming is required. The application can be used right away after completing the diagram.
For additional speed some authoring systems have the possibility to translate the diagram to a programming language such as C.
See also: authoring language.

authorization

The granting of access rights to users of a *network*. Users can be restricted in the number of applications, files and devices they may use.

authorware

1. Software to develop *multimedia* titles. With it can be combined video, sound, music, etc. to form a title. What is in the title is recorded in a script written in the *authoring language*.
2. A brand name of a program as described in 1.

auto power down

A technique developed in Sweden to prevent energy wastage. When a system is left idle for some time, it shuts off power-consuming components, placing them in standby mode which uses little energy. With each component users can specify the duration of time before standby mode is activated. A keystroke or moving the *mouse* is all it takes to make the system fully operational again.

auto trace

A technique for converting a picture from *bitmap format* to *vector format*. This is done by tracing the contours of the picture and translating this information into mathematical vector formulae.

auto-panning

A feature some programs offer for moving the contents of a *window* along with the mouse *pointer* when the pointer is placed outside the window.

autoexec.bat

A *batch file* executed by *MS-DOS* each time a computer is (re)started. In this file the user can place commands that he or she wants executed at startup. Autoexec is an abbreviation for auto execute. The *extension* .bat is an abbreviation for batch file.

automatic display power down

When a computer system is left idle for some time, it shuts off power consuming components, such as the display *monitor*. The monitor is then in standby mode which uses little energy.
See also: auto power down.

automatic document feeder

ADF - A *scanner* accessory that automatically feeds pages into a scanner. Without it, manual feeding of each page is necessary.

automatic rollback

A *database* safety feature that restores a database to its last known consistent state in case of a system *crash*. All incomplete updates are automatically invalidated.

autonomous unit interface

See: attachment unit interface.

AUXiliary

AUX - An extra input *plug* on an amplifier. With it an additional sound source can be connected.

AZERTY

A French language keyboard layout. The first six alphabetic keys at the top left of the keyboard read the string AZERTY.

B

B-ISDN
See: Integrated Services Digital Network.

back
Binding margin of *white space* to the left or right of the text. On odd numbered pages it is to the left and on even numbered pages to the right of the text.
See also: gutter; layout.

back light
1. Light behind an object to be photographed.
2. Background light used in LCDs.
See also: liquid crystal display.

back slant
Italic letters that *slant* to the left instead of to the right, in other words, a mirrored italic.

backbone
The main *network* that carries most of the data traffic. The backbone is the part that connects networks (LANs) to each other. They can all be in one building or in different parts of the world.

background noise
Noise present in a system caused by internal or external sources of interference. The noise caused by the signal itself is not considered to be background noise.
See also: burst noise; impulsive noise.

backslash
\ - A left slanted stroke, used in *file* names on the MS-DOS file system. Its function is to delimit *directory* and file names. For example: \DOS\HELP\DOSHELP.HLP.
See also: Microsoft disk operating system (MS-DOS).

backup
Copy of *hard disk* files for safety purposes. The copies are stored on

magnetic tape or *optical media*. If the hard disk is damaged or files are inadvertently deleted, they can be restored from this backup.
See also: full backup; incremental backup.

ballistic effect

A feature in *mouse* software to accelerate or decelerate the movement of the mouse *cursor* depending on the speed used to move the mouse. When the mouse is moved slowly, the cursor movement is decelerated, when the mouse is moved quickly, it is accelerated.
The deceleration is practical for precision work such as drawing. The acceleration comes in handy when going from one end of the screen to the other. In most mouse software the ballistic effect can be adjusted by the user.

banding

The effect visible when a *printer* or *monitor* cannot correctly display a hue or color *gradient*. The gradient is displayed as distinctive bands. This occurs when the printer or display does not have enough different color or *gray scales*.

bandwidth

The transmission capacity of a connection. The bandwidth is the difference between the highest and the lowest possible signal *frequency* that can be transmitted. The larger the bandwidth, the more information can be transmitted. The bandwidth determines which communication types are possible (*video*, *data*, *audio*) and the number of simultaneous *channels* that can be accommodated. The bandwidth is expressed in *Hertz*.
See also: guaranteed bandwith; broad band.

banner

1. Typographic term. A large, wide headline that runs across the full width of a newspaper page.
2. *Network* term. The page printed at the beginning of a print job. This page is generated by the network and contains job and user information.

base line

An imaginary straight line underneath a string of letters, which runs along the base of the non-descending letters, such as f, h, i, k, l, m, n, r, x and z. The c and o appear to rest on this line but in reality hang through it. Most *desktop publishing* programs allow the user to manipulate the baseline. This is necessary when text in different columns

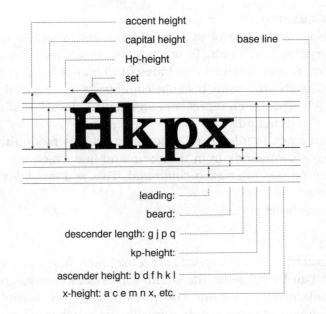

accent height
capital height　　base line
Hp-height
set

Ĥkpx

leading:
beard:
descender length: g j p q
kp-height:
ascender height: b d f h k l
x-height: a c e m n x, etc.

have the same line distance but the lines are not in *alignment* because, for instance, one of the columns has a heading with a different line space.

baseband

A form of *data communication* where only one *channel* exists in a connection. The signal is transmitted without any processing. This allows the necessary hardware to be simple and inexpensive.

Baseband is applied in *Ethernet* and *ARCnet*. Because all devices in a baseband *network* are connected to the same channel, a *protocol* such as *Token Ring* or *CSMA/CD* is needed to assure correct delivery of messages. The protocol corrects the situation when several senders transmit a message simultaneously.

Broadband is a technology whereby several signals are transmitted simultaneously over the same connection. With baseband this can be emulated by multiplexing.

See also: multiplexer.

batch file

A *file* that contains a batch of commands to be executed by the *operating system*. The operating system processes the file from start to finish. This is called *batch processing* as opposed to *interactive* processing where processing stops after each command to obtain a new command from the user.

batch processing

Batch processing is one of two possible modes in which an *operating system* executes commands. In batch mode, commands are read from a *file*. Execution of commands continues until end-of-file is reached.

It is called batch processing because commands are grouped together to form a batch. This batch represents an amount of work that is executed at the user's command.

The second mode is *interactive* processing. In this mode the operating system reads commands from the command line which the user types. The system pauses after each command. This is a one-by-one mode of execution.

See also: batch file.

baud rate

Unit for *data transmission* speed over a telephone line using a *modem* or telex. The baud represents the number of signal changes per second. Via a standard telephone line 600 rates of baud *full-duplex* and 1800 baud *half-duplex* are possible. Historically the number of signal changes equals the number of bits per second. However, with the most recent modems, more than one bit can be coded per signal change. This makes data transmission rates possible that exceed the *baud rate* (currently up to 28,800 bits per second). This effective line speed is still called baud rate although this is formally incorrect.

See also: bit rate.

Bayonet-Neil-Concelman

See: BNC.

BCN 1

A European standard for video tape. The tape width is one inch.

beat

1. The base unit of rhythm. The music *tempo* is determined by the number of beats per second.
2. In jazz, playing exactly on beat without *syncopation*.
3. A form of pop music originated in 1962 in England. Beat evolved from the Blues and Rhythm & Blues.

benchmark

A method for comparing results or performance. One result is taken as baseline and all other results are compared to it. This method is often used to compare the performance of computers of different type and/or brand.

Bernoulli

A type of *removable hard disk*. The Bernoulli storage technique does not require physical contact between the read/write heads and the rotating disk. This makes the disk more shockproof and safer to transport.

beta release

A program in its final test phase. A beta release is distributed to a limited number of users for field testing. This way the developer corrects and improves the program based on the user experience before it is officially released to the public.

Betacam

Sony's professional video recording and playback system. The tape width is half an inch (17.2 mm).
See also: Betacam SP; magnetic tape.

Betacam SP

Sony's video recording and playback system for professional use by Sony. The tape width is a half an inch (17.2 mm). This system records analog *component video*. It has a higher quality than standard *Betacam*. The system has been extended since its first release to include digital PCM-sound, a wider tape for clarity and *serial* digital input and output. Betacam SP will soon be capable of recording digital component video.
See also: analog; pulse code modulation; magnetic tape.

bevel join

A manner of flattening the outer point of a join. One of the styles of drawing joins available in illustration software.
See also: miter join.

bevel join

Bézier curve

A line (also called *path*, curve or vector) defined by a mathematical formula. The line is defined by four points: two *anchor points* and two directional points. Bézier curves are fundamental to vector-oriented programs.

Paul Bézier developed the curves for car manufacturer Renault to automate car design.
See also: anchor point; path; vector format.

bilevel

A scanning technique that can distinguish only black and white. It is also called *binary* scanning because color information is recorded in two values only.
See also: two-tone scanner.

binary

Arithmetical system based on two numbers: zero and one. All computer data is represented in binary. Some other arithmetical systems are: octal (base 8), decimal (base 10) and hexadecimal (base 16).
See also: digital.

binary digit

See: bit.

bind (to)

See: link (to).

bird's-eye view

View of a three-dimensional *scene* as seen from the position of a flying bird. It is a view from the air with the horizon in sight. This view is also called helicopter view.

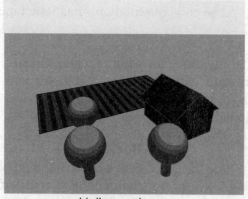

bird's eye view

bit

The smallest unit of data a computer uses to process information. A bit can have two values: zero or one. All computer data is represented by combinations of bits. A combination of eight bits is used to represent a letter or digit. Such a group of eight bits is called a *byte*.
The word bit is a contraction of *binary* and digit.
See also: digital.

bit block transfer

A method of moving picture element blocks in the computer *memory*. Graphics adapters that use this technique perform better than the ones that move picture elements *bit* by bit or *byte* by byte.

See also: pixel; video memory; video adapter.

bit rate

The number of bits that can be transmitted per second, abbreviated to 'bps'.

See also: baud rate.

bitmap

1. The representation of an *image* as an array of bits. Each cell in the array corresponds with a position of a picture element in the image. In its simplest form a cell contains one *bit* that indicates whether the picture element is visible or not. When a color image is represented, more bits are needed per picture element. The additional bits contain a code for the color of a picture element.

   A disadvantage of bitmaps is visible when an image is enlarged. Individual picture elements can be enlarged but not the number of elements. This causes loss of sharpness and jagged edges. Another disadvantage is that bitmap files are often voluminous.

2. A type of screen display where each picture element corresponds to a location in *video memory*. Each element contains information concerning visibility and color.

See also: bitmap format; bitmap font; jaggies; vector format.

bitmap font

A *font* where characters are stored as bitmaps. This is an array of bits in which the bits are activated according to a *pattern*. It is comparable to embroidering letters with cross-stitches. When the font is enlarged, it looks jagged. For this reason a bitmapped *font file* must be created for each required size.

See also: bitmap; jaggies; Adobe type manager (ATM); outline font.

bitmap format

A type of graphics *file format*. Its characteristic is that picture element data is stored as an array of bits. Some bitmap file formats are: *TIFF*, *BMP*, *PCX*, *PIC*, *GIF*, TGA.

See also: truevision targa (TGA); vector format.

bits per pixel

bpp - The number of bits used to code color information of a picture element (*pixel*). One *bit* can code two colors, two bits code four colors,

four bits code 16 colors, etc. Eight bits per color (red, green and blue) are used to display a full color *image*. In 32-bit color graphics adapters 24 bits are used for color information; the remaining eight bits are used for the *alpha channel*.
See also: pixeldepth.

blanking interval

The interval a *videodisc player* shows a blank screen while searching for the next video segment (*chapter*) or *frame*. During this interval the *monitor* receives no new video signals. Sometimes some information about the disc that is playing is shown to fill the gap. A better solution, applied in some players, is to hold the last shown image on screen until the following frame can be displayed.
See also: videodisc; blanking level.

blanking level

1. The signal level sent by a *videodisc player* during the *blanking interval*. Mostly the level is zero resulting in a blank screen.
2. The signal level at the time of a horizontal or *vertical blanking interval*. It is always zero to prevent *distortion* of the screen by the electron gun while it moves to its starting point.

See also: blanking interval; horizontal blanking interval; vertical blanking interval.

bleed off

Text or graphics that run off the *page area*, leaving no white margins. This effect is impossible on *laser printers* because they have a required minimum print margin of 10 millimeters. On a laser printer a bleed off can only be realized by printing on a larger paper size and then cutting off the excess.
See also: type area.

blend

A tool in a drawing or image *editing* program for blending two shapes and/or colors.

blend

blitter

A *chip* that performs *bit block transfers*. It is optimized for this operation and therefore performs it faster then a general processor like the *central processing unit* (CPU). Blitters are part of *graphic coprocessors* that enhance computer performance by relieving the CPU of graphics operations.

blitting

Blitting means executing a *bit block transfer*. It is used, for instance, for moving shapes on a graphic screen.
See also: blitter.

blur

A tool used in a drawing program to create a softened effect that is comparable to wiping over a pastel drawing, thereby blurring colors and outlines.

normal   blur

BMP

A graphic *file* in *bitmap format*. It can be recognized by the file name *extension*, which contains the letters 'bmp'. Files in this format were first used in the Microsoft *Windows* environment, for example, to display a background image (the wallpaper). BMP files are also used in the *OS/2* environment.
See also: file format.

BNC

Bayonet-Neil-Concelman. A bayonet connector for:
1. connecting devices in an *Ethernet* network with coax cable;
2. connecting video equipment.

BNC connector

body size

Size of a *font* in points or millimeters. Several opinions exist as how to define the body size:
- The height of a letter including some *white space* to prevent the descending and ascending letters from touching.
- The distance between ascending line and descending line.

- The total vertical space needed.
- Capital height plus descender.
- Ascender plus descender plus floating accent above capitals (Europe).

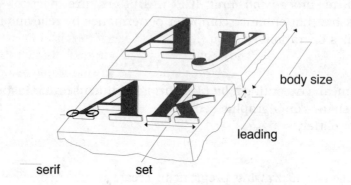

At the moment there is no international standard on body size.
See also: typographic measurements.

body text
The main text of a publication. The body text is the largest part of the text of a book, magazine, etc. In general, *font* sizes used are between 8 and 12 points.

bold
The letter printed fatter than the standard *roman* letter. Several variations of bold exist, ranging from semi bold to extra bold. Each of these gradations can be designed individually, but can also be produced by electronically deforming the standard letter. In the latter case the end result often deviates from the original design. The individually designed bold fonts are therefore preferred by most users.

bookmark
An electronic bookmark is a feature supported in some word processors and *multimedia* programs. The user creates bookmarks with descriptive names. Later on, the marks can be listed and from this list a jump can be made to the desired location.

Boolean operations
Functions on two bits using Boolean logic. In arithmetic there are functions such as multiplication and subtraction. Similarly, Boolean logic has functions such as AND, OR, NOT and XOR. Boolean logic uses only two values: true or false. When a function is carried out on two values, the outcome is also true or false. For example, the AND function

is defined as: when both values are true the result is true, otherwise it is false. So, true AND true = true, and true AND false 1 false. For each operation a truth table can be made, which is comparable to a multiplication table.

Boolean logic has many applications in computer programming. Instead of true or false, a computer deals with zeroes and ones, but the same logic applies. Boolean functions are among the fastest functions a computer can perform. Graphic applications use Boolean functions to edit their screens. A shape with the AND function can be added. An XOR function using a shape on itself erases it. Shapes are combined using the OR operation.

The Boolean logic was developed by English mathematician George Boole in the mid-19th century.

See also: binary.

boot (to)
In day-to-day use this means to start or restart a computer.

Formally it is the name for the process that prepares the computer for use after power-on or pressing Ctrl-Alt-Delete. Initially a small program in computer ROM executes. It only knows how to load and execute the program located in the boot *sector* of a floppy or a *hard disk*. This program contains instructions for loading the *operating system*. When it is loaded, the operating system executes startup files like *config.sys* and *autoexec.bat*. The system is then ready to use. This process has similarities to the expression 'to pull oneself up by one's bootstraps', hence the name of the startup process.

See also: cold reboot; warm reboot.

border
See: frame.

boundary fill
A tool in a drawing program used to fill a bounded area with a color or pattern, for example to fill a circle with red. The limits of an area are defined by adjoining areas that are of a different color.

See also: seed fill.

branching
The different paths on offer to a multimedia program user in order to browse through the contents of a production. The intersection at which it is possible to choose between alternative paths is called the branching point. A branching point is connected to a subject or leads to another branch point.

breakdown
See: cue sheet.

breakup
Visible interruptions of the video signal caused by damage to the video tape.
See also: video errors.

breathing
The incorrect expansion or shrinkage of a moving animated object between two *key-frames*.

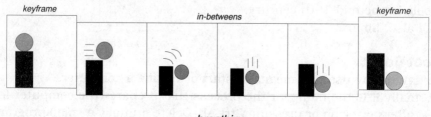

breathing

bridge
A software connection between two networks. A bridge can only be used when two networks use the same *protocol*.
See also: gateway.

broadband
A form of *data communication* that allows transmission of several simultaneous signals through one cable, accomplished by using frequency *multiplexing*. This divides the cable in channels, each with its own frequency. A connection can be made through each *channel* allowing data to be transmitted independently. The total cable *bandwidth* and channel bandwidth is expressed in *Megahertz* (MHz).
Broadband can transmit *analog* data. For example an *analog video* channel can be combined with a *digital* data channel.
Broadband allows two-way communication. This is done by dividing the channel into a forward and a reverse channel.
Cable TV is using a broadband *network*. All channels are available simultaneously, although most TV sets can only display one channel at a time. Up to now only one-way traffic has been possible on the cable TV net. This will change. Currently there are experiments with two-way traffic. This will create new possibilities such as *interactive* TV, TV shopping, playing games at a distance, *video conferencing*, TV

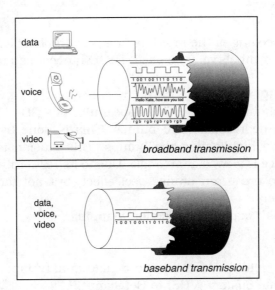

surveillance, etc. In 1994 a project was started in Orlando (USA) to research all these possibilities.
See also: baseband; Integrated Service Digital Network (ISDN), multi-plexer.

broadcast quality

Quality level of video equipment and video recordings, in compliance with the quality requirements that a network needs to broadcast. The equipment must at least produce the screen *frequency* and screen lines as specified in standards such as *Phase Alternating Line* (PAL), *National Television Standards Committee* (NTSC) or Séquentiel Couleur à Mémoire (SECAM).

Broadcast Video U-Matic

BVU - Semi-professional video recording and playback equipment. It uses three-quarter inch cassettes (190.5 mm).

buffer

A location in computer memory for temporary data storage.
See also: spooler.

bug

A fault or defect in computer software or hardware. A tale from the early days of computing when computers contained relays (instead of transistors) is that a computer broke down because a bug had been caught between the contacts. Defects are said to be caused by 'bugs' ever since. The eliminating of defects is consequently called 'debugging'.

bullet

A large dot preceding of the first line of a *paragraph* or listed item as a marker. Other symbols may be used, for instance a square or a star.

bump mapping

A method for changing the surface appearance of a 3D-object so that it seems to have depressions and bumps. This is done by *shading* the depressions and highlighting the bumps. This illusion is only visible when the surface is viewed at an angle. Due to its regularity, this method can be used to create an orange peel effect, but not for landscaping mountain scenery.

See also: normal; mapping; reflection mapping.

bumping up

Copying a low-quality video tape to a high-quality tape, for example from *Video Home System* (VHS) to Betacam-SP.

burnt-in time code

A *time code* recorded on tape together with the video material. The code is always visible during playback.

See also: window dub.

burst

In *data communication,* the quantity of signals considered as a unit.

burst mode

A technique used in *data communication* to accomplish a high transmission capacity over a small period of time. For a *burst transmission*, the sender obtains exclusive access to the transmission medium, temporarily halting any process that would otherwise interrupt the transmission. The sender transmits and releases the exclusive access. This frees the medium to traffic again so that all halted processes can be resumed.

burst noise

A considerable excess of a desired sound level.

See also: noise; background noise; impulsive noise.

burst transmission

A technique whereby transmission of data is interrupted at regular intervals. This allows devices with different transmission speeds to be connected.

bus

In a computer, the connection between the *central processing unit* (CPU), main memory (RAM) and the peripheral devices.

The bus has an *address* part that signals the location in memory to or from which *data* is sent or read. Data are sent over the data bus. The number of wires in the bus determines what the largest memory address is and how many bits are sent in *parallel* over the data bus. The more sent in parallel, the faster the system.

A characteristic of the bus is that all connected devices receive all signals. Only an addressed *device* (or devices) processes the signal. So, like a bus, the signal visits all stops along the way.

Widely used buses are: ISA, *NuBus*, *EISA*, MCA, Local Bus, PCI.

See also: random access memory; bus network.

bus mouse

A *mouse* connected to an add-on mouse *card*. This takes up an *extension* slot. An alternative is a mouse that connects to a *serial port*. The choice depends on what is needed most: a free expansion slot or a free serial port.

See also: serial mouse.

bus network

A *network topology* whereby all devices are connected to a common cable. Each *device* characteristically receives all messages sent over the cable. Each message has an *address*. Only a device with the same address can process the message. *Ethernet* is an example of a bus network.

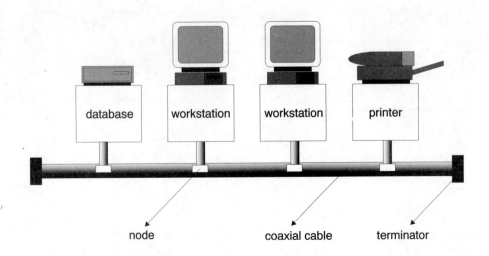

A bus network is suitable for medium sized networks. Connecting devices to a bus network is easy, although sometimes the common cable must be extended. A disorder in a device has no effect on the rest of the network.

button

1. A part of a *dialog box* the user can *click* on or off with the *mouse* to execute the function described in the button label.
2. The *mouse button*.

See also: radio button.

buy

The video material that will be used in the final edit.
See also: master tape.

byline

A line with the author's name underneath the title of a (magazine) article. The byline can also be found at the beginning or end of the article.

byte

A group of eight *bits*. This is the unit many computers use to store *data*. The name is a contraction of 'by eight'.

Eight bits allow the storage of up to 256 variables (*binary* 00000000 through 11111111). Some computers use a different number of bits per byte. For instance, a pocket calculator has four-bit bytes and a Bull mainframe computer uses nine-bit bytes.

See also: binary.

C

C

A programming language developed by Bell Labs (1970). The programming language is adapted as a *ANSI* standard (X3J11) and as an *ISO* standard. It has enormous flexibility and, because it executes the code quickly, C is used often to develop complex programs. C++ which succeeds C makes *object oriented* programming possible.

C-MAC

A *component video* transmission standard for MAC video signals combined with analog audio. It is used in the United Kingdom and Norway. See also: multiplexed analog components.

cable TV network

A network that transports TV signals. Compared to the telephone network, a cable TV network has a considerably larger transmission capacity, resulting from the *bandwidth* difference: 450 MHz for cable TV and 4000 Hz for a telephone line.

Currently, the transmission of TV signals does not use the total transmission capacity. The remaining capacity can be used for *interactive* applications such as: *pay TV*, tele-working, surveillance, *video conferencing*, etc.

In the future it will allow two-way communication among subscribers. Cable TV networks may become an important component of the *information highway*.

cache memory

A fast memory *buffer* for increasing system performance. There are two kinds:

1. The processor cache is a buffer between the *central processing unit* (CPU) and central memory (*random access memory*). The cache increases system performance because less time is needed to access its *data* and because some *parallel* processing is applied in loading the cache. The CPU executes instructions from the cache while the memory manager copies blocks of instructions between the cache and RAM. The processor cache can be located in the microprocessor (internal cache) or can consist of fast memory chips located on the motherboard (external cache).

2. The disk cache is a memory buffer located in RAM between programs and the *hard disk*. Performance increase results from the fact that programs often need the same data repeatedly. When a program reads data from the disk, it is copied to the cache. If it needs the data again, it is supplied from the cache. Since accessing RAM takes only a fraction of the time to access the disk, a large speed gain is attained.
See also: access time; cache RAM.

cache RAM
Chips designed for use in a cache. They are called Static Random Access Memory chips. The *access time* is 15 to 25 nanoseconds.
See also: cache memory.

calibrate
Deriving a set of corrective *parameters* to adjust for a device's deviation from ideal or consistent values. To give an idea what can be adjusted: some display monitors can compensate for the *ambient light* and the degradation of the *phosphor* layer.
See also: color management.

camcorder
The combination of a video recorder and *camera* in one housing. With a camcorder one can film a *scene* and immediately play it through the viewfinder or a connected *monitor*.
See also: video cassette recorder.

camera
A device for recording images. Two kinds of recording media exist:
1. Photographic *film*. This is used in movie cameras and still cameras.
2. *Magnetic tape* or disk or *flash memory*. These are used in video cameras, digital cameras and camcorders. The image is recorded electronically using a *charge-coupled device* (CCD) which converts light into electric pulses.
See also: analog video; still video; digital photography; camcorder.

Canadian Advanced Broadcast Systems Committee
A Canadian commission with the following goals:
1. Development and marketing of *high definition television*.
2. Distribution of data via television.
3. Study of new media possibilities.
The commission is founded by the Canadian government, the Canadian Broadcast Corporation, TV stations and Cable TV operators.

candela

Cd - Unit of light intensity. The unit is derived from the light intensity radiated by one candle.
See also: lumen; lux.

cap height

The height of the *upper case* letter (capital height) measured from the *base line* to the cap line (top of the upper case letter). The cap height determines the text placement on a page.
See also: base line.

capstan

A spindle that keeps a *magnetic tape* playing at a constant velocity.

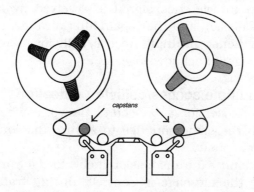

caption

A descriptive text accompanying a graphic or table. The caption is often typeset in a different *font* than used in *body text*.

card

An electronic board that adds a *device* or an *interface* to a device to a computer. The card is plugged into one of the extension slots the computer has for this purpose. Examples of add-on cards are: additional *memory*, *video adapter*, *sound card*, *hard disk* controller.
See also: PCMCIA; adapter.

carriage return

A handle or key on a typewriter that moves the carriage to the beginning of the next or the same line.
In word processing programs line endings are automatic. When a word is typed that does not fit into the current line width, it is moved to the next line. The carriage return (also called hard return) is used to mark the end of a *paragraph*. When it is inserted, the *cursor* moves to the next line.

carrier (signal)

An electric signal with a constant *frequency*. The carrier is modulated to code the *data* that is transmitted. This principle is used in radio and TV broadcasting and in *modem* and *network* connections.
See also: data communications.

carrier sense multiple access/collision avoidance

CSMA/CA - A pro*tocol* for a *baseband* network (where all devices transmit through the same *channel*) to ensure that only one sender transmits simultaneously.
Before the sender starts a transmission, it sends out an interference signal. It waits a while so that all the other components have enough time to receive it and then transmits the message. If, during transmission, an interference signal is received by the sender, it cancels the transmission and tries again after a random interval.
See also: carrier sense multiple access/collision detection; carrier sensing; carrier (signal); acknowledge.

carrier sense multiple access/collision detection

CSMA/CD - A *protocol* for a *baseband* network (where all devices transmit through the same *channel*) to ensure that only one sender transmits simultaneously.
Before the sender starts a transmission it checks if a transmission is in progress. If not, the message is sent. If, during transmission, the sender detects that another transmission has started, the transmission is canceled. Both senders attempt retransmission after a random interval.
CSMA/CD is more efficient than *Token Ring*, because in a Token Ring network time is lost by giving all components a chance to send instead of only those that need to.
See also: carrier sense multiple access/collision avoidance.

carrier sensing

Carrier sensing is done by a *network* component before sending a message to detect whether a transmission is already in progress. Carrier sensing is part of the *CSMA/CD* protocol.
See also: baseband; carrier (signal).

cartridge

1. The protective plastic housing containing *magnetic tape*.
See also: tape cartridge.
2. The container for ink or toner used in printers.
3. A printer extension that contains additional fonts.

cast animation

An *animation* where only certain elements are moved instead of the whole *image*. Such an element is called a *cell* in computer animation. See also: frame animation.

catalog

A list of available objects, such as files, programs, etc. on a storage medium. Information is made available as to the location of files and the amount of space they occupy.
See also: directory.

cathode ray

Electron ray that creates light emitting *dots* on the *phosphor* layers on the inside of a display screen. The movement of the ray around the screen is controlled by the *deflection* unit.
In a monochrome *monitor* there is one cathode ray. In a color monitor there are three, one for each phosphor layer *(red, green, blue)*.
See also: cathode ray tube.

cathode ray tube

CRT - A vacuum tube that displays the picture of a TV or computer *monitor*. Inside there are light emitting *phosphor* layers that are activated with a *cathode ray*. In computer jargon CRT is the synonym for a display monitor.

CCIR

See: Comité Consultatif International des Radiocommunications.

CCIR 601

CCIR Recommendation 601 - The international standard for digital *component video*. The specifications are:
- The signal is recorded in the *4:2:2* format.
- The *color difference* (*YCrCb*) coding as well as the *red, green, blue* (RGB) coding can be used to represent color.
- The electro/mechanical *interface* is defined in the *CCIR 656* standard.

CCIR 656

CCIR Recommendation 656 - The international standard on interfaces for digital *component video* (defined in *CCIR 601*).
The standard defines:
- The blanking and *sync signals*
- The *parallel* and *serial* interfaces. The electrical characteristics of each pin are specified as well as the connector type.

CCITT

See: Comité Consultatif International Téléphonique et Télégraphique.

CD-A

See: Compact Disc Digital Audio.

CD-DA

See: Compact Disc Digital Audio.

CD-drive

A CD-ROM player. It is connected to the computer via an *interface* card. To the user the CD-ROM *drive* behaves like a *floppy disk* or *hard disk*. With it, the user has access to large amounts of *data*, for example an entire encyclopedia can be stored on one CD-ROM.

Two trends are evident: The latest models play CD-ROMs at increasingly high speeds and support increasingly more CD formats. Quadruple speed drives exist today, whose rotation speed is four times the speed of the original *audio CD* player. However, when the player reproduces sound the player has to slow down to single speed, otherwise a high-pitched sound would be heard. An increasing number of CD formats have emerged. To name a few: audio CD, CD-ROM, *Photo CD*, Video Disc, etc. The latest models can handle many of them.

See also: Compact Disc; Compact Disc Read Only Memory; quad-speed.

CD-E

See: Compact Disc Erasable.

CD-Graphics

See: Compact Disc Graphics.

CD-i

See: Compact Disc Interactive.

CD-R

See: Compact Disc Recordable.

CD-Ready

See: Compact Disc Ready.

CD-ROM

See: Compact Disc Read Only Memory.

CD-ROM-XA
See: Compact Disc Read Only Memory Extended Architecture.

CD-RTOS
See: Compact Disc Real Time Operating System.

CD-S
See: Compact Disc Single.

CD-V
See: Compact Disc Video.

CDDI
See: Copper Distributed Data Interface.

cell
1. A sheet of acetate film a cartoonist uses to draw animated figures on. The sheets are transparent so they can be placed on top of each other to form a complete picture. Each layer contains a separate animated figure. Because it is independent of the other figures and the background, sheets can be reused when the movement of the figure needs to be repeated.
See also: cast animation.
2. An element in a *spreadsheet* program. A cell contains *data* or a formula and is identified by a column letter and a *row* number. For instance, cell B5 is in column 2, row 5.
3. A data *packet* of fixed size as used in the *cell switching* protocol.

cell switching
A transmission technique that divides the traffic in packets (called cells) of 53 bytes. A *cell* contains address information and *data*. Cell switching is fast because packets are small and fixed in size. It combines the advantages of *circuit switching* and *packet switching*. It is suitable for *analog* and *digital* signals.
Cell switching is applied in ATM (*asynchronous transfer mode*) networks.

center
The horizontal and/or vertical *alignment* of text or objects, so that the distance (of the text) to the left and the right and/or top and bottom margin is equal.

central processing unit

CPU - That part of a computer which performs the logic, computational and decision-making functions. In other words, it is the brain of the computer. In a *personal computer*, the CPU is contained in a single *chip*, the microprocessor.

Centronics

See: parallel port.

channel

The connection between a sender and a receiver for transmitting *data*. When only one channel is available in a *network*, it is called a *baseband* network. A multi-channel network is called a *broadband* network.
See also: bandwith; cable TV network.

chapter

A data segment on a *videodisc*. A chapter represents a random addressable piece of data. The data in a chapter can only be accessed sequentially. The end of a chapter is marked with a *chapter stop*. Chapters are used in *level one videodiscs*.

chapter stop

A code that marks the end of a *chapter* on a *videodisc*.

character

A symbol in a *font*.
See also: character set.

character box

The maximum area used to display a *character* on the screen.

character matrix

The number of *dots* in the horizontal and vertical direction used to form a *character* on a text screen or a matrix *printer* (for example: 9 * 14).
The character is formed by turning on dots in a matrix that follow the shape of the character. The characters have fixed width and height, so an 'l' takes up the same space as an 'm'.

character set

A *character set* is a definition of which characters are represented in a computer and how they are coded. Mostly one *byte* is used to represent a character, allowing 256 different characters to be defined. For each number between 0 and 255 a character (letter, digit, etc.) is assigned.

Several character sets exist. A few include: ASCII, Extended ASCII, EBCDI, Greek alphabet, mathematical symbols, etc.
See also: American Standard Code for Information Interchange.

charge-coupled device

A *device* to convert light to electric signals. It consists of light-sensitive (photoelectric) cells connected to an electric circuit. Charge-coupled devices are applied in *scanners,* (still) video cameras and *digital* cameras.

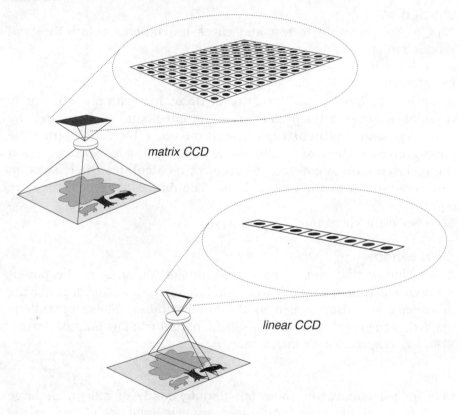

matrix CCD

linear CCD

A charge-coupled device receives light reflections from an object via a lens system into the photoelectric cells. The stronger the light intensity is, the higher the voltage of the electric signal. This way, light and dark areas are represented by different electric signals.
To capture color images scanners and video cameras are equipped with three types of photoelectric cells, each type sensitive to one of the colors red, green or blue.
See also: still videocamera; digital photography; red, green, blue.

check box
A control in a *dialog box* that consists of a square box and a choice text. An 'X' in the box means the choice is selected, blank means it is not selected. Check boxes are used when a user can choose from one or more nonexclusive options. A dialog box is a *window* that a program uses to exchange *data* with a user. The use of dialog boxes is standardized in the *Common User Access* directions.
See also: graphical user interface.

check disc
A *videodisc* produced to test and check its contents before the final production starts.

checksum
A method to ensure the integrity of *data*, for example when it is transmitted over a telephone line. The checksum is computed by applying some mathematical operation on a block of data. The checksum is appended to the block before transmission. To see if the received data is correct, the receiver recalculates the checksum and compares it to the received one. The data is correct if they are equal.
See also: error correction.

child window
A subwindow that cannot be moved outside the area of the parent *window*. Operations on the parent window such as maximizing, moving or closing are also applied to the child window. These operations applied to the child window respect the parent window boundaries.
See also: graphical user interface.

chip
Slice of semiconductor material, usually made of silicon. A large number of circuits (transistors, memory elements) are etched on the slice forming an integrated circuit. The circuit *density* has increased over the years from dozens to millions. Chips are produced in large numbers and are therefore inexpensive. The design of a chip, however, is very expensive.
See also: central processing unit; application specific integrated circuit; very large scale integrated.

chooser
A software tool on a *Macintosh* computer to configure peripheral devices.

chord

1. Short straight lines used as an aid in forming a circle. This is done by drawing short tangent lines along the circle radius.
2. In music, three or more notes that sound in harmony.
See also: tone.

chroma keying

A technique to combine two *video* images. Areas in the top image in a predefined color let the bottom layer shine through. The prerequisite is that both images are synchronized. An example is the TV weather report. What the viewer sees as the weather map is in fact a blue screen. The blue in the screen is replaced by the map using chroma keying.
See also: sync signal.

chrominance

The color component of a video signal. Together with the *luminance* component it forms the TV image. Chrominance and luminance are separate for compatibility with black-and-white TV. Such a TV shows a color broadcast in black-and-white by ignoring the chrominance component. In other words: the chrominance component is an addition to the black-and-white standard.

cicero

See: typographic measurements.

CIE

See: Commission International de l'Eclairage.

CIELab

A color representation model based on the human vision system. In this model each unit along the lightness (L) and color (a, b) axes represents the smallest change a human can perceive. The variables are defined as follows:
- lightness (the black-and-white component).
- an 'a' variable that places the color along a red-green axis.
- a 'b' variable that places the color on a blue-yellow axis.
This choice of variables is based on a theory of color opposites: that a color never has both green and red characteristics simultaneously, nor blue and yellow simultaneously. The advantage of CIELab over *CIEXYZ* is that no matter which color is being considered, a small change in the numeric value produces a proportionally small change in the color perceived.
See also: Commission International de l'Eclairage.

CIEXYZ

A color representation model developed by the *Commission International de l'Eclairage* (CIE). The model is based on the human perception of color. The CIE color system standardizes the three basic components that make up color as it's experienced by the human nervous system: the light source, the object, and the observer. In 1931 the CIE collected *data* about the color perception of several observers with normal color vision and then used that data to define an imaginary standard observer. Likewise, it defined several standard light sources. It then developed algorithms to derive three imaginary, primary constituents of color—X, Y and Z—that can be combined at different levels to produce all the colors the human eye can perceive. The color of an object can then be defined in terms of X, Y and Z for a specific light source and observer. The resulting color model, CIEXYZ, has spawned a series of other CIE *color models*, all of which are mathematically related.

Color models like RGB (*red, green, blue*) and CMY(K) (*cyan, magenta, yellow, black*) reproduce a given color differently depending on the conditions. For example: a color composed of 10% black, 50% cyan and 30% magenta looks less vibrant in the dark then in full light. Also that color looks different on yellowish paper with a fibrous structure than on smooth white paper. A color produced at the printers can differ from the *laser printer* version due to different ink composition. To compensate for these differences, a reference model is required such as the CIE model. When the color reproduction conditions are known, the RGB or CMYK model values are derived from the CIE model values combined with the *device profile* information.

The CIE model has several variations of which CIEXYZ and *CIELab* are best known. The various CIE-based systems can be transformed from one *color space* into another by a simple calculation. The word CIE model used by itself usually refers to CIEXYZ.

All *color management* programs use some variation of the CIE model to keep colors consistent across devices.

cine-oriented image

An *image* is cine-oriented when it is printed on a microfilm in the same orientation as a movie is recorded on *film*. The top of the image is at right angles with the longitudinal direction of the film.

See also: comic-strip oriented image.

cine-oriented image

Cinepack

A *lossy compression* method for *digital video*. The method was developed by SuperMac Technology.
See also: coder/decoder.

circuit switching

A type of *data communication* where a fixed *channel* is assigned to a connection. All traffic goes through the channel until the connection is terminated. The advantage is that once a connection is made, messages travel at maximum speed unhindered by other traffic. The disadvantages are that the cable occupancy is not optimal when nothing is sent through a connection and that the number of connections is limited to the number of channels in a cable.
See also: packet switching; cell switching; guaranteed bandwith.

CISC

See: complex instruction-set computing.

clef

A symbol used in *staff* notation. The clef is at the start of staff and determines the pitch of the note placed on that line. From that the pitch of the notes on the other lines is derived.
Some clefs are: the violin clef (the g clef) the alto clef (the f clef) and the bass clef (the c clef).

click

To press and release a *mouse button* without moving the mouse *pointer* off the choice.
See also: double click.

client

In a *network* the program or *device* that uses the services of another program or device (the *server*). The server can be located anywhere in the network.
See also: client/server.

client/server

The client/server architecture is a labor division between a *server*, which offers specialized services and a *client* which uses them. This architecture improves efficiency, i.e.:
- enhanced speed when fast hardware is used in the server;
- speed enhancement resulting from *parallel* processing;
- sharing of expensive hardware;

- *network* traffic reduction. For example: to *query* a central *database* the client must bring all its data to its location. With a database server only the result of the query travels the net.
See also: dedicated server; peer-to-peer network.

clip
A fragment of video or audio material.
See also: video clip.

clipboard
Memory area for temporary *data* storage that allows data exchange between programs, between documents or within a single document.
To use it one first selects part of the document. The selection is copied to the clipboard using the copy or cut command. Cut deletes the selected portion after copying. One moves to a new location in the document or switches to another application and copies the clipboard content with the *paste* command.
The clipboard was introduced by the *graphical user interface* programs. Included with Microsoft *Windows* is a program for viewing the clipboard content or saving it to a *file*.

clipping
An operation on a graphic *image* to make it fit in a *frame* or *window* too small for its size.
See also: shielding.

clock
A computer component that generates electrical pulses at a high *frequency*. Its purpose is to synchronize various operations.
See also: central processing unit.

clocking
A technique to synchronize sender and receiver during synchronous transmissions.
See also: synchronous transmission.

close box
In Microsoft *Windows*, every *window* has a *system menu* in its top left corner. It is a square box with a minus in it. When clicked once with the *mouse*, the system menu opens. When it is clicked twice the window closes. If an application's main window is closed, it terminates.
On a *Macintosh*, each window has a close box in its top left corner, with the sole purpose of closing the window and returning to a previous level.

close up

Film or photo *shot* from close by showing clearly all details of a subject. For example: a shot that only shows the face of an actress.
See also: medium shot; long shot.

closed circuit

A private *network* of TV cameras and monitors. It is mostly used for surveillance. Another example of use can be found in universities where closed circuits are used to make connections between buildings and lecture rooms.

closed path

A free-drawn line where begin and end are connected. The *path* encloses an area that can subsequently be filled with a color. The color fill respects the boundaries defined by the path, which is often not possible when the path is open.

closed system

A computer system that is incompatible with other systems. In the past each manufacturer made systems that could only run software designed for that system. The major disadvantages of closed systems are:
1. They require special trained staff to make software. Few trained personnel results in a software development backlog.
2. Exchange of information with other systems is troublesome because of incompatible *file formats*
3. Costs of software development are high because there is little chance of selling it often.

Under pressure of user demand most manufactures have made their systems compatible with an open standard.
See also: conversion.

cluster

A logical storage unit on a floppy or *hard disk*. For example, on a hard disk a cluster can be 2048 bytes, (= four sectors of 512 bytes each). On a *floppy disk* a cluster is often the same size as a *sector*, i.e. 512 bytes.
See also: track.

CMYK

See: cyan, magenta, yellow, black.

coax

A coax cable consists of a central copper conductor, covered by a plaited copper

coat. There are several qualities, each with a different transmission capacity. The capacity increases with cable thickness; a thicker cable is more expensive and more difficult to lay. Coax cables are often used in networks, for example cable television networks. The cable is suitable for *broadband*.
See also: fiber; unshielded twisted pair.

code book encoding
A technique to *compress* or *decompress* signals using a table of values to compress and reconstruct the original digital signal.

codec
See: coder/decoder.

coded image
An *image* with a certain digital structure that makes storage and *editing* easy.

coded set
A group of codes that identifies long text elements. A list of airport names can be represented by a coded set of three letters. For example, Paris-Charles De Gaulle is coded as 'CDG'.

coder/decoder
Codec - A software and/or hardware application which is used for coding and decoding electronic and *digital* signals. A hardware application, for example, is the digital-analog *chip* on a *sound card*. This chip converts *analog sound* to digital and back to analog again for playback. Software codecs are used in *Video for Windows* and in *QuickTime*. These codecs can (de)*compress* large amounts of video and audio data. *Cinepack* and *Indeo* are examples of codecs.

cold reboot
Restarting a computer system by pressing the reset button or by switching it off and on. This drastic intervention, which causes loss of *data* stored in RAM and can corrupt the *hard disk*, is all too often needed, for instance after software and/or hardware malfunction.
See also: warm reboot; boot (to).

collaborative screen sharing
The *interactive* usage of files and applications during *video conferences*. Conference attendants can edit available information publicly. This accomplishes instant exchange of ideas.

collinear

A *Bézier curve* is collinear when its directional points are in line, in which case the curve becomes a straight line.
See also: vector format.

collision

When several stations in a *network* send *data* at the same time over the same *channel*, a collision occurs causing signal *distortion*.
See also: carrier sense multiple access/collision avoidance.

colophon

A specification of design, print, edition, author(s) and editor(s) in (electronic) books and magazines.

color balance

The proper ratio of color components to reproduce gray on a *printer* or white and gray on a *monitor* correctly. No color may dominate or else a *color cast* will be visible.
See also: red, green, blue.

color bars

A video picture made of colored bars. The purpose is to *calibrate* the *luminance*, *chrominance*, *saturation* and *color balance* of connected devices.

color cast

A color cast is visible in a picture or print if one color dominates, i.e. when there is no *color balance*.
See also: gray balance.

color corrector

A device for adjusting colors of a video signal. The results are measured with a *vectorscope*.

color cycling

An *animation* technique where the animation effect is obtained by changing the *color lookup table*. This is done by sequentially assigning colors to *image* elements. The assignment of color is done in the color lookup table of the video card. During animation the colors in the table are rotated. For example: the color of element 1 is assigned to element 2, element 3 is assigned the color of element 2, etc. The effect is particularly vivid in *gradients*. Some animation programs have a *menu* option to activate this effect.

color difference

A technique for combining the three color components (*red, green, blue*) into two signals and which requires less capacity to transmit. It is used in the *Phase Alternating Line* (PAL) video system.

color filter

A colored filter made of light-transparent material like glass, synthetic material or gelatin. Color *filters* are applied to add color effects or to correct color aberrations while creating picture material (photo, film or video). Filters are available in all sorts of colors and tones. The working of a color filter is based on subtractive color mixture, for instance a red filter is transparent to red and blocks blue light. RGB color filters are used for *color separation* in reproduction photography and in *scanners, still video* and *digital* cameras.
See also: color synthesis; red, green, blue.

color graphics adapter

CGA - A video standard for IBM compatible computers. The *resolution* is 640 * 200 pixels. It displays 16 simultaneous colors selected from 64 possible colors. The 64 colors are available in four groups of 16 colors. Such an group is called a palette. The current video standard is SVGA, which, like all successors to CGA, is still capable of displaying CGA images.
See also: video adapter.

color lookup table

A table in a *video adapter* used as an aid to display color pictures. Nowadays adapters display 256 simultaneous colors. these are selected from a quarter of a million available colors. Initially 16 colors in 16 shades are available in the lookup table. When a picture requires 24 shades of a color these are added to the lookup table replacing color shades that are not needed.
This way, nearly all pictures can be displayed accurately as long as they contain no more than 256 different colors. In a picture that does contain more colors, the extra ones are replaced by colors with the closest resemblance.
See also: color cycling.

color management

Adjusting hard- and software in such a way that colors remain consistent while they travel through scanners, monitors, software, desktop printers to a final output *device*.
For example: To work with color photos, one must *digitize* the *image*

using a red, green and blue (RGB) *scanner*. For offset printing, the image is converted into the cyan, magenta, yellow and black (*CMYK*) model.

To make colors match, they are represented in a reference color model like *CIELAB*. Together with the color characteristics, as found in the device profiles, the color manager can convert colors so that an application can match its color output to that of the output device.

Some color management applications are: *ColorSync*, *FotoTune*, *ColorSense* and *Efi*.

See also: calibrate; red, green, blue; cyan, magenta, yellow, black; device profile; process color; color synthesis; cathode ray.

color models

A color model is a method for representing the color spectrum as a mixture of a limited number of base colors. For example the RGB model uses red, green and blue to reproduce a color picture. The components are mixed to produce all the other colors. A color model like RGB produces different colors from the same original depending on the environmental influences (like *ambient light*) and the medium a picture is reproduced on (quality of the *monitor*). To address these problems, objective color models, such as *CIELab*, are developed. CIELab is based on the human perception of color. These models are used by *color management* programs to ensure that colors look the same when displayed on a monitor or printed on a page.

See also: red, green, blue; hue, saturation, luminance; CIEXYZ; cyan, magenta, yellow, black.

color noise

Distortions in the color component of a video signal. They are caused by the lack of color *bandwidth* or are the side effect of *color subsampling*. Color noise causes colored bands in the picture.

See also: video errors.

color portability

This is the goal of *color management* applications: to ensure that colors look identical whether displayed on screen or printed on a printer. For example: a picture is digitized with an Agfa *scanner*, edited on a *Macintosh* and printed on a Xerox color printer. The color manager must ensure that colors stay the same throughout.

See also: calibrate.

color resolution

A measure for the color sharpness of an image used for video systems.

color scanner
A device that digitizes a color image making it processable with a computer. The accuracy of color reproduction depends on the *pixeldepth* (the number of bits per picture element (pixel)). When the pixeldepth is eight *bit*, 256 colors are recognized, 24 bits allow for 16.7 million colors and 36 bits allow for 68.7 million colors.
See also: scanner.

color separation
The representation of a color picture as mixes of a limited number of base colors. For example, to print a color picture its colors are separated in cyan, magenta, yellow and black. A color image is printed in four runs, one for each base color.
See also: cyan, magenta, yellow, black; red, green, blue.

color space
The colors a device can be reproduce or the colors that can be represented in a color model. The color space often is a subset of the complete visible color spectrum. This implies that not all colors can be reproduced.
See also: Commission de l'Eclairage, CIELab, color management.

color subsampling
A technique for reducing the *bandwidth* of a video signal, for instance to reduce the capacity needed to transmit the signal. The resolution color component of the video signal (the *chrominance*) is reduced to a value lower than the resolution of the brightness component (*luminance*) before transmission. The original resolution is restored when the signal is displayed. This can cause *color noise*.
See also: color resolution.

color synthesis
The reproduction of colors by mixing a few base colors. What colors are used as base colors depends on what is mixed: light or substance.
1. Light mixture is used whenever an *image* is displayed on a screen (TV, computer *monitor*). The base colors are red, green and blue. Mixtures of these colors reproduce virtually all colors in the spectrum. Red, green and blue mixed in a 1:1:1 ratio produces white light.

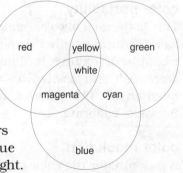

This is why the mixture is also called additive color mixture: the more of each color component is used, the lighter the color becomes.

2. Substance mixture is used whenever a picture is printed. The base colors are cyan, magenta and yellow. Mixtures of these colors reproduce a substantial part of all colors in the spectrum. Cyan, magenta and yellow mixed in a 1:1:1 ratio produce a dark brown that is nearly black, the reason this is also called a subtractive mixture: the more of each color component is used the darker the color becomes. Black is added to the base colors to obtain a solid black color.

See also: process color; cyan, magenta, yellow, black; color separation; color models.

colorization
The coloring of a monochrome original.

ColorSense
A program for *color management*. The program is designed for simple applications and works in concert with Apple's *ColorSync*. ColorSense makes colors match between scanners, monitors and printers.

ColorSync
A *color management* system used on a *Macintosh* (*System 7.x*). ColorSync uses the *CIEXYZ* color model and the *device profiles* supplied by the peripheral manufacturers. ColorSync is a very successful standard since nearly all manufactures support it.

column balance
A tool in publishing programs for spreading text over columns in such a way that all columns have equal length.

column gutter
The *white space* between columns.

COM
In the *MS-DOS* system these three letters symbolize a *serial port*. Usually COM is followed by a digit (e.g. COM1) to specify the serial port precisely. For example: configuring a communication program uses COM2 to specify that the *modem* is connected to the second serial port.

comic-strip oriented image

An *image* is comic-strip oriented when it is printed on a microfilm in the same orientation as a comic strip is printed. The top of the image is in line with the longitudinal direction of the film.

comic-strip oriented image

See also: cine-oriented image.

Comité Consultatif International de Téléphonique et Télégraphique

An organization that develops standards for *data communication*. CCITT is on of four organizations that form the International Telecommunication Union (ITU). The ITU resides in Geneva and reports to the United Nations.

Comité Consultatif International des Radiocommunications

An international standards organization that develops standards for *audio* and *video* equipment. It also provides recommendations.
See also: CCIR 601; CCIR 656.

command.com

The *MS-DOS* component that interprets commands. Commands are typed by the user or are read from a *file*. Commands are translated to calls. The MS-DOS operation system executes the functions implicated by a command. Commands are said to be internal or external. Internal means the command is handled internally by command.com, for example: DIR, DEL, TYPE, etc.
External means that to process the command a separate file is loaded in *memory* and executed. External commands supplied with MS-DOS are: XCOPY, FORMAT, etc. In general: an external command is any file with *extension* .EXE or .COM (provided it contains valid machine instructions).
See also: Micosoft disk operating system (MS-DOS).

Commission International de l'Eclairage

CIE - An international standards organization in the field of illumination. CIE has developed an objective color model that is used in *color management* to make a color look the same in all presentation environments.
See also: color models; CIELab; CIEXYZ.

common action

Common actions are defined in the *Common User Access* standard as actions every program should provide for interacting with a user. Examples are: OK, Cancel and Help. The OK action executes an action; the Cancel action stops the action at hand and returns the user to the previous level; the Help action supplies the user with information about the action at hand.

common command language

CCL - The command language used for accessing the *on-line* European databases. These databases are managed by the *European Community Host Organization* (ECHO).

Common User Access

CUA - A standard prescribing how a program should interact with the user. Characteristic is that the application surface is contained in a *window*. The user can size, move or hide the window. At the top of the window is a horizontal *menu* bar containing the main options. When a option is activated a submenu pops-up. To the user it appears that this submenu is pulled down from the menu bar, hence the name pulldown menu. The submenu provides the user with actions or sub menus to choose from. Selection of a submenu item results in the pop-up of another submenu.

To exchange information a program uses a *dialog box*. This is a sub window containing items (called controls) for data entry or display. Examples of controls are:
- *check boxes* to let a user select one or more options;
- *radio buttons* when a user must choose from excluding options;
- *buttons* to execute actions;
- list boxes to choose one option from a predefined list.
The standard also prescribes standard behavior for example:
- when a irreversible action is ordered the user must confirm or cancel it;
- when a program presents options to a user a set of defaults must be
  supplied by the user to keep typing to a minimum.
CUA is developed by IBM and is, among others, applied in the graphical user interface *Windows*.

Community Research and Development Information System

CORDIS - An item in the European *VALUE* program. CORDIS comprises a set of databases where historical and current *information* regarding European technology and research programs is stored. Information is available on energy, environment, training and education, science in information and communication, regional development, etc.

CORDIS gives access to the following databases:
- acronyms database;
- comdocuments database;
- news database;
- partners database;
- programmes database;
- projects database;
- publications database;
- results database.

VALUE and CORDIS are subordinate to DG-XIII (Directorate-General) which resides in Luxembourg. DG-XIII develops and executes policy in the field of telecommunication, information market and research exploitation. CORDIS is accessible to all European citizens and organizations. The databases are published on *CD-ROM* and available *on-line* via the *European Community Host Organization* (*ECHO*) also residing in Luxembourg.

See also: Valorization and Utilization for Europe.

Compact Disc

CD - A plastic *disc* with a silvery reflective layer that contains digital data in the form of non reflective pits. The data is read using a *laser* ray. The disc diameter is 12 cm (4.72 inch) and has a capacity of 650 MB or an audio playtime of 72 minutes. CD is very successful. The reasons are: unprecedented noisless audio reproduction; no wear when the disc is played; reasonable resistance to damage.

Compact disc is used for audio, *multimedia*, games, *Photo CD*, storage *(CD-ROM)*, etc. Many of these application use a specialized disc format.

See also: CD-A; CD-i; videodisc; High Sierra Standard.

Compact Disc Digital Audio

CD-DA - *Compact disc* containing audio. This is the first application of the CD technology. The disc has a 12 cm (4.72 inch) diameter and there are two variants: one has 550 MB (or 63 minutes audio) capacity, the other has a 650 MB (or 72 minutes audio) capacity. Both types are defined in the *ISO 9660* standards. A variant is CD-single. Discs are 8 cm (3.15 inch) in diameter and have a 150 MB storage capacity (18 minutes audio).

Compact Disc Erasable

CD-E - A recordable and erasable disc. They are also called *magneto-optical* discs. The Sony *MiniDisc* is an example of this format.

Compact Disc Graphics

CD-Graphics - A CD that contains audio, video and graphics mainly

used for *Karaoke*. When the *disc* is played, a *video clip* of a popular song is shown. The music is without vocals. The graphics show the lyrics of the song and emphasize which word is to be sung. The music is mixed with the voice of the participant.
See also: Compact Disc.

Compact Disc Interactive

CD-i - A *compact disc* that contains *audio*, *video*, *computer graphics* and a presentation program to show the material and interact with the user. The program presents a *menu* to the user. The user chooses from this menu by moving a *pointer* with the *trackball* supplied with the player and clicks on the appropriate option to select it. The player then shows the material associated with the selected option. Current CD-i applications are movies, games, video clips, references, courses and training.
CD-i's remarkable achievements are:
- The ability to *compress* video material to a fraction of the original size while maintaining a reasonable display quality.
- The possibility of interaction.
CD-i is invented by Philips. Its specifications and directions for developers are described in the so-called *Green Book*.
CD-i requires a specialized player that is connected to a normal TV set.
See also: multimedia; interactive; 3DO.

Compact Disc Plus

CD-Plus - *Multi-session* Music *Compact Disc*. A standard CD-Format. *Audio* and *data* are recorded on the same disc. CD-Plus discs can be played on an Audio CD-player and on a *CD-ROM* player. In the latter, it is possible to retrieve the data on the disc in addition to listening to the music. The audio (recorded following the *Red Book* specifications) fills the disc except the last track which is reserved for data.

Compact Disc Read Only Memory

CD-ROM - A *compact disc* in computer readable format. When inserted in a CD-ROM *drive* it is handled in the same way as a floppy or *hard disk*. For instance, it is possible to issue a DIR command to find out the contents of the disc. Besides a standard *MS-DOS* or *Macintosh* file system a CD-ROM can also contain *audio tracks*. These are identical to tracks on an *audio CD*. A *multimedia* program can use this facility to play CD quality music.
The capacity of a CD-ROM is 650 megabytes. CD-ROMs are used when large amounts of *data* are involved. Applications are:
- a CD-ROM with one year's worth of full-text articles from computer magazines;

- a movie *database* including clips from films;
- electronic multimedia magazines.

The possibilities of CD-ROM are greater than *CD-i*. However, it requires some computer literacy not required for CD-i.

Compact Disc Read Only Memory eXtended Architecture

CD-ROM-XA - An extension to CD-ROM that makes it possible to simultaneously reproduce *video* and *audio*. XA has a capacity of 9.5 hours stereo sound (19 hours mono) as opposed to a CD-ROM that can only contain 72 minutes of audio. XA discs can be played by a *CD-i* player. XA was developed by Philips, Sony and Microsoft.

See also: Compact Disc Read Only Memory.

Compact Disc Ready

CD-ready - A CD-i *disc* that can be played in a standard CD audio disc drive.
See also: Compact Disc Interactive.

Compact Disc Real Time Operating System

CD-RTOS - The *operating system* that is used by *Compact Disc-interactive*. It is derived from *OS-9*.

Compact Disc Recordable

CD-R - A *compact disc* that can be recorded once. It is not necessary to record the entire disc in a single session. Multiple sessions are possible that record only a part of the disc. The recorded disc is readable by standard *CD-A* and *CD-ROM* (XA) players provided it is recorded in a single session. *Multi-session* discs require a player that understands the format. CD-R is similar to *write once, read many* (WORM) discs. The difference is that WORM discs are not readable by CD-players.

The specifications for CD-R are defined in a standard called *Orange Book*. CD-R is becoming increasingly popular. Applications are: archival backups, CD-ROM mastering, small-scale distribution of data etc.

See also: Photo CD.

Compact Disc Single

CD-S - A *compact disc* with 8 cm (3.13 inch) diameter and 20 minutes audio recording capacity (150 megabytes). Older CD players require an *adapter* to enlarge the diameter to 12 cm (4.7 inch) to play the single.

Compact Disc Video

CD-V - A *videodisc* developed by Philips for *analog video* and digital or analog audio. The disc was introduced in 1987 and was since then known as Video Long Play and Laser Vision. Its current name is Laser Disc.

There are three formats:
- CD video single, diameter 12 cm (4.7 inch), single-sided capacity 6 minutes video with digital audio or 20 minutes audio.
- CD Video EP, diameter 20 cm (7.9 inch), single- or double-sided playable; capacity 20 minutes video and audio per side.
- CD Video LP, diameter 30 cm (11.8 inch), single- or double-sided playable; capacity 60 minutes video and audio per side. This format has a gold-colored version for digital sound and a silver-colored version for *analog sound*.

companding

A technique for enhancing the image quality when digitizing video images.
See also: frame grabber.

compandor

A compandor increases the transmission capacity of telephone channels by compressing the audio signal before transmission and decompressing it afterwards. Compandor is a contraction of compressor and expander.
See also: compress.

compile (to)

The translation of a program written in a programming language, such as *C* or Pascal, to machine instructions, i.e. program instructions the microprocessor understands. In computer jargon: to translate *source code* to *object code*. To make an executable program from an object code it must first be 'linked' - a procedure to connect a program with standard routines located in libraries.
See also: link (to).

complex instruction-set computing

CISC - A type of microprocessor that processes high-level complex instructions. CISC's advantage is that less instructions are needed to perform a task, reducing the programming effort. CISC's disadvantage is the extra processing time needed to decode and interpret the instructions. Complex instructions require a complex microprocessor consisting of an increasing number of transistors; this makes the microprocessor design more difficult.
See also: reduced instruction-set computing; central processing unit.

component video

A video signal type where brightness (*luminance*) and color (*chrominance*) signal are separated. This allows a higher picture quality than is possible when the signals are combined into one signal as in *composite video*.

composite video

A video signal type where brightness (*luminance*) and color (*chrominance*) signal are combined into one signal. The picture quality is less than is possible when the signals are separated, because the signals interfere, resulting in *distortion*. Several techniques exist to combine the signals, for example *National Television Standards Committee* (NTSC), *Phase Alternating Line* (PAL) and *Séquentiel à Couleur Mémoire* (SECAM).

See also: component video.

compound document editor

A program that integrates objects of many types into one (composite) document. Possible objects are: text drawings, charts, spreadsheets, video, sound, etc. An additional option allows importing objects made with other applications. The compound editor is used as multimedia *authoring* tool.

compress

A technique for reducing the size of files. The compression program replaces long strings of reccurring data with short codes. Depending on the file content, size reductions as high as 80% are possible. A file in its compressed form must be decompressed before it can be used by an application.

Some applications are:

- Disk doublers. This program type doubles the storage capacity of a *hard disk* by compressing all files. The compression and decompression process is completely transparent to the user and to application programs.
- File transfer. To reduce the transmission time of files over a telephone line, most modems have built-in compression and decompression.

For data files, compression must be lossless, i.e. decompression must reproduce the original file. Video files are so large that, to keep their storage requirements within reasonable limits, *lossy compression* is used to attain higher compression ratios. In this case decompression does not reproduce the original but instead a picture of a lower quality.

See also: lossless compression; fractal image compression.

compressed audio

Audio that is compressed for storage on *videodisc* allowing many hours of recording time. To attain high compression ratios, *lossy compression* is used.

compression ratio
The ratio between the size of a *file* in its compressed form and in its uncompressed form.
See also: compress.

computer graphics
The creation and *editing* of graphics with a computer. Several graphic types exist:
- *photorealistic* images;
- line drawings (drawings, diagrams etc.);
- real time images (live action, *animation*, *virtual reality*);
- *simulation* (still or animated images for scientific applications).

computer graphics metafile
A *file format* to store graphic images based on the *vector format*.

computer-aided design
The production of technical drawings with the aid of computer applications. CAD is applied in architecture and manufacture. Computer-aided manufacturing is the process of setting-up manufacturing machinery through the computer from the designs.

computer-aided publishing
Computers are applied nowadays in all stages of the publishing process. Text, pictures, graphics are all entered in the computer. The *layout* is made with a publishing program. The result in *digital* form is delivered to the *printer* who can print from it without further processing.
A novel trend is electronic publishing. This kind of publication is put onto a *CD-ROM* or is available through a *modem* from an electronic information service. The introduction of computer-aided publishing has ensured that nearly all publishing tasks can be done from the desktop. Publishing costs are thus significantly reduced.

computer-animated graphics
Animated graphics that are created and played back on a computer.
See also: animation.

computer-assisted instruction
The use of (*multimedia*) computer applications to instruct people.

concurrence
The simultaneous transmission of *video* and *audio*.

condensed type

The narrow version of a *font*.
See also: extended type.

confetti

Small colored speckles in the video display caused by *drop-outs* or other *video errors*.

config.sys

A *file* that instructs *Microsoft disk operating system* (MS-DOS) during system start-up and on which additional files must be loaded and/or which system *parameters* must be set. The additional loaded files extend MS-DOS. For example: to use a PC in a *network* a program is loaded from config.sys. Thereafter, files stored on a remote PC appear to be stored on a local *hard disk*. Users can easily change config.sys since it is an ASCII file.
See also: boot (to); American Standard Code for Information Interchange.

configuration file

A file that contains set-up *parameters* of an application on an *operating system*.
See also: config.sys.

connection oriented protocol

A data communication *protocol* that requires a connection to be made between sender and receiver before transmission can begin. An example is a telephone conversation. One party has to dial a number, the other party has to answer before a conversation can take place.
See also: X.25; connectionless protocol.

connectionless protocol

A data communication *protocol* that does not require a connection to be made between sender and recipient before transmission. In this protocol *network* components continuously monitor their communication lines to see if a data *packet* addressed to them has arrived. In this protocol all data is divided into packets which contain addresses of both sender and addressee (recipient). A component knows a packet is destined for it by comparing the destination *address* to its own and then retrieves it from the data stream.
An example of this protocol is the *Transmission Control Protocol/Internet Protocol* (TCP/IP).
See also: connection oriented protocol; packet switching.

constant angular velocity
CAV - A technique for writing *data* on an *optical disc* where rotational speed is the same without regard to the position of the track on the disc. With CAV a track near the center of the disc contains the same amount of data as a track near the edge. Only half the disc's data storage capacity is used this way, because an outside track has more capacity than an inside track. CAV allows fast access data because *tracks* are divided into fixed lengths (called sectors); these start on fixed locations and therefore are directly addressable. CAV is, among others, employed in hard disks and *videodiscs.*
See also: constant linear velocity.

constant linear velocity
CLV - A technique for writing *data* on an *optical disc* when the rotational speed depends on the position of a track on the disc. With CLV, a track near the center of the disc contains less data than one near the outside. With CLV the disc's data storage capacity is fully utilized, because each track is completely filled. There are no unused positions on the longer *tracks* towards the outside, as is the case with *constant angular velocity.* However, rotational speed must decrease when moving from the center to the outside. Data are stored on a spiral track. This makes locating data more time consuming, because the track is divided into fixed length units (called sectors) that do not start at fixed locations and therefore are not directly addressable. CLV is therefore less suitable where fast access is required. CLV applied to *CD-DA* and *CD-ROMs.*
See also: videodisc.

constrain
A drawing program tool which facilitates the drawing of predefined shapes such as circles, squares or straight lines. The chosen shape (circle, square or line) can sometimes deform into an ellipse, oblong or raggedy angled lines. Once in position, the required shape can be restored with the shift or control key.

Consultative Committee International for Telephone and Telegraph Communication
CCITT - An international committee which defines European standards for *modem* and telephone communication.

continuity
The maintaining of consistency between scenes when recording a film or computer *animation.* For example, a *button* that was active at the end of a *scene* must still be active at the beginning of the next scene.

contrast range

The difference in brightness between the lightest and darkest areas of a picture. The contrast range of a recording medium determines the amount of detail that can be recorded. The contrast range of *charge-coupled devices* as used in a video camera is higher than that of photographic film.

See also: luminance.

control point

See: anchor point.

Control-S

A *video control* system by Sony with functions comparable to commonly used remote control devices with one difference, namely that wires are used for conveying the control signals instead of infra-red signals. Control-S is mostly used to control monitors. When several monitors are interlinked they can all be controlled at the same time.

control-track

A track on a video tape for checking and controlling the tape speed.

See also: magnetic tape.

convergence

The maintenance at right angles of horizontal and vertical lines on a TV or computer screen.

conversion

1. The changing of signals to *analog* or vice versa.
2. The changing of *file formats.* Program manufacturers are inclined to create new trends of file formats for each application they create, leading to the plethora of file formats that exists today. File conversion is done by specialized programs or by using the available import or export options of an application.
3. The changing of a file for transfer to a different computer type and/or *operating system.*

Conversion can be complex. It is not always possible to reproduce exactly the features of the original format to the designated format. In such cases, mostly with graphic files, the resulting data can be faulty.

coordinate system

A system of axes for specifying the location and scale of objects. Two or three axes are used depending on whether the object representation is two or three dimensional. In 3D-modeling three coordinate systems are

used: *world coordinates, modeling coordinates* and *eye coordinates*. *World coordinates* are absolute, the other two systems define coordinates relative to a particular angle of viewing.

Copper Distributed Data Interface

CDDI - A *token-passing* network that uses *unshielded twisted pair* wiring (copper wires). It supports transmission speeds up to 100 megabits per second. CDDI is a variation on *Fiber Distributed Data Interface* (FDDI) that uses optical fibers for wiring. CDDI's advantage is its use of low-cost copper wiring *(10Base-T)*.

coprocessor

Mathematical microprocessor designed for speeding up floating point calculations and standard mathematical functions like sine and cosine. The coprocessor cooperates with the CPU in the following way: when the CPU executes a program and encounters a coprocessor instruction it sends it to the coprocessor and awaits a completion signal. Often one coprocessor instruction is the equivalent of many CPU instructions.

Applications such as spreadsheets and *computer-aided design* programs perform significantly better when a coprocessor is present. However, when a program is constructed the special coprocessor instructions must be included otherwise it cannot use the coprocessor. See also: central processing unit.

copy stand

A flat plate with lamps on either side; a photo or video camera is placed above the plate (vertically), allowing the user to view the plate. It is used for recording flat images, slides and *3D* objects on photographic or video material.

CORDIS

See: Community Research & Development Information System.

cordless mouse

A type of *mouse* which uses radio impulses to send signals to the computer instead of a wire, thereby allowing the user greater freedom of handling.

courier

A type style widely used in many typewriters and printers. The characters are non-proportional, i.e. have a fixed *width*. Courier is a member of the family *Egyptian* family of type styles.
See also: type classification.

courseware
A package of teaching materials comprising of various items to follow a course, such as: videodiscs, video tapes, floppy disks, textbooks etc.

crane
A *camera* platform fixed to a mechanical arm that can be moved in any direction (up and down and from side to side) either manually by hand or mechanically. It is used to take *shots* of or from a high viewpoint.

crash
A program or hardware defect which renders a computer unusable. An example is the so-called *head crash*, where the floating read/write head of a *hard disk* makes contact with and scratches the metal plate. After this the hard disk must be replaced.

crawl
1. Text that moves horizontally or vertically over a screen, for instance the credit titles at the end of a *film*. In computer jargon this is called *scrolling*.
2. A *video error* visible as a *glare* arround the bright parts of an image. It is caused by low-quality recording.

crescendo
A musical term indicating a gradual increase in the volume. It is abbreviated to 'cresc' or 'cr'.

cropping
Removing unwanted parts of an illustration (which need not be printed).

cross platform
A qualification of applications and files that can be used on different computer systems and/or *operating systems.* For example: Adobe *Acrobat* produces documents that can be processed by DOS, *Windows, Macintosh* and *UNIX* systems.

Cross-Interleaved Reed-Solomon Code
A fault detection and correction technique that handles errors in data blocks with lengths of up to 3,500 bits. It is applied to CD-ROMs, where it creates a large tolerance for

cropping

manufacturing faults as well as those caused by scratches on the CD surface due to wear.
See also: Compact Disc Read Only Memory.

crunching
A form of file compression.
See also: compress.

CSMA/CA
See: carrier sense multiple access/collision avoidance.

CSMA/CD
See: carrier sense multiple access/collision detection.

cubic mapping
A technique creating realistic light reflection for a *3D* object. Six photographs (shots) of the object are required: top, bottom, left, right, front and back. The program projects these shots onto the inside of an (imaginary) cube. The 3D object is then placed in a side cube. All light reflections on the object then come from the bitmaps that represent the outside world.
See also: mapping; reflection mapping.

cue sheet
A list of *synchronization* points linking *video* to *audio*. A synchronization point is, for instance, represented by the sound of the *clap board* at the beginning of a *scene*. Breakdown is a synonym for cue sheet.

cursor
The cursor marks the location on screen where the next typed *character* will be inserted. Depending on the program, the user can use a variety of shapes ranging from the simple blinking underscore or block of the non-graphic programs, to the pointing finger, cross, hour glass or other symbols used in different graphic software.

cut
Film and *video* term. To change scenes in a film without *transition*.
See also: wipe.

cyan, magenta, yellow, black
CMYK - Cyan, yellow and magenta are the three base ink pigments (colors) used for color in printing. By mixing these pigments in different ratios a great number of colors in the spectrum can be reproduced. The closest approximation to black that can be attained (by mixing the

three pigments in a 1:1:1 ratio) is a very dark brown. To achieve solid black therefore, black is added as the fourth base pigment. CMYK are called process colors because each color requires a print run, so four runs are needed to print a full color picture.
See also: color synthesis.

cybercop
A person who investigates illegal practices on national and international computer networks. Cybercops track down *cyberpunks* (also called 'hackers'), search for and destroy viruses, suppress illegal software copying, etc.
See also: cyberspace.

cybernaut
See: cyberspace.

cybernetics
Research in communication that compares human and animal brains with those of machines and electronic devices. This knowledge is employed in the construction of machines, especially where it concerns control and feedback as, for example, robots. Computers are used in research to simulate mechanical processes and the outcome of the process and quality control, e.g. flight simulators.
See also: simulation.

cyberpunks
People that use computer systems of others without permission, also known as hackers.
See also: cyberspace.

cyberspace
The vast and almost incomprehensible world of connected information networks such as *Internet*. Cyberspace gives access to almost in-exhaustible information and knowledge sources. However it is necessary to have the time, money and skill to 'surf' the net. People who regularly delve into cyberspace are called cybernauts.
The word Cyberspace was coined by the author William Gibson in his novel Neuromancer. In this book people use a futuristic network by connecting their brains directly to it.

cyclic redundancy check
A method for detecting faulty *data* in a *file*, for instance during telephone transmission.

cylinder

The set of stacked *tracks* that can be processed simultaneously by the read/write heads of a *hard disk*. A hard disk consists of a pack of several (metal) plates, both sides of which are used for *data* storage. Each surface in the pack has its own read/write *head*. Data is first stored on a track on the top surface of the top plate, then on the same track on the bottom etc. This minimizes the head movement, which speeds up the process.

D

D-MAC

A video transmission standard, consisting of MAC video signals and NICAM digital sound.
See also: D2-MAC; multiplexed analog components (MAC); near instantaneously companded audio multiplex (NICAM).

D1

A standard for *digital video* recording based on the *CCIR 601* standard. The videotape has a 19-mm width and a standard recording time of 94 minutes. The advantages are: the high chrominance *bandwidth* for high-quality *chroma keying* and the possibility of making several *generations* with little quality loss.

D2

A standard for *digital video* recording in composite PAL and NTSC signals. The standard prescribes 19-mm videotapes with a recording time up to 208 minutes. The videotape and the recording size are different from *D1*. The composite PAL or NTSC signals are digitized using eight bits.
See also: composite video; Phase Alternating Line (PAL); National Television Standards Committee (NTSC).

D2-MAC

A new TV system that will replace current systems such as PAL, NTSC and SECAM. The improvements are better *video* and *audio* quality (CD quality). Furthermore, it is possible to include speech in different languages simultaneously.
Also signals can be sent simultaneously for the traditional screen proportion 4:3 as well as the new screen proportion 16:9 (wide screen TV). TV receivers adjust automatically to the signal.
D2 MAC is already in use in The Netherlands, Germany and France. It is considered the forerunner of *High Definition Television*. D2 MAC is not related to the *digital video* standard *D2*.
See also: D-MAC, multiplexed analog components (MAC); Phase Alternating Line (PAL), National Television Standards Committee (NTSC); Séquentiel Couleur à Mémoire (SECAM).

D3
A standard for *digital video* recording in composite PAL and NTSC signals. It requires 1-inch videotapes that have a recording time of up to 245 minutes.
See also: composite video; Phase Alternating Line (PAL); National Television Standards Committee (NTSC).

dash
The term dash refers to the horizontal stroke used in pairs in text to mark a break in sense, or (incorrectly) to the *hyphen* used to link words or to break a word at the end of a line. There are two ways to set a dash, using either an unspaced em-dash which is as wide as the type is high, or a spaced en-dash (half the *width* of the *body size*). The hyphen is an unspaced en-dash.
See also: space.

data
A universal name for 'facts' (entries, items). They exist everywhere: on paper, in someone's brains, digitally filed in the computer, etc.

data communications
The electronic exchange of *data* between computers. This involves coding, decoding and checking.

data dictionary
A collection of *data*, comprising an *information* system. Examples of these kinds of data are files, transactions, reports, data flows and their relationships, as well as that between the data and the user.

data exchange format
DXF - File format for 2-D and 3-D drawings. This format, originally designed for the technical design program AutoCad, has gradually developed into an exchange standard.
See also: file format; vector format.

data glove
An electronic glove, which is used as control in *virtual reality* devices. Inside the glove are directional sensors which transmit the user's movements to the computer. The computer uses the *data* to control objects in the virtual environment.

data redundancy
Redundant *data* or excess of data. In compression algorithms based on

data redundancy, white spaces in texts or areas of identical color are replaced by a short code.
See also: compress.

data suit
An electronic suit that registers the position and movements of the user. These movements are made visible in a virtual environment using a graphic *image* generated by the computer. An electronic glove is frequently part of the suit.
See also: virtual reality; data glove.

database
A collection of structured and related *data*, such as occurs in the linking of articles to orders. This data can only be processed with an appropriate database program.
See also: database management system.

database management system
DBMS - A computer system for storing, managing and controlling access to huge amounts of *data* in a *file* (*database*). Filed data can consist of computer data, photographs, illustrations, sound, moving pictures etc. Characteristic of a DBMS is that, apart from managing the data itself, it also maintains the relationships between data.
It is very important to ensure the integrity of the file. Consequently, exhaustive checks on data entry have to be performed. Moreover, data must be filed in such a way that unauthorized users cannot gain access.
See also: database publishing.

database publishing
The assembly and publishing of *data* using a *database*. There are publishing programs which import raw data and assemble and format it. *Layout* characteristics assigned to a particular item are automatically applied to other items, for example when composing a catalog. Direct mail is a good example of database publishing.

datagram
A *data communication* term for a data *packet*. The packets consist of the network address of receiver and sender, and the data.
See also: connectionless protocol.

Datanet 1
A public nationwide *network* of the Dutch telecommunication company (PTT), consisting of special copper wiring. Computers with modems can

communicate via Datanet 1 for the rapid and interference-free transmission of large amounts of *digital data*. Part of Datanet is the text communication system Memocom.

dataspeed
The effective speed, which two *modems* use to exchange *data*. The speed depends amongst others on the technical features of the modems and the quality of the telephone line. Modern modems are equipped with a visual display of the effective speed per second.
See also: baud rate.

dBrn
See: decibel above reference noise.

DD1/ID1
A standard for computer data recorders and *backup* systems, using *D1* videotape as storage medium.

DD2
A standard for computer data recorders and *backup* systems, using *D2* videotape as storage medium.

deadlock
A network situation where a blockage occurs due to several users (or processes) using facilities exclusively. An example: P is exclusively using facility F. In order to continue working it needs facility G. G however, is exclusively in use by Q. Q, on the other hand, needs facility F to be able to continue. Both P and Q are now blocked, because they are waiting for each other to release the required facility.

decibel
1. The unit of sound that is one tenth of a Bel unit.
2. A unit of voltages or sound levels. The logarithmic relationship between a measured value and an established reference value. In acoustics, an increase of one decibel is equal to sound intensity increase that is just barely audible.

decibel above reference noise
dBrn - The number of *decibels* exceeding a reference value.

decimal tab
Tabulator specification that aligns numerical data on the decimal point, ensuring that the decimal point is in the same position on every line.

decoded audio signal

An *audio* signal generated after *demodulation, error correction* and digital/analog *conversion*. The best-known application is the *compact disc* player.

See also: Cross-Interleaved Reed-Solomon Code; digital-to-analog converter.

decompress

To decode a compressed file to bring it back to its original length and *file format*.

decorative type

A *type classification* of fonts differing widely in appearance and therefore difficult to classify within other type categories. The decorative aspect takes precedence over the legibility.

dedicated server

A network term that describes a *server*'s characteristics. A dedicated server is a computer used solely to regulate *data*, traffic, etc. Generally a powerful *personal computer, Macintosh* or *Unix* machine is used.

On a dedicated server the network versions of programs are installed and data files can be stored. Medium sized and large networks often use dedicated servers for increased performance.

See also: peer-to-peer network; client-server.

default

Standard option. For example, when printing a *file*, the default states that only one copy is to be printed, unless the user specifies how many copies he or she wants.

definition

The level of detail or sharpness on a television screen.

deflection

Technology applied to monitors whereby the deflection of *cathode rays* is increased by a deflection unit. The broader this deflection (angle of spread), the flatter the *monitor* can be.

defragment (to)

To restructure a *hard disk*. Fragmented files, with *data* spread over several locations on the hard disk, will be joined to form one block. When a disk becomes too fragmented, it will be at the expense of system performance.

delete

Wiping text or illustrations from *memory* with the delete *key*. Fortunately, if pressed by mistake, the deletion can usually be corrected with an *undo* command.

delta-YUV

DYUV- A method for economically storing digital photographic images. The principle is that the human eye is better able to perceive differences in *luminance* than differences in color. Consequently, half as much color information is stored with this method than of luminance. This saves considerable file space.
See also: YUV.

demand priority

An access method in networks, employed in 100Base-VG. This method regulates a *collision* free way for several devices to use the same cable. In other access methods such as *CSMA/CD* and *CSMA/CA*, *data* packages (bursts) may have to wait for each other or may even collide. In *multimedia* applications this can be very disturbing, for when a data package of a multimedia session has to wait for a free connection, the picture continuity at the receiving end will be disrupted. In demand priority, a *star* topology is used with the *hub* as the center. In this structure each station is connected to a hub and each time a station wishes to send, it has to ask the hub's permission. The hub will maintain the connection until the transmission is finished. This is called *guaranteed bandwidth*.
See also: broad band.

demodulation

The extraction of sound information from a modulated *carrier*.

demultiplexed

The splitting of a compound signal into several single signals.

densitometer

An instrument for measuring the differences of blackness of the lightest and darkest parts of a photograph or the *density* of ink on a printed image.

density

1. A logarithmic value indicating the relationship between striking and reflected light from a surface. With transparencies, it indicates the level of transparency. The value of density describes the blackness of negative or positive film or photographic paper. The density of the ink during the printing process can also be measured in this way.

2. Indication for the number of *tracks* on a storage medium. This number determines the storage capacity.

depth cueing

A method for creating the impression of extra depth during rendering based on the theory that distant points appear darker but less sharp than points close by.
See also: render (to).

depth of field

A photographic term. It is the zone in which everything photographed is rendered sharply. This zone is partly in front of and behind the point at which the lens is focused.
The depth of field is calculated by the lens *angle* and the *iris* diameter. This depth of field is varied by changing the iris diameter. By reducing the opening of the iris, a large depth of field is attained, whereas increasing the iris diameter reduces it. When the depth of field is shallow it is necessary to precisely adjust the *camera* to the distance in order to avoid fuzzy, out-of-focus pictures.
See also: f-stop.

derivative work

A new piece of work derived from an existing copyrighted work. The original work can either be changed or extended to create the new piece of work.
For example: a multimedia product which is derived from a book. In this example moving images, sound, search and menu structures and so on are added. In most cases the derivative work enjoys copyright protection.

descender length

The length of that part of a letter that descends below the *base line*.

descenders

Letters which partly decend below the *base line*: g, j, p, q, y.

desktop

A working surface on which all elements of a *graphical user interface* are displayed. Examples of these elements are: a graphically pictured wastepaper basket to *delete* files and a *clipboard* in which temporary information can be stored. The desktop also displays graphical representations of the files and programs.
See also: graphical user interface.

desktop accessories

Utility programs such as a clock, notepad, calculator or card-tray. These programs are generally available in a *graphical user interface*.

desktop publishing

DTP - An application whereby a (personal) computer is used to produce high-quality printed or camera-ready output for commercial printing. The power of DTP lies in its *WYSIWYG* characteristics which allow the manipulation of text and images on screen. The printing industry initially rejected DTP because of its limited graphics features. However, after major improvements, DTP has now become standard for professional as well as office print production. Consequently, a great deal of printing can be economically done in-house.

desktop video

DTV - The production of video programs using a (personal) computer. The software controls the *auxiliary* equipment for *editing* and affects machines as well as video recorders. In most installations, the video material is recorded on cassettes. Modern systems utilize *non-linear* media such as hard disks for video and audio recording. Other parts consist of add-on cards for generating *video effects*.
See also: editor; non-linear video.

device

A computer consists of a series of auxiliary systems with a microprocessor as the *central processing unit*.
These subsystems or devices are classified as internal or external. A *hard disk* is an example of an internal device. The *mouse, monitor* and *printer* are external devices.

device drivers

Programs which, in cooperation with the *operating system*, control devices such as printers, scanners, tape streamers, *CD-ROM* drives etc.

device profile

A term used in *color management* systems. The device profile is a device-independent description of the colors which a device (*scanner, monitor* or *printer*) can reproduce. For example, by scanning the included test color card a profile of the color capabilities of a scanner and the deviations are established.
The device profiles are used by the color management system for automatically correcting deviating colors.
See also: calibrate.

diacritical mark
Marks used in phonetics or in foreign languages which are placed either above the letters such as accent aigu, accent grave, accent circumflexe, diaeresis, tilde, etc. (é, è, ê, ë, ñ) or beneath such as the cedilla (ç - in French) which indicate the correct pronunciation of a letter.

dialog
Part of a computer program where the interaction between user and computer takes place.

dialog box
A pop-up *window* within a program which allows the user to make choices such as determining values or opening files. It is possible to return from the dialog box to the original document or alternatively to activate a submenu. A dialog box can also give error messages or warnings.
See also: graphical user interface.

Didot system
European typographers' measure (4.51278 mm) based on the French Imperial foot, divided into twelve Didot points and still in use. It is somewhat wider than the Anglo-Saxon pica measure of approx. 4.217 mm, which is also divided in 12 (pica) points.
See also: typographic measurements.

differential backup
A *backup* copy of all files that are new or have changed since the last complete backup copy.
See also: incremental backup.

diffuser
1. A photographic term. A filter type that diffuses light to soften it. The filter consists of a gelatin substance.
2. A software tool. Contrasts are softened to create a blurred picture.
See also: scrim; gobo; key light; fill-in light.

diffusion filter
A software tool. Contrasts are softened to create a diffuse picture.
See also: filters.

normal   diffusion

digital
Digital is derived from the Latin word digitus meaning finger. Digital means making calculations with *data* represented in digital form, for

example 1-2-3-4-5, etc. or 0,5-1-1,5-2-2,5-3 ..., with no values in between as in *analog* techniques. Counting on your fingers is digital. Computers work with digital data based on the *binary* (base 2) system which uses only two values, 0 and 1, or translated into electrical signals, on or off. See also: bit.

digital audio tape

DAT - *Magnetic tape* used both as a storage medium for computer *data* (especially for *backups)* and for *audio* applications. Data is registered in *digital* form using a rotating recording *head*.
Its advantage is that large amounts of computer data can be stored. The amount that can be stored is generally expressed in gigabytes.
See also: tapestreamer; helical scan.

digital highway

See: information highway.

digital photography

A type of photography where pictures are digitally recorded. The recording technique is basically the same as with *still video*. The pictures are recorded with a *charge-coupled device* (CCD).

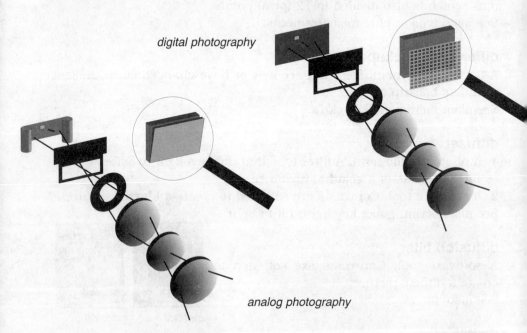

digital photography

analog photography

Digital photography is developing at a very fast pace. As yet, high-resolution digital color photography is a problem. Most existing professional systems need to make a separate recording for each of the three primary colors (*red, green, blue*). That makes it impossible to photograph moving objects in color.

digital signal processor
DSP - A *chip* that processes *analog* signals after digitizing them. DSPs differ from other chips (such as microprocessors) in the following ways:
1. They are optimized, so extensive calculations are quickly executed.
2. They are programmed using their own *operating system*. This makes them of general purpose. To add more functions to a DSP only a software upgrade is required. The hardware does not need changes. DSPs are used for *data communication* and processing digital audio/video.

digital studio camera
A digital camera back developed by Leaf Digital Systems together with software accessories. The system is used for video recording, color calibrating and *editing*.
See also: digital photography.

digital video
Video material in *digital* format (the other format is *analog*). The advantages of digital video are:
- images can be edited to the *pixel* level;
- it makes *non-linear video* possible;
- it can be combined with other *data* in digital format.
In digital format music, text, speech and video can be recorded combined on a single medium. This is the foundation for *multimedia*.
See also: analog video; Video for Windows; QuickTime; Motion Picture Experts Group; digital video interactive; 4:2:2.

digital video effects generator
DVE - Hardware for *editing* video pictures. A *frame grabber* captures the picture and a *genlock* brings it back to *analog* form. Especially used in scene *transitions*.

digital video interactive
DVI - A standard for compressing and playing digital *full-screen* and *full-motion* video pictures. It also has specifications for the user *interface*. DVI has a compression rate of 100:1 and is a form of *lossy compression*.
DVI technology consists of:
- a *chip* set for recording and playing audio and video;

- software specifications and routines for the use of DVI functions. These functions are meant for:
- manipulating and *editing* video pictures;
- the use of text, sound and animation;
- *file formats* for audio and video;
- compression and decompression algorithms.

These four functions are the basis for the designing and production of *multimedia* systems and author software. IBM and Intel have patented this technology, which was originally developed by the American media giant RCA.

See also: compression ratio; authoring language.

digital-to-analog converter

DAC - A unit, in computers generally a *chip*, that converts *digital* values into *analog* signals. The best-known application is the digital-to-analog converter of the *compact disc* player, where the digital signal is converted into an analog signal, which then becomes audible. In computers these converters are used, for example, to convert digitally recorded pictures into an analog video signal.

See also: random access memory digital-to-analog converter (RAMDAC); analog-to-digital converter.

digitize

The *conversion* of illustrations, photographs, video pictures and/or text into digital values.

digitized font

Typeface that is digitally designed and stored.

digitizer

A tablet (generally pressure sensitive) with a special *pen* which is connected to the computer. Sometimes a puck (a type of *mouse*) is used instead of a pen.

Its specific functions are:

1. Tracing drawings whereby the combination of pen and tablet transmits the coordinates of the drawing to the computer. These coordinates are converted into digital values making it possible to display the traced drawing on the screen and to process it in programs.
2. Activating *menu* commands. Specific computer commands can be activated by touching specially marked places on the digitizer with the pen.
3. The pen can serve as replacement for the mouse.

See also: pen-based PC.

digitizer board
An add-on *card* for computers. This card is provided with special *chips* for digitizing *analog* signals, such as stills or moving video pictures. See also: frame grabber.

diminuendo
A musical term that indicates a gradual decrease of the sound volume in a composition. The abbreviation is 'dim'.

dingbats
A collection of characters, consisting of symbols such as arrows, stars, a telephone, a pointing finger, etc. Hermann Zapf designed these symbols and they are officially called ITC Zapf Dingbats.

DIP switch
Dual-In-line Package - Small switches in a computer, printer or other *device* used for optional settings.

direct memory access
DMA - A facility in personal computers that circumvents the microprocessor when *data* is transferred between *devices* and the internal *memory*. Consequently, data transfer is faster. See also: central processing unit.

DIP switch

direct mode
A modem feature that enables direct transmission of *digital data*, without *error correction* or data compression.

director
The person to whom the artistic direction of the shooting and *editing* of a *film* or *video* production is assigned.

directory
A list that provides information on the location of program and *data* files on a storage medium (diskette, *hard disk*, etc.). This information can be sorted, e.g. alphabetically or chronologically.

disc
An optical storage medium. Optical discs allow a high writing *density*. The *data* is recorded in so-called pits. The areas between pits are called

lands. Pits and lands have a different reflection level, which allows the *laser* reading *head* to distinguish them. Each *transition* from *pit* to land and vice versa represents the *binary* number 1.

These discs often contain many errors because they are generally produced cheaply and in large numbers. This is solved by installing intelligent *error correction* methods in the playback equipment.
See also: Compact Disc.

disc production work order

The technical specifications of a *master tape*. These specifications are needed for making copies.

disc warp

A bend or other *distortion* of the horizontal surface of an *optical disc*.

discrete cosine transform

DCT - An element of a compression method used for moving pictures. DCT is a mathematical process that changes picture data according to a code scheme. The result is suitable for so-called *lossy compression*. This is a compression method that results in high compression ratios, at the expense of only a slight loss of picture data.
See also: compress.

discretionary hyphen

Hyphen indicating where long or unusual words must be divided, such as foreseeable: fore-seeable and not foresee-able.

This hyphenating method operates independently from the hyphenating program and takes priority over it. It can be manually inserted (as a code) and in some cases is generated by word processing or publishing programs.

disk recorder

A *hard disk* used as storage medium for video recordings. By applying compression techniques several hours of moving pictures can be stored on the disk.

display

Small *monitor* which shows commands to and messages from devices.

display cycle

The movements required by an electron beam to project a *character* or picture on screen.
See also: cathode ray.

Display PostScript

A version of the *page description language* PostScript for use on displays. It translates *PostScript* commands to graphic and text elements on screen. Normally a *file* is not converted into PostScript until it is ready for printing. If a PostScript file contains an error, this file will have to be regenerated from the beginning.

Display PostScript makes it easy to change a PostScript file because of its ability to display and edit the file on screen. This requires a lot of computing power and it therefore runs only on high-end computers.

dissolve

Picture *transition* where one picture slowly fades into the next until it is completely replaced by it.

distortion

An undesirable mutilation of an *audio* or *video* signal which can occur during signal transmission.

See also: noise.

distribution medium

A storage medium used for the distribution of software. Much used distribution media are diskettes, *Digital Audio Tapes* (DAT) and *Compact Disc Read Only Memory* (CD-ROM).

dithering

The *simulation* of a gray tone or color hue using grid patterns of different colors. This technique is sometimes applied in order to reproduce more colors on a screen or a printer.

See also: interpolation.

documation

Automation to make information from documents available. Microfilms and/or magnetic or optical discs are used to store this information. A user can browse through this information with a *terminal* or a PC.

document type definition

DTD - Information at the beginning of an SGML document describing its structure and the *data* categories. Defining a document this way makes it possible to structure and print text information from various documents or databases uniformly. Briefly: information is more quickly available, can be better controlled and more easily exchanged.

See also: Standard Generalized Markup Language.

Dolby surround sound

A system developed by Dolby Labs, for four-channel sound. Initially it was used in movie theaters. Nowadays it is also used in TV, amplifiers and other consumer products. Dolby surround sound uses two channels, which split four-ways using special codes. Despite the extra codes, surround sound can be played on standard stereo equipment, albeit without the surround effect.

Three logos are in use by Dolby surround sound:

1. The Dolby surround sound logo for soft and hardware. The sound is coded as described above.
2. The Dolby surround Pro Logic logo on hardware. An advanced version of the decode *chip* is applied, which improves sound quality.
3. The Dolby stereo logo is used in movies. Besides Dolby surround a *noise* reducer is also applied.

dolly

1. A *camera* platform on wheels.
2. A camera movement where the camera is fixed on a tripod with wheels, which is moved forward or backward.
3. Name for a camera movement in a 3D *modeler*.

dongle

See: hardware key.

door swing

A *video effect* where the *image* is rotated along a certain axis, for example, a vertical axis rotates the image like a revolving door.

dot

1. The picture on a screen is composed of *pixels* (picture elements). These pixels are drawn on the screen by the *cathode ray*. The well-known VGA video standard displays 640 pixels horizontally and 480 pixels vertically.
2. The print quality of printers and imagesetters is often indicated as *dots per inch* (dpi).

dot pitch

See: triple pitch.

dots per inch

dpi - Unit for the *resolution* of printers and imagesetters. The number of pixels per inch (2,54 cm) is measured. The higher the number of pixels, the higher the resolution and therefore the print quality. The standard for *laser* printers has been 300 dpi for some years. This standard has moved up to 600 dpi and will increase in the future. Imagesetters mostly work with a resolution or 2400 dpi and higher.

dots per line

dpl - Unit for the *resolution* of monitors. The number of pixels (picture elements) per horizontal line is measured. The VGA video standard has a resolution of 640 * 480. This indicates that each of the 480 screen lines consists of 640 pixels.

double buffering

Technique to make screen composition (and therefore the movements) of computer *animation* more fluid. Two screen *buffers* are used, which are displayed alternately. In the invisible screen buffer a new picture is composed, while the visible screen buffer shows the picture that was composed earlier. Then the invisible buffer is displayed and the visible one becomes invisible (where a new picture is immediately composed), and so on. In this way pictures can be displayed rapidly without jerking, which improves the quality of the animation.
See also: frame buffer; persistence of vision; animating on fields.

double click

Clicking the *mouse button* twice in succession. In a graphic environment this will generally activate a program or function, or display a *file*.
See also: graphical user interface.

double spread

See: spread.

download (to)

Copying a *file* from the *host* computer to the remote computer over a telephone line. When a file travels to the host computer from the remote computer, it is called an *upload*.

downloadable font

Font that is sent to the *printer* before or during the printing of documents where it is stored in its *memory* until needed for printing.

downstream

See: upstream.

drag

An operation with the *mouse* whereby the *mouse button* is kept pressed down while the mouse is being moved. Dragging a particular point of an element will result in the element being either relocated or changed in shape or size.

drive
Computer part that is a permanent or removable housing for a storage medium for digital data.

driver
See: device drivers.

drop initial
Enlarged first capital at the beginning of a text, which fits perfectly into the print area. The top of the *initial* aligns with the capital height of the *body type*, while the base aligns with the baseline of the body type a line lower down.
See also: cap height.

I n the heart of the large island of Niphon and in a mountainous and wooded region, fifty leagues from Yokohama, is hidden that marvel of marvels—the necropolis of the Japanese Emperors.

drop letter
See: drop initial.

drop-frame
Video term, specific to NTSC. The *frame* speed in NTSC is often indicated on various counters as 30 *frames per second*, while the effective speed is 29.7 frames per second. As a result, the timing of the counters is not entirely accurate. Correction can be done by regularly dropping frames. Two frames are dropped per minute, except on minutes that are a multiple of ten.
See also: National Television Standards Committee (NTSC).

drop-out
1. An error during the reading of a *binary* character on a magnetic medium. Generally caused by irregularities in the magnetic layer such as dust or dirt, or by inadequate contact between the read/write head and the tape.
2. A short interruption of *data* transmission. This can be caused by a defect in the system or the presence of too much *noise* in the signal.
3. Interference of a video signal. The term drop-out indicates the reason for the interference (damage to the emulsion of the video/audio tape) and its consequence (a blank part in a scan line in the video picture).
See also: video errors.

drum machine
An electronic musical instrument that imitates the sound of a drum.

drum scanner
A *scanner* that scans an original that is stretched around a drum. The drum rotates while the original is scanned and converted into digital values. This is the best and most expensive type of scanning device.

dub (to)
1. To copy a video or audio tape.
2. To insert voices or *sound effects* during the *editing* of a film or video production.
3. To make a new audio *track* in another language.

See also: post production.

dynamic data exchange
DDE - An internal communication *protocol* which programs *Windows* and *OS/2* environments. They are used to exchange *data* and commands between applications. In Window DDE it is extended with OLE (*object linking and embedding*). In OS/2 it is extended with *OpenDoc*.

dynamic focusing
This technique ensures that the pixels at the *monitor*'s edges are exactly round, thus preventing *distortion*.

dynamic range
The distance between the lowest and highest sound volume.

dynamics
Animation technique which attempts to make movements appear natural. Apart from laws of nature such as gravity, friction, wind, etc., the animated object's characteristics such as weight and smoothness have to be taken into account. Using this technique the computer can, for example, calculate the flapping of a flag in the wind. Applied mostly to 3D-animations.

DYUV
A video compression format for *digital video*. It is a combination of the digitized *YUV* signal (color and luminance for *PAL*) and a compression technique, where the differences between adjacent pixels are determined (rather than the differences between frames). However, its disadvantage is that when contrasts between pixels are high, the

picture will *smear*, causing loss of contrast and *definition*. DYUV is one of many video compression formats supported by CD-i.
See also: Compact Disc Interactive; compress.

E

E-mail
See: electronic mail.

ECHO
See: European Community Host Organization.

EDI
See: electronic data interchange.

edit decision list
EDL - An electronic log which lists the beginning and end of the scenes to be edited including the desired special effects, based on the *SMPTE-time code*. EDL is applied for pre-editing (*off-line*) on inexpensive equipment. Thereafter, the *editing* process is executed, based on the list, on more expensive equipment (*on-line editing*).
See also: Society of Motion Picture and Television Engineers (SMPTE); off-line editing.

editing
Compiling a film- or *video clip* into the sequence of images and sounds destined by the *director* or producer. Editing includes cutting pictures and sounds and adding special effects and *transitions*.
See also: off-line editing; on-line editing.

editor
A function of computer software for adapting/revising documents, for example, a *pixel* editor to edit an *image* pixel by pixel and a text-editor for word processing.

educational design
The combined expertise of hardware, software, theory of education and didactic to create a *interactive* program design within education objectives.

Efi
Electronics for imaging - A *color management* program. It accomplishes adequate color processing by using *device profiles* in order to match colors between devices. Efi is the first name of Azary, the founder of Efi.

Egyptian
A class of type faces that are characterized by:
- angular *serifs*, that are almost as thick as the ascenders;
- serifs with an acute angle with the ascender or *descender*.

Many typewriters use an Egyptian type. Well known Egyptians are *Courier* and Clarendon. Egyptian typefaces originate from England where they were introduced in the nineteenth century. The name comes from the resemblance between the serifs and the way the hands of people were pictured by the ancient Egyptians.
See also: type classification.

EISA
See: enhanced industry standard architecture.

electronic data interchange
Standard for exchanging business documents in digital form by means of *data communication*. Documents are orders, order confirmations, invoices, customs forms, etc. The documents are translated into a prearranged format before transmission.

electronic field production
EFP - Making video recordings on location using portable equipment.

electronic gun
Electrostatic unit in the back of a cathode-ray tube that generates the *cathode ray*. The cathode-ray projects the TV picture on the screen.
See also: dynamic focusing.

Electronic Industries Association
EIA - An American organization for *data communication* standards, comparable to the *CCITT* in Europe. The standards from these two organizations often are identical.
See also: Comité Consultatif International Téléphonique et Télégraphique.

electronic mail
E-mail - Sending mail over a computer *network*. This can be confined to the users of the local network, but there are also worldwide nets (for example the *Internet*). Fervent E-mail users often refer to regular mail as Snail mail (Standard Air or Land) to express their opinion on how fast they feel regular mail works. E-mail is a step towards the creation of the paperless office, because it dispenses with nearly all internal printed document exchange. At the same time it supplies the

user with an advanced filing system. A memo can be found by specifying a few keywords and takes a few seconds.

electronic photography

Photography or filming that uses some form of electronic medium for storage instead photographic film. Examples are *flash memory* or *floppy disk*. The recordings can be *analog* as well as *digital*.
See also: digital photography.

em-space

See: space.

emboss filter

A tool that creates a three-dimensional effect by adding shadow to a text or color area. This makes the area appear to stand out.
See also: filters.

normal   *emboss*

emulate (to)

To imitate the workings of a hardware or software system by another system. For example, the DEC VT-100 is a dumb *terminal* with which many systems know how to communicate. A *personal computer* can, by use of a communication program, appear to be a VT-100 terminal to these systems. Another example is running an executable program intended for an Intel microprocessor or another microprocessor having a different machine language. A software tool can make it appear to the program that it runs on a Intel processor.

en-space

See: space.

Encapsulated PostScript

EPS - A format to record graphical material. EPS is a *vector format* with formulas expressed in the *PostScript* language. To display a EPS file on screen *Display PostScript* must be supported by the *operating system* (as is the case of *Unix* and *NeXTstep*). To accommodate other operating systems often a copy of the picture is also supplied in *TIFF* or *PICT* format. This allows viewing, enlarging or reducing the picture but it cannot be altered.
See also: file format.

end-of-tape marker
EOT - Mark at the end of the recordable section of a tape. The marker can be a reflective strip, transparent tape, holes in the tape or a bit pattern. See also: magnetic tape; leader.

enhanced graphics adapter
EGA - A video standard for IBM-compatible computers. The *resolution* is 640 * 350 *pixels.* It displays 16 simultaneous colors selected from 64 possible colors. The 64 colors are available in four groups of 16 colors. Such a group is called a palette. The current video standard is *super video graphics array* (SVGA). However, all *video adapters* are still capable of displaying EGA images. EGA was introduced in 1984.

enhanced industrial standard architecture
EISA - The name for a *32-bit* bus used in personal computers that improves on the ISA *bus* in transmission capacity and speed, while maintaining complete compatibility. However, to take advantage of EISA's capabilities, specially designed hardware must be used. EISA was meant to succeed ISA but failed to do so, because of the high costs of EISA machines. ISA will most likely be succeeded by local bus systems such as VESA or PCI or the new plug-and-play concepts. See also: Video Electronic Standards Association.

environmental immersion
See: virtual reality.

EPS
See: Encapsulated PostScript.

equalize filter
A tool for decreasing the difference in brightness between the brightest and darkest area of an image, mostly a scanned photo. Equalizing is sometimes needed to make reproduction possible.

ergonomics
Scientific research of the human body and mind in order to create healthy and productive working environments. Ergonomics studies the effects of monitors, chairs, tables, illumination, noise level, etc. on the people that work with it/in it.

error burst
A series of errors in a *bit* stream.
See also: burst; noise; error correction.

error correction
A technique to detect and correct errors in *data*. This is applied in all levels of computing. A computer's memory contains hardware that tests constantly for *parity* errors. In data communication, data is added to each message to check if data has been corrupted during transmission. See also: checksum; Cross-Interleaved Reed-Solomon Code; cyclic redundancy check.

ESPRIT
See: European Strategic Programme for Research and development in Information Technology.

establishing shot
A film *scene* of some duration for familiarizing the viewer with the surroundings and the atmosphere.

Ethernet
An often used *network protocol* for *LAN* applications (developed by Intel, DEC and Xerox). In the *OSI* model Ethernet is positioned as the data connection layer. Ethernet is characterized as follows:
- data is transmitted in packets;
- *bus* topology;
- it uses *CSMA/CA* or *CSMA/CD* protocol for save data delivery;
- cabling is thick or *thin Ethernet* or unshielded twisted pair;
- the maximum transmission speed is 10 MB/s;
- Ethernet is an *IEEE* standard.

Nowadays multimedia and graphics applications easily consume Ethernet's transmission capacity. Therefore a successor has been developed: *Fast Ethernet*.
See also: 100Base-VG; baseband.

European Broadcast Union
A union of European broadcast organizations that coordinates their production and technical interests. EBU commissions advise the CCIR. See also: Comité Consultatif International des Radiocommunications.

European Community Host Organization
ECHO - The host organization of the European Union (founded in 1980). ECHO contributes to the creation of a common market for information services in context of the IMPACT program. ECHO's main objectives are to:
- provide multilingual, objective information about European information services;

- guide and train users, mainly in regions where electronic information is seldom used;
- serve as a distribution channel for advanced services.

ECHO resides in Luxembourg. The organization has a helpdesk which solves problems users have. ECHO also provides access to the CORDIS *database*.

See also: Information Marketing Policy Actions (IMPACT); Community Research and Development Information System (CORDIS).

European Strategic Programme for Research and Development in Information Technology

ESPRIT - A European program for pre-competitive research of information technology.

ESPRIT has three objectives:

1. Developing a technological foundation that gives the European information industry a competitive position relative to Japan and the USA.
2. Stimulating co-operation between European companies, research centers and universities on the subject of information technology.
3. Contributing to the development of international standards.

eventstore

A electronic memory where the editing actions are stored during the editing of a *video clip*.

expand

See: decompress.

expanded memory manager

A *driver* program that makes *expanded memory* available to applications in a MS-DOS computer. With MS-DOS a program called EMM386.EXE is supplied that converts *extended memory* into expanded memory.

See also: Micosoft disk operating system; memory.

expanded memory system

EMS - Hardware that gives application programs access to extra memory. EMS has been developed when MS-DOS computers were restricted to 1 MB. With EMS additional memory could be added. This memory can only be used for storage, not for running programs. Due to limitations in the computer system, EMS memory is divided in blocks of 64 KB. Only one block can be accessed at a time. The hardware of EMS memory contains a mechanism (called paging) to switch between blocks very fast. To MS-DOS and application programs the 64 KB block appears to be within the 1 MB range but in reality it is located on the expanded memory board. The block in the 1 MB range is called the page frame.

Nowadays computers do not have the limitations of their predecessors. EMS has therefore outgrown its use. Extra memory is now supplied by *extended memory*.

See also: Micosoft disk operating system.

expander
See: synthesizer.

extended graphics adapter
XGA - A video standard for IBM-compatible computers. The *resolution* is 1024 * 768 pixels. It displays 256 simultaneous colors selected from 262,144 possible colors. In the VGA *mode* (640 * 480 resolution) 65,635 simultaneous colors are possible. The simultaneous colors are available in groups of colors. Such a group is called a palette. XGA was introduced in 1989.

The current video standard is *super video graphics array* (SVGA).

See also: video adapter; video graphics array (VGA).

extended memory specification
XMS - A standard that gives application programs access to extra *memory*. This memory is used for storage and for running programs. Extended memory requires at least a *16-bit* processor. With the coming of *32-bit* processor all of the capabilities of expanded memory are available in the microprocessor (the paging mechanism).

XMS is linear addressable. This means all available memory can be addressed by the microprocessor without having to resort to address virtualization as EMS has to do.

See also: memory.

extended type
The broad version of a typeface.

See also: condensed type.

extension
A part of a MS-DOS file name that can be used to classify the file content. For example in file name README.TXT, TXT is the extension. The extension is between one and three characters long. In the example TXT indicates that the file contains text.

On a *Macintosh* a file has two hidden extensions or attributes, each four characters long: file type and creator. The list below shows a selection of the most important extensions in multimedia:

bmp   *Bitmap*, graphic format;
avi   *Audio Video Interleaved*, *digital video* (*Video for Windows*);
fli   *animation* format, maximum 256 colors, developed by Autodesk;
gif   *Graphic Interchange Format*, 8 bits lossless *image compression*, developed by Compuserve.
jpg   Joint Picture Experts Group, 24 bits lossy image compression;
mid   Musical Instrument Digital Interface;
mov   movie format, *QuickTime* digital video;
mpg   *Motion Picture Experts Group*, digital video, lossy compression;
pcx   PC Paintbrush, graphics format;
tga   Truevision Graphics Adaptor; graphics format;
tif   *Tagged image file format*, graphics format;
wav   Wave, sound format (Windows).

external memory
External memory is all memory but the central memory (RAM). Examples are: hard and floppy disk, optical disc, digiital audio tape cassettes, etc.

extreme close up
A *shot* where the object is larger than the screen.

extreme long shot
A *shot* of an object from an extreme large distance, for example: an aerial shot of a car in a mountain landscape showing only the dust cloud.
See also: close up; medium shot; long shot.

extruding
A technique in a design program for composing a three-dimensional object from two-dimensional objects. To compose a *cylinder* one uses a

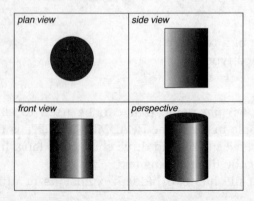

extruding

flat object to define how it looks from each viewpoint; a circle for the top and bottom view, a rectangle for the front, back and side view. The design program computes from this the cylinder that subsequently is available for viewing from every conceivable viewpoint.

See also: lofting.

eye coordinates

In a design program a three-dimensional object can be represented in eye coordinates, which gives depth to the object. Eye coordinates are relative to the user's viewpoint and are computed from the absolute *world coordinates*.

See also: coordinate system.

F

f-stop
A series of standardized lens openings that are expressed as numbers (f1.8, f2.6 ... f22). Each number represents a logarithmic value for the light intensity. The light intensity level depends on ratio between the focal distance and diameter of the chosen diaphragm (*iris*). For example: a lens with a focal distance of 90 mm and diaphragm diameter of 20 mm gives an f-stop value of 90:20=4.5:1=f4.5.
A small f-stop value corresponds with a large lens opening and a small focus depth. To obtain a desired focus depth the f-stop is set; every next stop doubles the amount of light that passes through the diaphragm.
See also: depth of field; angle.

faces
A 3D-term. The planes in a *wire-frame* model.
See also: mesh; vertices.

fade-in/out
To gradually make a picture visible (fade-in) or invisible (fade-out).

fade-up/down
Increase (up) or decrease (down) of sound volume or video brightness.

Farb Bild Austatung Sychronization
German term that refers to the TV signal transmitted within TV studios or from the studio to the transmitter.

Fast Ethernet
A fast variant of *Ethernet*. Some characteristics are:
- transmission speed of 100 megabits per second;
- *unshielded twisted pair* cabling.
Fast Ethernet competes with *FDDI* and *CDDI*.
See also: 100VG-AnyLAN; 100Base-T.

fatbits
A software tool to enlarge each *pixel* (resulting in enlarged version of a picture) and edit them individually.
See also: pixel; bitmap.

FDDI
See: fiber distributed data interface.

feature
A *film* with a playtime of 60 to 120 minutes.
See also: short.

feature connector
The extra connector (20 or 26 pin) on VGA adapters giving direct access to all video signals. Some video capture boards do use it enabling the mixing of video with computer output.

Federal Communications Commission
FCC - American organization that tests and certifies equipment on radio and electrical interference. Class A equipment is for use at home, class B equipment (restricted) is for use in the office or at home. Each electrical appliance requires an FCC certificate before sale is allowed.

feed cable
A cable that connects a picture source (for instance a *camera*) to a *monitor*.

fiber
A cable used in *data communication*. Data is sent in the form of light pulses. Fiber distributed data interface (FDDI) is a *protocol* that uses optical fiber. Its characteristics are:
- expensive;
- higher speed and capacity compared to copper;
- insensitive to electrical interference.
See also: unshielded twisted pair; coax.

fiber channel
A yet-to-be developed superfast *network protocol* for use on *optical fiber* as well as copper wire. It is a joint initiative of IBM, Sun and Hewlett-Packard. There are already transmission capacities of 266, 512 and 1062 *Mbit/s*. Eventually speeds of two and four gigabits could become available.

Fiber Distributed Data Interface
FDDI - An ANSI standard for a *token-passing* network that uses *optical fiber* for wiring, although a copper wire version exists. It supports speeds of up to 100 *Mbit/s*, tenfold the speed of *Ethernet*. FDDI equipment is expensive and is used therefore only when traffic increases, for instance the connection between two *LANs*.
See also: American National Standards Institute.

field

1. A video *image* is built up in two stages; first the even horizontal lines are displayed from top to bottom, then the odd lines. Such a half image is called a field and two of those fields form a *frame*.
2. An element in a database *record* which contains data concerning one attribute of the object the record represents.

field dominance

The field dominance defines which *field* of a *frame* is read first.

field frequency

The *frequency* in which *fields* are displayed on the screen. For NTSC this is 59.94 Hz and for PAL and SECAM 50 Hz.

See also: Herz; refresh rate; National Television Standards Committee (NTSC); Phase Alternating Line (PAL); Séquentiel Couleur à Mémoire (SECAM).

figure space

See: space.

file

A set of *data* stored on electronic medium. The *operating system* or applications assign meaning to the contents of files.

file allocation table

A table on a disk the *operating system* uses to find out where files are located and where free space is available.

file format

The structure of a file content. Most developers design an unique file format for their applications. This has led to a plethora of file formats. However, this means brisk business for developers of file *conversion* programs. To alleviate the problem, applications have the ability to deal with most of the popular formats through their import and export functions.

See also: vector format; bitmap format.

file manager

An application program for *file* management. Functions are available for copying, moving, deleting and viewing files. The possibility to maintain the *directory* structure is also available, such as creating and removing directories.

See also: operating system.

fill
Percussion or other music to fill the transition between two music fragments.

fill-in light
The use of lights to fill-in shadows of an object after exposure with the *key-light*. The fill-in light is widespread and less intense than the key-light.

fillet
A tool in a design program to round a right angle with an arc. Most CAD programs have a specially designed function for this.
See also: computer-aided design.

fillet

film
Recording medium for images. When producing a film (movie) many pictures are taken by a *camera* and recorded on a strip (25 *frames* per second). When this strip is transported in front of the light in a projector the picture comes to life. Popular film formats are 8 and 16 mm for consumer use and 35 and 70 mm for professional use.

film chain
Optical equipment for copying a film frame or a slide on to a video tape. The original is projected on the lens of a video *camera*. The video camera then records it.

filters
1. Tools used in photography to process pictures during shooting and printing.
2. Software tools for editing images. Examples are diffusing, granulating, blurring, etc.

See also: color filter; diffusion filter; add noise filter; emboss filter; blur; equalize filter; mosaic filter; outline filter; sharpness filter; smear.

finder
The *Macintosh* application that manages the *desktop*. It is used to manage objects like *folders*, *files* and the *clipboard*. Common operations are: copying, moving and opening files.

firmware
Software which is stored in unerasable *read only memory* (ROM). The software controls hardware components. Firmware is used in PCs, printers, modems, add-on cards, etc.

fixed disk
See: hard disk.

fixed focus
A *camera* lens with fixed focus and fixed *depth of field*. The depth of field ranges from 70 cm to infinity.

flash
Emphasized text to attract attention, for example by adding a *frame* or *reversed* printing.

flash memory
Memory made of EPROMs or EEPROMs (erasable programmable *read only memory*). It is also called non-volatile memory because its *data* can be held indefinitely. The *access time* is very short: it is measured in nanoseconds (comparable to the access time of RAM), not in milliseconds as is the case with hard disks.
Flash memory can be erased by ultraviolet light (EPROM) or by electrical current (EEPROM) whereafter new data can be stored. The erasing process is very slow and therefore flash memory is used for applications reading mainly data, for example in add-on cards to hold setup data or as credit card-size key-cards.

flat shading
To color a 3D-object in flat planes, creating an angular unrealistic *image*, allowing a quick check of the lighting effect.
See also: shading.

flatbed scanner
A device that scans a document situated on a glass plate by moving a light underneath it. The reflected light is transformed into digital information with a *charge-coupled device*. A flatbed *scanner* is easier to use than a *hand-held scanner* because the device moves the sensor at constant speed, which is hard to achieve by hand. The ease of use comes at a price; flatbed scanners are more expensive than hand-held scanners.

flicker
1. The flicker that is visible when two *fields* of a still-video *frame* do not coincide.
2. The flicker that is visible when the frames of moving video are displayed in a *frequency* which is too low.
See also: refresh rate.

floating palettes

A feature in graphical design and drawing applications giving users fast access to frequently used palettes and/or tools. Along with the document *window*, small windows open filled with icons. These icons symbolize a color palette to apply or a tool to use. They are said to be floating because they are always visible even when they are not *active*. Normally, non-active windows are covered by the active window.
See also: graphical user interface.

floppy disk

A flexible magnetic disk in a protective housing. Before hard disks were feasible they were the only means to store programs and data. Now that every PC has a *hard disk*, they are mainly used for distributing software and exchange of data. Floppy disks exist in 5.25-inch and 3.5-inch diameter, both available in double *density* and high density format. The storage capacities are:
5.25-inch DD - 360 KB
5.25-inch HD - 1.2 MB
3.5-inch DD   - 720 KB
3.5-inch HD   - 1.44 MB
The 3.5-inch disk exist also in an extended density format with a storage capacity of 2.88 MB. The disk most used is the 3.5-inch disk with a capacity of 1.44 MB.

floptical disc

A flexible magnetic disk with a 3.5-inch diameter that has a 20 MB capacity when used in a specialized *drive*. This drive uses optical techniques to acquire the necessary precision to handle this level of data *density*. The floptical drive can also read and write standard 3.5–inch disks.
See also: floppy disk.

flowchart

A diagram for clarifying the workings of a process by showing how information or goods flow through a system. It consists of a set of boxes of various shapes, interconnected by a set of directed arcs. The arcs indicate flow of control while the boxes indicate actions, processes or decisions. Flowcharts are, for instance, used to document programs and to describe production processes in a factory, etc.

flush right

See: right justification.

flutter

High-pitched sound produced when a recording is played back. It is caused when the motor of the mechanical playback device is running at irregular speed or by faults in the recording.
See also: wow; drop-out.

fly-by

A *bird's-eye view* on a three-dimensional environment. It is used to show architectoral models from the inside and outside.

fly-in

In video a transitional effect where one picture is reduced, making it disappear into the next picture. To add perspective the disappearing picture is rotated into the depth.
See also: video effects.

fly-through

A *video* or *film shot* of a 3D-animation, the *camera* floats in one continuous movement over and through a location.

flying erase head

A *head* in a video recorder that erases the tape obliquely. This makes smooth transitions between scenes possible, because the read/write heads use the same *angle*. An ordinary head erases vertically causing frayed transitions and significant *noise*.

flying height

The standard distance between a *hard disk*'s read/write heads and the surface of the platter.
See also: head crash; landing zone.

focus servo

The mechanism that keeps the read/write heads on track in an *optical disc* player. The mechanism can compensate for irregularities in the disc surface and vibrations caused by the motor.

folder

Name for a container of files (*directory*) on a *Macintosh*. Folders are a way of organizing files. For example, one can use a folder to group related files together. Each folder can hold other (sub)folders; these, in turn can also contain folders. This way a hierarchy of folders can be created.

font

Derived from the period when lead was used in printing: a set of printing type of one *style* and size. For example, an 11 *point*, bold Times *Roman*. The point defines the size and the word bold defines the style. Possible styles are for instance, *normal*, *bold* and *italic*.

The distinction between font and type stems from the period when lead was used for typesetting. With the introduction of scalable fonts this distinction has become diffuse. There still are fonts for each style, but a font of a particular style is scalable to all sizes.

See also: multiple master.

font cache

An area in computer *memory* a type manager uses to speed printing and displaying fonts. A type manager makes fonts from outlines on demand. To make a font available the *outline font* is transformed into a *bitmap font* and stored in the cache. When the same font is requested at a later time, the transformation step is skipped and the font is supplied from the cache. The cache is limited in size. When it is full the least-used font is removed to clear space for a new font.

font file

A *file* containing a *font* definition.

font metric

Size characteristics of a *font* such as *width* and height.

font substitution

The replacement of unavailable fonts by the closest resembling *font*, a feature offered by many word-processing programs. The program matches fonts on characteristics such as stroke *weight*, *style* (*normal*, *italic*, etc.) and type class. When the program makes a poor choice it can change the document's *layout* dramatically. A font can become unavailable when one changes to another printer, uses the document with another wordprocessor or transfers the document to another computer platform.

See also: SuperATM.

footer

Line(s) of text at the bottom of each page, for instance showing the page number or the title of the current chapter.

foreground processing

In a *multitasking* environment, such as Microsoft *Windows*, where several processes (programs) run simultaneously, there is one foreground process; all the others are background processes. The foreground process receives the input the user types, i.e. the process that has the focus. To keep the foreground process as responsive as possible, it is given higher priority than the background processes. So, when the foreground process needs processing time at the same time as a background process, it is granted to the former. Most operating environments allow the foreground and background priorities to be adjusted.

formatting

1. Making a magnetic disk (floppy or *hard disk*) ready for use. For a hard disk two stages are needed. In the first stage (called low-level format) the *tracks* are recorded and divided in sectors. Tracks are checked for defects and marked unavailable if they do. In the second stage (called high-level format) sectors are grouped in clusters and file system tables are added. After low-level formatting a disk can be high-formatted for any *operating system*. After high-level formatting the disk is specific for an operating system.
2. Processing needed to give a text its final appearance, for instance, when a document is made ready for printing, the text is *spread* over pages, *header* and *footer* lines are inserted, etc.

forward prediction

A video compression technique that reduces the amount of data by recording only the differences between two adjacent frames. To eliminate visible *video errors* caused by the compression as much as possible, forward prediction techniques are used.
See also: compress; interframe compression.

Fourier transforms

A technique for *digital video* compression.
See also: compress.

FotoTune

Agfa's *color management* program.

fractal image compression

A technique for *digital video* compression. After compression an image is defined by a (small) set of mathematical formulas, called *fractals*. The original image is reproduced by 'playing' these formulas. The advantage of fractal compression is the high *compression ratio* without noticeable loss of image quality. The disadvantage is that it takes a

long time to derive the formulas from the picture. Once they are established the image is reproduced quickly.
See also: compress.

fractals

A fractal is an *image* made of patterns that are reduced copies of the larger *pattern* they are part of. A reduced pattern is itself made of reduced copies. This recurring reduction is repeated until a pattern is invisibly small. A fractal is created from a mathematical formula that is repeatedly executed. As it turns out, phenomena in nature (such as the shape of mountain, a tree or a coastline) itself consists of similar repeating patterns. Fractals are used to create beautiful pictures and they also play a role in image compression.
See also: fractal image compression.

fragmentation

After using the *MS-DOS* or *Macintosh* file system for some time the situation can arise that the space individual files take up is no longer on one consecutive area on the *hard disk*, but instead it is scattered in several areas on the disk. The time to access files increases with the level of fragmentation, because of the required additional movement of the read/write heads. Therefore, a defragmentation program needs to be run periodically.
See also: defragment (to).

frame

1. One picture of a (*video*) *film*. Frames are shown with a speed of 25 or 30 *frames per second*, thus creating the illusion of movement. Frames on television are built-up in two stages: in the first stage the even lines are shown, the odd ones in the second. Such a half screen is called a *field*.
2. One picture of an *animation*.
3. A rectangular area in a document produced by a wordprocessor or a publishing program that contains an illustration or a text. A frame's main features are: the body text flows around it and it can be surrounded by lines in different styles.
4. An amount of *data* that is sent as a unit over a *network*. Besides the data the frame also contains control information such as addresses and *synchronization* bits.
5. An amount of information on a *videodisc* that also includes error checking and synchronization data.

frame animation

Animation technique where for each *frame* a complete new drawing is made. This is very time consuming. *Cast animation* addresses this problem by working with several *layers*, each containing a separately animated character or other element.

frame buffer
Area in computer *memory* containing an instance of a screen image. There are several buffers, each containing a different image. This speeds up displaying these images on the screen and switching between them. The *frame buffer* is read by a conversion chip which translates the buffer content to video signals suitable for display on the screen or for recording with a video recorder.
See also: random access memory digital-to-analog converter; double buffering.

frame differencing
A method for image compression used in graphic computer applications. Temporary encoding is combined with local encoding so that only differences between sequential frames are recorded. This method is used in *production-level video*.
See also: compress.

frame grabber
A computer add-on *card* used for digitizing still and motion video images. Possible sources are: video-players, video cameras or *still video cameras*. Most frame grabbers can grab and *digitize* a single frame of playing video tape. The lowest quality is low-resolution black and white; the highest quality is 16.7 million colors in *high resolution*.

frame relay
A high-speed data communication *protocol* used in WANs (*wide area network*). It is a *packet switching* protocol. Frame relay is suitable for transmitting data and images, but not for speech or multimedia. A packet switching protocol is not particularly fast; however, frame relay uses smaller packets resulting in less *error correction.*

frames per second
In *film* and *video*, the number of frames per second that can be shot by a *camera* or shown by a projector.

frequency
The speed at which signal changes value, usually expressed in *Hertz*. One Hertz is one change per second.
See also: amplitude; waveform.

Frequency Modulation synthesis

FM-synthesis - A method for producing artificial sound. The FM-synthesis is based on the technique used to transmit radio signals over the FM-band. Sounds are produced by combining a number of sine waves. When only a few sine waves are used (as in cheap sound cards) the sound is often unnatural.

fringing

Incorrect display of colors on a screen. This is most noticeable at the edges of an *image* element. It is caused by inaccurate projection of the red, green and blue color rays.
See also: red, green, blue; cathode ray tube.

full backup

Copying (a selected portion of) files on a *hard disk* to a *backup* medium (such as tape). Backups are made to prevent loss of *data* when the hard disk breaks down. The difference between incremental and *differential backups* is that files are backed up even if they have not changed. After backup the *archive bit* of all backed-up files is switched off to indicate that a safety copy has been made. The full backup is the reference point for incremental and differential backups that only backup files that have changed since the last (full) backup.
See also: differential backup; incremental backup.

full duplex

A form of *modem* communication where signals are sent over a (telephone) line in both directions at the same time.
See also: half-duplex.

full immersion

See: virtual reality.

full-motion video

When used in the context of *digital video* display, it means that video is shown at the same speed as on TV (25 or 30 *frames per second*). This frame rate is not possible on ordinary PCs. It requires lots of *memory* and specialized graphics hardware to show full-motion video. This is necessary because an enormous amount of *data* is involved. To play digital video on standard hardware the frame rate is lowered and the picture is reduced to a small size.
See also: full-screen video; Phase Alternating Line (PAL); Séquentiel Couleur à Mémoire (SECAM); National Television Standards Committee (NTSC).

full-screen video

Digital video that is shown covering the entire screen. On ordinary PCs this is not possible because of the enormous amount of *data* involved. To show full-screen video, hardware has to be added or upgraded.
See also: full-motion video.

full-text index

An index created to speed up searching through a document set in order to find information pertaining to a subject. The index (called the inverted file) is created with a computer program. The program enters a reference to every word in the documents in the index, creating a file whose size approximates the size of the document set. This can be very time consuming. An alternative to full-text *indexing* is keyword indexing, where documents are identified by manually assigned keywords. This creates a small index.

full-text retrieval

A technique for searching through a document set, where every word in the set is compared to the ones the user specified in order to retrieve information pertaining to a subject. Documents that contain matching words are presented. To speed up searching, a *full-text index* is created. An alternative is keyword searching. Here words are compared to keywords that identify the document.
Full-text retrieval is characterized as follows:
- Any conceivable combination of words can be used in a search.
- When search words are too general, too many documents are retrieved. This is called noise.
- There is a risk of not finding a document that, although it pertains to the subject, does not contain a matching word, because synonyms are used.
Keyword retrieval is characterized as follows:
- Searching is limited to the predefined structure of the assigned keywords. When interests shift, information that seemed unimportant at the time may now qualify for a keyword.

function

A part of a program that is called to return a single value. A function may need input *parameters* to produce the result. These must be specified when the call is made. For example, a function to calculate the circumference of a circle uses parameter radius to calculate the circumference.
See also: programming languages.

fuzzy logic

A mathematical technique for dealing with imprecise *data* and problems that have more solutions than one. Contrary to its name, fuzzy logic is a very precise subdiscipline in mathematics. Although it is implemented in digital computers which ultimately make only yes/no decisions, fuzzy logic works with ranges of values, solving problems in a way that more resembles human logic. It enables mathematicians and engineers to simulate human thinking by quantifying concepts such as hot, cold, very far, pretty close, quite true, most usually, almost impossible, etc. It does this by recognizing that measurements are much more useful when they are characterized in linguistic terms, than when taken to the fourth decimal point. The central idea of fuzzy logic is probability of set membership. For instance, referring to someone 175 cm/5 ft 9 in tall, the statement 'this person is tall' (or 'this person is a member of the set of tall people') might be about 70% true if that person is a man, and about 85% true if that person is a woman. This way, fuzzy logic reduces a spectrum of numbers into a few categories called membership groups.

Within five years virtually all consumer goods will have fuzzy logic. Already fuzzy logic is inside video camcorders (to reduce the motion of the camera), in washing machines (to figure the optimum mix of washing conditions for that weight and filth). Fuzzy logic chips are made by several manufacturers.

G

G.Series
A series of standards describing audio equipment and the transmission of audio signals.

gaffer
Someone who builds up and dismantles *film* or *video* sets.
See also: grip.

gain
The increase or decrease of signal strength or the amplification factor in *decibels* (dB).

gamma
A rate of strength. A value to indicate the contrast of a photograph reproduced on photographic material or on a *monitor*. Low gamma indicates low contrast. The gamma value is determined according to the gradation curve. A steep curve produces a high gamma (high contrast). The gamma of an electronic picture can be adjusted per component (RGB, CMYK), color, across the entire picture, for half-tones, shadows segments or highlights.
See also: contrast range; red, green blue; cyan, magenta, yellow, black.

gamma correction
Adjusting contrast in an *image*.

gateway
A link between two networks. A gateway is used if the networks to be linked use different *protocols*. A PC is often used as a gateway, with one adapter for each network type.
See also: bridge.

general MIDI
A standardization of channel numbers for MIDI. General MIDI allows exchange of MIDI files while retaining the original sounds. For example: a piano still sounds like a piano after transferring the MIDI *file* to another computer and does not sound like a guitar or other instrument.
See also: musical instrument digital interface.

generation

Indication of the number of times *audio* and *video* material has been copied from one medium to another. As copying analog audio and video material adds *noise* and causes other deficiencies, there is a maximum number of generations. Digital material can be copied infinitely because each copy is identical to the original.

genlock

A device that synchronizes *analog video* signals from an external source (such as a video cassette recorder) with *digital video* signals, so they can be merged. It is possible to program where in the new picture, the video *image* or the computer image are to appear. Applications are, among others, *tele-conferencing* and the adaptation of computer-graphics for video *editing*.
See also: alpha channel; chroma keying; overlay; authoring.

geographic information system

GIS - System for storing maps and demographic data digitally. The advantages, among others are:
- easy adjustment of geographic and demographic data;
- integrating small parts into a whole;
- visualizing future changes. For instance, GIS data is used in design programs that can produce a spatial view of a housing project.

geometry

The mathematics of the properties of three-dimensional objects such as dimensions and coordinates, lines, angles, surfaces and solids. With the help of mathematical methods, the angle of rotation and elevation of objects are examined and/or created. Geometry is of great importance to applications such as CAD (*computer-aided design*) and GIS (*geographic information systems*).
See also: coordinate system; virtual reality.

GIF

See: Graphic interchange format.

gigabyte

Approximately one billion bytes.
To be precise, 2 to the power of 30 = 1,073,741,824 bytes.

glare

The reflection of *ambient light* on the surface of a screen, which makes it difficult to distinguish the display.
See also: anti-reflection surface panel.

glass master

A glass disc on which the data of a *master tape* are stored in the form of *pits*. From this male mold a number of female discs are made, the copies (pressings) of which—called *stampers*—are used for *replication*.

glitch

Deformation of video pictures due to interference by external devices or the corruption of the source signal. Whenever a glitch is recorded, the effect is irreversible.
See also: video errors; artifacts.

glyph

1. A symbol or pictogram for conveying non-verbal information.
2. A system of coding in the form of printed symbols which, when scanned, are referenced by the computer and converted into data on screen.
3. Bar codes on paper documents that give information when scanned. After scanning a glyph in, a table can show a formula in a spreadsheet.

gobo

A photographic term. A black screen positioned in such a way that it deflects the light of one or more studio lights. This prevents light entering directly into the camera lens. It can also create shadow effects.
See also: scrim.

going down

A term used when a computer system completely stops functioning. This can happen due to a *bug* or an error. At the moment of going down current *data* are often damaged. If files are regularly backed up, they can be restored from tape.
Normally, a system is shut down because the system operator or technician wants to change or maintain the system.

Gouraud shading

A method for coloring a 3D-representation with color *gradients* to achieve certain visual effects.
There are utilities which are used to avoid huge and complicated calculations. The main procedure is triangulating the area to be colored. The real colors are calculated at the angles of the triangle; the rest of the trangle is then filled with the relevant color gradients. However, there are some disadvantages to this procedure. The gradients are not shown as fluid as they should be.
See also: shading.

gradient

A gradual changing of color and/or *gray scale*. A gradient may cause problems when printed. If a *printer* or recorder does not have sufficient *resolution*, it may generate *banding*.

gradient (fill)

A color fill of an object with one or more color shades. In illustration, programs can be varied according to angle and type of *gradient*. Color gradients are also applied in 3D-coloring.
See also: shading.

grain

The light-sensitive silver particles of a photographic *film* form an irregular pattern called the grain. The more sensitive the photographic material is to light, the larger the grain. The fineness of the grain structure determines how many lines per millimeter can be reproduced.

graphic coprocessor

GCP - An extra processor, usually installed on a *video adapter* which provides a higher processing speed by converting computer data for *monitor* displaying.

graphic file format

See: file format; bitmap format; vector format.

graphic interchange format

GIF - A graphic *file format* of the *bitmap* type. GIF has been developed by Compuserve, an American *on-line* network. GIF files are compressed using the LZW-algorithm. File transmission via a *modem* is much faster when the file has been compressed.
See also: compress; Lempel-Ziv-Welch.

graphic mode

A method where each *pixel* on the display is controlled individually by the computer. This is in contrast with text *mode* where complete characters are sent to the display. The graphic mode is increasingly applied, among others caused by the emergence of the *graphical user interfaces.*

graphical environment manager

GEM - A *graphical user interface* by Digital Research (now owned by Novell). Programs have to be specially written in order to be run by GEM.

graphical user interface

GUI - A graphical 'command center'. From this center, commands can be given to the *operating system* or to the software. GUI is a kind of *desktop* where functions and elements are displayed graphically instead of textually.

All elements can be activated with a *mouse button*, which serves as an alternative to the keyboard. This makes the use of the computer and software easier and more pleasant for most people.

See also: Macintosh; Windows.

gray balance

The necessary balance in printing between the process colors cyan, magenta and yellow. An equal amount of cyan, magenta and yellow makes gray. When one of the three colors dominates, no gray forms. Consequently, the gray balance is not correct. The gray balance is closely related to the *color balance*. When the gray balance is not correct, neither is the color balance.

gray scale

1. A scale from white to black of graduated gray values. This scale is used for *verifying* a graphic production process.
2. Set-up of a *scanner* or *digital camera*. The picture will be more realistic when more gray scales can be produced, in particular when printing a photo. In practice, a minimum of 256 gray scales is used.
3. A paper gray scale (for example from Kodak or Agfa), used in (digital) photography as a measure for the exposure of the lightest and darkest areas in a scene. Sometimes gray scales are imitated by screening a picture like a newspaper photograph. This, however, is another technique.

See also: half-tone; screen (to).

gray-scale scanner

A *scanner* that converts the colors of a picture or photograph into a digital picture composed of gray scales. The number of gray scales varies per scanner and per *pixeldepth*, this means the number of bits by which one pixel is described.

A 1-bit scanner can read black-and-white pictures; an 8-bit scanner can read 256 gray scaled pictures.

Gray scales must not be confused with *half-tone*, which simulates gray scales by screening a picture like a newspaper photograph.

greeking

Displaying text as gray bands. It is used for quickly showing a *layout*, because this way the screen builds up promptly. When pages are shown in reduced size (e.g. thumb nail size), the software usually applies greeking. This expression originates from the traditional graphic trade, where Greek texts often were used by designers to simulate text in a designing phase.

Green Book
A book of standards by Philips, published in 1988, containing information and instructions necessary to develop a CD-i application. This book describes the disc, the playback equipment and the system software. The CD-i structure allows all related CD formats to be played on a CD-i player (except *CD-ROM*).
See also: Compact Disc Interactive.

grid
A systematic division into planes bounded by vertical and horizontal construction lines. Such a grid is used in many *desktop publishing* and drawing programs. For easier determining of the position and dimensions of an element, the lines can often be made 'magnetic'.
See also: guideline; snap to.

grip
A person in a *film* or *video* production responsible for mounting the *camera* on places indicated by the *director* or camera man. The camera can simply be mounted on a *dolly* or *crane*, but sometimes it is more complicated requiring special constructions on moving cars, flying helicopters, etc.

group (to)
Combining two or more elements within an illustration or page making them behave as one element when edited.

guaranteed bandwidth
Guaranteed transmission capacity of a connection.
See also: bandwith; 100Base-VG; broadband.

guideline
Vertical and horizontal construction lines on a display. These lines are used in many *desktop publishing* and drawing programs. It allows easier determining of the position and dimensions of an element. The lines can often be made 'magnetic'.
See also: snap to; grid.

gutter

A designation for white space on a page. A gutter may point to a *header margin*, middle white, *column gutter*, *back margin* and *tail margin*.

H

H.261
A *CCITT* standard for video compression.
See also: H.320.

H.320
An umbrella standard for *video conferencing*. The standard defines the communication between various video conferencing devices. The image *resolution* is 352 * 288 pixels and is called Common Intermedia Format.

hacker
See: cyberpunk(s).

hair-space
See: space.

hairline
An extremely fine rule with a thickness of 0.1 mm or less. *Laser printers* with a *resolution* of 300 dpi are not able to print rules that give less than 0.08466-mm (1/300 inch) thick.

half duplex
A term used when *data communication* between two computers is one-way at any given time.
See also: full duplex.

half-tone
1. In graphics: a gray or color value which is reproduced with dots whose size and frequency determine the intensity of the (color) *shade*. This technique is used for monitors, scanners and in print. Half-tone must not be confused with *gray scale* (contour) which represents real shades of gray.
See also: gray scale; line-art.
2. In music: the value of the smallest possible interval between tones in the diatonic scale, for instance e and f (between mi and fa) or b and c (between ti and do) also between notes with a sharp (upward) or flat (downward) notation and the following full note.

The chromatic scale is made up entirely of ascending or descending half-tones.

Ascending: c - cis - d - dis - e - f - fis - g - gis - a - ais b.

Descending: c - b - bis - a - as - g - es - f - e - es - d - des - c.

hand-held scanner

A manually operated hand-sized digital *scanner*.

handshaking

The exchange of signals for establishing communication between two devices. The handshake synchronizes the devices so that a device only transmits when the other is ready to receive.

hard disk

A rigid aluminum disk with a magnetic coating. Read/write heads record *data* to or read data from the disks. Hard disk is the generic term used for the built-in, non-removable type of disk which has a much larger capacity than a diskette. There is, however, an intermediate form, the *removable hard disk*, which has the same capacity but is exchangeable. Another variant is the 'hard card' which is a hard disk mounted on a *plug-in* card that fits in an extension slot of the computer.

In the 1980s a hard disk was also called a Winchester, the name IBM gave to the technology used in the first hard disks.

See also: track; cluster.

hard space

See: space.

hardware

The physical equipment of a computer system (as opposed to the software, or programs) This can consist of the basic computer plus extensions: monitor, printer, mouse, keyboard, cables, etc.

hardware key

Also known as dongle. A connector, sold together with a computer program, which serves as a key in order to secure access to the program. The connector contains a circuit which holds a code. When the connector is attached to the *parallel port* a program can retrieve the code. Without the code the program will not run. The dongle prevents illegal copying of software.

hashing

A method for referencing and accessing *data*. The key which identifies

the data is translated into the numbered location where the information is stored on disk, thus enabling fast access.
See also: indexing.

head

The electromagnetic or optical part of recording and/or playback equipment which writes or reads the tape or disk. There are three types of heads: read-heads, write-heads and read/write-heads. The alignment of read- or write-heads is linear for hard disks and can be linear or rotating for tape.
See also: flying erase head; helical scan.

head crash

This occurs when the read/write *head* comes into physical contact with the rotating disk, for instance after a collision with a dust grain. The head scratches the disk rendering the *data* unreadable. A *hard disk* suffers 'total loss' after a *crash*.
See also: flying height; landing zone.

head end

Equipment which controls the two-way traffic connections of a *broadband* coaxial network. Its task is to route signals from the upstream (i.e. from the network nodes) to the downstream channel (to the nodes). Its secondary function is the distribution of available bandwidths across the channels.
See also: cable TV network.

head frame

The first *frame* number of the *video* or *audio segment* of an image.
See also: chapter; videodisc.

head gap

See: flying height.

head mounted display

HMD or visette - A helmet with two built-in screens, one for each eye. Stereoscopic vision (*3D*) is simulated by presenting the left and right images from slightly different angles. The visette is used for VR (*virtual reality*) programs.

head tracking

The sensing and measuring of head movements with the *head mounted display* of *virtual reality* system.

header

1. *Data* format: the technical instructions found at the beginning of a data *file*. These instructions are also called *header information*.
2. In typography: running headline at the top of each page of a publication containing reference information such as publication, chapter or article title, date or word reference, etc.
3. Term in digital imaging which refers to the information at the beginning of a CD-ROM *sector*. The information contained in the header indicates where the CD-ROM player can access the data necessary for playback.

header information

(Usually invisible) information at the beginning of a data *file* that an application program needs to process and print the file, consisting of details such as program title, *file format*, etc. The *header* is visible under certain circumstances, for instance in the case of *PostScript* files which are encoded in ASCII. A separate program is usually needed to access the header.

See also: American Standard Code for Information Interchange.

header margin

Margin above the type-area of a page.

helical scan

The manner in which a video head scans *magnetic tape*. By moving the tape across the head and simultaneously rotating the head, the speed necessary for writing and reading the video images is reached. The video head is positioned at 30 degrees to the tape transporter. The resulting angled track allows an increase in the tape surface available for processing. The video head reads one *frame* per rotation. By using two heads each *field* can be read separately. If the tape is mounted around the video head, this results in a spiral form, which explains the term helical.

Hercules graphics card

HGC - A *video card* introduced by Hercules Computer Technology in 1982, which has since become a recognized standard. The Hercules standard allows only monochrome reproduction with a *resolution* of 720 * 348 *pixels*.

Hertz

Hz - Hertz is the name given to wave *frequency*. Hertz is equal to one impulse per second.
See also: refresh rate.

Hi-8

Video system on 8-mm tape developed by Sony. This format is suitable for semi-professional use.

hidden-line removal

A method for rendering a *3D* wire model as a solid object. This method makes the surfaces invisible which would also not be visible to the naked eye. The simplest solution is to decide which surfaces would normally be visible to an observer from a particular angle. The angles away from the observer are then eliminated.
The method can be inaccurate with objects that are placed in front of each other (the background objects then shine through the objects in front). Only by applying complex calculations can realistic representation be achieved.
See also: wire frame; modeler.

hierarchical link

The linking of two objects, referred to as the parent and the child. Any changes made to the parent are automatically inherited by the child, for instance if a hand moves, the position of the fingers will also change, whereas the fingers can move without affecting the position of the hand.
See also: inverse kinematics.

high definition television

HDTV - A television standard for high picture quality. The high quality is obtained by doubling the number of scan lines from 625 to 1250. The picture *resolution* is therefore considerably higher. Another distinct change is found in the dimensions of the TV screen. The current *PAL*, *NTSC* and *SECAM* screens have a height:width ratio of 3:4. In HDTV this is 9:16. This wider format agrees better with our natural way of seeing.
The HDTV technology brings about many more changes besides an improved TV screen. New graphic processors, new compression techniques and even new *color models* are being developed. HDTV, besides TV, will undoubtedly also have a great impact on other media.
See also: television signal standard.

high DOS memory

Memory capacity of DOS PCs between 640 KB (conventional) and 1 MB.
See also: expanded memory system; extended memory specifications.

high memory area

HMA - The 64-KB area of *memory* in DOS PCs which lies immediately
above the first *megabyte*. This area can only be directly accessed by 16-
bit processors.
See also: Microsoft disk operating system.

high resolution

A high number of dots (per inch) reproduced on screen, paper or *film*.
The higher the dot *density*, the higher the definition and sharpness of
the image.

High Sierra Standard

The first CD-ROM standard named after the area near Lake Tahoe in
the Sierra Nevada, where this standard was conceived. This standard
later became the official *ISO 9660* standard.
See also: Compact Disc Read Only Memory.

high-density compact disc

HDCD - A *compact disc* of the second generation, also called Multimedia CD. Two types are developed by Philips/Sony and Toshiba
(1994) respectively. The HDCDs have a high data *density* namely
3.7 gigabytes (Philips/Sony) and 4.2 gigabytes (Toshiba). The
Philips/Sony HDCD uses a double layered disc; the Toshiba HDCD is
double sided. In both cases the capacity doubles. For comparison: a
first-generation CD holds only 650 megabytes of information. The
higher storage capacity is obtained using a red *laser* with a shorter
wave length.
The capacity of HDCD allows recordings of movies with a play time of
more than two hours in normal *broadcast quality* (*PAL*, *NTSC*). For this,
compression method MPEG-2 is used (MPEG-1 attains one half the
resolution of broadcast quality). The high-density compact disc with
accompanying players is expected to be available to the public by the
end of 1996/beginning of 1997.
See also: Motion Picture Expert Group; television signal standard.

high-performance file system

HPFS - The method of *file* organization used by *OS/2* systems. Fast
access to the storage units is achieved via the *cache memory*. This
system allows file names of up to 254 characters.

hints

Font description that contains important typographical *information* concerning the characters of a particular font. These hints are used to present the deformation of the characters when transformed from *vector* to *bitmap format* for output. Most clearly the benefit can be seen when rendering small type at low screen or *printer* resolutions.

hit point

The decisive *scene* in a movie where, for dramatic effect, supporting music needs to be introduced or changed.

HMSF

Hours:Minutes:Seconds:Frames.
See also: time code.

hologram

Three-dimensional *image* reproduced through a combination of lasers.

holostore

A system for storing three-dimensional images, where light-sensitive crystals are used which can distinguish patterns of light.

horizontal blanking interval

The time needed for the electron beam of a screen to travel from the end of a scan line to the beginning of the next one. At the end of the final scan line a so-called *vertical blanking interval* starts.
See also: cathode ray.

horizontal scaling

Distorting the relationship between the height and width of an object or text along the x-axis by expansion or reduction. This distorts the original *font* appearance.
See also: scaling.

host

The central computer that controls the dumb terminals of a *network*.

hot key

A key or key combination that starts the execution of a function within the resident program. A good example is the *screen dump* routine, where the routine itself may not appear on screen and must therefore be activated by a hot key.

hot text
A bold or colored key word or text which, when activated, performs a programmed task.

hot-spot
Extreme highlight in an *image*, usually caused by light reflection.
See also: video errors.

house style
The recurring use of predetermined typographical design.

hub
Equipment used as the point of distribution within a *network*. The point at which the various cables join. The hub is used in systems with a *star* configuration. There are two types: active and passive. An active hub bumps up the signals, whereas the passive hub merely transmits the signals received from the terminals to the *server* and vice versa.

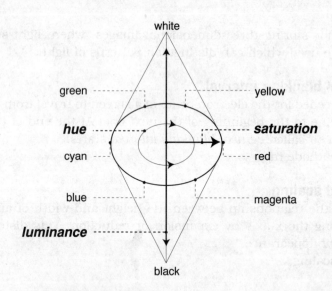

hue, saturation, luminance
HSL - system for defining colors as applied to screens and pigments.
- Hue refers to the color (yellow, blue, etc.)
- *Saturation* refers to the strength of a color (*shade*). A pigment becomes saturated by adding white pigment. On screen a color becomes saturated by adding white light. As applied to print: the lower the screen percentage the lower the ink coverage therefore the higher the saturation.

- *Luminance* refers to the amount of black present in a color and therefore its intensity: the more black the lower the luminance.
See also: color synthesis; color models.

hue, saturation, value
See: hue, saturation, luminance.

Huffman encoding
A much used compression *algorithm* that causes no loss of *data*. This algorithm replaces long recurring code strings with short codes. Two methods are applied in compression programming. Either the existing code tables are used to replace code strings or a code table is generated during the compression process, based on the data to be compressed.
See also: compress.

hybrid computer
A type of computer incorporating *analog* and *digital* components. The converters that transform analog data to digital and vice versa are linked. This allows the processing of analog as well as digital data.
See also: digital-to-analog converter; analog-to-digital converter.

hypertext
An application which allows digital texts to be used interactively. *Interactive* means the ability of the user to select and sequence the *data* on offer. The underlying principle is the prior linking of words or terms between different text files. These links are made between words and terms which are logically or contextually associated. The key words are highlighted on screen by appearing in a bold face or in a different color. The user can make the linked text appear by activating the key word(s). The hierarchical structure allows the user to penetrate the available information at ever increasing levels of depth and width.

hypertext link
A link made between words or terms in different text files. These links enable the user to select the available information interactively.
See also: hypertext.

hyphen
Short horizontal stroke indicating the division of a word at the end of a line. Also used to link words or parts of words to each other.
See also: dash.

I

i.txt
See: interactive teletext.

ice-cap
A cooler mounted on an Intel 80486 processor to prevent overheating. Mostly processors with *clock* speeds of 33 MHz, 50 MHz and up run the risk of heating up over the critical 85 degrees Celsius mark. The risk of malfunctioning or even breakdown is considerably higher at high temperature.

The ice-cap is made of a Peltier element for active cooling and integrated electronics that keep the processor on a constant temperature of 20 to 25 degrees Celsius.

icon
A graphic symbol that represents a program or function in a *graphical user interface*. By clicking the *mouse* on an icon a program is activated or a command carried out.

IEEE
See: Institute of Electrical and Electronic Engineers.

image
A digital reproduction of a picture. A *scanner* for instance can record this picture. A computer program can also generate an image.
See also: computer graphics.

image compression
A specific technique for *image* compressing.
See also: compress; Joint Photographic Expert Group; Moving Picture Expert Group.

image mapping
Applying a *texture* to a 3D-object and subsequent projection of the texture on the surface.
See also: mapping; reflection mapping; bump mapping; 3D.

image pacs
Specification for the five different *resolutions* used for recording images on a *Photo CD*. These five resolutions, expressed in *pixels,* are:

128 * 192   for contact printing and for use in directories of image bases;

256 * 384   for use as low-resolution images in publishing programs (OPI applications);

512 * 768   for display on television;

1024 * 1536   for display on High-Definition Television;

2048 * 3072   for photo printing and for use in publications.

See also: Pro-Photo CD; open prepress interface.

imager
Photo camera that shoots digital pictures. The picture is projected via the lens on the light-sensitive cells of an image sensor and converted into an *analog* signal. An *analog-to-digital converter* transforms the picture into a digital image that can be stored directly in the computer. An imager functions like a *scanner*, but has a variety of possibilities as a traditional photo camera, while a scanner has a fixed recording distance, maximum format and fixed exposure time.

See also: imaging.

imaging
1. Creating and/or *editing* an image (design) with a computer. An architect, for example, can convert his design into a *3D* CAD design, which can be shown from all sides, allowing the client to get a good impression. Another example is editing digital images with a computer.
2. *Digital photography* with an *imager.* An electronic method to store images in a computer for further processing without the use of *film.*

IMG
A graphic *file format* of the *bitmap* type. This format is used by GEM programs. The file format limits images to a maximum of 256 colors.

See also: graphical environment manager.

IMPACT
See: Information Marketing Policy Actions.

implementation
1. The final stage in the development of a computer application, where hardware and software are installed and readied for the end-users.
2. The process of adding new programs, devices and/or procedures to an existing application.

in-betweens

Animation term for images in between *key-frames*. These images are very time-consuming to make and therefore they are made by the *animator*'s assistants. In computer animation the computer takes over the creation of the in-betweens.

incremental backup

Backup copy of files created or changed since the last backup session (i.e. make a backup copy of all files of which the *archive bit* is on). After copying the backup program turns the archive bit off.
See also: differential backup; full backup.

incremental vector

A vector of which the end is defined as a shift relative to the starting point.

indent

Extra white space at the beginning of *paragraphs* to distinguish one paragraph from another. The traditional method prescribes that the indentation is the same as the used font size. This is called: with square white. When a text contains a lot of short paragraphs, indentation may decrease readability.

Indeo

A compression/decompression method (codec), developed by Intel, for *digital video* on a DOS computer. The codec is available in a software and a hardware version. An Intel 750i processor is applied in the hardware version.
See also: coder/decoder.

indexing

A technique for storing and retrieving *data* using a key. This allows retrieving a data *record* directly by specifying the key without having to read from the beginning of the file until the desired record is encountered. Indexing is building an index of keys that identify records along with references to the location of the record within the file. The key can be composed of one or more fields in the record. The index is stored together with the data.
See also: database management system; hashing.

inferior

Letter or figure in a smaller *font* placed just below the *base line*. In publishing programs the inferior's size and position are generally adjustable.

infinite loop
A programming *bug* causing infinite repetition of the same instructions.

info highway
See: information highway.

infomercial
A commercial in the form of a documentary with the following characteristics:
1. it is longer than usual;
2. it looks like an informative program.
See also: commercial; infotainment.

information
A set of *data* enhanced with coherence and purposes.

information highway
Name for (future) *broadband* data communication. Broadband allows transmission of large amounts of data. This makes applications such as *video-on-demand* and various forms of *interactive* programs feasible. The information highway is commonly viewed as the most important communication instrument for the 21st century's information society.

Information Marketing Policy Actions
IMPACT - A European program with the following objectives:
1. Creation of an internal European market for information services.
2. Assess the weak and strong sides of existing information services and boost the competitive power of European information suppliers.
3. Stimulate the use of advanced information services.
4. Encourage European cooperation with special attention to small- and medium-sized business and so-called underdeveloped regions.
5. Using results of other European or national programs in order to realize the objectives 1 to 4 described above.

information retrieval
Selectively (possibly from a remote location using a telephone or network connection) retrieving existing information from text, data and image files.

information-junkie
An individual addicted to *information*.

infotainment
Mixture of *information* and entertainment.
See also: infomercial; commercial.

initial
Enlarged first capital of a *paragraph*. An initial often takes up more than one line (two-line initial, three-line initial) and is divided in hanging (or dropped) and raised. Initials predate the invention of *typography* (monks' handwriting).
See also: drop initial.

> **I**n the heart of the large island of Niphon and in a mountainous and wooded region, fifty leagues from Yokohama, is hidden that marvel of marvels - the necropolis of the Japanese Emperors.

initialization
Set-up activities that a system, device or program requires. Before a new storage medium can be used for storage, a number of actions must be carried out. Also, when a program starts, registers and memory locations must be set-up. This is called initialization.

insert edit
The addition or overwriting of a video segment of an existing recording, without altering the *control-track*.

insert position
Location of the *cursor* in the text where newly typed text is inserted.

instant jump
A technique used in *LaserVision* videodisc recorders that allows jumping backward or forward a maximum of 50 frames without blanking the monitor.
See also: blanking level.

Institute of Electrical and Electronic Engineers
IEEE - An American organization that develops and establishes standards in the field of telecommunication, computers and local area networks.

instructional designer
A person who designs the instructive part of a multimedia production.

Integrated Services Digital Network
A national, European and worldwide digital telecommunication *network*, presently under construction, that will allow faster and more

voluminous *data* exchange. In Europe ISDN is constructed by the telecommunication companies of the EC countries.

ISDN can be interpreted as follows:

I - Integrated (and standard access)

S - Services (standardized)

D - Digital (fully digital communication)

N - Network (possibly switched).

In general, two connections are possible:

- The Basic Rate Interface, or BRI, provides two B channels (capacatity 64 Kpbs each) and one 16 Kbps D channel for a total of 144 Kbps. The two B channels can be used simultaneously, for talking and at the same time sending a fax or for *joint-editing*.
- The Primary Rate Interface, or (PRI), provides 23 B channels and one 64 Kpbs D channel (USA). In Europe, PRI includes 30 B channels and one D channel, with a total capacity of nearly 2 Mbits/s.

ISDN gives the opportunity of developing new products and services in the medical, social and economic field. The European PTTs (Post, Telephony and Telegraphy) have an agreement on which facilities will be uniformly supplied.

ISDN is only a small advance towards the digital world because its transmission capacity is too low for *multimedia* applications. For these applications *Broadband* ISDN (B-ISDN) is required, expected to become operational after the year 2000. This will allow for a wide range of applications in one network. Examples are: video conferencing, high-resolution TV, high-speed data transmission, etc. In B-ISDN transmission speeds from 64 Kbits/s to 135 Mbits/s will be supported.

See also: Memorandum of Understanding; videophony.

interactive

User participation during program use. The user decides tempo and sequence of the program. This also involves answering questions and choosing from options the program presents.

The program is designed to respond to the widest range of conceivable situations, but the user decides what course the program will take.

See also: branching.

interactive teletext

An *interactive* version of teletext where a telephone connection is used to give commands, also called i.txt. The TV viewer presses the telephone buttons to indicate which page must be shown. The telephone takes over the function of the remote control. Interactive teletext advantages over classic (linear) teletext are:

- the response time is only one second;

- the amount of information is virtually unlimited;
- the TV viewer can react to the presented information, for example to order or reserve products or services.

Interactive teletext was invented by Gustaaf van Ditzhuyzen and Fred Kappetijn in 1983 when they were employed by the Dutch publisher VNU.

interactive television

A two-way communication system that uses television, cable TV, telephone and other media. This technology allows the viewer to influence the course of a television program. Theoretically, it offers endless possibilities for new products and services. Today telephone, cable, TV and video companies and producers of PC and TV applications are competitors in the commercial interest involved in *interactive* television. Issues such as, will the PC be part of TV or TV part of the PC and who will have the strongest position if multimedia finally breaks through?, still remain to be solved.

See also: cable TV network; set-top box.

interactive video

Integrated video and computer techniques allowing the viewer to decide what videos are played.

interface

An interface is a link between hardware or software components. SCSI (*small computer system interface*) is an example of a hardware interface. Microsoft *Windows* is an example of a software interface.

See also: graphical user interface.

interframe coding

See: interframe compression.

interframe compression

Compression method for moving pictures such as *animation* or *video*. By coding empty areas or areas in one color, *data* is compressed. The compression standard of the *Motion Picture Experts Group* is based on interframe compression.

See also: compress.

interlace flicker

The interlace technique for monitors produces a flickering display caused by the difference in brightness of the odd and even scan lines.

See also: interlaced/non-interlaced; refresh rate.

interlaced/non-interlaced

Interlaced is a technique used in monitors where a *cathode ray* draws a scan line at each vertical passage. First the even then the odd scan lines. Generally used for high *resolutions* (1024 * 768 pixels). Its disadvantage is that it produces a flickering display.

With non-interlaced the cathode ray, when passing vertically, scans all lines on the screen one after another. Non-interlaced screens present a more settled *image* than interlaced screens.

See also: interlace flicker; refresh rate.

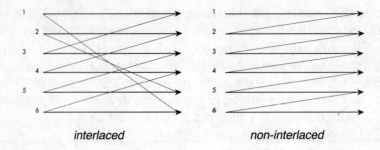

interlaced   non-interlaced

interleaving

Integrating various types of data into one recording. On CD-i, for instance, video, audio, text and data are recorded combined to create animations with accompanying sound. Its *operating system* (CD-RTOS) is designed to detect and correctly reproduce the various data types.

See also: Compact Disc Interactive; Compact Disc Real Time Operating System; audio video interleaved.

intermediate materials

All media selected for use on a *videodisc*, such as film and video pictures, 16-mm films, 35-mm slides, etc.

International Electrotechnical Commission

IEC - An international standards organization, closely related to the ISO, that consists of several electrotechnical committees from countries all over the world.

See also: International Standards Organization.

International MIDI Association

IMA - Distributor of MIDI specifications.

See also: Musical Instrument Digital Interface.

International Standards Organization

ISO - An international organization founded in 1946 and residing in

Geneva. The ISO sets up international standards in every field except for electric and electronic applications. This area is served by the IEC (*International Electrotechnical Commission*).

As far as information technology is concerned ISO and IEC are joined together in JTC1 (joint technical committee). The very extensive field of activity is divided among more than 160 technical committees (TCs) and approximately 2300 subcommittees and work groups. These committees and work groups are staffed via the national standards organizations of approximately 80 member countries.

International Telecommunications Union

ITU - An international organization which develops standards for the telecommunications industry, including *video conferencing*. The ITU resides in Geneva, Switzerland. The organization is responsible to the United Nations. The Telecommunications Standardization Sector is a division of ITU.

Internet

A worldwide *network* of computers interlinked via satellites and telephone networks. Through Internet all kinds of networks can communicate.

Internet was founded in 1969 by the Pentagon under the name ARPAnet. It was further developed when a number of large universities started to create a network. The communication between universities was through telephone lines.

The network grew when the government and various companies and institutions joined. In mid-1995 an estimated 35 million computer users have access to the Internet.

Internet consists of three parts:

1. E-mail. With the E-mail system, electronic messages can be sent all over the world.
2. Usenet. Electronic newsgroups exchanging questions, discussions and experiences on all kinds of subjects.
3. Public Databases. Users consult databases for every conceivable subject. Examples are university libraries and shareware databases.

Internet uses TCP/IP.

See also: Transmission Control Protocol/Internet Protocol; cyberspace; electronic mail.

internetworking

The communication between, not necessarily similar, networks. Linking is realized through bridges and gateways.

See also: bridge; gateway; protocol.

interpersonal communication

Direct and real time communication between individuals through computers, usually using *multimedia*. Applications are, amongst others, *video conferencing* and *joint-editing*.

interpolation

1. A video term for calculating an intervening value in a range of known numbers. Interpolation is used as soon as a long signal interruption occurs while reading an *optical disc*. In that case no information is supplied; however with interpolation an average value is calculated based on the signal received before or after. This prevents display interruptions.
2. Scan and print technique. Also used for calculating an intervening value in a series of known numbers. This technique is applied to achieve an apparent higher *resolution* when printing on paper or reading pictures with a *scanner*. This optical effect is realized by computing the extra dots based on the values present. The newly calculated dots are placed as an average between the dots present.

See also: dithering; anti-aliasing.

interruptible display

A function in programs that interrupts building-up the screen as the user starts a next process. It eliminates waiting until the screen is fully built-up after a previous process has been completed. Consequently, this function accelerates the operation considerably.

intraframe coding

See: intraframe compression.

intraframe compression

A term for compressing a still as a part of a video compression. Redundancy in consecutive pictures is used to decrease the amount of *data*.

A typical intraframe method is the *discrete cosine transform*.

inverse color highlighting

See: reverse video.

inverse kinematics

A 3D *animation* technique. A link type that, besides a *hierarchical link*, also contains a feedback mechanism.

For example: when the fingers (= child object) of a hand (= parent object) are moved, the hand will also start moving from a given *point*. On a point further away, the arm will also start moving as a result of the feedback mechanism.

iris
1. Photography. An adjustable lens opening made of metal blades sliding together, that regulates the amount of light that enters the lens. The diaphragm is adjustable to diaphragm numbers *(f-stops)*. These are international standard values indicating standard lens openings.
2. Video term. A video *transition* effect where the image of the current screen disappears from the screen in spirals.
See also: video effects.

IRIX
A *operating system* based on *Unix* (release 4) by the Silicon Graphics corporation. IRIX is used for Mips' RISC processors.
See also: reduced instruction-set computing.

ISDN
See: Integrated Services Digital Network.

ISO
See: International Standards Organization.

ISO 9660
See: High Sierra Standard.

isolation
A technique for simultaneous shooting with several video cameras. Each video camera is connected to its own video recorder. During video *editing* the shots are combined.

italic
Oblique font variation based on a *roman* type. An italic variation is designed separately. An oblique letter is not always an italic. Some oblique fonts are romans, while some italics are practically straight. Romans that are made oblique electronically are not italics either.
See also: slant.

J

jack
See: plug.

jaggies
Jagged letters on a screen or a printed page caused by enlargement of a *bitmap* image.
See also: bitmap format.

jewel box
A synthetic container for *compact discs* that has the form of a flat box, consisting of three parts which are assembled by clicking them together:
1. a transparent cover that can hold a removable information sheet;
2. a transparent bottom;
3. a holder with clips to clasp the CD.

jewel case
See: jewel box.

jitter
A small interruption in an information stream. Interruption can arise due to a small deviation in the playback speed of audio equipment.

Joint Photographic Experts Group
JPEG
1   A compression standard for *still video*. To attain a high *compression ratio* data is omitted from the compressed image. This causes a quality loss in the decompressed image that depends on the compression ratio.
2. A group of experts that develop algorithms for compressing photos and video stills. This group also defines ISO (*International Standards Organization*) and CCITT *(Consultative Committee for International Telegraph and Telephony)* standards for the application of the algorithms.
See also: JPEG++.

joint work

A piece of work made by several authors and published in such a way that the individual contributions cannot be distinguished.

joint-editing

An ISDN (*Integrated Services Digital Network*) application with two transmission channels. Users can have a voice connection through one *channel* and view/edit a shared computer file through the other channel.

joy stick

A little stick for moving the *cursor* or other movable objects on the screen. Generally used in computer games.
See also: roller controller: touchpad.

JPEG++

An extension to the JPEG algorithm where parts of a still image are selected as foreground or background. The compression level of the defined foreground and background can be set separately. Only a small amount of *data* is lost during compression.
See also: Joint Photographic Experts Group; lossy compression.

jukebox

A playback installation containing several CD-ROMs or videodiscs, comparable to original record jukebox.

jump cut

An artificial *transition* in a *film* or *video shot* as a result of sudden changes in the camera angle, shooting distance or unexpected movements within the picture. Sometimes a jump cut is deliberately used.
See also: video effects.

justification

The adjustment of word and letter *spacing* to make text lines of equal length. The left and right text margins draw a straight line.
Generally the word spacing is set when the text lines are justified. It is also possible to adjust the letter spacing, but this is less pleasing, because the letter appearance differs from line to line.
Large word spacing lacks aesthetic appeal and therefore hyphenation is given priority. Publishing programs allow adjustable spacing size. When word or letter spacing exceed the limits, the relevant text line will be marked for manual correction later.
See also: rivers.

K

Karaoke
Singing along with a musical band. Sometimes the text can be read from a screen. The music can be registered magnetically (tape) or optically.

keeper
See: buy.

kerning
Reducing or enlarging the *spacing* between certain letter combinations. Reducing is called *negative spacing* and enlarging is called positive spacing. Characteristic is that the degree of adaptation of every letter combination can be different. Take for example the combinations VA and rn. The V and A must have a negative spacing because the amount of white is too disturbing, while the r and n need a positive spacing because otherwise an m could be read. Kerning should not be confused with ordinary spacing because with that the degree of negative or positive spacing is the same between each letter combination.

key
A musical term. The key is determined by the note with which a composition ends and the possible sharps or minors. If a composition is played half a tone higher or lower the key changes and with this the number of sharps or minors. If the correct sharps or minors are not played, some tones sound too high or too low. This is caused by the whole and half intervals which appear on pre-arranged places in a scale as well as a composition.
See also: half-tone.

key-frames
1. Some images from a *film* or *video* production that show the outlines of the events.
2. *Animation* term. The images that fulfill a key function because they mark the beginning or the end of a movement. In a drawn animation it is the *animator* who draws these key figures completely. The images between the key-frames are called *in-betweens*.

(See picture next page)

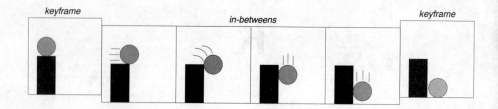

keyframe   in-betweens   keyframe

key-light

Term from photography. In a video or film production the main light serves as the primary lighting of a performance. This is a very intense light with an aimed beam; *quartz lighting* is used. This type of lighting is also used in *digital photography*.
See also: quartz iodide light.

key-signal

A signal which indicates the beginning of each separate image in a video signal. Also, the end of each video line is indicated.

keying

Overlapping video images with the use of electronic techniques.
See also: chroma keying; genlock; alpha channel.

keypad

A small remote control device for a *videodisc* recorder. With this, only *level one videodiscs* and *level two videodiscs* are operated.

keystone effect

A deformation of a projected picture. Deformation occurs when a slide, film, video or computer picture is displayed while the lens of the projector is not at right angles with the projection screen. For example, when the lens is slanted upward, the top of the picture will be wider than the bottom.

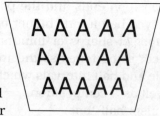

killer application

A computer application that is so useful by itself it justifies any collateral purchases. For example: the first word processing programs were the reason many people decided to buy a computer. Later on they found that the computer was useful for other tasks. Another example is *Mosaic*, a program for browsing the *Internet*. Mosaic has made accessing the Internet easy and visually attractive, and therefore raised the popularity of the Internet tremendously. *OS/2* is an *operating system* that still has no killer application, i.e. an application that only runs with OS/2 and is very useful and so could make the operating system popular.

kilobyte
KB - About 1000 bytes. To be exact: 2 to the power of ten = 1024 bytes.

kiloHertz
1 KHz = 1000 *Hertz*.

kp-height
The distance between the top of the *descender* of the letter k and the lowest point of the ascender of the p.
See also: base line.

L

LAN
See: local area network.

landing zone
Synonym for 'take-off zone'. An area on the *hard disk* where the combined (read/write) *head* is parked the instant the disk stops rotating. This to prevent damage to the magnetizable surface of the disk (for example during transport of the hard disk).
See also: flying height.

lands
The flat areas on an *optical disc* between the *pits.* These areas are not burned in by the *laser* beam during the *mastering* process. In this area the laser beam is reflected completely, whereas pits are areas which are extinguished through interference.

landscape
See: portrait.

laptop
This is the general name for portable computers. The first models were too big and heavy to travel with comfortably. Nevertheless a modern laptop is bigger than 20 * 30 centimeters and weighs more than 3.5 kilograms.
See also: notebook pc; palmtop; pen-based pc.

laser
See: light amplification by stimulated emission radation.

laser printer
With this type of *printer* the image is created by *laser* beam. On those spots the beam touches the paper toner particles are attracted which creates a print. The development of the printing quality of laser printers has not yet stopped. The most advanced printers have now *resolution* of 1200 *dots per inch* (compare: the resolution of an imagesetter is 2400 dpi or higher). A laser printer can print many fonts. Moreover, laser technology makes possible the printing of illustrations and *half-tone* printing of reasonable quality.

laser videodisc
See: videodisc.

LaserDisc
See: Compact Disc Video.

LaserVision
LV - An analog *videodisc* system developed by Philips. The videodisc is used to reproduce color video images and two-channel sound. The operation normally takes place by means of an *interactive* program which is also placed on a videodisc. Unlike the other *data* this program is stored digitally.

A videodisc is 30 cm in diameter and it looks like a large *compact disc*. The data is written and read by the CAV-principle (*constant angular velocity*). The information is scanned by *laser* beam. Information can be stored on both sides. A LV-videodisc contains on each side an input capacity of 54,000 stationary images or 35 minutes *full-screen, full-motion video* with two sound *tracks*. At the beginning of the nineties Phillips changed the name LaserVision to LaserDisc.

See also: LaserVision read only memory; Compact Disc Video.

LaserVision Read Only Memory
LV ROM - The digital brother of *LaserVision*. LaserVision *Read Only Memory* is an *interactive* digital system based on a *videodisc*. Not only is it possible to store two sound channels and 54,000 (*analog*) images on each side of a LV ROM but also 324 megabytes of computer *data*. These may include alphanumeric characters, graphics and/or software. The data is loaded into the computer memory of the videodisc player and can be mixed with video images.

lathe
A function within a *3D* or graphics program: The rotation of a two-dimensional figure around its horizontal or vertical axis. For example: A spherical shape can be created through rotating a circle.

See also: extruding; lofting..

layering
This technique is used in sound reproduction. Different sound sources are combined to reproduce a richer sound.

layers
This term is used in several kinds of programs to indicate that an *image* can be build up with different layers. This offers the advantage that the

layers can be operated and changed independently. With complex drawings all layers, except the one to be changed, can be turned off. This results in a better view and the screen builds up faster.

layout
A term to indicate how to compile a page, such as defining the size and position of illustrations, choosing colors and fonts and fixing supporting elements such as lines, boxes and shadings etc.
See also: typography.

LCD
See: liquid crystal display.

lead-in
Introductory text preceding the main text.

leader
1. The first part of a *magnetic tape*. This part precedes the 'beginning-of-tape' indication. It is used to wind the first part of the tape on a reel.
2. The first images of a *film* or *video* production, often along with opening titles.

leading
Originally a small piece of lead between two succeeding lines to create extra *spacing*. Nowadays it has a different meaning. In *layout* programs spacing is the same as line interval which means the *space* between the base lines of two succeeding lines. The space between the lines and the body size make up the leading.
With automatic leading the spacing is usually 20% of the body size. Of course it is possible to change the leading.

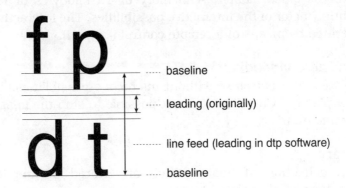

baseline

leading (originally)

line feed (leading in dtp software)

baseline

..stification

..e *alignment* of text within a column. On the left side of the text the first letters are placed in a straight line beneath each other.

Lempel-Ziv-Welch

LZW - A lossless algorithm compression. The basic principle is to look for similarities between *character* codes such as *spacing* which is subsequently changed into shorter codes. The LZW algorithm was developed in 1977 and still forms an important basis for contemporary compression methods, especially with *on-the-fly compression/decompression*.
See also: compress.

level one videodisc

A *videodisc* with little *interactive* possibilities. A level one videodisc is composed of segments *(chapters)*. The *videodisc player* can only be stopped at fixed places on the videodisc. The videodisc player can again be started with the starter of the remote control *(keypad)*. To jump to a certain position on the videodisc it is necessary to enter a *frame* number on the remote control at a frozen image.

level three videodisc

The use of a *videodisc* with almost unlimited *interactive* possibilities. This is possible because the interactive program is operated by an external computer. The *videodisc player* is connected to the computer as a separate *device*.

level two videodisc

The use of a *videodisc* with a considerable amount of *interactive* possibilities. There is an operating program on the videodisc which uses the microprocessor and the internal *memory* of the *videodisc player*. During the *mastering* process the operating program is written onto the *glass master*. A memory of 10 kilobytes or less means a limiting factor of the interactive possibilities. The interactive program is operated by means of a remote control *(keypad)*.

level zero videodisc

The use of a *videodisc* without *interactive* possibilities. The user can only play the videodisc. It is not possible to stop the image or to enter a *frame* number.

library

1. A collection of books which are stored in one location and subsequently ordered by a certain system.

2. The term from the programming knowledge. A collection of standard *functions* and *procedures* which can be used for the development of computer programs. An important advantage is that a well-stacked library can shorten the development of software considerably. Some *programming languages* go with a library and some can be made by the programmer.

ligature
A composing technique originating from the time lead was used. A ligature is a fixed combination of two or more combined letters (especially with the letter f), made to effect a correct position (for example ff, lf, ffi and sometimes also fb, fh, fj, fk.

light
Thin letter belonging to *roman*. There are several gradations of light.

light amplification by stimulated emission of radiation
LASER - A light source which emits an extremely narrow and intense beam of light of high optical quality. It is used to write (burn into) or to read *data* (by exposure after which the reflected light is measured). For example a laser is used in devices such as a *laser printer* and the read *head* of optical units.

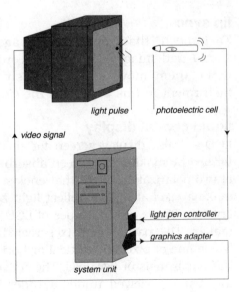

light pen
A *pen* containing a photoelectric cell. The user can indicate certain points on the display and execute the desired action. See also: pen-based pc.

line pairing
A *video error* because of which the lines from the even *field* cover the lines of the odd field and not between.

light pen

line-art
Each image which is build up from black and white and no gray tones (continuous tone). *Half-tone* images also belong to this because the *grid* of a half-tone consists only of black and white.

linear play

1. Sequentially playing a recorded series without any form of interaction. For example: playing an audio CD from beginning to end.
2. A *videodisc* of 30 centimeters in diameter which is operated according to the *constant linear velocity* principle.

line-art

linefeed

This term refers to a soft return a *word processor* places because there is not enough space at the end of a line for a word or part of a word so that this word (part of a word) is placed on the following line by the program.
See also: leading.

link (to)

The process in which the object codes and libraries that form part of a certain application are combined. After this the application can be used independently.
See also: compile (to); library.

lip sync

To indicate that sound and image move simultaneously. Because sound and images are often recorded separately, it is necessary to make them move simultaneously (to synchronize). An important instrument in this process is the *clap board*.

liquid crystal display

LCD - A flat display screen for use in notebooks, etc. The picture is formed by making the screen absorb or reflect light. The screen is made of two polarization filters that enclose liquid crystals. The liquid crystals make a *pixel* absorb or reflect light by applying a electronic field to the crystals. There are two types of LCD screens: passive matrix and active matrix. The passive matrix screen has one transistor that controls a whole line of pixels in vertical or horizontal direction. The active version has one transistor per pixel. The active version has faster screen updates and can be viewed under a wider angle. Active matrix, however, is substantially more expensive than passive matrix and has a larger power consumption. To enhance the visibility of the screen, backlighting is applied. These are lights that are mounted along the edges of the screen.

local application numerical control

LANC - *Video control* method used by Sony and other producers of video

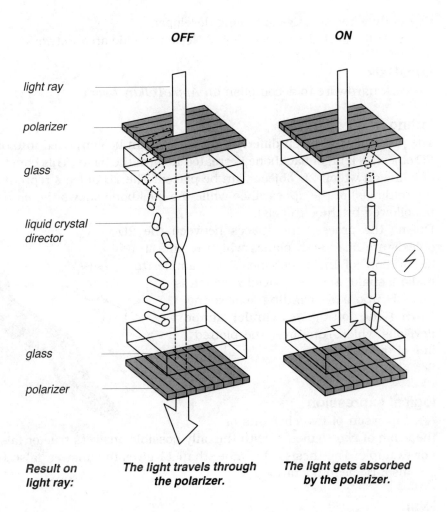

	OFF	**ON**
Result on light ray:	**The light travels through the polarizer.**	**The light gets absorbed by the polarizer.**

devices. The operating communication runs by means of a two-way system and can carry other protocols (such as *Control-S*). Among others the information sent contains *HMSF* time codes and numerical data.

local area network

LAN - A system which connects computers by means of a cable network. This network may also include printers, CD-ROMs, modems and other devices with the purpose to have connected devices communicate with each other and make available expensive peripheral units to several users. Such a network is usually tied to one location and does not use national or international networks like ISDN or a public switching telephone network.

Currently wireless LANs are being developed.
See also: Integrated Services Digital Network; wide area network.

LocalTalk
Network hardware to accomplish an *AppleTalk-network*.

lofting
The process with which different 2D objects can be converted into one 3D object. A kind of backbone is created to form the basis. This consists of a line on which 2D objects can be placed. The 2D objects reproduce the outline(s) of the appearance while the backbone shows the *path* to be followed by the outline(s).

During the process the spaces between the 2D objects are filled with planes which results in a 'decoration' of the backbone. For example: to make a snake a circle is needed which is placed upon a winding backbone. During the lofting, a cylinder shape develops which runs over the plotted line of the backbone.
See also: extruding.

logical expression
A comparison of two elements or the value of two elements, with the only possible answers true or false. For example: The thesis 10 is more than 11 gives the answer 'false'.
See also: Boolean operations.

login
A command which has to be given by the user on a *workstation* to enter a *network*.

logo
A single piece of type comprising a name or product reproduced in a special design with the aim of creating a trademark.

logout
A command given by a user on a *workstation* to end a session on a *network*.

long play
Term used for videodiscs recorded and played according to the *constant linear velocity* principle.

long shot
A *shot* from great distance, for example a person within his surroundings. Such an overall picture is often used as starting *point* of a *scene* and simultaneously serves as reference point for the next takes.
See also: extreme long shot; medium shot; close up.

longitudinal magnetic recording
See: magnetic tape.

longitudinal time code
LTC - A video *time code* recorded as a sound signal on a linear track. The code is not visible on the screen.

look-up table
LUT - A table of comparison for the colors cyan, magenta, yellow and black. This table is used for the initial color corrections during the scanning of color images. These tables incorporate the factors paper, ink and printing press. Deviation in reflection of light of the pure ink colors can be corrected with this table. For example: The pure ink color yellow in an original would theoretically only reflect red and green light and totally absorb blue light. In practice however a small part of the blue light is also reflected. Uncorrected, the scanned image would produce a pollution of color. In the example the digital values would give too much blue and the final reproduction would be less yellow than the original.

loop
An instruction or series of commands in a computer program that repeats itself, for example to check if a number appears in an arithmetic series. With a graphic image of the operation of the program in *flowchart* programs a loop can be applied to indicate that a certain procedure must be repeated.

lossless compression
Method of compression in which no *data* is lost during compression of a *file*. After decompression an exact copy of the original is available.
See also: compress; lossy compression.

lossy compression
Method of compression in which original information is lost. After decompression an exact copy of the original is not available. An example is compression based on the JPEG-standard (*Joint Photographic Experts*

Group). This method is often used for storage of large image or sound files. The method is based on the assumption that a limited loss of *data* is unnoticed after decompression of the file. The advantage of this method is that a higher *compression ratio* is reached in comparison to *lossless compression*.
See also: compress.

low frequency suppression

The suppression of a *frequency* lower than 20 *Hertz*. These frequencies are not audible. Negative effects of these low frequencies are the increase of power consumption and mechanical vibrations.

low resolution

A small number of dots on a screen or on the print of a *printer*. The lower the number of dots, the coarser the image or print.
See also: resolution.

lower case

The normal reading letter without capitals. The term lower case refers to the location of the small letters in the type case of the hand typesetter.

LPT

The female connector of 25 poles at the rear of a computer for the connection of the *printer*. Because communication with the printer takes place with 8 bits simultaneously, another term is *parallel port*.
This is contrary to the *serial port* with which communication takes place *bit* after bit. Nowadays the parallel port is also used for the connection with other devices: tape streamers, hard disks, network adapters, etc.

lumen

1. Internationally accepted unit of luminous flux. One lumen is the luminous flux which a light source emits with the luminous intensity of one *candela* in a certain angle.
2. Photography. Measure for luminous flux of a certain light source which renders a certain *density* of photographic material. That density is similar to the density of the same material by means of a standard bulb with a luminous flux of one lumen.
See also: lux.

luminance

1. Theory of color. The impression of color which is formed because a pure color black is added (*subtractive color synthesis*) or light is

removed (*additive color synthesis*). The more black is added to a color the more the brightness diminishes. And also: the impression of color of an image in full sunlight is brighter than in the shadow (lower intensity of light). With the graphic printing process the brightness is influenced through adding black ink to a color. With monitors (light colors) the brightness is influenced through reducing the light intensity.
2. Video term. The component of brightness in an image signal. With a desired black-white processing an image can still be created because the brightness is present separately.

See also: chrominance; color synthesis; YCC.

lux

A unit of illumination of a light source. It measures the light source on top of an object. The luminous intensity of one lux is caused by a luminous flux of one *lumen* on top of a surface one square meter.
See also: candela.

M

Macintosh

A computer introduced by Apple in 1984. This computer uses the Motorola 68000 CPU-family (*central processing unit*). Characteristic of the machine is the Macintosh *graphical user interface* which was primarily designed by Xerox and introduced for the first time in 1981. The Macintosh uses a graphic screen with symbols which are found on a desk: maps, sheets of paper, a waste paper basket. The computer is mainly operated with a *mouse*. The Macintosh software generally links well with the graphical user interface, so that working with new software is easy to learn. The operating programs are of similar structure and mostly use the same menus and keyboard commands. Because of this set-up the Macintosh gained the reputation of being 'user friendly'. The Macintosh is often used for graphical and multimedia applications.

macro language

Computer instruction languages which do not belong to the standard languages such as BASIC, COBOL, FORTRAN, Assembler etc. Mostly these kinds of languages belong to a certain application to automate hand editing. They include possibilities for comparisons, leaps and calculations. An example of such a language is to be found in the *word processor* WordPerfect.

See also: authoring language; Restructured EXtended eXecutor.

magnetic card

A *card* with a magnetizable stripe attached to it. On this magnetic tape stripe all kinds of *data* can be registered. The magnetic card knows different applications, such as a credit card or parking card. The card can also be used as *memory* of a computer (magnetic card memory).

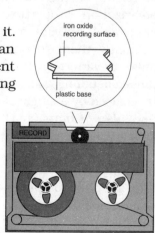

iron oxide
recording surface

plastic base

RECORD

magnetic tape

A tape covered with a thin layer of magnetizable material on which *data* can be registered. This registration is done through polarizing selective parts on the tape.

magneto-optical disc

An *optical disc* which can be written several times (optical rewritable). This method combines the characteristics of magnetic input media such as floppy disks and tapes with the characteristics of an optical disc such as *CD-ROM* and WORM. The regular optical discs can only be written once, while magneto-optical media are rewritable.

See also: write once, read many; magneto-optics.

magneto-optics

An input method in which *laser* techniques and magnetic techniques are combined. Thus, an erasable input medium with a high *density* can be formed. With this technique a laser beam polarizes the magnetic surface of a *disc*.

A magneto-optical disc (MO-disc) consists of four layers. There is a crystalline metal alloy that is a few atoms thick and rests on a thin aluminium layer. The alloy and the aluminium layer are protected on each side by a layer of transparent plastic.

An MO-disc is read using a low-energy polarized laser beam. The laser light is reflected by the aluminium layer. When light is reflected the direction of the polarization is modified by the crystalline layer depending on the state of individual crystals. This difference in polarization direction makes it possible to distinguish between the ones and zeroes of a bit pattern.

An MO-disc is written in two passes: first the crystal layer is heated by a high-energy laser beam to a critical temperature (the Curie level) which resets the polarization properties of each crystal, effectively erasing any previous data by replacing it with zeroes. In the second pass the magnetic head modifies the polarization properties of each applicable crystal, effectively changing them to ones. In the most advanced MO-drives this time-consuming two-pass process is replaced by a single pass.

See also: Compact Disc Read Only Memory.

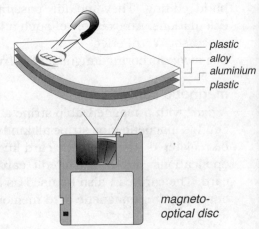

plastic
alloy
aluminium
plastic

magneto-
optical disc

magnify

With graphic computer applications it means the enlargement of the dimensions of a projected image with a certain factor. This enlargement can take place on a *monitor* or projection screen.

mailing
Term for printed advertising or information sent addressed by post.

majuscule
See: upper case.

mandatory entry field
A certain field in a user's *interface* which asks for input from the user. The user must give a legitimate input to continue application. An example of such a field is the input of a password.

map
See: folder.

mapping
With this function is indicated how a *texture* (image) is pasted on the surface of an object. In this mapping function not only scale and orientation of the texture are laid down but also (with *3D* objects) the way in which the texture follows the object. An example of the last function: the texture of a snake skin must follow the 3D object of the snake when the snake moves.
See also: reflection mapping; bump mapping.

markup
A code for parts of a text and elements of a document such as chapter, heading, subheading and paragraph. Producers of software tend to use their own codes with the result that a uniform structure and exchange of text files are made difficult. A known initiative to reach a general standard for text codes is SGML.
See also: Structured Generalized Markup Language.

master font
The making of an *outline font* for use on printers and monitors is based on one master font. Other type sizes are scaled proportionally on the basis of this master font. Each *type size* has its characteristics which change when a letter is made larger or smaller. This may sometimes result in a diminished quality in relation to the master font. For the benefit of readability and in order not to deviate too much from the original design several techniques are used to adapt the letters.
See also: hints; multiple master.

master tape
Term for a videotape, audio tape or film which is edited. A 'master' is

used to make copies for distribution and screening. After that it is usually kept in a safe place. If the tape is of great value there is usually also a *protection master*. If it concerns an interactive *videodisc* there is also an integrated interactive program. The master tape is then used to produce a *glass master*.

See also: intermediate materials.

mastering

The optical recording process for manufacturing a *glass master*. The video and sound material to be recorded are located on the *master tape*. To manufacture a glass master a small *laser* beam is pointed on a rotating *disc*. This disc is covered with a thin layer of photosensitive material. During the recording the *analog video* information is modulated into a *digital* signal by means of a *pulse code modulation*. The digital signal is used to turn the laser on and off. When the laser is turned on, a *pit* is burned into the disc.

See also: photoresist.

Mbit/s

Megabit per second, to be precise: 1,048,576 bits per second. A unit which indicates the speed of transmission. The term is often used to indicate the speed of *network* connections.

Measures to Encourage the Development of the Industry of Audiovisual Production

MEDIA - A European Committee development program which has the following objectives:

- To create a common European audio-visual market in the field of cinema, television and video and in broadcasting by satellite and cable.
- To promote European techniques and culture in the world audio-visual market by creating a European distribution system and production structure.

MEDIA

See: Measures to Encourage the Development of the Industry of Audiovisual Production.

media control interface

MCI - A standard control system for *multimedia* applications. Through MCI a multimedia program can operate the different multimedia files and devices. Commands such as play, stop and record are used.

medium shot
A *shot* between a *close up* and a *long shot*, for example the shot of a person from head to waist.

megabyte
About one million bytes.
To be precise: 2 raised to the power of 20 = 1,048,576.

megahertz
MHz - 1 MHz = 1,000,000 *Hertz*.

Memorandum of Understanding
MoU - A document set up by the European telephone companies which supplies a harmonized introduction of a European ISDN (*Integrated Services Digital Network*). Among others it is arranged such that a number (of many) ISDN facilities will be introduced uniformly. These facilities are indicated with 'Priority 1'. They contain:
- CLIP: Calling Line Identification Presentation. This facility passes the number of the caller to the called user. For this purpose most ISDN telephones have a small *display* on which the number is made visible.
- CLIR: Calling Line Identification Restriction. With this facility the caller can prevent the number being passed on.
- DDI: Direct Dialing In: With this facility the user can dial direct to the user who is connected with a private system or telephone exchange. This form of direct dialing is also already available on the existing telephone network.
- MSN: Multiple Subscriber number. The facility to link different numbers to one connection. This makes it possible, for example, to reach two different applications through two different numbers, even if they are on the same computer.
- TP: Terminal portability. This facility offers the possibility of plugging the telephone into another *socket* during the conversation.
Priority 2 includes:
- AOC: Advice of charge
- CCBS: Completion of calls to bust subscriber
- CD: Call deflection
- CFB: Call forwarding busy
- CFNR: Call forwarding no reply
- CFU: Call forwarding unconditional
- COLP: Connected line identification presentation
- COLR: Connected line identification restriction
- CONF: Add-on-conference call
- CUG: Closed user group

- CWL: Call waiting
- ECT: Explicit call transfer
- FPH: Freephone supplementary service
- HOLD: Call hold
- MMC: Meet me conference
- MCID: Malicious call identification
- 3PYT: Three party service
- SUB: Subaddressing
- UUS: User-to-user signaling

memory
The part of the computer where *data* is stored. Mostly the internal memory is meant. With external memory is meant disk drives, tape streamers etc.

memory bank
A logical unit of *memory*. The internal memory of a computer is divided into so-called memory banks, mostly the size of 1, 2 or 4 slots for memory *chips*.
See also: single-inline memory module.

menu
A *window* on the *monitor* with several functions from which the user can choose by means of the *mouse* or keyboard. There are different kinds of menus such as:
1. *Pull-down menu*. This consists of a main menubar at the top of the screen from which the submenus can be 'pulled down'.
2. Pop-up menu. This menu can be called at any spot on the display by pressing the *mouse button*. An advantage compared to the pull-down menu is that the mouse does not have to be pushed upwards to pull down a menu.

mesh
A *3D* object consisting of a number of dots with planes in between. The planes are usually triangles because this type of plane can be calculated the fastest.
See also: wire-frame modeling.

metafile
A way to describe illustrations. Specific with a metafile is that not only *bitmap* but also *vector format* can be used in one *file*. It was originally developed by the American National Bureau of Standards as an agreement for the exchange of illustrations in government publications. An example of a metafile is Windows Metafile (WMF).

metronome

An aid with playing music. The device gives an audible click on every count. The metronome is used by musicians to keep the right speed of performance for a piece of music.

microfiche

A rectangular piece of celluloid (105 * 108 mm) which contains a large number of photographic information. This information is reduced so much that it can only be read with a special device, the microfiche reader.

microprocessor

See: central processing unit.

Microsoft disk operating system

MS-DOS - An *operating system* of *16 bits*, developed by Microsoft. The companies IBM and Novell have their own versions of DOS. It is (still) the most applied operating system of personal computers, although it loses ground fast to newly developed *32-bits* operating systems such as *OS/2, NeXTstep, Unixware*, Windows NT etc.

Microsoft mouse

A *mouse* standard developed by Microsoft. Specific is the use of two buttons. There exists also a standard for a mouse with three buttons. See also: mouse system.

MiniDisc

MD - A magneto-optical storing system developed by Sony. The specifications which are needed for the development are taken down in the *Orange Book* 1.

minimize

The replacement of an open *window* by a pictogram. All windows relating to one specific computer application disappear from the display and the application is then presented by the pictogram. Through clicking the pictogram the application can be brought back on the display. Thus the space needed for the representation of the program is minimized.
See also: graphical user interface.

minutes, seconds and frames

MSF - A form of time codification used in *multimedia* applications and in audio CD.
See also: time code.

mirror

1. Opposite pages or parts of pages are printed in such a way that they are mirror images.
2. The placing in mirror image of (part of) an illustration, photo or text. This option can be used in graphic, painting and image editing programs.

See also: register (to).

miter join

A term used in graphic programs. The term refers to an angle which is limited or mitered. With sharp angles in thick lines it is often better to use a miter joint because otherwise an enormous point appears at the outside of the angle. With an obtuse angle the point will not be that large, so a miter joint will be less necessary.

miter join

See also: bevel join; miter limit.

miter limit

A term used in graphic programs. The miter limit shows the number of degrees of an angle with which the angle is limited. Especially with thick lines in which a sharp angle is made an enormous point would appear at the outside of the angle. The lower the number of degrees of the miter limit, the sharper the angle in which the program changes from a sharp angle to an obtuse angle.

See also: miter join; bevel join.

mix (to)

Audio and *video* term. Combining two or more audio or videotapes to one single audio- or videotape.

mode

1. General. Indication for a mode.
2. Specific. Way of functioning or the mode of a *video card* in a computer system.

See also: graphic mode.

modeler

A program or part of a program with which a *3D* model can be built. In general two types can be distinguished: *solid modeling* and *wire-frame modeling*.

modeling coordinates
One type of coordinate systems with *3D* applications. With this type each object has its own modeling coordinates. By shifting, rotating or changing the scale of the complete modeling coordinates in relation to each other the objects are repeatedly converted to a place in the *world coordinates*.
See also: coordinate system.

modem
Contraction of MOdulation and *DEModulation*. A *device* between computer and telephone network which converts *digital* computer signals into *analog* telephone signals and vice versa. Thus, it is possible to exchange *data* between computers via the telephone network. The modem checks, corrects, compresses the data and controls the speed of which they are sent.
See also: dataspeed; baud rate.

modern
A *style* of type with contrasting thick and thin strokes, serifs at right-angles with curves thickened in the center, radical changes from thick to thin. Examples: Bodoni, Bauer, Onix.
See also: type classification; old style type; serif.

modify
The electronic changing and adapting of characters. Examples are: to *slant*, to widen or to make narrower a *character* or to make it thinner or thicker. It is also possible to create new characters. The disadvantage of modifying is that it often creates a letter of less quality than the original.

moiré
1. *Video* term. An unwanted optical phenomenon, with which two regular patterns interfere. The finer the patterns, the more intensive the effect. An example of the moiré effect is seen with television images. A person with a fine-striped jacket causes a flickering image. The cause is often found in a too limited *resolution* of the video screen to show details well.
See also: video errors.
2. Graphical term. In printing moiré can be caused when the screens of different printings shift slightly in relation to each other or if the screen files are not correct. As a result an unwanted pattern may become visible. It can usually be avoided by changing the screen angle.

monitor

A monitor is the same as a television screen but with a higher *resolution* and without a receiver. A monitor makes visible video signals coming from a computer or video recorder. The video signals can be reproduced in different resolutions. A monitor is able to process *analog* or *digital* colors. With processing analog colors a continuous variable voltage is used to reproduce many colors.

The digital method uses digital color wire-frames which can be switched on and off. Digital monitors can be used with CGA and EGA. A monitor uses two reproduction techniques: *interlaced* and non-interlaced.

See also: cathode ray tube; video adapter.

monochrome display adapter

MDA - The first video standard of IBM, a black-and-white *video adapter* which can only process alphanumeric characters and symbols.

monospace

A kind of *spacing* with which the type spacing of each *character* is equal, independent of the character used. Some OCR-programs (optical character recognition) need this to recognize text.

morphing

An image processing method with which an image is changed into another image by means of *animation*. The shape and also the color is adjusted in small steps in such a way that the beginning image changes fluently into the last image. This method became known to the public through a *video clip* of Michael Jackson.

Mosaic

Computer program to browse through the *Internet*. It is primarily aimed at the use on the *World Wide Web* (= set of documents that are interlinked using *hypertext* techniques). Mosaic is developed by the American National Center for Supercomputer Applications (NCSA).

See also: Internet.

mosaic filter

The processing of an *image* through software, with which the image is divided into small uneven planes. In combination with *shading* it looks as if the image is built up from small mosaic tiles.

See also: filters.

normal   *mosaic filter*

Motif

A *graphical user interface* developed by Open Software Foundation (OSF) for the operating system *Unix*.

motion blur

A way to make speed, path and motion in *animation* more flexible without raising the number of images per second. In the path of an object a vague *blur* is drawn in the shape of the object. This helps the eye to fix on the path of the object, otherwise the unwanted effect of what is called *strobing* would occur. See also: animating on fields.

motion blur

Motion Picture Experts Group

MPEG

1. A group of experts who developed an *algorithm* for compression of moving images. The group is also working on the arrangement of ISO and CCITT standards for the use of algorithms in programs.
2. MPEG is also the name for the standard of the developed algorithm. It is divided into MPEG 1, 2 and 4.

   MPEG 1 is intended for compressing *full-motion video* and audio on a compact disc. The image resolution is at best half the resolution used in the *PAL* and *NTSC* television standard. The required data transmission capacity is 150 kilobytes per second.

   MPEG 2 is intended for transmitting digital video via the cable network and for future use on the *high-density compact disc*. The image resolution is the same as in existing television standards. The required data transmission capacity is 2 to 16 megabits per second. This is substantially higher than MPEG 1.

   MPEG 4 is intended, among others, for video telephony. The image quality is fairly low. This requires less data transmission capacity: 10 to 64 kilobits per second.

See also: compress; International Standards Organization; Consultative Committee International for Telephone and Telegraph communication.

motion video

The opposite of *still video*. Motion video stands for recording and reproducing moving pictures. The general term video usually refers to motion video.
See also: still video.

motion-control photography
With *multimedia* the use of one or more computers to operate the movements of a *camera* accurately.

mouse
Peripheral unit. A small device fitting in the palm of the hand, with which software can be operated. The mouse is used to move the *cursor* over the display and to give instructions. Moving the cursor is done by dragging the mouse over a flat surface. The movements of the mouse are passed on to the computer via a built-in rotating ball-bearing or optical sensors. The instructions are passed on by pressing the buttons on top of the mouse.
See also: graphical user interface.

mouse button
The *button*(s) on a *mouse* with which the display can be operated. The *Macintosh* mouse has one button. A mouse for an IBM-compatible computer has a standard two buttons. There are also mice with three or more buttons. The extra button(s) can be programmed by the user for specific operations.
See also: Mouse Systems mouse.

Mouse Systems mouse
The operating standard for a *mouse* with three buttons.
See also: Microsoft mouse.

MS-DOS
See: Microsoft disk operating system.

muddy media
Multimedia applications of low quality. Little thought is given to the possibilities multimedia has to communicate. Examples are:
- *content* with little meaning;
- underdeveloped system of interactivity;
- excessive use of color;
- short on typographical knowledge.
See also: typography.

multi using
The possibility of allowing different users to work with one and the same computer simultaneously and independent of each other. All users have a keyboard and a terminal and share all facilities and files of the computer system to which they are connected.

multi-session

A term used with CD-ROM recorders. A CD-ROM recorder which is suitable for multi-session can read *data* recorded at different times on the same *compact disc*. This is especially advantageous with *Photo CD* because new photos can be added to the compact disc at different moments.
See also: single-session.

multi-station access unit

MAU - A *device* which enables terminals, printers, PCs and other devices to be linked in a star-shaped *network*.

MultiFinder

A part of the *operating system* for the *Macintosh*. This part makes it possible to load different programs simultaneously into the *memory*.

multimedia

The integration via computer technology of individual media such as film, video, music, language, photos, databases, spreadsheets etc. into one product which is stored on one *digital* carrier. Multimedia products usually have an *interactive* structure, although batch-oriented applications are possible.
Multimedia products are at present most commonly used in commerce (presentations, marketing), education (interactive teaching programs) and in the entertainment industry (games).
See also: multiple media; hypertext.

multimedia compact disc

See: high-density compact disc.

Multimedia Marketing Council

MMC - A group of hard and software manufacturers who determine the specifications of DOS computers for *multimedia* applications.
See also: multimedia personal computer.

multimedia personal computer

MPC - A *personal computer* whose hardware configurations conforms to the MMC's specifications for multimedia hard- and software. MPC divide into two categories, level 1 and level 2. The specifications for a level 2 MPC (published in May 1993) are higher than for a level 1 MPC (published in 1990).
The minimum configuration specification for both these levels are listed below:

	Level 1	Level 2
RAM	2 MB	4 MB
Processor	386SX 16 MHz	486SX 25 MHz
Floppy disk	1.44 MB 3.5 inch	1.44MB 3.5 inch
Hard disk	30 MB	160 MB
CD-ROM	150 KB transfer rate 1 second access time	300 KB transfer rate 400 ms access time CD-ROM XA ready multi-session
Sound	8-bit, 8 voice	16-bit, 8 voice
MIDI playback	MIDI playback	
Video	640 * 480 * 16	640 * 480 * 16
Ports	MIDI, joystick	MIDI, joystick

multimedia system

Electronic equipment used for compiling transparencies, photographs, animations, film and video stills, sound and computer data into a new product. The computer usually manages the process, thus enabling the integration of *digital* and *analog* techniques into one digital product. See also: authoring.

multiple master

Digital technique developed by Adobe Systems for describing *outline fonts* based on three sets of data: the *weight* of the letter (from *light* to *bold*), the *width* (from *condensed* to *extended)* and the *style* (*serif* or *sans-serif).* These three characteristics may be altered individually and on a sliding scale.
See also: master font.

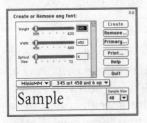  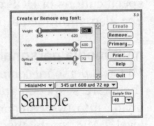

multiple media

The combination of different products into a package. The most common type of package is a book accompanied by a diskette or *CD-ROM.* There is a great difference, therefore, between multiple media and *multimedia,*

where different media types are integrated on one *digital* carrier.
See also: multimedia.

multiplexed
A method with which two or more separate signals are led simultaneously via the same *channel*.

multiplexed analog components
MAC - A proposed standard for the transfer of television signals. The *luminance* and *color separation* signals are sent after each other. On receipt the signals are combined (*multiplexed*) to one unit. In this way the total tape width of the different signals is kept so that color interference which does occur with *PAL* and *NTSC* standards can be prevented.
See also: color difference; television signal standard; D2-MAC.

multiplexer
Device which divides a *data communication* connection into different channels. There are several techniques:
- Multiplexing separation of *frequency*. With this technique signals are sent simultaneously on different frequencies.
- Multiplexing time separation. Only one signal is sent each time, however, it is possible to create more channels through dividing the data in packets and sending in turns a *packet* for each *channel*.

multitasking
The computer carries out different tasks simultaneously. This may be in the same program, for example the calculation of an already defined three-dimensional figure by the computer while the user is already working on a new illustration. Multitasking is also possible with different programs simultaneously.

multithreaded
A technique which can be described as '*multitasking* within one program'. It means the possibility of simultaneously processing different tasks within one application. With this the performance of a computer can be increased.
It is an advanced programming technique which is present in the *operating system OS/2*.

Musical Instrument Digital Interface
MIDI - A standard for the operation of electric musical instruments. At the center is a (personal) computer in which the musical *data* is stored. The data communication is *serial* and bi-directional; it can be passed

on from *device* to device. A MIDI-connection consists of a round DIN *plug* with four pegs.

See also: International MIDI Association.

mute

1. With audio and image recorders the possibility of reducing the volume to a certain level by pressing a *button*. The original sound level is not influenced.
2. With multimedia and telephony, it means temporarily switching off the sound.

N

National Association of Broadcasters
NAB - An American organization of owners of radio and television stations, suppliers and other companies which are involved with the broadcasting network in America.

National Television Standards Committee
NTSC - An American committee which defines standards for color television broadcasts and video. The most important standard of this committee is called the NTSC standard. Japan has adopted this standard.
NTSC works with 525 video lines and screen *frequency* of 59.94 Hz. In Europe the TV standards PAL and SECAM are used.
See also: Phase Alternating Line (PAL); Séquentiel Couleur à Mémoire (SECAM); television signal standard.

native signal processing
NSP - Processing large amounts of *data* in real time by a microprocessor instead of a *digital signal processor* (DSP). The microprocessor has to be extremely powerful to accomplish this as the data flow involved with *video* and *audio* requires a lot of processing power. Sun was the first company to manufacture a microprocessor with NSP capabilities (the 64-bit Ultra *Sparc*).

near instantaneously companded audio multiplex
NICAM - A system with which it is possible to add sound with stereo CD quality to the existing TV signal. Compression techniques are used to be able to stay within the channel. This system is only used in Europe.
See also: D-MAC.

Nebraska scale
A scale division to mark interactivity, originally intended to classify *laser* discs. Nowadays, it is also used to classify other systems. The scale is designed by the Nebraska Videodisc Design/Production Group.
The scale division is as follows:
- Level 0: a non-interactive, linear product, for instance a feature movie.
- Level 1: limited search facilities such as fast forward and rewind, decelerated or double speed.

- Level 2: a system with a microprocessor that reads programs from *hard disk* or ROM cartridge. This allows limited interactivity.
- Level 3: a system where the microprocessor is replaced by a complete computer system. The disc player and computer are separate, inter-linked devices. Full interactivity is possible.
- Level 4: the same as level 3 with the difference that the disc player and computer are placed in one housing (e.g. *CD-i*).

See also: level one videodisc.

neckline
Spacing underneath a heading.

negative spacing
Reducing the *spacing* between characters. The degree of reduction between all characters is equal. The opposite of negative spacing is positive spacing, also called *tracking*.
See also: spacing; kerning.

Netware
A system of network protocols and functions developed by Novell.

network
See: local area network; wide area network

network adapter
Electronics in the shape of a PC feature *card* with which communication within a *network* is made possible. The type of *adapter* depends on the network *protocol* used. There are cards for *ARCnet*, *Token Ring* and *Ethernet*. Because over the past years ever more computers are connected to a network, most computers are supplied with a network adapter. Mostly this is an Ethernet adapter because of the great popularity of this protocol.

network topology
The way in which a *network* is structured, especially concerning the type of connection and the type of cables. The most common network topologies are: *ring*, *bus* and *star*.

NeXTstep
The first totally *object oriented* operating system. NeXTstep is an operating system based on *Unix* which originally only operated on NeXT-hardware. Nowadays it also operates on Intel processors which appeared after the 80486. Because of the object oriented *shell* of

NeXTstep, the operating system is easy to use. It offers software developers an enormous amount of pre-defined objects (for 2D/3D graphics, file management, multimedia and financial models), which can be used in programs written in the programming language Objective C.
See also: object oriented.

node

1. A term which indicates a link or a node in a *network* (computer, *printer*, *hub* etc.)
2. A linking spot in a *Bézier curve*.

noise

A disturbance which influences the sound or video signal and causes an unwanted change in the information in the signal. In some cases, it is possible that a unit or system's performance is seriously impaired.
See also: noise power emission; burst noise.

noise power emission

Audio term. An unwanted noise produced by a sound source. The degree of noise is measured in *decibels*.
See also: noise.

non-breaking space

A spacing which cannot be broken off. Such a spacing, also called a *hard space*, is meant to keep words that belong together on the same line.
See also: space.

non-interlaced

See: interlaced/non-interlaced.

non-linear

A method with which digital data is stored in such a way that they can be read in a random order. There is no reel-time such as with magnetic audio- or videotapes. The data is stored on a rotating medium such as a *hard disk* or in a *memory bank*.
See also: non-linear video.

non-linear video

Storing video images on a *non-linear* medium (such as a *hard disk*). The video images are edited by changing the starting point and the end

point and the order of the excerpts. It is not necessary to make a copy
to view the result. While the tape is played, the images are looked up
and shown super-fast.
See also: non-linear.

normal

A geometrical concept. A line which is at a right angles to a surface (or
can be projected at a right angle) is called the normal. The normal
shows the curve of the surface.

notebook pc

A portable computer, the size of a standard piece of paper (21.0 * 29.7 cm)
which weighs 3 kilograms or less.

NTSC

See: National Television Standards Committee.

NuBus

A fast *bus* (32 bits) used with *Macintosh* computers.

numeric processing unit

See: coprocessor.

O

object code

Technically speaking object code is machine language with which a computer is controlled directly. The *source code* is converted into object code through compiling. Object code is a semi-finished product. It can operate on its own by adding functions which are located in so-called libraries. This process is called linking.
See also: compile (to); link (to).

object linking and embedding

OLE - A method to link files in MS-Windows and share the information in these files. There are two methods: linking and embedding. Linking offers the more possibilities. OLE is a relatively new technique which has to be developed further. A competitive technique is *OpenDoc* which is developed by Apple, IBM and Novell.

object oriented

1. Programming. A way of programming with which a program does not exist of separate programming lines, but of several objects. Such an object has a specific function and consists of several programming lines. An object is not restricted to one program but can also be used in other programs. With the aid of these objects, new programs can be written faster. An example of an object-oriented *operating system* is *NeXTstep*.
2. Applications. Operating procedure in a graphics program with which figures are built up out of objects. These can exist of lines, circles, squares or other shapes. Then properties can be allotted: color, thickness, etc.
   A feature is that the *bitmap* pattern is not saved but instead a series of numbers describing the object.

oblique

A slanted variant of a *roman*. The difference between an *italic* and an oblique is that the italic is a separately developed *font*. This is not so with an oblique; the characters of a roman are slanted without adaptation.

abcde
ABCDE
12345

Helvetica normal

abcde
ABCDE
12345

Helvetica oblique

octave

A music term. The grouping of a series of notes consisting of 13 succeeding half notes. In Western music the octaves start and end with the same note and are octaves divided into eight basic intervals (c-d-e-f-g-a-b-c). These intervals contain five added *half-tones:* ais or bes, cis or des, dis or es, fis or ges, gis or as to form a chromatic scale (ais and bes, cis and des etc). have the same pitch. Between the e and f and between the b and c no half-tones have to be added because the intervals in between these are already half steps.

ODI

See: open data-link interface.

off-line

The status of a connection. Off-line means that a connection is broken. This can be used for printers to feed paper, change adjustments etc. See also: on-line.

off-line editing

The pre-editing of video images on cheaper equipment (contrary to *on-line editing*) through entering the starting and end points of scenes and the effects to be added in an *edit decision list*.

old style type

Collection of type sizes with the characteristics: *serif*, the short cross line at the end of a stroke of a letter, even change from thin to thick, diagonal center line. Readable letter. Examples: Garamond, Goudy Oldstyle, Times New *Roman*.
See also: type classification.

on-demand system

A system with which *information* or service is delivered on request.

on-line

The status of connection. On-line means that a connection is operational so that through this connection an order can be carried out. *Data* can be sent between modems, a file can be printed on a printer, etc.
See also: off-line.

on-line editing

The *editing* process with the original videotapes in a completely equipped editing room. Because of the high costs of this editing process the editing is first done mostly *off-line* on less-expensive equipment after which the *on-line* editing takes place automatically by means of the produced *edit decision list*.

on-the-fly compression/decompression

A method with which (de)compression of a *file* takes place during writing to and the reading of a storing medium. An advantage of the method is that the user does not have to do anything to (de)*compress*. The method works on the background and is invisible to the user.

open data-link interface

A standard of the Novell company which makes it possible to use different *network* protocols over the same network card and cable, for example *TCP/IP* and IPX/SPX.

Open Look

A *graphical user interface* (GUI) developed by AT&T and Sun, built around the *X-Windows* system.

open prepress interface

OPI - A technology developed by the company Aldus to exchange *image information* between high-end and low-end systems during *layout*. This is based on a *PostScript* description, combined with OPI-information. An image is stored in *high resolution* on a central computer. To process the image on low-end workstations a version of a *low resolution* is used, which increases the speed of processing. The high-resolution image is adapted automatically on the background by a central computer. The high-resolution image is used for printing. The two versions of the image 'recognize' each other through the OPI information.

open system

System by which (part of) the *source code* is released because other producers can develop programs for this system. Also, *file formats* can be exchanged with other systems.

Open System Interconnection

OSI - A standard for *data communication*, developed by the *International Standards Organization* (ISO). The ISO model is divided into seven *layers*. Before a *network* is able to function, it is necessary that different techniques cooperate. There need to be cables, connections, network structures, agreements on data transfer and on the programs which are to be used on a network. In the OSI model in every one of the seven layers, one of the required components is described. For

example, in the first layer the transfer medium and the hardware are described. The definition of the layers in the OSI model is as follows:
1. physical layer;
2. data linking layer (such as linking protocols);
3. network layer (the type of network);
4. transfer layer (the protocol used for the transfer of data);
5. session layer (the method of communication);
6. presentation layer (possible adaptation and conversion of a connection);
7. application layer (the use of an application of the above-mentioned facilities).

The layers 3, 4 and 5 are closely linked.

OpenDoc

An *object oriented* technique which makes it possible to compile documents from files which are made in different programs. It is possible to retain the linking made, so that later changes in one *file* are automatically made in the linked files. OpenDoc can be used in different operating systems. The initiators of OpenDoc are: Apple, IBM, WordPerfect Corporation (now Novell). OpenDoc is a direct competitor of *object linking and embedding* (OLE) from Microsoft.

operating system

A collection of cooperating programs to operate a computer system. Many of these systems have been developed. Some of the most well known are: Microsoft disk operating system (MS-DOS), *Apple Macintosh system, Unix, Operating System/2* (OS/2), VMS and VME.

Operating System/2

A 32-bit *operating system* for personal computers. Originally this system was developed by Microsoft, and later further developed by IBM. One characteristic of this operating system is that in the *graphical user interface* not only DOS and *Windows* but also *OS/2* programs can be used.

optical center

The optical center of a page is situated about 10% higher than the geometrical center.

optical disc

A storing medium with a high storing capacity which can be read by means of a *laser*.
See also: Compact Disc Read Only Memory; magneto-optical disc.

optical fiber
See: fiber.

optical media
Data banks which are read by *laser*. With this *memory* medium data is stored digitally encoded. This code can be applied by means of microscopic pits and the relevant spacing, or by means of magnetic techniques: *CD-A*, *CD-E*, *CD-i*, *CD-R*, *CD-V*, CD-WORM, *CD-ROM*, *Photo CD*, *LaserVision* and *LaserDisc*.

Orange Book
The data and instructions needed for making a *Compact Disc Recordable* (CD-R). CD-R can be distinguished in magneto-optical systems, CD-R/Write/Erase and CD-R-WORM. The specifications of the first two systems are described in the Orange Book 1, the specifications of the CD-R-WORM in the Orange Book 2.

org chart
See: flowchart.

original equipment manufacturer
OEM - Suppliers who supply the equipment as a semi-manufactured product to other companies. Thus it is possible a PC is sold with the *hard disk* of an OEM manufacturer.

orphan
The last line of a *paragraph* which appears on its own at the top of a page. Typographically unwanted.
See also: widow; wrong overturn.

OS-9
The real time *operating system* on which the operating system of CD-i is based (CD-RTOS).
See also: Compact Disc Real Time Operating System.

OS/2
See: Operating System/2.

OSI
See: Open System Interconnection.

outdent
First line of a *paragraph* which indents on the left margin.

outline

1. *Flowchart* diagram. Outline or main classification in levels of a flowchart diagram, with which the lower levels can be made invisible and can be called on individually.
2. Word processing. Outline of, for example, the *layout* of chapters or paragraphs.
3. Graphics. Outline description of, for example, fonts or illustrations. See also: vector format.

outline filter

The *editing* by means of software of an illustration to which a dark line is added to the contours of an object.

outline font

Outline fonts reproduce the outline of each *character*. They are composed of lines and *Bézier curves*. These are mathematical descriptions which do not depend on *resolution* and hardware. Outline fonts are based on the description of one *master font*.
Examples of outline fonts are *True-Type* and *Type 1*.

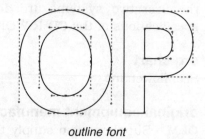

outline font

outline format

See: vector format.

outro

A musical end (finale) in an *audio* or *video* production.

over-dub

The production of a new soundtrack to replace an already existing soundtrack.
See also: dub (to).

over-the-shoulder

OS - Also called 'over-shoulder'. This is a take in *video* or *film* productions with which the *camera* looks over someone's shoulder at another person or object.
See also: close up; medium shot; two-shot; long shot.

overhead scanner

A *scanner* looking like an overhead projector, especially meant to read in overhead sheets and films and to convert them into digital values. With overhead scanners, the light falls through the document to be read on and is not reflected. Scanning takes place from a head with a lens positioned above the document.

overlay

1. Placing two images on top of each other on a *monitor* with which the position, order and degree of blending can be defined. It may concern two *digital* images from different sources of an *analog video* image and a digital computer image.
2. A transparency placed on a paste up with instructions such as color indications etc.

See also: superimpose; genlock; alpha channel.

overlay module

Part of a computer application which is not put in the *memory* until functions are called upon. After the part is used it can be overwritten by another part which is needed. With this technique the memory space can be used very efficiently. For the operation and loading of the modules a so-called 'overlay manager' is needed which does have to be constantly present in the memory.

overscan

Images that more than fill the *monitor*. With this technique the received images can be enlarged with 2 to 10 percent. Because of this a small part of the images is also rendered on the invisible part of the screen, behind the frame of the monitor. Thus, there is no black frame around the *active* image.

See also: underscan.

P

packet

A packet with *data* which is sent through a *network*. Each packet contains data about the sending and receiving station, the data to be sent and information about how to treat the sent request and the *error correction*. The size and *content* of the packet may be different and depends on the program used and the network *protocol*.
See also: datagram; packet switching.

packet switching

A *data communication* term. A technique with which a message is divided into packets of equal size. Each *packet* starts with the *network address* (to which the packet must be sent) and the sender (from which station it is sent). When the data packet arrives on the network, it is first processed with a mathematical formula which creates a *checksum*. Next the packets are sent one by one. The packets may follow different routes through the network. When a packet arrives it is again processed with the same mathematical formula. By means of the checksum it is then possible to check if the data packet is still undamaged. If this is the case an ACK or *acknowledgment* is sent to the sending station. If this is not so, a message is sent to the sending station to send again. Examples of protocols that work based on packet switching are *X.25* and *frame relay*.
The advantage of this technique is an optimal use of the network, because it is not necessary to make an exclusive connection to send a message. If it is busy on the network, then the message is sent via another route (switched). Switching means that packets can be sent by different routes. This happens in such a way that the fastest route is always chosen.
A result of switching is that the packets do not always arrive in the same order in which they were sent. The receiver then has to reconstruct the original message by means of the order information in the packet. Because of this, the switching network is not suitable for sending, for example, sound. Here *circuit switching* must be used.

page area

The position of the *type area* including the spacing.
See also: gutter; layout.

page description language

PDL - A page description language encodes and describes the *layout* of a page. Such languages mostly use vector information because in that way scaled characters and fluent lines can be created. Finally the files are converted into a *bitmap* file which can be printed. Examples of page description languages are: *PostScript* of Adobe Systems, PCL of Hewlett-Packard and CaPSL of Canon.

page memory

A part of a *video memory* in which the information is stored to reproduce a complete video page. If a *video adapter* has enough memory capacity, different images can be stored simultaneously. This makes it possible to switch very fast from one *image* to another.

paint brush

A function in graphics, paint or *image* processing programs with which the same effects can be reached as with a paint brush. Differences can be used in the brushstrokes (oil or water colors, etc.).
See also: air brush.

paintbox

1. General indication for *pixel* oriented illustration systems used by video images as input and output.
2. The name of a specific computer system of the company Quantel.
See also: pixel.

PAL

See: Phase Alternating Line.

palette shift

An unwanted color change of an *image* with graphic computer applications. This is caused because more colors are used than a *monitor* or monitor *mode* can process.
For example: the use of more than 256 colors with the *graphic mode* VGA (*video graphics array*).

palmtop

Also called hand-held computer. The smallest version of the *personal computer*. Although the basic functions are available there are limitations compared to its big brothers. As storing medium, a so-called *memory card* is used, an electronic storing medium the size of a large credit card.
See also: PCMCIA; laptop; notebook pc; pen-based pc.

panning

With graphic computer applications the viewing of an *image* which is too big to fit on a *monitor* at once. By moving from one side of the image to the other side the total image can be viewed. The image shifts as it were over the monitor.

paragraph

Part of a text which is preceeded by and ends with a hard return.

parallel

Parallel is used when computer *data* is not sent *bit* after bit by one or more bytes. For this it is necessary that different signals are sent in parallel. This communication runs through a *parallel port*.

parallel computer

A computer with more than one microprocessor which results in an enormous computer capacity.
See also: central processing unit.

parallel port

A port on a computer which makes it possible to send computer *data* *parallel* to another computer or *device*. For example with personal computers a parallel connection on the computer consists of a DA-25 connector and on the *printer* of a Centronics-36 connector. Each time a *byte* is sent through eight connections, the other connections are used for check signals which are sent back to the computer. On larger computers more bytes can be sent simultaneously with parallel connections.

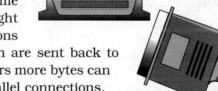

parameters

Additions (in the form of variables, specifications, commands etc.) to a computer command. The term is used in different specialties. For example: with *data communication* is meant a fixed number of variables for checking the data stream and with printing fixed variables for checking the printing process.
For example: within the *operating system* DOS the command FORMAT means that a computer must format a disk. As parameter to the command FORMAT can be given a: /F:720. The computer receives through these specifications the command to format disk a: with a storing capacity of 720 kilobytes.
See also: Microsoft disk operating system; formatting.

parity
A simple way to detect errors in asynchronous *serial* connections. An extra *bit*, the parity bit, is added to each *character* sent. With even parity checks the parity bit indicates if the number of ones is even. Thus, it may be a matter of even or odd parity. Parity is being used less nowadays. Newer, faster checking techniques have been developed such as MNP and V.42. These calculate check digits over a great number of bytes.
In the computer *memory* a parity bit is also used for checking purposes.
See also: asynchronous transmission.

parser
The translation of a computer input to logical concepts. A parser can be, for example, an *algorithm* for the syntactic analysis of a sentence. A sentence is analyzed into structural formulations. It can also be a program or routine which interprets the input of a user from which it decides what actions have to be taken.

partial immersion
See: virtual reality.

particle animation
Technique with which the *animation* of many equal particles is easily carried out. The particles move according to physical forces governing gravity, wind, turbulence, etc. Among others, this technique is used with the animation of rain, snow and explosions.

partition
1. An area in the working *memory* which is assigned a certain form of processing or task with multiprogramming.
2. A separate part of the internal memory of a *hard disk* which can be addressed. Thus the hard disk of a *personal computer* can be divided into different partitions, each with its own storing capacity and disk name.

paste
To insert copies or clipped texts or images in a *graphical user interface*.
See also: clipboard.

path
A unit of linked segments or curves in a vector-oriented image.
See also: vector format.

pattern
That which returns regularly as form, image or event.

pay TV

A TV service, via television cable networks or satellites, which is only open to subscribers. The subscriber can decide what to see by sending commands via the cable: a movie, a documentary, a musical program, news or whatever. Considering the fast-developing technology and the continuing tendency in society towards further individualization, in the future pay TV may grow into a full service.
See also: cable TV network.

PCMCIA

Contraction of Personal Computer Memory Card International Association. The memory card, an American finding, consists of a card as large as a credit card which contains a *flash memory*. The card can be placed in the computer via a special slot. Nowadays the cards are also used to accommodate devices such as modems, network connections and hard disks.

PCX

An often used graphic *file format* of the kind *bitmap*. The format has different variants: monochrome, 16 colors, 256 colors and 16.7 million colors.

pedestal up/down

With *multimedia* applications the moving up and down of a *camera* placed on a pedestal.

peer-to-peer network

A type of *network* in which the linked computers can function simultaneously as *server* and *workstation*. Thus the peripheral units of a workstation become available for all other workstations.
See also: dedicated server.

pen

A pointing and input pen which is used with touch-sensitive devices. The pen writes on a special *monitor* or *digitizer*. In this way commands can be given and the *cursor* can be moved.
See also: pen-based pc; light pen.

pen-based pc

This type of *palmtop* is a kind of electronic slate-pencil and slate. As a *pointing device*, a certain type of *pen* is used with which to write on a LCD-display. In this way, commands can be given and written text inserted.

Pentium

The successor of the 80486-microprocessor of Intel. For commercial reasons this *chip* did not get a figure name as with its predecessors but a letter name (which is better to protect).

The Pentium has a combined RISC/CISC architecture and a bus-width of 64 bits. With the aid of the CISC architecture, the chip emulates the 80486DX processor. Because of this, DOS will still remain the most frequently used *operating system*. In addition *Windows* NT and different *Unix* variants can also be used.

See also: central processing unit; reduced instruction-set computing; complex instruction-set computing; 64 bit.

persistence of vision

A characteristic of the human visual system through which separate static images get a moving character if they are shown with a certain speed after each other. Because of this, media such as *film*, *video* and *animation* could come into being.

personal computer

1. Generic name for a computer that can function independently (not in a *network*) and is used by one person at a time. The *operating system* is on *hard disk* or *floppy disk*. Size and weight makes the system non-portable.
2. A computer with an Intel (compatible) microprocessor running the MS-DOS (PC-DOS) operating system.

See also: Microsoft disk operating system; central processing unit; workstation.

Phase Alternating Line

PAL - A television standard which is especially used in Europe. It is based on NTSC, but in the PAL standard 625 rules are used on 50 *Hertz*. In addition, color shifting in the signal is prevented by turning around the phase of the *color difference* signal after each line. The total tape width of the signal is 5.5 MHz for *luminance* and 1.3 MHz for each color difference signal.

See also: National Television Standards Committee.

Phong shading

A method to color a *3D* picture. Characteristic for this method is that the color (combination) of each *dot* on the surface of the objects is calculated. To prevent too many calculations, the normals over the surface are inserted. This method renders the most flowing forms and the most beautiful incidence of light of all *shading* methods.

phosphor

A substance, applied to the interior of a *cathode ray tube*, which makes the picture visible. Phosphor emits light when it is bombarded with electrons. On a color screen for each picture element (*pixel*), phosphor in three colors (*red, green, blue*) blends to create the final color.

Photo CD

An optical *videodisc* (*compact disc*) for digital storing of photos. The videodisc can be written fully in different sessions (*multi-session*). The digitally stored images can be shown on a television screen by means of a special recorder, a Photo CD-recorder or a Compact Disc Interactive-recorder. Moreover, it is possible to read the stored images into a computer for processing. A CD-ROM-recorder is needed. The system is developed by Kodak. The basis is formed by photographs taken with a traditional *camera* on photographic film. The photographs are printed, scanned and afterwards placed in five resolutions (*image pacs*) on compact disc. The maximum is 100 per CD. Photo CD is a *Compact Disc Recordable* on which the images are described according to Kodak's own *YCC* format. See also: Pro-Photo CD.

photo detector

An electronic part in the reader of *optical media*. The light which is reflected by the *disc* is recorded by the photo detector and converted into electric signals.

photomultiplier

A type of photo-electric cell. A tube which contains materials (metallic joints) that react through the influence of light by means of a change of resistance or generating tension without a tension source. If the cells (and also the light-sensitive materials) are put under tension because of the incidence of light, that tension will change by changing the variation of resistance. A change in current intensity is produced which can be measured. In this way light is converted into signals. The technique is used in scanners, light meters and electronic cameras.

photorealistic

Photorealism tries to attain a true-to-life rendering of *3D* representation. This means that light incidence, shadow, luminance and other facets of the true world are allowed for.

photoresist

A light-sensitive layer applied to a *glass master*. During *mastering* of a *videodisc* production, *pits* are burnt into this layer by *laser*.

PIC

A graphic *file format* of the type *bitmap*. Among others, it is used by the graphic program PC Paint. A limitation of this format is the number of colors which can be stored: 256.

pica

See: typographic measurements.

picon

An *icon* which reproduces an extremely reduced image of a linked graphic *file* (an illustration, animation, video images).

PICT

A graphic *file format* used in *Macintosh* applications. The PICT format is a *vector format*. Two main types can be distinguished:
- PICT or PICT1, can register objects in eight fixed colors: white, black, cyan, magenta, yellow, red, green and blue;
- PICT2 is an extended version of the PICT1-format and known an 8-bit version and a 24-bit version. The first can store 256 colors, the second 16.7 million colors.

picture in picture

PIP - A function which shows a small screen within a screen filling picture with a picture from another signal source. With this method, two image sources can be viewed simultaneously.

picture stop

An instruction with which the moving image on a *videodisc* recorder can be stopped at a *chapter* which is fixed beforehand. Such instructions are put in codes on the videodisc immediately. A *level one videodisc* uses these kinds of instructions.

piezo electric force transducer

A crystal *monitor* that passes operating signals by means of touching. This process is effected with crystals which produce an electric tension through touching.
See also: touch screen.

pilot project

An experimental project which precedes a larger project. For the most part a pilot project is tested in a smaller form to learn from it, before starting the larger project. Sometimes a pilot project also serves to investigate whether a larger project is warranted.

pit

A microscopic hole in the information layer of an optical storing medium. These holes or pits are burnt into the surface by a *laser* beam and together they make up the registered information. The areas between the pits are called *lands*. The difference in depth between the pits and lands is the basis on which zeros and ones are realized.
See also: ablation; photoresist.

pixel

The smallest graphic element with the reproduction of an image on a *monitor*. This element has the form of a *dot* with a specific color and/or intensity. Together the image dots make up the video image. The values of the pixels are stored in a so-called *bitmap*. The value of a dot fixes the color of a pixel on the monitor. The highest value which is used in a *video adapter* is never higher than 8 bits per primary color (*red, green, blue*). In scanners and film recorders 12 bits per primary color are also used.

pixel density

The number of pixels per inch or centimeter in the horizontal or vertical direction. The *density* is indicated by *dots per inch* (dpi) or *dots per line* (dpl).
See also: resolution.

pixeldepth

A unit which indicates how many bits are used for the description of the color of one *pixel*. When colors are used on a computer, the maximum number of colors which can be converted by a *scanner* or shown on the *monitor* by a graphic *card*, can be made up from the number of bits.
A pixeldepth of
- 2-bit color gives 4 colors (2 to the power of 2);
- 4-bit color gives 16 colors (4 to the power of 2);
- 8-bit color gives 256 colors (16 to the power of 2);
- 16-bit color gives 65,536 colors (256 to the power of 2);
- 24-bit color gives 16.777 million colors (256 to the power of 3).
With 32-bit graphic cards the extra 8 bits are not used for the description of colors but for video processing.
See also: bit; pixel; scanner; alpha channel.

pixellation

Blurred or undetailed pictures with digital images. This poor quality is caused because the *pixels* are so large that they can be seen individually.

plasma panel
PP - A *monitor* formed by a grid of electrodes in a closed flat space. This space is filled with gas. When a potential difference is caused by two nearby electrodes, the gas ionizes and a light emission occurs on that spot.
See also: liquid crystal display (LCD).

plug
A connector to create a connection.
See also: jack.

plug-in
A program meant as an extension of another program. The two programs work as one unit. Examples are: extra *filters* in PhotoShop, Additions in Pagemaker and XTensions in QuarkXPress.

point
See: typographic measurements.

Point of information/sale
POI/POS - An individual *interactive* computer program which offers the public *information*, advice or product on a *monitor*. This may take place in commercial surroundings (department store, stock-exchange), service institutions (job centers, city hall, post office) or recreation institutions (museum, exhibition). Mostly the monitor is a *touch screen*. Sometimes a *printer* is connected to a POI or POS which makes it possible for the user to take information or confirmation of an order with him or her.

point of view
POV
1. In three-dimensional applications the position of the viewer in relation to the objects.
2. A *camera* position which reproduces what an actor in a *film* sees. The viewer steps, as it were, into the shoes of the actor. This technique is often used in horror movies or thrillers to increase the excitement of the viewer.

point size
See: body size.

point-to-point
An exclusive communication link between two devices.

pointer
An arrow-shaped *cursor* which can be moved with a *mouse*, arrow keys or *pen*. With this, menus and elements can be activated and frames, illustrations and text can be moved and other commands given.
See also: graphical user interface.

pointillism
An effect in several image-processing programs. It means copying (imitation) of pointillism from the art of painting. Primary (pure) colors are placed next to each other in dots or small spots.
See also: filters.

normal   *pointillism*

pointing device
Peripheral equipment (*mouse*, *pen* of *digitizer*) used with programs with a *graphical user interface*.

polyline
In graphic applications a series of connected lines.

pop-up menu
See: menu.

portable document file
See: Acrobat.

portrait/landscape
By portrait is meant a page printed in such a way that the height of the *page area* is larger than its width. The text lines run parallel with the shortest side of the paper. Portrait is the *layout* which is most often used. *Landscape* means that by normal reading of a text the width of the paper is larger than its height.

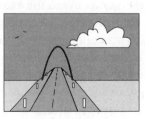 

landscape   *portrait*

post production

The phase of production in which *film* and *video* images is processed into the final result. This includes *editing*, dubbing, *bumping up*, *audio dubbing*.

PostScript

A programming language with which laid-out pages can be described. PostScript describes the total *layout* of a page. The position, layout of text, lines, colors and other layout *data* are described accurately. The first version of PostScript was published by Adobe Systems in 1985 with the indication Level 1. PostScript is vector oriented, which means that the language uses mathematical formulas to describe illustrations and text. An important advantage of this method is that scalable fonts and fluent lines can be worked with.

Besides the programming language, there is the software interpreter which takes care of the arranged description. The interpreter is mostly built into a grid image processor. This is a *device* which, with the aid of the interpreter, takes care of the interpretation of PostScript descriptions to a *bitmap*, a description in dots by which the laid-out page can be printed on a device (*printer*, imagesetter).

The PostScript descriptions are stored in ASCII text. For this and other reasons the language is independent of hardware which nowadays is seen as an important advantage. Also because of this, PostScript has grown into a generally accepted standard, although there is also criticism. This criticism is mainly directed at the lack of speed and the rather poor color processing in Level 1.

In 1992 Adobe Systems came out with a new version, Level 2. Among others, the additions and improvements are related to color processing, grid files, *memory* control and processing speed. To make colors of the reproduced image identical to the colors of the original, a universal *color model* is added in Level 2. Based on this model it is possible to remove nearly all the differences in color of an input medium (*scanner*) and those of an output medium (printer).

Level 2 also has the so-called accurate screen technology (AST), a technique to adapt grid files with which problems like *moiré* can be prevented. Also the processing speed is improved, for example, through the application of compression techniques. Because of this, the communication with output media procedes faster. Finally, Level 2 deals more efficiently with the available memory because larger and more complex files can be processed with the same memory space.

See also: Display PostScript; page description language; American Standard Code for Information Interchange; calibrate.

powerline
An indication for a function in some graphic programs with which a line can be drawn which runs from thin to thick and vice versa.

PowerOpen
A *Unix*-variant which is especially meant for the PowerPC-microprocessor. PowerOpen is developed by Apple and IBM and is based upon IMB's *AIX* and to a lesser degree on Apple's *A/UX*.

PowerPC
The power PC is a RISC processor and designed and produced by IBM, Apple and Motorola. The *chip* design is based on the IBM's Power architecture. The PowerPC's main feature is intended for use with *Macintosh* and PC computers. In the PowerPC line three models have been available since 1994: the MPC601 for use in *desktop* machines, the MPC603 for use in notebook computers and MPC604 for use in workstations and servers. Work has started on the MPC620 which will be twice as fast as the MPC604.
See also: reduced instruction-set computer.

PowerPC Reference Platform
PReP - A generic standard, defined by IBM in 1993, for *PowerPC* computers. It describes technical specifications for add-on cards, input-output systems and parts of the system software. If an *operating system* conforms to the PReP standard, it is guaranteed to run all PReP-PowerPC models.

pre-roll
A method to prevent errors when there are only two video recorders available during video *editing*.
To show a perfectly moving image from a stationary position (pause or stop) a video recorder needs some starting time. For this reason, the videotape is rewound in a small part in the video recorder. The image can then reach the required quality standard. When the point is reached where the recording tape has to take over the images of the reproduction tape, the video recorder is started. The rewinding and starting on time is called pre-roll. This function is present on most (semi)professional equipment.

preferences
Set-ups within a program which can be saved so that the next time the program is used these set-ups do not have to be entered again.

prelim

A page containing *data* on the printed matter, mostly a right-hand page at the beginning of a book or report. The data on a title page include: name or names of author(s), title, subtitle, name of translator, illustrator, photographer, name of publisher and year of publication.

premastering

Videodisc term. Generating a *master tape*. During this process all video and sound fragments are collected on a tape. By simulating the programmed interaction the *interactive* program is tested. When the tests lead to an acceptable result, the interactive program is recorded on the master tape.

PreP

See: PowerPC Reference Platform.

presentation graphics

Software applications for making graphical presentation material such as stills, sheets, video images, printed pictures etc.

primary display

With the use of two monitors on a computer this term indicates the *monitor* which is active when starting the system.

primitives

Simple geometrical figures in flat surfaces as well as dimensionally:
1. Two-dimensional, flat surface. Figures such as squares, circles, triangles, ovals, etc.
2. Three-dimensional. Figures such as spheres, pyramids, blocks, tubes and planes. These are usually directly available in a *modeler*.

With *solid modelers* primitives are used consisting out of mathematical formulas. In wire-frame modelers the primitives are available in the shape of wire-frame models.
See also: geometry.

print queue

A queue of printing commands which occurs when different printing commands are given. This may happen when a printer is linked to a *network*. In the print queue, priority can be given to certain printing commands.
See also: spooler.

printer

Device which can print documents made in a computer on paper or other material.

pro-Photo CD

The pro-Photo CD is a *Photo CD* for professional applications. The difference with the consumer's version is the size and *resolution* of the images. On a regular Photo CD only miniature materials in five fixed resolutions can be registered. On the pro-Photo CD also negatives of 6 * 6, 6 * 7, 6 * 9 cm and 4 * 5 inch in a *high resolution* can be registered.

procedure

A part of a computer program which is activated after a command. Together the procedures form a set of standard instructions which are present in a *library* or which can be stored. When calling a procedure, in most cases *variables* can be given. Contrary to a *function* however, a procedure does not return values.

production control room

A control room for *video*, *film* and TV applications. In such a room there is a series of monitors, mixing consoles, control panels and extensive communication facilities. In this room all images of the active video cameras are shown on the monitors so that at any moment the *director* can decide which *camera* will give the actual image.

production-level video

PLV - Within DVI technology (*digital video interactive*) the method for video compression with the highest image quality. The video compression is performed with powerful computers; the decompression with the DVI system. PLV is a form of *intraframe compression*.

professional graphics adapter

PGA - A graphic color standard with a *resolution* of 640 * 480 *pixels*, introduced by IBM in 1984. There are 256 colors (from a pallet of 4096) which can be shown on the screen simultaneously.

program information file

PIF - A *file* which can be made in *Windows*. In this file important *information* can be stored for applications in Windows. That information may be the name of a program, a *path* name, the required *monitor mode*, etc.

Programmers Hierarchical Interactive Graphics System

PHIGS - An ANSI and ISO standard for programming applications which use two or three dimensional graphics instructions.
See also: American National Standards Institute; International Standards Organization.

programming languages

Computer instruction languages which, in most cases, are standardized and used worldwide. The languages are artificial, meaning they are not based on natural languages (although many English words are used). The research and development of programming languages is a continuous process.

Programming languages are divided into generations. Those used most are the third-generation languages such as BASIC, COBOL, C, PASCAL, FORTRAN etc. Growing is the so-called *object oriented* programming.

prompt

One or more special symbols which mark the beginning of a command line. These symbols are used with character-oriented operating systems. The prompt usually shows which of the external memories (for example *hard disk*) is being worked on at that moment.

proportional spacing

A way of *spacing* with which the amount of spacing is decided upon separately for each *character*. The i gets less spacing than the w. In traditional printing (lead printing) characters are also printed proportionally. In computer programs proportional spacing occurs automatically, allthough all kinds of adjustments are possible. This modern way of spacing is usually not of a better quality than the traditional handwork. Typewriters for the most part do not give a proportional script and the spacing is similar for each character. The opposite of proportional spacing is *mono-space*.

See also: kerning.

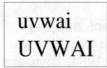

proportial spacing

mono spacing

props

The materials needed for the equipment of a *set* with film or video productions. It concerns movable objects (furniture, crockery) and personal possessions of the actors (a pipe, wallet or whatever).

protection master

A copy of the *master tape* which is safely put away in a safe-deposit box. Where problems with the original arise, this extra copy can be used.

protocol

A set series of arrangements and rules on the way in which the exchange, error control and compression of computer *data* should take place. Protocols are used with networks and telecommunication.

With networks, the protocols used most often are *Ethernet*, *ARCnet*, *Token Ring* and *LocalTalk*. Protocols with higher speeds are *CDDI*, *FDDI*, *ISDN* and *ATM*.

In *telecommunications*, the best-known protocols are X-modem, Y-modem, Z-modem and Kermit.

prototyping

Rapidly developing an operational trial version of an application. All features are present but are not fully implemented. The purpose of the prototype is to check whether or not a design satisfies the user's needs. See also: authoring/scripting.

pull-down menu

See: menu.

pulse code modulation

PCM - A *digital* modulating process which has been given a series of applications:

1. *Videodisc*. PCM is used with the recording process of an *optical disc*. This process takes care of the encoding of *binary* numbers to a pulse train. The pulse train is recorded as a *pit* pattern on an optical disc.
2. Sound. A method of storing sound digitally, used in *Hi-8* recorders and in different audio digitizers.
3. *Data* transmission. Converting *analog* telephone signals to *digital* format is done with PCM. With this the signal is measured 8000 times per second and each measurement is encoded with 8 bits. Thus a stream of 64 kilobits per second is created.

See also: encoding; sampler.

pushpin

A *glyph* with the shape of a pushpin. It is used in the graphical user interface *Open Look* to keep visible a *menu* or pop-up screen.

Px64

See: H.261.

Q

quad right
See: right justification.

quad-speed
A *CD-ROM* player which processes *data* four times as fast as a single speed CD-ROM player, which has a throughput of 150 kilobytes per second. This means that a quad-speed CD-ROM player has an processing speed of 600 KBps.
See also: CD-drive.

quartz iodide light
A type of bulb with a high light output applied in studio lighting. The bulb itself is made of glass/quartz glass, is filled with halogen gas and contains an electric wire. This wire is heated to an extreme temperature by an electrical current, which generates a high light intensity.
See also: key-light.

quartz lighting
A very bright source of light, such as a halogen lamp, used for lighting in video and film productions.

query
A consultation of a *database*. The contents of the database is not changed through this.

QuickTime
A system expansion developed by *Apple* to *compress* and *decompress* digitized video images and to display them on a *monitor*.
The first version of QuickTime did not exceed 12 images per second on a 1/16th part of the screen. Improved versions are released regularly. The ultimate goal is FSFM, *full-screen full motion,* which enables 25 full screen images per second (normally video images run at 25 *frames per second*). QuickTime was initially developed for Macintosh but has now also been adapted to MS *Windows*.
See also: digital video; coder/decoder; QuickTime VR.

QuickTime VR

A program by Apple Corporation which creates virtual *3D*-sceneries. *QuickTime* VR employs two technologies:
- the panoramic movie technology for making and surveying a 360 degree scenery.
- the object movie technology for viewing objects from all sides by moving and rotating them.

A panoramic movie is composed from a series of photos that are shot from a fixed position covering 360 degrees. It is also possible to start from computer generated (rendered) images. A panoramic scene takes up less than one MB storage space. Users can zoom in and out, navigate from scene to scene and change the viewpoints. The perspective is automatically adjusted during these actions. Using authoring tools, text,, video and/or audio can be linked to the image. These links are presented to users as 'hot spots' they can activate (e.g. with the mouse) to instruct the program to present the linked data. The authoring software is only available for the Macintosh. The run-time software is available for Macintosh as well as for Windows starting from QuickTime version 2.0.

QWERTY

The acronym for the most common keyboard layout. The letters on the first six keys in the top left-hand corner of the keyboard spell QWERTY.

R

R4x00

A type of microprocessor developed by MIPS Technologies Inc. The R4000 and the R4400 are RISC processors and have a *bus* width of 64 bits. The chips are mainly applied in *Unix* systems, such as that of Silicon Graphics. Software designed for other processors can also be used by applying MIPS-ABI (Application Binary Interface). The R4200 model can be applied to PC mother boards.

See also: central processing unit; reduced intstruction-set computing; 64 bit.

radio buttons

A *graphical user interface* component. A number of push buttons located in a *window* which can be selected, one at a time, by the user.

radio frequency

RF - The antenna signal consisting of high-frequency electrical vibrations transported by cable networks or by air. In this RF signal, the video signal is modulated into a *channel* with one *frequency*. So various TV signals can be transported via one cable because each signal operates on a different frequency.

radiosity

A method to *render 3D* images. The method was originally invented to imitate diffuse light effects. The method is mainly based on techniques derived from thermal science (such as heat reflection) but calculations are based on light intensities instead of heat. The method is especially suited for simulating light entrance in buildings; the images which then occur are very realistic. When an *image* is being calculated, a relationship between light intensities and colors is processed. When adjusting the *camera* position, the same system of ratios can be used time after time. Therefore this method is ideal for *fly-throughs*, provided that the visual elements remain unchanged.

See also: shading.

ragged-right setting

Text with left *alignment* and lines varying in length because the right-hand side is not aligned. This alignment has two variations: the free flow and the English flow. The free flow does not hyphenate words; the English flow does hyphenate words.

In the heart of the large island of Niphon and in a mountainous and wooded region, fifty leagues from Yokohama, is hidden that marvel of marvels - the necropolis of the Japanese Emperors.	In the heart of the large island of Niphon and in a mountainous and wooded region, fifty leagues from Yokohama, is hidden that marvel of marvels - the necropolis of the Japanese Emperors.

RAM-drive

This is a part of the RAM *memory* configured to serve as a temporary disk drive. A major advantage is the high access speed. The danger is that the stored data is lost when the computer is switched off or jams. A RAM drive is also called virtual drive.

See also: drive; random access memory (RAM).

RAMDAC

See: random access memory digital-to-analog converter.

random access memory

RAM - Electronic *memory* in the form of chips with read and write capabilities. It is used, for example, as internal working memory in computers.

random access memory digital-to-analog converter

RAMDAC - A *chip* on a graphic card (*video adapter*). This chip converts the digital information from dots to *analog* information, so that it can be displayed on the screen.

ray-tracing

A display method for *3D* images. This method is based on a reversed structure of the path along which light beams usually travel. In nature, light beams travel in every direction. They travel via refractions and reflections and ultimately reach the retina upon which the image is formed.

Ray-tracing is the reverse process. Light beams are projected, as it were, from the eye of the viewer. The projected beams are affected in the same way as natural light beams in the physical world. They can disappear in the background, be reflected by shiny surfaces, be deflected by transparent materials or hit a light source. The final color (intensity) is determined based on the beam's 'experiences' in the physical world. This color is displayed on the screen.

Ray-tracing is a slow method, mainly aimed at imitating accurate mirror and lens effects. However, the images tend to be somewhat lifeless, which is a disadvantage.

See also: render (to).

reaction shot
A picture of a key figure's face to show his/her reaction to the content or action of the previous *scene*.
See also: point of view.

read only memory
ROM - A type of *memory* which only allows perusal of the text or image. It is used, for example, to store system software (ROM-BIOS).
See also: random access memory.

real estate
The (still) available recording space on a *videodisc* or video tape.

real image
A real world *image* captured by a video *camera*, *still videocamera* or movie camera.

real-time compression
See: on-the-fly compression.

real-time system
An undelayed *operating system*. A real-time operating system is often used to run stand-alone (mechanical) applications, such as industrial control systems. These are systems that must always finish processing on time and so are clearly time dictated.

real-time video
RTV - Video compression techniques in the *digital video interactive* (DVI) standard that *compress* at normal speed. These compression techniques are used during application development in order to have a correct impression of the video frames to be used. The *production-level video* (PLV) compression method is used for the final version.

reboot
Restarting the computer without disconnecting the power.
See also: boot (to); warm reboot; cold reboot.

record
A group of *data* concerning the same item or subject and that is treated as an entity in a *database*. This data is divided over *fields*. A record in an address file, for example, can consist of the following fields: name, address, city and telephone number.

recorded voice announcement

RVA - A recorded voice that is used in an intercom or play unit that can rewind and replay.

Red Book

The standard published by Philips and Sony in 1982 that describes the physical format of the Compact Disc Audio. This standards book is called 'CD Digital Audio and CD + Graphics'.
See also: Compact Disc Digital Audio.

red, green, blue

RGB - Color system used in screens and photography. The colors are built up of red, green and blue. Phosphorus on the inside of the tube lights up and the colors are formed on the screen.
See also: color synthesis; cathode ray; cathode ray tube; phosphor.

redirected restore

Placing a (part of the) spare copy somewhere other than from where it has been copied.
See also: backup; tape streamer.

reduced instruction-set computing

RISC - A type of microprocessor that, compared with *reduced instruction-set computing* (CISC), has a limited, but optimal, instruction set. A number of applications (mainly graphic applications) can therefore be processed quicker. However it has the disadvantage that the programs are bigger, because a number of complicated instructions have to be supplied by the applications themselves. CISC microprocessors contain most of these instructions themselves.
See also: central processing unit.

redundant array of inexpensive discs

RAID - A storage technique patented by IBM in 1977. A RAID consists of a number of linked hard disks allowing greater storage capacity.

reflection mapping

Placing a *texture* on a *3D* object to serve as a reflection. The texture in this technique is an image of the environment, seen from the object. Besides calculating reflections such as *ray-tracing*, this method has the additional advantage of shorter calculation times. This technique causes a problem for animations because when the environment around the object changes, the reflection does not change along with it.
See also: cubic mapping.

refresh rate

The *frequency* with which the information on a screen is rewritten. The higher the frequency, the more stable the image. At a frequency of 70 *Hertz* (Hz), images are rewritten 70 times per second. Televisions have a standard frequency of 50 Hertz. A TV image is built up in two stages, first the even horizontal lines and then the uneven horizontal lines. Television and video (*PAL*) operate at 25 *frames per second*. 25 complete images are written at 50 Hertz. At 100 Hertz, 25 video images are rewritten on the screen twice.

See also: interlaced/non-interlaced.

register (to)

1. Allows columns on facing pages or on the front and back of a page to align accurately. The columns are mirrored in relation to each other. This enhances a stable image of the page, especially when the paper is translucent.
2. The correct positioning of the colors in four-color printing.

remote access

Working on a *network* at a geographical distance. Remote users are linked to the network via *modem* and PC. This method is applied by teleworkers.

See also: teleworking.

remote controller

A device to control remote equipment.

removable hard disk

A disk for data storage which has the same characteristics as a *hard disk*, but which is placed in a casing from which the disk can be removed.

render (to), rendering

The process that calculates a photo realistic image from *3D* objects and their *attributes*. It can also be the name of a program or program module that carries out the render process.

See also: ray-tracing; radiosity; z-buffer.

Renderman Image

3D *file format* designed for the Renderman render application. This format is considered the *PostScript* standard of the 3D modeling environment.

See also: rendering.

repeater

A device applied in *Ethernet* for amplifying signals. This is necessary to maintain signal quality for long-distance connections.

replication

The process of making copies of original optical discs. The discs are pressed with a mold under high pressure and at high temperatures. The environment in which the process takes place must be completely clean (sterile). The next step is to metallize the *disc*. The side of the disc that has already been provided with small *pits* is covered with aluminium to create a reflecting layer. This process takes place in an airtight space. The disc is then sprayed with a protective varnish coating and provided with a label. It is then accurately centered to punch the hole in the middle of the disc.

See also: mastering; glass master; stamper.

Research and development in Advanced Communications technologies in Europe

RACE - A European program that researches *broadband* networks (called Integrated Broadband Communications Network (IBCN)). The network must be capable of transporting vast amounts of differing information (from computer files to HDTV) at the same time. The RACE program is divided into two phases. The first phase (1987-1992) explored the possibilities. The second phase (1991-1995) prepares *implementation*. RACE researches into: (in order of decreasing priority)

1. networks and standards, including mobile networks and the division of intelligence and functionality between network and terminal;
2. public exchange;
3. expansion of glass *fiber* transmission capacity;
4. integrated optics;
5. European *pilot projects* for new services;
6. radio transmission for mobile networks;
7. private communication (video-phone, fax, rediffision);
8. production techniques for integrated optics and broadband glass fibers;
9. customized *very large scale integrated* (VLSI) chips for mobile devices.

The RACE program has been completed. In the early part of 1995 it was followed up by the *Advanced Communications Technologies and Services* (ACTS) program. To characterize the difference between the programs: RACE's objective was to develop the infrastructure; ACTS objective is to develop applications for Integrated Broadband Communications Networks.

See also: European Strategic Program for Research in Information Technology.

resolution

A standard for the level of sharpness of a screen image or a print. The resolution of a screen is indicated by the number of *pixels* (dots) per line. A resolution of 1024 * 768 *dots per line* (dpl) means that there are 1024 dots on each of the 768 horizontal lines.

Prints are expressed in *dots per inch* (dpi). An inch is 2.54 centimeters. A *laser printer* usually has a resolution as of 300 or 600 dpi, e.i. 90,000 or 360,000 dots per square inch. Scanners often have a resolution of 2400 dpi or higher. The higher the resolution of a screen or printer, the sharper the image.

resource sharing

Equipment and data in a *network* that can be shared by users. This can be the *hard disk* in a *server*, a *printer*, a *modem*, a fax, etc.
See also: peer-to-peer network.

restore (to)

The retrieval of a spare copy to replace a lost original.
See also: back up; redirected restore; tape streamer.

Restructured EXtended eXecutor

REXX - A macro programming language aimed at automated use of the operating system *OS/2* and the applications that run on it. A variation of REXX is AREXX used on the Commodore Amiga computers.
See also: macro language.

retrace

The short period of time that an electron bundle is turned off while the electron beam in a *cathode ray tube* is being repositioned. A screen image is constantly built up of image lines projected by an electron beam. When the electron beam arrives at the end of a line or a *field*, the beam is turned off and positioned at the next line or the next field.
See also: cathode ray; blanking interval.

reverse video

A way to highlight a character, field or cursor on a screen. The colors of the element to be highlighted and the background are switched. For instance: a red character on a black background is changed into a black character on a red background.

reversed

Reversing contrasts. What is white becomes black and vice versa.

rewritable consumer time code

A *time code* format, developed by Sony and implemented in the *video system control architecture* (*VISCA*) standard. This standard is comparable to the *SMPTE time code* and so measures in Hours:Minutes:Seconds:Frames.

right justification

Text whereby the lines flow freely on the left, and align straight along the right margin. This kind of *typography* is used, for example, for captions placed to the left of a picture or image. Also called flush right, quad right or range right.
See also: alignment; left justification.

ring

A *network* structure (topology) in which each device (*workstation* or peripheral) is linked to the next one. All devices are connected within one ring-shaped network. A message sent through a ring-shaped network goes through each station in the ring until it reaches its destination.

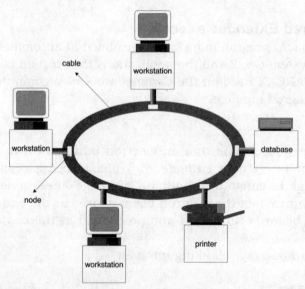

A ring network is not suitable for a large network, because it would take too long to transmit a message. Furthermore, only a limited number of devices can be connected. Another disadvantage is that when one computer fails, the ring is interrupted and some devices can then not be approached. Some ring network examples are: Apple's *LocalTalk* and IBM's *Token Ring*.
See also: bus; star.

RISC
See: reduced instruction-set computing.

ritardando
A music term indicating that the *tempo* is to be reduced gradually. Ritardando is the opposite of *accelerando*. It is often abbreviated as ritard.

rivers
A phenomenon whereby extreme word spaces appear in a text block. This happens when text is justified without hyphenation, and is placed in narrow columns. In this case, lines with few words are spaced with white gaps almost as long as the words themselves. This affects easy reading. The maximum length of word spaces can usually be specified for justified text in *layout* programs. A warning appears when this maximum is exceeded.

> In december 1877 kwam een jong mens op het redactiekantoor van Sientific American en toonde de daar aanwezigen een eenvoudig toestelletje van eigen vinding dat hij de vorige dag voltooid had. Na een beknopte inlichting te hebben gegeven, draaide de

rivers

RJ-45
An 8-pins telephone connector usually used as a connection in the case of *unshielded twisted pair* cables (UTP).

Rock Ridge format
A proposed standard for CD-WO (write-once CDs) to provide *directory* structures that can be updated when files are added to an *optical disc* at a later date. This method is already used in *multi-session* Photo CDs.

roller controller
A control device for CD-i players developed by Philips and which is especially suitable for games. The device can be compared to a *trackball*, but has more functions.
See also: Compact Disc Interactive.

roller-feed scanner
See: sheet-fed scanner.

roman
Originally one of the first typefaces that replaced the gothic letter (15th century). The roman is a *serif* letter that in the course of time has been further developed and on which numerous variations are based. Today

the term is often used to indicate a letter *style*, namely the *normal* style. The other styles such as *italic*, *bold*, etc., are derived from the roman version of a typeface.
See also: type classification.

roman numerals

These are roman letters, used to indicate numbers. The numbers one through four, for example, can be represented by roman numerals: I, II, III, IV.

rotoscope

1. A method which allows basing *animation* on the motion of an object recorded on *video* or *film*. To achieve this the film or video image is projected under the *animator*'s drawing surface. By projecting the frames one by one the animator can trace the motion and make smoothly flowing animations.
2. A device with which film images can be projected on the bottom of a glass surface. The animator is then able to trace the images. The traced images serve as a guide to let objects move. The (patented) device was invented by Max Fleischer in 1917.

router

A device that connects networks. The networks may or may not be similar. A router has the same functionality as a *bridge* and a *gateway*, but has the additional feature of sending traffic along the most expedient route. To do this, a router uses information on message traffic, utilization and rates of a connection.

row

A horizontal row of fields in a table or *spreadsheet*.
See also: cell.

RP 125

SMPTE Recommended Practice 125 - Standard for the *parallel* digital connection along which *component video* signals are transmitted. It is the predecessor of *CCIR 601* and *CCIR 656*.

rules

Horizontal and vertical lines used to separate or frame text and images, e.g. column lines.

run around

The flow of text around a picture. There are various possibilities. The text can flow around one side or both sides of a picture, the text can run along a straight line beside or around the picture or it can follow the contours of the picture.

run-time
A limited version of an application development program. It runs the application developed with the full version incapable of altering the application. Run-times are supplied to secure an application and to enhance performance. When the design module is not present, additional resources are available to run the application.
Run-time versions must sometimes be purchased separately and sometimes they are distributed free of charge.

rundown
A rough *outline* of the contents of a video program when no script is needed, e.g. for an interview.

running head
A heading repeated on each page, used for example to indicate the author or the title of a chapter.
See also: header.

S

S/DIF
See: Sony/Philips Digital Interface.

safe area
The area that is guaranteed visibility on TV. *Overscan* and the frame of the TV housing can cause parts of the picture to become invisible. When a film or video is made, this has to be taken in account. For example: titles must not be located outside the safe area.

sample-playback
See: synthesizer.

sampler
A technical facility that converts existing *analog sound* into digital information. The digital information can then be processed with a computer. See also: sampling; sampling rate.

sampling
The technical *procedure* whereby an *analog* signal is gauged via high *frequency* measuring and then converted to *digital* values.
See also: sampling rate.

sampling rate
The number of times per time unit that an *analog* signal is sampled, i.e. is converted into a *digital* signal. For instance: a *Compact Disc* signal is measured and converted 44,100 times per second. This is done via the *adaptive differential pulse code modulation* (ADPCM) technique.

sampling-synthesizer
See: synthesizer.

sans serif
A kind of typeface that has no *serifs* and little variation in line *width*. Examples: Helvetica, Univers, Futura, Franklin Gothic.
See also: type classification.

abcde	abcde
ABCDE	ABCDE
12345	12345

Futura Regular   *Helvetica Regular*

saturation

A color science term. The best color saturation is when no white has been added to the color; it is then a pure, undiluted color.
See also: hue, saturation, luminance; color synthesis.

scalable font

A *vector format* font. The font can be scaled without losing its quality because it is constructed by means of mathematical calculations.

Scalable Processor ARChitecture

SPARC - The SPARC microprocessor was developed by Sun and Weitek. The *chip* is used mainly by Sun and manufactured by Weitek and Texas Instruments. The SPARC is a *reduced instruction-set computing* (RISC) type and mainly uses the SunOS control system, but other *Unix* versions are also supported.
See also: central processing unit.

scaling

1. Enlarging or reducing an image or part of an image in graphic computer applications. The change of scale takes place by multiplying the coordinates of the image by a constant value.
2. Enlarging or reducing a typeface.

scan converter

A peripheral to convert high-resolution computer images into compatible signals for TV systems such as PAL, NTSC or SECAM.
See also: Phase Alternating Line; National Television Standards Committee; Séquential Couleur à Mémoire.

scan rate

The speed with which a *scanner* can read a page. Page scanners measure the speed in seconds per page and hand scanners measure in inches per second. The speed depends on, for example, the selected *resolution*.

scan resolution

The *resolution* in which an image that is to be scanned must be stored and processed. This resolution is expressed in *dots per inch* (dpi).

scanner

A peripheral for computers used for optical scanning of images and text. A special light source illuminates the object to be scanned. The light is converted by a photoelectric cell into an *analog* electronic signal. An *analog-to-digital converter* converts this signal into digital values. This is usually done in a *bitmap format*. Besides converting an image from analog into digital signals, the (print) colors are transformed into red, green and blue. The colors *red, green, blue* (RGB) are the standards for building a color image on a screen. By means of additional software the image can then be processed and, if necessary, converted to another format.

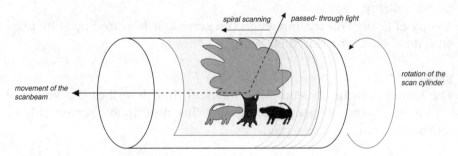

drum scanner

Various scanners can be distinguished:
1. by design: *flatbed scanners, drum scanners, overhead scanners, sheet-fed scanners, hand-held scanners;*
2. by number of gray values or colors: *two-tone scanners, gray-scale scanners, color scanners;*
3. by function: image scanning, optical character recognition.
See also: charge-coupled device; cyan, magenta, yellow, black; red, green, blue.

scanning velocity
The speed with which a *laser* beam scans the data tracks on an *optical disc*. This speed is usually expressed in meters per second.
See also: constant angular velocity.

scart
A connector for audio and video signals found on TVs and video recorders. Also known as Euro connector.

scene
An uninterrupted *video* or *film* recording. A scene is usually recorded (*shot*) a number of times in order to obtain the best possible version. Each attempt is called a *take*. When the right take is found during *editing*, it is called a *buy*.

screen (to)

Converting a *half-tone* image (such as a picture) via photographic or electronic means into an image built up of dots of varying sizes. The tints in the original are converted into small or large dots. The darker the tint, the larger the dots. This method simulates the *saturation* of a color (light and dark).
See also: gray scale.

screen dump

A copy of (a part of) the image on the screen. It is stored *pixel* by pixel on a *hard disk*, or printed on paper.

screen font

The *bitmap font* in the computer *memory* that describes the shape of characters based on points (bitmaps). This description serves only to represent a font on the screen.

screen refresh

See: refresh rate.

screen-sharing

See: joint-editing.

scrim

In the case of *video* or *film* productions, a mesh of metal wires placed in a light source in order to improve the lighting of a *scene* or subject to be recorded. The wire network is usually circular and distributes and dims the light.
See also: diffuser; gobo; key light; fill-in light.

script

1. A kind of typeface characterized mainly by the fact that its *style* is based on handwritten letters. It is a very recognizable, unique letter. Examples: Mistral, Script, Zapf Chancery.
2. An important tool in the development of a multimedia application. The script describes the functions and course of the under development. Described are:
   - content and set-up;
   - level of interactivity;
   - use of video, audio and animation;
   - interface design.

In short: the script describes the desired application in a nutshell.
See also: multimedia; authoring/scripting; story board.

Script X

A *multimedia* script language developed by Apple and IBM. By using Script X, developers can design hardware-independent and software-independent (multimedia) applications, for the purpose of allowing these Script X designed applications to make maximum use of the possibilities offered in the hardware environment.

scroll bar

Part of a *graphical user interface*. A bar along the side of a screen in which symbols are located. These symbols can be moved with the cursor. When moved, the content of the *field* shifts as well.
See also: scrolling.

Scroll-lock key

A key on a keyboard that ensures that the *cursor* is anchored at a certain spot. When the reader moves through the text, the cursor does not change position while the text rolls over the screen.
See also: scrolling.

scrolling

Moving text or images horizontally or vertically on a screen. Data that otherwise would not be visible because of the limited dimensions of the screen, can now be perused.
See also: scroll bar.

SECAM

See: Séquentiel Couleur à Mémoire.

secondary display

When two screens are connected to one computer, this indicates the screen that is inactive when the system is started up.

sector

A section of a *track* on a storage medium (disk or tape).

seed fill

A way to fill an uninterrupted and one-color space with a specific color in drawing and painting packages.
See also: boundary fill.

segment

A straight line or curved line as part of a vector-oriented image.
See also: curve; vector format.

segue
The switchover from one program segment to another in video or audio presentations.

select (to)
Activating a certain part on the screen by means of a mouse or keys. For instance: selecting part of a text, illustrations, frames or lines.
See also: active.

semiconductor industry association
SIA - A cooperative of *chip* manufacturers.

sequencer
1. A part of a program that sorts *records* according to desired specifications.
2. A device that drives digital music instruments, usually according to the *Musical Instrument Digital Interface* (MIDI) standard.

Séquentiel Couleur à Mémoire
SECAM - *Composite video* standard used in France, Russia, the Eastern European countries and some African countries. SECAM consists of 625 image lines and has a raster *frequency* of 50 Hz. 819 so-called 'scan lines' are used to scan, which ensures a better image quality than NTSC or PAL.
See also: field frequency; National Television Standards Committee; Phase Alternating Line.

serial
In series. A way to transfer data between computers and peripherals. The signals are transferred per *bit*. To enable this, computers have one or more *serial ports*.

serial mouse
A type of *mouse* that is connected to a computer via a *serial port*, as opposed to the *bus mouse* that is connected to one of the extension slots via a *plug-in* card.

serial port
A port on a computer for connecting peripherals, such as a *mouse*, *modem*, *printer* and such.

serif
A thin line, bracket or flourish at the top and/or bottom of a letter. Originally only meant for decoration, but also of importance for easy

reading. A serif letter is often preferred for run-on text. Typefaces without serif are called *sans serifs.*

server

A computer in a *network* that provides service to other computers in a network. For instance: data server, print server, mail server.
See also: client; client/server; dedicated server; peer-to-peer network.

set

The location where *video* or *film* recordings are made.

set-top box

A device that makes *interactive television* possible. It is a box with a control panel situated between the antenna cable and a television set. The set top box, or set-top, facilitates two-way communication between the consumer and the information provider via the cable. The TV viewer can select certain channels (feature films, documentaries) for which the customer pays extra. Two-way traffic can also be used for various types of service, e.g. for security services, medical care, and such.
See also: cable TV network; pay TV.

SGML

See: Standard Generalized Markup Language.

shade

A term used for determining a color impression. Shade usually means the *saturation* of a color. When mixing paint or ink, it can be made a shade lighter by adding white. Monitors make shades lighter by increasing the value of the two RGB colors that at that moment have the lowest value. For instance: the color bright red is represented on a screen by lighting up the red *pixels* to maximum strength. The green and blue pixels are dark. By increasing the light strength of the green and the blue pixels, the shade becomes lighter.
See also: color balance; red, green, blue (RGB); hue, saturation, luminance.

shading

Coloring a three-dimensional representation based on light sources and a viewpoint in the *eye coordinate system*. There are various methods to color: *flat shading, Gouraud shading* and *Phong shading*. The purpose of shading is to apply light and dark effects on the objects present in a three-dimensional image, in such a way that a somewhat realistic representation is created. In general, the following steps are followed:

1. The color of the object is determined. Either a fixed color is determined for the whole object, or an 'image map' is applied.
2. The standards of the object are determined.
3. The relationship between the standards and the angle of light incidence is determined. The smaller the angle between the two, the lighter the color value becomes.
4. Shadows and reflections of other objects are determined and included in the color value.
5. If some objects are transparent (e.g. a window), the color of the transparent objects in the background (sun, blue sky) is determined first. This, too, is calculated in the final color value.
6. The color value is then complete and is displayed.

Steps 4 and 5 do not always have to be carried out; this depends on the complexity of the program.

shared whiteboard
A white board as used in video conferences. It allows graphical presentation and exchange of ideas. The white board is visible to all conference participants and can be edited by any of them.
See also: collaborative screen sharing.

sharpness filter
Algorithm to improve the sharpness of an image.

sheet-fed scanner
A *scanner* that feeds documents through the scanner on rolls, just as a document is fed through a fax machine. The optical scanning section does not move. This type of scanner has the disadvantage that only single pages of a certain size can be used.

shell
A kind of command center, which can be seen as a switch between the user and the *operating system*. Its purpose is to simplify communication between the user and the control system. Often the user can switch from one application to another without the necessity to close applications.

shielded twisted pair
STP - A cable consisting of two insulated pairs of two wires each twisted around each other. Interference sensitivity is reduced by the twists.
See also: unshielded twisted pair.

shielding
1. In graphic computer applications, making all image elements within a certain field invisible.
See also: clipping.
2. A metal casing, installed around certain electronic components to isolate an electrical or electromagnetic field.

Shift key
A key on the keyboard marked 'shift'. Used in combination with other keys, this key carries out a number of special tasks. A capital letter is displayed when used in combination with letter keys. In combination with the other keys, the top *character* on the key is displayed. Some keyboards have a ShiftLock key, with which the Shift function can be locked in. More common is the CapsLock key, with which only the capital letter function is switched on and not the special characters.

shoot
Recording images on *film* or *video*.
See also: scene; set; take.

shooting ratio
The ratio between the amount of recorded video or film material and the amount that has been used in the final product.
See also: footage.

short
A film or video production with a duration of 1 to 35 minutes.
See also: feature.

shortcut
A special key or key combination with which a certain command can be carried out without first having to choose a *menu*. Shortcut keys allow faster work with a user interface.

shot
An image recording made with a film or video camera, possibly supplemented with synchronously recorded sound.

show reel
A compilation of films or videos made by a studio or an individual filmmaker/director/producer to give an impression of his/her competencies.

shower door effect

An unwanted side-effect of video compression (e.g. MPEG and *Indeo*). It is as if one is looking at a *scene* through multifaceted glass. Some parts of the screen show movement while others are still. The problem aggravates as the *compression ratio* rises.
See also: lossy compression; Motion Picture Experts Group.

shrink

See: compress.

side notes

Short notes in the margin of a text page.

simplex

A term used when one-way only communication can take place between computers via a *modem*.
See also: half duplex; full duplex.

simulation

A type of *interactive* computer program which imitates a real situation. This can vary from a flight *simulator* (as a game or as a training tool for pilots) to a model of an ecological system in which the influence of certain chemical or organic compounds is studied.

simulation sickness

Sickness symptoms that may occur after working with a *virtual reality* system for a long period of time, e.g. in a flight *simulator*. Complaints that may occur are dizziness, disorientation and vomiting.

simulator

A device or computer application with which reality is imitated. In the case of a device, the appearance and movements of reality are precisely imitated. Such a device is a flight simulator, for example. This is a complete copy of a cockpit, which can tilt in all directions in accordance with the flight commands given by the pilot to the simulated airplane.
See also: virtual reality; simulation sickness.

single inline memory module

SIMM - A *memory* module on which a series of memory *chips* is mounted. It usually has rows of eight or nine chips with a capacity of 256 kilobits, 1 megabits or 4 megabits. The module is connected to the mother board via a contact slot
See also: chip; 9-pin chip; 3-pin chip; single inline package.

single inline package

SIP - A *memory* module on which a series of memory *chips* is mounted. It usually has rows of eight or nine chips with a capacity of 256 kilobits, 1 megabits or 4 megabits. The module is connected to the mother board via a pin connector.
See also: single-inline memory module.

single-frame controller

SFC - A device that accurately controls a video recorder for single-frame recordings. The correct recording position is determined via a *time code*. The device is usually used to record (computer) animations. While making animations, the computer automatically records an *image* as soon as it has been fully processed.
See also: single-frame recorder.

single-frame recorder

A video recorder that can handle single-frame recording.
See also: single-frame controller.

single-session

A term used to indicate a certain type of *CD-ROM* player. The player can only read information that is written to a *compact disc* for the first time. It is no use adding *data* to the same CD at a later date when using this kind of CD-ROM player. When data is added to a CD-ROM several times a *multi-session* player is needed
See also: Photo CD.

slant

Slanting a *roman* electronically. An electronically slanted letter should not be confused with an *italic* font. The real italic is a separately designed letter, based on the roman typeface. It has a different appearance than the slanted font. The real italic is usually preferred to the slanted font, because the latter affects the design of the letter. Some fonts have an electronically slanted version called *Oblique*. Characters can be slanted to various degrees.
See also: back slant; modify.

slide scanner

A device used for scanning slides and converting them into digital images.

slow motion

Displaying images at a slower speed than they were recorded, which slows down the image motions. On TV, slow motion is mainly used during sports broadcasts. When making *feature* films, slow motion can be used to emphasize dramatic effects.

small capitals

Not a reduced capital, but a unique typeface. They are capitals that more or less meet the *x-height*. They are, comparatively, somewhat broader than capitals and have approximately the same line *width* as small letters. Small capitals are usually applied to abbreviations or to emphasize words. They can be found mainly in *roman* or medieval typefaces.

small computer system interface

SCSI - Pronounced 'skoozy'. A *parallel* interface to which a maximum of eight peripherals (devices) can be connected in series. Each device has its own identification number.

small computer system interface-2

An improved version of the SCSI *interface*. The bus width has been expanded from 8 bits to 32 bits which allows a throughput of up to 20 megabytes per second.

smear

1. Blend. Software *algorithm* that blends adjoining colors in an image.
2. Multimedia. An effect whereby right angles in a picture are stretched to left or right.
3. Graphical process. Ink stains on prints. The wet ink can easily smear when too much ink is used or the print work is handled too soon, resulting in dirty or damaged prints.

See also: filters.

SMPTE

See: Society of Motion Picture and Television Engineers.

SMPTE time code

Image number for video systems developed by SMPTE, based on an LTC *time code* in the form of HH:MM:SS:FF (hours:minutes:seconds:frame: numbers). The coding agreements are stipulated in ANSI/SMPTE 12M-1986. This time code has a compensation for the so-called *drop-frames*.

See also: Society of Motion Picture and Television Engineers (SMPTE); American National Standards Institute (ANSI); longitudinal time code (LTC).

snap to ..

Many graphic programs make magnetic lines (guide lines, column lines, etc.) and sometimes magnetic parts of an image. This helps to accurately position elements on a page. When an element is dragged in the direction of a magnetic line it will be drawn towards the line from a certain distance. The magnetic line and the closest *parallel* line of the placed element will then fit exactly.
See also: guideline.

sneakernet

The alternative to using a network: put a file on a (removable hard) disk and start walking. The sneakernet is often used when a *network* transports graphic files so slowly that it is faster to walk. Sneakernet is the successor of the 'frisbee network' where only diskettes (that were thrown) were used.

Society of Motion Picture and Television Engineers

SMPTE - An American organization with international branches. Broadcasting companies, equipment suppliers and representatives of the film and television world are members of the organization. The organization has various committees that draw up guidelines and make recommendations, e.g. *RP 125* for *CCIR*. The *SMPTE time code* is very well known and widely applied.
See also: Comité Consultatif International des Radiocommunications.

socket

1. A connection in which a *plug* can be placed.
2. A slot in which an expansion *card* can be placed.
3. A data communication standard, with which an application can make easy use of the *Transmission Control Protocol/Internet Protocol* (TCP/IP).

soft fonts

See: downloadable font.

softbot

A contraction of 'software robot'.
See also: agent.

solid modeling

A method to build *3D* objects. The method uses *primitives* such as round, square, flat, etc., for building an object. The primitives are changed into the desired object by means of *Boolean operations*.
See also: modeler; wire frame.

Sony/Philips Digital Interface

S/DIF - The consumer version of the *AES/EBU* standard for connecting stereo, digital and audio signals electrically. A smaller connection *plug* (mini-DIN) makes everything less robust than the professional version.

sound card

An expansion *card* which enables the computer to produce sound and music. The audio can be sent to external equipment.

sound effects

All sounds added to a sound track, with the exception of music and voices.

See also: audio track.

sound power level

Lw - The volume of an audio signal expressed in decibels. The number of *decibels* is calculated based on the sound intensity of the signal measured in watts per square meter.

See also: sound pressure level.

sound pressure level

Lp - The tension of an audio signal measured in decibels. The number of *decibels* is calculated based on the pressure of the audio signal measured in pascals per square meter.

See also: sound power level.

source code

The legible text in which a computer program is written. The text is drawn up according to the rules of a programming language. The source code is used to change and extend a program. The users usually do not get the source code but a compiled version, so that they can not make any changes.

See also: compile (to); programming languages.

space

Division in the form of a white space. There are various types of spaces. No consensus about the *width* of spaces can be found in professional literature. The following distinctions can be made:

- Ordinary word space.
- Fixed space, hard space: between two text segments that constitute a whole. If this space is at the end of a line both text segments are moved to the next line so that they remain together, e.g. US $500 and December 5th.

- Square, em-space: its width is equal to the letter size in use. An 8-points letter has an 8-points-wide em-space.
- Half-square, en-space: its width is equal to half the size of the letter in use. An 8-points letter has a 4-points-wide em-space.
- Number space: its width is equal to the number size in use.
- Thin space, narrow space, half space: its width is 1/5th or 1/6th of the size in use.
- Fat space, wide space: its width is 1/3rd of the size in use.
- Hair space: its width is 1/8th to 1/12th of the size in use.
- Line space: a white or empty line.

See also: body size.

spacing

Enlarging or reducing the white spaces between letters. *Tracking* (also called positive spacing) means enlarging the white spaces and *negative spacing* means reducing the white spaces. In both cases the extent to which the white spaces between letters is enlarged or reduced is the same. A specific type of negative spacing is *kerning*.

SPARC

See: Scalable Processor ARChitecure.

spectral colors

The visible colors of the spectrum. These are the colors made up of one wavelength.

spin-coating technique

A method for applying an extremely thin and even layer on an optical medium. A small drop of fluid is placed in the middle of a *disc*. The disc is then rotated at high speed. The fluid is thus distributed over the entire disc surface and then dried.

See also: optical media.

spline curve

In graphic applications this is a curve drawn by the computer. The user specifies a number of points, after which the computer determines and draws the ideal line along those points.

See also: Bézier curve.

normal line

spline

spooler

A *memory* component in a printer or computer in which a document waiting to print is stored temporarily until the task can be carried out. In the meantime, the computer can be used for other tasks.

spotlight
A type of light source that projects a highly intensive beam of light. This light source is mainly intended to give a *scene* extra depth (because a dark shadow is created behind the illuminated object). See also: ambient light.

spreadsheet
A program that divides the screen in rectangular fields. A horizontal row of fields is called a row, a vertical row is called a column. The fields are divided by a code consisting of a letter for the columns and a number for the rows, so A1, A2, etc.
The contents of the fields can be a text, a number, a mathematical term or a function. By filling in fields, calculations can be executed and models can be built up. The user has, as it were, a huge computation sheet in front of him/her and can let the computer execute all sorts of calculations with the values he/she has entered.

square-pixel digitizing
A correction to the height:width ratio of TV signals in a *frame grabber*. Without this correction, the circle of the test screen would be egg-shaped. PAL has a 7% *distortion*, NTSC can distort up to 11%.
See also: Phase Alternating Line (PAL); National Television Standards Committee (NTSC).

staff
Five closely placed horizontal lines on which symbols and musical notes are positioned to indicate their pitch.

stamper
A metal plate with the negative of a glass *CD-ROM* mold (*glass master*). This plate is used as a die for manufacturing the final compact discs or videodiscs.
See also: replication.

Standard Generalized Markup Language
SGML - A standard designed by the *International Standards Organization* for structuring *information* (ISO-standard 8879). With SGML are registered the essential properties of documents and texts. SGML identifies and codes document elements such as titles, subheadings, paragraphs and tables. The codes are linked to the original document.

The user can define the rules and relations for structuring the *data*. These are recorded in the *document type definition* (DTD).

In an SGML document the data is stored in a neutral format (*ASCII*) so it can be run on various operating systems. SGML is becoming more and more popular mainly due to this feature. SGML was used principally on the *Unix* operating system, but this is changing. Various manufacturers of popular programs (WordPerfect, Framemaker, *Acrobat*) have announced they will include SGML facilities in their products. Also an SGML wordprocessor called Author/Editor is available in a *Windows* and a *Macintosh* version.

See also: American Standard Code for Information Interchange; markup.

star

A *network* structure (topology) within which all devices (workstations and peripherals) are connected to one central device. This can be a computer or a *hub*.

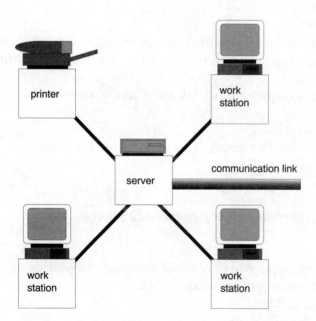

star topology

The star structure is suitable for medium-sized and large networks. Expansions are easy to implement because devices can simply be connected to the central device. The advantage of the star structure is that a network manager has easy access to the connected devices via the central device. Its weakness, however, is the 'hub'. When it fails, the workstations connected to the network are cut off.

See also: network topology.

statistical multiplexing

A *multiplexer* that distributes its capacity over the connected channels. The capacity is only used for the channels that are transmitting data at a given moment. No capacity is reserved for the channels that are not transmitting. A higher transmission capacity can thus be achieved for the occupied channels.
See also: multiplexing.

status line

A line, often at the bottom of the screen, which displays information concerning the open document. For instance, page number, line number, mouse or cursor position, etc.

step backward

In *multimedia*, this means putting the combined read/write *head* back a step in a storage medium. The step size can be a *frame* or a *segment*.
See also: step forward; frame; track reverse; track advance.

step forward

In *multimedia*, this means putting the combined read/write *head* a step forward in a storage medium. The step size can be a *frame* or a *segment*.
See also: step backward; track advance; track reverse.

step frame

Playing a *videodisc* forward or backward frame-by-frame.
See also: videodisc.

still frame

A (stationary) video image (one *frame*, 1/25 second).

still video

A recording technique whereby a *still videocamera* records an *image* as one stationary *analog video* image.
See also: motion video.

still videocamera

A photo *camera* to record *still video* images. The (reflected) light of an object is projected via the lens of a camera onto the light-sensitive fields of a *charge-coupled device* (CCD) and converted into an electronic *analog image*. The analog image is usually stored on a 2–inch magnetic disk. The analog image can be converted via a special *card* in a computer, into a *digital* image for further computer processing.

The quality of still video images is similar to that of TV images (it has a *low resolution* compared to printed matter). In the past still video systems could make color images in one recording sooner than digital systems.

At present the main applications are cable news, computer presentations and journalism. Most important to the latter are fast processing and the ability to transmit images over telephone lines and/or by satellite.

See also: digital photograpy.

sting

A short musical theme or a jingle, usually found in television *commercials*. A sting is designed to attract the viewers' attention.

storyboard

A graphic representation of the general storyline of a *film* or *video* production. The story *outline* is sketched on paper as a comic strip. Actions, sound and main developments appear as captions under the pictures. Storyboards are used, inter alia, in the production of movies and commercials.

See also: script.

stretch

A fast movement effect created by pulling an image centered between two *key-frames* in both directions simultaneously. The image stretches and blurs, thus achieving the illusion of movement.

See also: motion blur.

frame 1   frame 2 - stretch   frame 3

strike

In film and video productions, this term means removing all stage property (*props*) from the *set*.

stripe

Installing a signal on the *time code* channel of a videotape. The tape is not exposed during the process. For proper *editing*, the whole tape must have a time code before editing commences.

stripe pitch

The shortest distance between two points on a screen. The shorter the distance, the sharper the points and lines on the screen.
See also: resolution.

strobing

An effect in the human visual system that could be described as 'object duplication'. The effect occurs when not enough images per second are used in a *3D animation*.
A characteristic of the human visual system is that it anticipates the continuation of an action based on a previous observation. The expected image is made visible in the human brain. When the expected and the actual continuation of the action do not correspond, it looks as if there is a second object. The visual system is helped to synchronize the expected and the actual image by means of *motion blur*. This prevents the double image.

style

The style in which a letter is displayed, e.g. *italic*, *bold* or *condensed*. *Layout* programs can usually apply a style option to a normal *roman*. The graphic profession does not tend to *modify* letters by means of software because the original letter design is affected. If a bold Helvetica is required, Helvetica Bold is preferred. This typeface has its own *spacing* which allows a better letter picture and word picture.
See also: modify.

subhead

A heading after a headline, e.g. to indicate a *paragraph* or an article.

subscript

See: inferior.

subtractive color synthesis

See: color synthesis.

suitcase

A help program for the *Macintosh*, with which *font* packages (suitcases) can be loaded. PrePress companies and service agencies often have many fonts. These take up quite a large amount of *memory*. It is therefore preferable to load only the fonts that are needed.

super storyboard
Documentation that describes all audio, video, graphic and logic control elements of an *interactive* videodisc program.

super video graphics array
SVGA - An extension to the VGA standard for image display, which has now become a standard extension. The image *resolution* has been increased to 800 * 600 points. A number of graphic cards for SVGA also have a resolution of 1024 * 768. The SVGA specifications have been standardized by the Video Electronics Standards Association (VESA).

super video home system
S-VHS - An improved version of the *Video Home System* (VHS). More image lines are recorded, resulting in a sharper image. The physical composition of the videotape itself is different; it has less *noise* and more *generations* can be made.

Super-video
S-video - A video format, whereby brightness (*luminance*) and color (*chrominance*) are transported separately according to the *YC* method. The standard connection is a four-pin DIN *plug*.

SuperATM
An extension of the *Adobe Type Manager* program. If certain *fonts* are not available when exchanging documents, SuperATM can imitate the fonts. The fonts may look slightly different than the original fonts, but the font *width* is exactly the same, so the document *layout* does not change.
SuperATM uses the *multiple master* font technology to imitate the appearance of various fonts. Font widths for approximately 1300 fonts are available.

SuperCockpit
The virtual sight system which is being developed by the U.S. Air Force. See also: head mounted display; virtual reality.

superimpose
Placing two video or computer images from different sources one over the other on one screen and displaying them together. For instance: a graphic generated by a computer or subtitles over a video image. Super-

impose is applied in, for example, video *editing* and when using a computer and a *videodisc player* combined. Superimpose is also called *overlay*.
See also: genlock; alpha channel.

superior
Relatively small letters. They are raised above the *base line* and placed in the text. This is useful when typing mathematical equations and marking notes.
See also: inferior.

superscript
See: superior.

surface modeling
A method to build *3D* objects. With this method, the objects are built up of mathematical comparisons. The objects thus created cannot be opened out, as can be done in *solid modeling*. Yet this method can best be compared to solid modeling.
See also: modeler.

SVGA
See: super video graphics array

sweetening
A term used in *film* and *video* productions for:
1. Tuning an audio signal for purposes of eliminating *noise* in order to get the best possible sound.
2. Adding elements such as laughter, applause, music and *sound effects* to a sound track.

switcher
A device to switch from one or more video sources to another, such as video recorders and cameras. The device is usually located in a control room.
See also: production control room.

swivel
The rotating stand on which a *monitor* is placed.

symmetrical compression
A compression method is symmetrical when decompression is done by reversing the compression process, i.e. the *file* created after decompression is identical to the original.
See also: asymmetrical compression; compress; decompress.

sync signal

A signal that is used to synchronize two *video* recorders. The *synchronization* signal is often controlled by a *time-base corrector*.

synchronization

A *film* and *video* term. Ensuring that corresponding *audio* and *image* tapes run exactly *parallel* as of a fixed starting point. Tapes that do not run parallel result in an asynchronous reproduction.
See also: clap board.

synchronous transmission

A type of *serial* data transmission whereby characters are sent in one package. The exact time at which a package is sent is determined by the transmitter and the receiver. That is why the term synchronous is used. Synchronization and control characters are added to the data package, so that it can be checked whether the data has been received correctly and whether a garbled package has to be resent.
See also: asynchronous transmission.

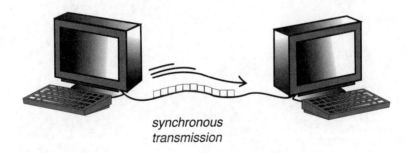

synchronous transmission

syncopation

A musical term that indicates a rhythmic accent that is dropped unexpectedly. The accent then lies just before or just after the count.

synthesizer

An electronic musical instrument that is able to reproduce the sound of ordinary musical instruments, as well as other unconventional sounds by using complex wavelengths. Synthesizers usually have a built-in keyboard. If not, they are called expanders. Synthesizers using digital sounds to create voices are called *sample-playback* or *sampling-synthesizers*.

SyQuest

A type of *removable hard disk.*
See also: Bernoulli.

System 7.X
See: Apple Macintosh system.

system bus
See: bus.

system menu
Every *window* in *Windows* and *OS/2* applications has a *menu* in the upper left-hand corner where some system commands can be approached.

T

tag

This term is mostly used for a collection of set-ups. An example is a text-tag. In this tag several text adjustments are combined, like *font*, *body size*, *leading*, tabs, *alignment*, etc. Using this, it is possible to install various set-ups in one action. A synonym for tag is typogram. Another example is a ColorTag. In a ColorTag the color characteristics of several devices like monitors, scanners and printers are stored. ColorTags are used within the *color management* software *FotoTune*.

Tagged image file format

TIFF - An often used graphic *file format* of the *bitmap* type. This file format is usually used for scanning images. The format has many variations, which often leads to exchange problems.
The format contains information about the used *resolution*, the number of gray scales or the number of colors. Because the files are very large, they are compressed automatically by a number of programs. Unfortunately, not all these programs use the same compression method, which also can lead to problems.
TIFF-files are divided into 3 main types:
- black/white TIFF;
- gray TIFF (256 *gray scales);*
- color TIFF (up to 16.7 million colors).
See also: compress; gray scale.

tagging

The marking of a *file* or *directory* so that it can be processed subsequently, for instance to erase, copy, move or backup it.

tail margin

White margin at the bottom of a page.
See also: layout.

take

The shooting/recording of a *scene* on video or film material. Often, several takes are made to be able to select the best *shot* during the *editing*.

take-up reel

A reel on which film material or magnetic tape is spooled during recording and/or reproduction.

Taligent

A purely *object oriented* operating system that is under development by Apple and IBM. It is a completely open and extendible operating system. This allows developing of extensions in the form of object libraries to add extra functionality to Taligent.

tally light

A tiny (red) indication light on the front of a video camera which indicates that the camera is recording. The light is used to indicate to the person(s) about to be filmed to look in the right direction. This is especially important in situations where various cameras are on the *set*.

tape cartridge

A *magnetic tape* on a reel in a solid protective housing. Different types of tapes are used depending on the recording/playback equipment, for example *digital audio tape* (DAT) or *data cartridge*.
The magnetic tape is often used as a storage medium because of its high storage capacity. The access to the recorded data is slow, however. The tape must be frequently spooled backward or forward.

tape streamer

A device connected to a computer, through which a *magnetic tape* can be read, written or erased. The most important function of a tape streamer is making *backup* copies of files in a computer system.
See also: digital audio tape.

TCP/IP

See: Transmission Control Protocol/Internet Protocol.

Tech.3235-E

The standard of the *European Broadcast Union* for the set-up and transmission of TV images. This standard is called *Phase Alternating Line* (PAL).
See also: television signal standard.

telecommunications

Communication which takes place over a long distance with the help of electric and electronic means. Forms used are: beam transmission, radio, satellite, cable and modem connections.

telecommuting
See: teleworking.

teleconferencing
A meeting by two or more persons in different locations. These persons communicate by means of image or sound connections.
See also: video conferencing.

telematics
Contraction of TELEcommunication and inforMATICS (computer science). The combination of these two technologies makes it possible to control remote computers.

telemetry
Remote measuring and presenting of variables such as temperature, pressure, speed, digital processes, etc. This technique is used in space travel, in medical care and in cable television networks. Telemetry is handy for the registration of two-way communication, for example for information exchange and *pay TV*.

telerecording
Remote recording of still or moving images (photographs, television) and of technical measurements (space travel). The values of the measured or registered variables are converted to electric current or they are encoded in a *binary* code. The values are transmitted to a receiver and recorded on a data medium by means of a wireless connection. This is usually paper or a magnetic medium. An everyday application of telerecording is a video recorder.

television signal standard
The technical rules and guidelines for the set-up and transmission of television images. The three best-known standards are PAL, NTSC and SECAM. They are only compatible by using extra tools. A new, more advanced, but less used standard is MAC.
See also: Phase Alternating Line (PAL); National Television Standards Committee (NTSC); Séquentiel Couleur à Mémoire (SECAM); multi-plexed analog components (MAC).

teleworking
The performing of activities at a geographical distance on a computer that is connected through a *modem* to a computer of the central organization.
See also: remote access.

tempo

In music, tempo is expressed by the number of counts (beats) per minute. In film and video the tempo is expressed in *frames per second*.

tensioning

The fast forward and backward winding of the *magnetic tape* in a *tape streamer*. The purpose is to ensure that the tape is tightly wound on the reel, so that no slack arises during the *backup* copy.

terabyte

Well over a billion bytes.
To be exact: 2 to the power of 40 = 1,099,511,627,776 bytes.

terminal

A terminal or *workstation* is a combination of a keyboard and a *monitor*. Such a workstation is connected to a central computer system. In this way a number of people are able to work behind their workstation with the central computer simultaneously.

There are two kinds of terminals: dumb and intelligent. A dumb terminal has no processing capability of its own; it is only able to do something if it is connected to a central computer system. An 'intelligent' terminal does have its own processing capability.

A PC can serve as an 'intelligent' terminal.

terminate and stay resident

TSR - A program that is loaded and stays loaded into the internal *memory* (RAM) of a computer. At any moment, even when working with other programs, a user can call the TSR by pressing a determined key combination beforehand. An example of a TSR program is a screen capture program. Such a program makes a print of the current screen, but may not become visible on the screen itself.

See also: random access memory; screendump.

texture

An image, repeating or not, which is meant to be pasted onto a certain surface or object, in 2D as well as in 3D objects. Textures can represent natural or imaginary images, like a stone wall or a face. There are also procedural textures, which are calculated completely from formulas.

thick Ethernet

Thick coax-cable. This cable is expensive, but it has an important advantage that lengths up to 600 meters are possible without the need

for signal amplifying. The connection is made by clasping a *transceiver* to the cable.
See also: repeater; thin Ethernet.

thick space
See: space.

thin Ethernet
Thin coax-cable. This cable is cheaper than *thick Ethernet*, but the unamplified connection length is less. *BNC*-connectors are used for making connections.

thin space
See: space.

three-point curve
In graphical computer applications a shape where two points define the far ends of a curve and a third point defines the top of the image.

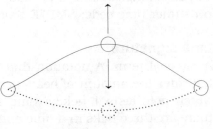

three-point curve

thresholding
In graphical computer applications converting gray-scale image data into *binary* image data. With this method all the image data above a certain level are represented by 1 (white) and all gray-scale image data below that level are represented by 0 (black)

thumbnails
Representing illustrations or pages in small size on one screen. This function is often used in image databases.

thumbpad
1. An electro-mechanical system that allows the user to move the *cursor* (or other graphic element) over the screen by rubbing his/her thumb over a pad. The pad registers direction of movement and the applied pressure. This is transmitted to the computer and as a result the cursor is moved.
2. A type of remote control for a CD-i player. It works as described above.
See also: Compact Disc Interactive.

TIFF
See: tagged image file format.

tilt up/down
A camera movement where the camera moves up and down vertically.

time base
The tuning of the horizontal and vertical *synchronization* pulses in a video signal.
See also: time-base corrector; sync signal.

time code
A system where a time mark and a frame number is encoded in every individual video frame. This allows precise *editing* to the frame level. An example is Hours:Minutes:Seconds:Frames (*HMSF*).
See also: longitudinal time code; vertical-interval time code; rewritable consumer time code; SMPTE time code.

time signature
A musical term. A notation that looks like a fraction. The numerator indicates the amount of beats per time, and the denominator indicates which note lasts 1 tick. A time signature of 3/4 often indicates that there are three ticks in a time and that a quarter note has the duration of one tick. A time signature of 12/8 indicates twelve ticks in a time and that an eighth note equals one tick.

time slot
A network term. A constantly repeating, fixed interval in which data can be sent over a network. When a time slot is full, the transmission is interrupted until a new one is available.
See also: token passing protocol.

time-base corrector
A device that synchronizes various video signals allowing them to be overlapped. The measuring of *synchronization* is done with a *waveform monitor*.
See also: time base.

title generator
A device or program for generating credit titles or subtitles. When software is used a *genlock* is needed to be able to edit the image and the titles.

toggle
A term used in various kinds of programs. It is a command allowing a user to choose between two possibilities.

token passing protocol

A token in the form of a unique combination of bits. This token goes round continuously in a ring-shaped *network*. If a *workstation* wants to transmit, it waits for the token. If the token arrives, the message is send. The receiver, for its part, answers when it gets the token.
See also: Token Ring; ring.

Token Ring

A ring-shaped network structure by IBM where devices communicate with each other using the *token passing protocol*. The transmission speed measures 16 megabits per second. The Token Ring-protocol is an IEEE-standard.
See also: network topology; ring; Institute of Electrical and Electronic Engineers.

tone

A gray or color value.
See also: gray scale; hue, saturation, luminance.

tone reproduction

The extent to which the *luminance* proportions in a subject and a recorded image are similar.

tone value

The *density* of a random point of a positive or negative image. The tone value gives no information about the color of the measured point.
The tone value of a point combined with the color of a point (based on *red, green, blue* (RGB) or *cyan, magenta, yellow, black* (CMYK)) determines the *saturation* or brightness of a color.
The tone value in photographic films reveals itself by a high or low density of the emulsion. CCDs in scanners and digital cameras register per color (RGB) the tone value of an image. The gray scales are converted into the individual colors during processing.
The tone value of an image can be influenced by a *color filter* during reproduction or (video) recording. After a recording the tone value can be adjusted with image manipulation software.
See also: charge-coupled device.

touch screen

A *monitor* that can be used as monitor and as pointing device. Processing can be done by touching the screen with a finger. A touch screen is usually a normal monitor with a front screen. The electric field or an infrared beam is broken by touching the screen. This allows the computer to localize the position that is touched and instructions can be executed. When infrared beams are used it is not necessary to touch the screen. Approaching it to a distance of 0.5 or 1 mm is enough. An advantage of touch screens is the interference sensitivity reduction. A keyboard, one of the most interference sensitive devices, is not needed. Touch screens are, among other things, used for the information displays at stations and airports. There are usually only a few actions needed to get the desired information. The use of touch screens is also increasing in computer-controlled machinery in factories and in commerce, for example, in the catering industry, utilities and tourism.

touchpad

A remote control used for CD-i players developed by Philips, especially suitable for games.
See also: Compact Disc Interactive; roller controller.

track advance

To move the read/write *head* forward to the beginning of the next track on a storage medium, in the context of *multimedia* applications.
See also: track reverse; tracks; step forward; step backward.

track reverse

To move the read/write *head* back to the beginning of the current track on a storage medium, in the context of multimedia applications. If the head is already located on this position then it is moved to the beginning of the previous track.
See also: track advance; tracks; step backward; step forward.

trackball

A *mouse button* alternative. It is a ball that can be moved with the palm of the hand or with the fingers. An advantage of this type is that one needs little space on the desktop. This is the reason the trackball is often used in laptops. A disadvantage is that the precise control of the *cursor* is harder.

tracking

1. Graphic process. This term means enlarging the white *space* between letters. The same enlargement is used for all letters. The opposite of tracking is *negative spacing*.
See also: kerning.
2. Video term. A disturbance in the video image caused by an incomplete read out of the control track or by a damaged control track. This can be caused by wrong tape tension, dirt or a faulty cassette.
See also: video errors.

tracks

Tracks on a disk or a tape magnetized by a write *head*. Tracks are used for storing data. In the case of disks, tracks are concentric rings. Audio tape has longitudinal tracks and video-tape has diagonal tracks.

Tracks can be read simultaneously if there is more than one head. A video and audio track can be read at the same time with the corresponding head.

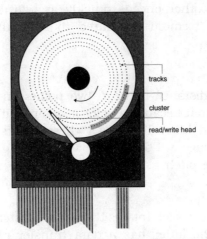

transceiver

A device that sends and receives information. It is the part of a *network adapter* to which the network cable is connected.

transition

See: video effects.

Transmission Control Protocol/Internet Protocol

TCP/IP - A *network protocol* allowing various computers and all kinds of networks communicate with each other. The name shows that it consists of two protocols. The basic protocol is IP (Internet Protocol), a *packet switching* protocol.

TCP complements IP. It checks and corrects errors by *tracking* down and recovering lost, mutilated and doubled data packages. It accomplishes a faultless connection between transmitter and receiver. The TCP/IP protocol has been developed by the American Department of Defense.

transponder

The part of a communication satellite that transmits sound, TV and data signals from one Earth station to one or more other Earth stations.

transpose

Musical term. The transcription of a piece of music to a higher or lower key.

tremolo

A musical effect, consisting of deliberately vibrating one or more musical notes. A tremolo on one note is achieved by repeating the note as quickly as possible. A tremolo on two or more notes is achieved by playing every other one as quickly as possible. When it is used by synthesizers, tremolo is related to a small change in the sound *amplitude.*

triple pitch

The smallest distance between two points on a color *monitor.* This is called triple pitch because a color is composed of the three basic colors red, green and blue. The closer these points are to each other, the sharper the image will be.
See also: stripe pitch.

triple-speed

A CD-ROM drive which rotates three times faster than a single-speed CD-ROM drive. The latter has a data transfer rate of 150 kilobytes per second. This implies that a triple-speed CD-ROM drive has a transfer rate of 450 kilobytes per second.
See also: Compact Disc; quad-speed.

truck

A *shot* where the *camera,* mounted on a mobile tripod, moves sideways.

TrueType

A technology for scalable fonts introduced in early 1991 by Apple Computer. At first it seemed that Apple would drop the comparable *Type 1* font technology by Adobe Systems after completing TrueType. Nevertheless at the end of 1991 it became clear that Apple would continue to support Type 1.
Besides Apple computers, TrueType is available for Microsoft *Windows* and for *OS/2* (by IBM). Microsoft and Apple have an agreement to further develop TrueType.
See also: outline font.

truevision targa

TGA - A graphic *file format* of the *bitmap* type. This format can record up to 16.7 million colors.

tumbling
A graphical effect where a video image rotates around its axis, while the axis itself also rotates.
See also: video effects.

TWAIN
Tool Without An Important Name - A software standard for entering image material into graphic programs (*Windows* and *Macintosh*). This standard is used by most *scanners, frame grabbers* and *still videocameras*.

tweening
An *animation* technology where a computer calculates and creates the images (in-betweens) that connect two *key-frames*.

two-shot
2S - In a video or film production a *shot* of two persons. Both persons have equal screen *space*.
See also: over-the-shoulder; close up; medium shot; long shot.

two-tone scanner
A *scanner* that presents an image or an object in black and white only. A black-and-white scanner is usually used for scanning *line-art* or text.

Type 1
A PostScript *outline font*, a technology developed by Adobe Systems. Type 1 starts from one outline description. Based on this description the fonts are proportionally scaled for use on monitors, printers, imagesetters, etc. Letters are adjusted with *hints* to get typographic sound, readable letters at low resolutions. Type 1 was elected as the standard for describing an outline font (ISO 9541) by the *International Standards Organization* in 1992.

type area
The *page area* where text and illustrations are placed, excluding page numbers, headers and footers.
See also: layout.

type classification
The classification of fonts by nature, origin and appearance. The total number of available digital fonts is approximately 15,000. For font classification several criteria can be applied, for instance, appearance and origin. A commonly used classification is defined by the Frenchman

Maximilien Vox. It is based on appearance, but the fonts in the first five groups are grouped on historical similarities. The Association Typographic Internationale (A.Typ.I.) has raised Vox's classification to a standard. The following font groups are defined:
- humans;
- garalds;
- reals;
- didones;
- mechanics;
- incises;
- manuares;
- fractures;
- exotics.

The simplest classification has six groups:
- *old style type;*
- *modern;*
- *Egyptian;*
- *sans serif;*
- *script;*
- *decorative.*

type size
See: body size.

typographic measurements
Typography has two specific measurement systems, the European Didot system and the English-American *pica* system. The *point* is the smallest unit in both systems. In the European system, twelve Didot-points make up a *cicero* or augustian. A Didot point is 0.376065 mm.

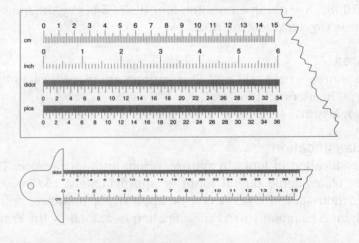

A cicero/augustian measures therefore 12 * 0.376065 = 4.513 mm. The cicero and augustian used to be different measurement units, but they are identical nowadays.

In the English-American system twelve pica points make up a pica. Opinions differ greatly on the correct thickness of the pica measure. A generally accepted standard is not available. Most publishing programs use the pica *point size* as defined in the *page description language PostScript*. This pica point equals 1/72nd inch (0.35278 mm). A pica measures therefore 12 * 0.35278 = 4.23 mm (1/6th inch). In some programs the point size is adjustable.

typography

The word is derived from the Greek word 'typos' (platform, relief) and 'grafyn' (to write). Typography originally mean 'to write a raised image'. There are different definitions of this term. One of the oldest and clearest is from Stanley Morison (1889 - 1967) in his book 'First Principles of Typography': 'Typography could be defined as the art of arranging printing material in accordance with a specific goal: to arrange the letters amongst themselves, to divide the white space and to arrange the type to help the reader in every possible way to better understand the text. Typography is a practical method to a primarily useful and only by coincidence aesthetic aim, because enjoying pretty images is seldom the main intention of the reader.'

U

underscan
A function to reduce a normal sized scanned video image by approximately 20 per cent. This makes the complete television image visible on a *monitor*. See also: overscan.

undo
A command present in many programs to recall an action. In some programs it is possible to recall a number of successive actions.

uninterruptible power supply
UPS - A current supply where the switch from mains supply to emergency supply takes place without any loss of current.

universal asynchronous receiver/transmitter
A *chip* that controls the *serial* communication of a computer. The chip is mainly used in personal computers.
See also: 8250 UART; 16450 UART; 16550 UART.

UNIX
A 32-bit *operating system*. Developed in the *C* language. In theory, it can be used on different computer systems platforms. Unfortunately some manufacturers developed their own version of Unix causing the compatibility to be imperfect.
Multi-user and *multitasking* are important features of Unix. This operating system is often used in a scientific environment and lately also in the business environment.
See also: multi-using.

UnixWare
A Unix-compatible 32-bit *operating system* manufactured by Novell. Well-known *Unix* features such as *multi-user* and *multitasking* are available incorporated. Unixware offers, in contrast with Unix, a useful Windows-like *graphical user interface*.

unplugged
People that cannot participate in the information society, due to their position in society.

unshielded twisted pair

UTP - A cable consisting of four pairs of two twisted wires each which, in contrast to *shielded twisted pair*, are not isolated. Cable consisting of two pairs of two wires each can be used in combination with telephone and *10Base-T*. It is a relatively cheap kind type of cable often used for *network* connections. There are several kinds of UTP-cables, divided into the categories 1 to 5. Cables of category 3 can transmit up to 10 Mbits/s. Cables of category 5 can transmit up to 100 Mbits/s. Compared to *thick Ethernet* cable the maximum distance where no signal amplification is needed is less.
See also: coax.

upload (to)

Copying a file from the remote (local) computer to the *host* computer. Contrast with *download.*

upper case

The capital letters of the alphabet.

upstream

The direction of data signals of a *cable TV network* seen from the *head end* (device that controls and checks the status of the transmission). Signals from the head end go downstream; signals to the head end go upstream.

upward compatible

A term used by computer manufacturers to indicate successors to an earlier mode. They are constructed in such a way that programs of the predecessor can also be used. The same applies to software. Without problems, a data file produced with earlier versions of a program can be used. The opposite is called downward *compatible.*

utility

A software tool that is used for executing specific actions.

V

Valorization and Utilitization for Europe
VALUE - A European program, the aims of which are protection, exploitation and promotion of research results in the field of technology. Value is developed and executed by DG-XIII (Directorate General) which has its residence in Luxembourg.
See also: Community Research and Development Information System.

VALUE
See: Valorization and Utilitization for Europe.

variable
The variable is an important part in a *programming language*. The variable name is a certain character/digit combination assigned by a the programmer. The variable refers to a place in the computer memory. The use of variables simplifies the programming.

vector format
A graphic *file format*. The most important characteristic is the use of mathematical formulas to represent objects. A *bitmap format* contains information about each individual *pixel*. There are no relations between these pixels. A vector file contains no information about individual pixels but does hold information about objects such as squares, lines and so on. For instance, a line is defined by the starting point, the end, the thickness and the color. The pixels that form the line are one unit. Modifications of the line take place by changing the formulas.

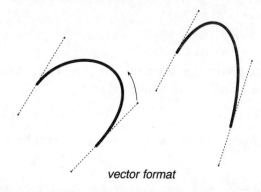

vector format

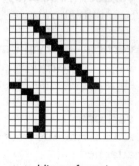

bitmap format

Therefore, the line stays smooth after modification. In a vector-oriented drawing program, the user is unaware of the underlying technology. The *graphical user interface* makes it possible to alter these formulas using simple manipulations (like moving a line with the help of a *mouse*), but the user is actually programming. Some vector formats are *PICT*, *EPS*, and DXF.

Vector format advantages are:

- Files are smaller. Individual pixels are not described, only the *outline*.
- There is less image degradation during modification because a mathematically described line always stays smooth. Bitmap formats often look jagged after modification. A vector format is *resolution* independent.

See also: Bézier curve.

vectorscope

A device that shows the status of the color signal of a video source. The device contains a round *monitor* upon which a pattern is drawn. With points of reference on the monitor the video device is adjusted until the image shown on the vectorscope coincides with the points of reference. The adjustments are set with a *color corrector*.

verifying

To compare data of a copy with the original data to check if the data is identical.

vertical blanking interval

In monitors, the short period the electronic beam needs to move from the last *pixel* in the bottom image line to the first pixel in the top image line. In this short period information can be sent, for example a *time code*.

vertical frequency

See: refresh rate.

vertical-interval time code

VITC - *Time code* that is integrated with the video picture. The code is situated on line 17 of a *frame* and consists of white dots.

vertices

A 3D term. The nodes in a *wire frame* model where two planes can be attached.

See also: mesh; faces.

very large scale integration

VLSI - A design and production technology of digital circuits with a very high integration *density*. This technology makes it possible to integrate large and complex circuits on a *chip*.

vibrato

A musical term that indicates rapid, small changes in the pitch of a note. With a wind instrument a vibration is played by blowing technique; with a violin vibrato, it can be produced by lightly moving up and down the fingertip(s) pressing the strings.

video

An electronically recorded and transported moving image. The word originates from Latin and means 'I see'.

video adapter

An add-on *card* translating digital data to the picture on a *monitor*. The digital information is translated to black and white or *red, green, blue* signals a monitor uses.
See also: random access memory digital to analog converter (RAMDAC).

video cassette

A housing of synthetic material for protecting *magnetic tape*. In the housing there are two spools each with a tape-end attached to it. Usually the tape is pulled off the cassette by the *video cassette recorder* a few centimeters, to be transported along the different heads.

video cassette recorder

VCR - A device that writes video signals to and reads video signals from *magnetic tape* in a cassette. There are *video cassette* recorders for the consumer market (*video home system* (VHS), Super VHS, *Hi-8*) and for the professional environment (*Betacam SP*, U-matic, *BCN 1*).

video CD

A *motion video* standard according to the specifications of the *White Book*. Video CD must not be confused with *Digital Video* (DV) or *full-motion video* (FMV). Video CDs can be read by any XA-compatible CD; however for displaying it needs a MPEG decoder.
See also: Motion Picture Experts Group (MPEG).

video clip

A video presentation, used to adorn a piece of music. A video clip is usually applied to popular music.

video conferencing

An electronic application allowing people to have a conference from a distance via the use of computers and communication equipment. The Video Conferencing Rooms play a central role. These are rooms where people are seated at a conference table. Communication equipment makes connections with one or more other Video Conferencing Rooms where the other conference participants are present. Using cameras and microphones the participants can hear and see each other. They can study the same documents and use the same computer programs. It is as if one is in the same room, in spite of the long distance.

Business trips are often time-consuming and tiring; the expectation is that video conferencing will gain popularity.

video control

System for remote controlling a *video cassette recorder*. Such a system can include the physical connection as well as the command structure. See also: Control-S; local application numerical control; video system control architecture (VISCA).

video controller

The graphical processor on a video card that translates digital data to monitor signals.
See also: video adapter; digital-to-analog converter (DAC).

video driver

Control software for a *video card*. The *driver* is the *interface* between application program and the video card.
See also: video adapter.

video effects

Manipulations with the *video image* in order to create special image effects.
See also: dissolve; door swing; fade-in; fade-out; fly-in; iris; jump cut; tumbling; warp.

Video Electronic Standards Association

VESA - A group of hardware manufacturers and software developers that create graphical and video card standards.

video errors

Irregularities that become visible during the reproduction of a video signal.
See also: breakup; color noise; confetti; crawl; drop-out; glitch; hot-spot; line pairing; moiré; tracking.

Video for Windows

A software package that enables PCs running Microsoft *Windows* to display and record video. For (de)compression of the video signals, codecs—such as *Indeo* or *Cinepack*—are used. Without hardware assistance during (de)compression, a picture size of 160 * 120 *pixels* (1/16th the area of a VGA screen) at 15 *frames per second* is possible on a PC equipped with a 80486 processor running at 33 MHz.
Video for Windows has been developed by Microsoft.
See also: digital video; coder/decoder; video graphics array (VGA).

video gain

The strength of a video signal.

video graphics array

VGA - The video standard introduced by IBM in 1987. The *resolution* is to 640 * 480 pixels in 16 colors, or 320 * 200 pixels of a palette of 262,144 colors.
See also: super video graphics array (SVGA).

video home system

VHS - A video system intended for use at home; it has a low quality. The sound signal is recorded on a single linear track. In HIFI-stereo recorders the sound is recorded on the video track in stereo.
See also: super video home system (S-VHS); video cassette recorder.

video memory

Memory part where *data* is stored for displaying on the *monitor*. Each *pixel* is represented by at least one *bit*. For color representation more than one bit is required.
See also: pixeldepth.

video mode

A specific *resolution* set-up for a video card, the number of colors and the controlling of a *monitor*. There are several set-ups possible depending on the video card. These set-ups are necessary for image reproduction on different monitor types.

video random access memory

VRAM - A kind of RAM-memory suitable for use in a video card. Because dual-ported memory is used, the central processor (CPU) and the graphic processor have simultaneous access to this memory. This results in a substantial screen display speed.
See also: video adapter.

video splitter
Device for splitting one video signal into several branches containing the same video signal.

video system control architecture
VISCA - A control *protocol* designed by Sony. The information stream in the protocol is set up in the same way as in *Musical Instrument Digital Interface* (MIDI).
See also: video control.

video-on-demand
See: on-demand system.

videodisc
A common name for an *optical disc* with colored video images and stereo sound. During the read out of a videodisc the same optical mechanism is used just as in compact discs. The discs have a diameter of 30, 20 or 12 centimeters. The 12-cm version can only be played single sided; the 20 and 30-cm versions can be played single and double-sided.
These optical discs are able to contain *analog* as well as *digital image* and sound information; however the control information is always present in a digital format. Videodiscs are divided in four levels; ranging from level zero to level three videodiscs. These levels represent the level of interaction of the program on the videodisc.
See also: level zero videodisc.

videodisc map
A table containing information about every video and sound segment used in a presentation. In this table, for instance, are the first and last *frame* numbers stored and sound specifications.
See also: chapter.

videodisc player
Playback equipment for videodiscs. The videodisc hardware element requirements are videodisc-level dependent.

videophony
A service combining sound and video over a telephone line allowing users to see and to hear each other.

videotex
An information system with communication possibilities via the telephone network. The service is often not free of charge, but on the

other hand, it offers a lot more possibilities than teletext. All kinds of information (commercial, tourist) can be obtained. Orders can be placed with companies and institutions that have a Videotex connection.

Viditel

An information service designed by the Dutch PTT and only accessible to subscribers. Access to Viditel is via a telephone-line, a computer and a *modem*.

Viditel looks like the teletext pages on TV. On every screen page, there are 25 text-lines of 40 characters each. Lines in common computer applications contain 80 characters. There are many thousands of information pages stored in the Viditel computers. An important supplier of information is the government giving information about the fiscal system, legislation, subsidies and so on. Companies, institutions and sometimes private individuals make use of Viditel. The aim is to provide customers with information about products and services. Viditel has the reputation of being slow. Developments are on the way to provide a better system which will be faster and provide more information per screen.

vidiwall

Several rows of monitors stacked on top of each other acting as one screen. Each monitor displays only a part of the total image.

virtual device interface

VDI - A graphical *interface* for high-level computer languages. This interface is recommended for ANSI standard.
See also: American National Standards Institute.

virtual drive

See: RAM-drive.

virtual memory

A technology for simulating more internal *memory*. A part of the *hard disk* is used as if it is internal memory. Therefore, it is possible to work with programs that need more internal memory than is present.

virtual reality

VR - A computer-simulated environment. Four levels of virtual reality are distinguished, each allowing an increasing 'immersion' of the user. The basic components of a VR-system comprise of: a reproduction system, a data file and the hardware and software tools to manage these components. The four levels of VR are:

1. *Desktop* systems. Two-dimensional images on an ordinary screen creating the illusion of a three-dimensional world with movement and other visual stimuli.
2. *Partial immersion.* This level is obtained adding 3D-simulations to desktop systems by means of a 3D-glasses, a *mouse* (with three or more degrees of freedom) or a *data glove*. With these systems specialized software is used to pick up objects with the glove or by clicking a *mouse button.*
3 *Full immersion.* This level creates a simulated reality in a true-to-life way. An essential part for obtaining this effect is the *head mounted display*, a helmet filled with electronics worn by the user. Through this the virtual world around the user can be observed. A user sees a stereoscopic three-dimensional image. Hand and body movements are registered with a *data suit.*
4 *Environmental immersion.* At this level the user is situated in a room with projections of the virtual world on the walls. Only light-weight stereoglasses are necessary for three-dimensional vision. The room is equipped with instruments allowing the image of the environment to be adjusted to the movements of the user.

See also: simulation.

Another VR-model is known as the AIP-cube. This model is developed by the MIT Media Lab. The letters A, I and P mean Autonomy, Interaction and Presence. To what extent each of the components is present is expressed as numbers between zero and one.

Autonomy (A) means the capability of a computer model to react to external stimuli.

The Interaction is equal to one if all *parameters* are used by the user; however, interaction is still limited by the computer's capabilities.

The Presence (P) indicates the level of immersion. The more tactile feedback a system offers, the closer P comes to one. Reality, by definition, has value one. A, I and P are three axes at right angles in a *coordinate system* from 0, 0, 0 to 1, 1, 1. Ultimate VR approximates reality at the point 1,1,1.

virtual space

An electronic generated environment, consisting of three-dimensional computer images. The movements and actions of a human visitor are registered and the image of the environment is adjusted accordingly.

Virtual Worlds Consortium

A co-operation for the research on and the promotion of the use of *virtual reality* technology. Members of this consortium are the US Navy, Boeing, DEC, Fujitsu, Microsoft, Ford and Sun Microsystems, etc.

See also: virtual reality.

VISCA
See: video system control architecture.

visual programming
A programming technique where the application interface is built by placing objects (such as buttons, check boxes, input fields, list boxes) on a form. This way the programmer sees immediately what screens of the final application will look like. Without visual programming it is neccesary to write many code lines before the application can be tested and the screening can be judged. Therefore, visual programming not only gives instant feedback on screen designs, it also reduces the programming effort in offering ready-to-use building blocks.
Programming of the content of the application code is associated with events. For example: when the user clicks on a *button* the program receives a button-down event. To specify what to do when this event occurs, the programmer selects the button and opens a *window* where the program code can be entered.
See also: programming languages.

visualization
The technique for presenting scientific insights in a graphical way (e.g. by using charts and diagrams). Often databases or spreadsheets supply the data for the charts.

voice mail
Software designed to send voice messages over computer networks.

voice over
VO - The voice of a narrator in a film or video production.

voice print
A recorded voice sample used to identify, mostly for security measures.

voice synthesizer
A device that imitates human voices.
See also: audio response unit.

volume
A unit of disk storage. A volume can be as large as the physical disk; it can also occupy a part of the disk allowing several volumes to exist on one disk. In a *network*, the available *hard disks*, CD-ROMs, etc. are also known as volumes. In *MS-DOS* a volume is made available for use by assigning a *drive* letter to it (such as A: B: or C:).

voxel

Contraction of VOlume piXEL. It is a three-dimensional pixel. Voxels are often generated by *3D* digitizers.

W

WAN
See: wide area network.

warm reboot
The restart of a computer by pressing Ctrl-Alt-Del. A warm *reboot* is faster than a *cold reboot*, because most hardware checks are skipped (no memory test, for instance).

A warm reboot is necessary when changing configuration (for example to load drivers to access a *CD-ROM*) or when the system locks after a program error or hardware conflict. When the warm reboot fails, it is necessary to resort to cold reboot (press the reset button or switch the computer off and on).

warp
Digital *video effect* where the *transition* to a new *scene* is carried out by rotating the next scene's picture while it comes to the front or by rotating and reducing the picture of the current scene whilst moving out of sight.

waveform
1. The graphical representation of a wave. The characteristics of the wave, such as *frequency* and *amplitude* are made visible.
2. A digital method for sound storage and manipulation.

waveform monitor
A device for measuring the characteristics of a video signal. These are the strength of a signal (*video gain*) and the 'sync pulses'. The adjustments of sync pulses are made through activating a *time-base corrector*. The colors are measured with a *vectorscope*.
See also: sync signal.

weight
There are a number of ways to describe the boldness of a letter, for instance regular, semibold and *bold*. This is also called the weight of a letter.

Weitek coprocessor
A powerful numeric *coprocessor* by the Weitek company, specially designed for CAD applications. There is a type designed for the 80386-microprocessors (the 3167-model) and one for the 80486-micro-processors (the 4167-model). The Weitek-processor is only able to use programs that are specially designed for it.
See also: 80x86DX.

weld
A function in some drawing programs which connects two lines to each other, also known as 'join'.
See also: path.

white balance
Calibrating a (still) videocamera to the light frequency that must be recorded as 'white'. The process is simple: screen-filling a white sheet of paper is recorded (placed against the background one wants to record). The *camera* corrects color casts in the subject if necessary. Most camera systems have an automatic white balance; color casts are corrected automatically.
See also: still videocamera.

White Book
The standard that defines how *data* must be recorded on a *Video CD*/Karaoke CD. A white book CD can record up to 74 minutes of audio and video using MPEG-1 compression.
See also: Motion Picture Experts Group.

white line
An extra white line, also called line space.

white space
An important element on a page: the not-printed parts. These are *back margin, header margin, tail margin* and *column gutter*.
See also: layout.

whole tone
Musical term. The length of an interval between two whole notes on a scale.
See also: half-tone.

wide angle
A lens with a short focal distance and a wide *angle*. This gives a picture a wider view than the normal view.

wide area network

WAN - A network connecting workstations at different geographical locations. A WAN often connects several *local area networks* to each other.

widow

A widow is the starting line of a *paragraph* and appears as the last line at the bottom of a page. From a typographical point of view this is unwanted. Word-processing and publishing programs offer widow/orphan protection. When a widow is found it is transferred onto the next page automatically.

See also: orphan; wrong overturn; typography.

width

The width of a *font*. To indicate the font width, the following names are used: condensed (narrow), regular and extended (broad), etc.

See also: width table; condensed type; extended type.

width table

A file containing information about the height and *width* of individual characters in every size and *style*. The width table is fully independent of the *font* and controls the placement of each *character* with respect to the next character. In this way documents can be made in the absence of the fonts used. The printing can be done on a *printer* or a typesetting machine where these fonts are present. An example of such a table is AFM (Adobe Font Metrics).

wildcard

Character (mostly a question mark or asterisk) that matches any character or group of characters. A wildcard is often used when searching functions are partly known. It is also handy as shorthand when specifying file names in commands.

Winchester

Technology used in hard disks units. The fast-rotating disk surface creates an air cushion, causing the read/write *head* to remain floating above the surface. When the disk stops rotating, the air cushion disappears. To prevent damage the head is parked on a part of the disk with no data on it (*landing zone*). Winchester disk units are sealed airtight. Pollution could cause a *head crash*.

window

Demarcated rectangular area on screen which can be made *active* and where commands can be executed or processing can be done.

window dub
Video *time code* visible on screen that is recorded on a track not in use for video. The display of the time-code can be switched on and off. It can be therefore used for *editing* purposes.
See also: burnt-in time code.

Windows
A *graphical user interface* for the *operating system* DOS developed by Microsoft.

Windows accelerator
A *card*, mostly with a fast graphical processor and VRAM *memory* to speed up displaying graphic screens. Since *Windows* is popular but also slow on standard hardware, manufacturers have concentrated on making Windows accelerators.
See also: video random access memory; video adapter.

Windows Open Services Architecture
WOSA - A name for a set of APIs that standardize the links between *Windows* applications, and between Windows and other platforms.
See also: application programming interface (API).

wipe
A fast fade-out of a film or video *image*.
See also: video effects.

wire frame
In many vector-oriented drawing programs and 3D-modelers it is possible to edit a wire-frame model of an illustration to speed up screen display during the making of an illustration. In the wire-frame only thin lines (with points) are visible. Colors, filling and differences in line densities are not visible.
See also: modeler.

wire-frame modeling
A method for building 3D-objects. This method uses wire frames for *editing*. An advantage of wire-frame modeling is the almost unlimited freedom in building objects.
See also: wire-frame; solid modeling.

wire frame

word processor
Program or program module which is used for the entering and *editing* of text. Publishing programs sometimes have a separate word-processor. Working with a dedicated word processor is often faster and more pleasant than word processing with a publishing program.
See also: desktop publishing.

word wrap
A function in a word-processing program. When a word does not fit entirely on a line, it is automatically placed at the beginning of the next line.

wordspace
See: space.

workstation
A general name for a computer with the following characteristics:
- it is connected to a network;
- programs are loaded via the *network* connection;
- it uses *Unix* operating system as a rule;
- it mostly contains a *RISC* microprocessor.
The distinction between PC and workstation has faded over the years, because PCs have become more and more powerful. PCs are now also equipped with RISC processors and can also run Unix.
See also: personal computer.

world coordinates
A *coordinate system* in 3D-applications. In this system all present objects are placed. All coordinates of these objects are relative to one zero-point, so everything 'fits together'. There is always only one system of world coordinates present.
See also: modeling coordinates; eye coordinates.

World Wide Web
WWW - Part of *Internet* developed by the Swiss Research Center CERN. The WWW is an extensive set of documents with *hypertext* capabilities. Hypertext is a technique that enables a user to jump to other documents.
WWW documents are written in the HyperText Markup Language HTML. Besides hypertext, HTML offers the possibility of adding illustrations, audio and video. In order to show or play these additions, the HTML browser has to run under a *graphical user interface*. *Mosaic* (available for *Windows* and *Macintosh*) is such a browser.

wow

A clearly audible varying pitch during reproduction of sound from a sound medium, such as a record-player. It produces a humming sound during the sound reproduction. This can be caused by the playback device or the sound medium.
See also: flutter.

write once, read many

WORM - An *optical disc* that can be written only once, but can be read many times thereafter. *Laser* technology is used in reading and writing the disc.
See also: optical media.

wrong overturn

Half a line at the top of a page. This is the end of the last sentence of the previous page. From a typographical point of view this is unwanted.
See also: orphan; widow.

WWW

See: World Wide Web.

WYSIWYG

What You See Is What You Get, meaning that it is possible to see on the screen what the printed page will look like.
Before publishing programs existed, documents were made up of codes. This had great limitations. When a code was inserted to print words in *bold*, the effect was not visible until the page was printed. It was also not possible to display illustrations, lines, different typefaces, etc. on screen.
In current publishing programs, the page as it will print is shown on the screen. However, what is seen on the screen does not always match exactly with what is printed. This concerns the difference in screen and the *printer resolution*.
See also: Display PostScript.

X

x-height

The letter height of the lower-case letters without ascender or descender, such as the x. The x-height is not the same as the body size (body size = x-height plus the length of the ascender and the descender). The larger the x-height in a certain body size, the shorter are the ascender and descender of a letter.

See also: lower case; base line.

X-Windows

An *operating system* independent *graphical user interface*. X-Windows is mainly used in *Unix*-systems.

See also: Open Look.

X.25

A *CCITT*-standard for networks based on the *packet switching* protocol.

XON/XOFF protocol

A *data communication* term. A software *protocol* which adjusts the speed of data transmission to the speed of the receiver. This prevents a faster transmission than the receiver is able to receive.

Y

YC

The *S-video* system signal (de)code method where the *luminance* (Y) and the *chrominance* (C) are separated. The letters YC are also the initials of the inventor of this (de)code process Yves C. Faroudj.

YCC

A compression technique used for storing files on Kodak Photo CDs. The Y stands for *luminance* and the two Cs for two-color channels. With YCC, high compression ratios are possible.

YCrCb

Indication for the digital *luminance* and the two-color difference signals (red and blue). The luminance signal is digitized at 13.5 MHz and the two-color difference signals at 6.77 MHz. This system is, for example, used in the *CCIR 601*-standard.

Yellow Book

Description of the physical format of a CD-ROM defined by Sony and Philips in 1985. Specified are the *sector* size, the rotational speed of the *disc*, reading and writing method and the sector addressing scheme. The physical format should not be confused with the logical format. The logical format describes the way the data are divided over the sectors and how the data can be retrieved by the computer program.
See also: Compact Disc Read Only Memory.

YIQ

An indication for the video signal in NTSC. The Y stands for the *luminance* and the I and Q stands for the *color difference* signals.
See also: National Television Standards Committee (NTSC).

YUV

Video signal type with *luminance* and two-color difference signals as used in *component video*. The U and V values combined with the PAL subcarrier produce the color signal.
See also: Phase Alternating Line (PAL); DYUV.

Y

Z

z-buffer

3D-image reproduction method. This method is based on *shading* and also makes use of a technology for determining which object is placed before, in front or behind other objects.

For every *dot* on the screen, the color and the depth of the last placed dot is registered. When a new object is drawn, it is determined whether the depth of the newly drawn dot lies in front or behind the earlier drawn dot. If the new dot is in front, then the new dot (color) is drawn. See also: render (to).

zapping

Switching from one to another TV channel using a remote control unit. This has created the so-called zapp-junkies. They switch continuously, searching for something that can capture their attention for more than three seconds and seldom succeeding.

zoomable icons

A (moving) reduced video-animation image. As soon as the image is clicked on (made *active*), it is displayed in a larger format. See also: icon.

Abbreviations
and
acronyms

1f	lower operating frequency
2BIQ	two binary, one quaternary
2CS	two carrier system
2D	two dimensional
2f	higher operating frequency
3D	three dimensional
3DP	three dimensional printing
3PM	three-position modulation
4GL	fourth generation language
A/D	analog to digital
A/UX	Apple unix
AA	author's alterations
AAAS	American Association for the Advancement of Science
AAD	analog analog digital
AAT	average access time
ABC	automatic brightness control
ABIC	adaptive bilevel image compression
ABR	automatic baud rate
ABT	advanced board technology
AC	author's correction
AC/DC	alternating current/direct current
ACCH	associated control channel
ACD	automatic call distribution
ACDI	asynchronous communications device interface
ACF	advanced communications function
ACK	acknowledgment
ACL	(1) access control list
	(2) audio communication line
ACR	(1) achromatic color removal and replacement
	(2) automatic carriage return
ACS	(1) access control system
	(2) alternate channel suppression
ACTS	Advanced Communication Technologies and Services
AD	anno Domini (in the year of our Lord)
ADA	(1) advanced design aids
	(2) analog to digital to analog
ADB	Apple desktop bus
ADC	(1) analog to digital converter
	(2) automatic device control
ADCCP	advanced data communication control procedure
ADD	analog digital digital
ADL	asymmetrical digital subscriber line
ADMA	advanced direct memory access

ADO	ampex digital optics
ADP	automatic data processing
ADPCM	adaptive differential pulse code modulation
ADPD	automatic display power down
ADPVM	adaptive delta pulse code modulation
ADR	automatic dialogue replacement
ADRM	analog/digital re-master
ADSL	asymmetric digital subscriber loop
ADSR	attack, decay, sustain and release
ADT	asynchronous data transfer
Advanced 21	Advanced Communication Network Development Center Inc.
AE	application entity
AEC	automatic editing control
AED	automatic error detection
AES	Audio Engineering Society (USA)
AF	audio frequency
AFC	automatic frequency control
AFE	Apple file exchange
AFF	audio file format
AFLICIO	American Federation of Labor/Congress of Industrial Organizations
AFP	AppleTalk filing protocol
AGA	advanced graphics adapter
AGC	automatic gain control
AGV	automatically guided vehicles
AI	artificial intelligence
AIB	asynchronous interface board
AIMS	auto indexing mass storage
AIP	average instructions per second
AIPLA	American Intellectual Property Law Association
AIS	automated imaging systems
AIST	Agency of Industrial Science and Technology
AIX	advanced interactive executive
AKA	also known as
AL	artificial language
ALC	(1) automatic level control
	(2) automatic light compensation
ALPAC	Automatic Language Processing Advisory Committee
ALU	arithmetic logic unit
ALVIN	autonomous land vehicle in a neural network
AM	(1) amplitude modulation
	(2) automated mapping

AMH	application message handler
AMI	access method interface
AMP	ampere
AMPS	automatic music program search
AMS	access method services
ANDES	architecture with non-sequential dynamic execution schedule
ANRS	automatic noise reduction system
ANS	advanced network & services
ANSI	American National Standards Institute
AO	analog output
AOC	advice of charge
AOC-D	advice of charge - during call
AOC-E	advice of charge - end of call
AOC-S	advice of charge - at call set-up time
AOQ	average outgoing quality
APD	auto power down
API	application programming interface
APLD	automatic program locate device
APNSS	analog private network signaling system
APPC	advanced program-to-program communication
APPN	advanced peer-to-peer networking
APR	automatic picture replacement
APSS	automatic program search system
APT	automatic picture transmission
AQL	acceptable quality level
AR	automatic reverse
ARCnet	attached resource computer network
ARM	(1) advanced RISC machine
	(2) asynchronous response mode
AROM	alterable read only memory
ARPA	Advanced Research Projects Agency
ARQ	automatic retry request
ARU	audio response unit
ARVIS	alternate reality vision system
ASA	(1) American Standards Association
	(2) Acoustical Society of America
ASCAP	American Society of Composers, Authors and Publishers
ASCII	American Standard Code for Information Interchange
ASI	(1) automated system initialization
	(2) Applied Systems Institute
ASIC	application specific integrated circuit
ASL	automatic stereo level

ASM	assembler
ASME	American Society for Manufacturing Engineers
ASME	American Society of Mechanical Engineers
ASR	(1) automatic send-receive set,
	(2) automatic speech recognition
AST	(1) accurate screen technology
	(2) automatic scan tracking
ASTA	Advanced Software Technology and Algorithms
AT	(1) advanced technology
	(2) absolute time
ATC	(1) authorized training centre
	(2) automatic tuning control
ATCC	American type culture collection
ATIS	advanced traveler information systems
ATM	(1) asynchronous transfer mode
	(2) Adobe Type Manager
atm	atmosphere
ATMS	advanced traffic management systems
ATR	(1) audiotape recorder
	(2) Advanced Telecommunications Research Laboratory
ATRC	Advanced Television Research Consortium (Philips, Thomson, NBC)
ATTS	automatic tape time selector
AU	(1) access unit
	(2) administrative unit
AUI	(1) autonomous unit interface
	(2) attachment unit interface
AUP	acceptable use policy
AUX	auxiliary
AV	(1) audiovisual
	(2) audio/video
AVA	(1) audio visual authoring language
	(2) International Audio Visual Software Fair Organizing Association
AVC	(1) audio visual connection
	(2) automatic volume control
AVCS	advanced vehicle control system
AVI	(1) audio/video interleave
	(2) automated vehicle identification
AVK	audio visual kernel
AVL	automatic vehicle location
AVR	automatic volume recognition
AVSS	audio-video support system

AVT	address vector table
AWE	advanced wave effects
B	(1) byte
	(2) Bell
b	bit
B&W	black and white
B-ISDN	broadband integrated services digital network
b/s	bits per second
B/s	bytes per second
B/W	black and white
BASIC	Beginner's All-purpose Symbolic Instruction Code
BB	black burst
BBS	bulletin board system
BC	(1) byte counter
	(2) binary code
BCB	block control byte
BCC	(1) block control character
	(2) block check character
BDOS	basic disk operating system
BEP	bit error probability
BER	bit error rate
BEX	broadband exchange
BFT	boundary function table
BGU	business graphics utility
BI-DI	bidirectional communications
BIDEC	binary to decimal converter
BIDI	bidirectional bus
BIFF	binary interchange file format
BIM	beginning-of-information marker
BIO	buffered input/output
BIOS	basic input/output system
BIP	bulk information processing
Bit	binary digit
BITBLT	bit block transfer
BIX	binary information exchange
BL	bit length
BLOB	binary large object
BMP	(1) bit mapped pattern
	(2) batch message processing
BNC	(1) baby 'N' connector
	(2) bayonet-Neil-Concelman
	(3) British national connector

BNU	basic networking utilities
BOCA	Borland object component architecture
BOD	bandwith-on-demand
BOF	beginning of file
BOPS	billion operations per second
BOS	basic operating system
BOT	boolean operation table
bpi	bits per inch
bpp	bits per pixel
Bps	bytes per second
bps	bits per second
BPU	branch protection unit
BRA	basic rate access
BRI	basic rate interface
BRR	bitrate reduction
BS	(1) backspace (character)
	(2) base station
BSA	Business Software Alliance
BSS	broadcast satellite system
BTSC	Broadcast Television Systems Committee
BVU	broadcast video U-matic
BW	black and white
C	(1) cyan
	(2) celsius
	(3) programming language C
C/N	carrier-to-noise-ratio
C/S	client/server
C7	common channel signaling no. 7
CA	(1) computer-aided
	(2) channel adapter
	(3) change accumulation
	(4) channel attachment
CACD	computer-aided circuit design
CAD	computer-aided design
CAD/CAM	computer-aided design and manufacturing
CAE	computer-aided engineering
CAGE	computer-aided graphic expression
CAI	computer-aided instruction
CAL	calibrate
CAM	(1) computer-aided manufacturing
	(2) common access method
CAMD	computer assisted molecular design

CAN	controller area network
CANARIE	Canadian Network for the Advancement of Research, Industry and Education
CAP	computer-aided publishing
cap	capital
CaPSL	Canon Printing System Language
CAPTAIN	character and pattern telephone access information network system
CAS	communicating application specification
CASE	computer-aided software engineering
CASS	conditional access subsystem
CAT	(1) computer-assisted typesetting
	(2) computer-aided translation
	(3) computer assisted telephony
CATV	(1) cable television
	(2) computer-aided TV
CAV	(1) constant angular velocity
	(2) component analog video
CAVE	computer-assisted visual education
CAX	community automatic exchange
CBMS	computer based messaging system
CBR	constant bit rate
CBT	computer-based training
CBX	computerized branch exchange
cc	cubic centimeters
CC	(1) colour compensating
	(2) compact cassette
CC filter	colour compensating filter
CCA	common communication adapter
CCCC	colour calibration, communication and control
CCD	(1) charge-coupled device
	(2) central control desk
CCDM	charge-coupled device memory
CCI	computer-controlled instruction
CCIR	Comité Consultatif International des Radiocommunications
CCITT	Consultative Committee International for Telegraph and Telephone communication
CCP	(1) communication control program
	(2) configuration control program
CCS7	common channel signaling no. 7
CCTV	(1) computer controlled television
	(2) closed circuit TV

CCU	(1) camera control unit
	(2) central control unit
CCW	counterclockwise
CD	(1) compact disc
	(2) call deflection
CD-DA	compact disc-digital audio
CD-E	compact disc-erasable
CD-I	compact disc-interactive
CD-R	compact disc-recordable
CD-ROM	compact disc-read only memory
CD-ROM XA	compact disc-rom extended architecture
CD-S	compact disc-single
CD-WO	compact disc-write once
CD-WORM	compact disc-write once read many
CDDI	copper digital data interface
CDE	control and display equipment
CDL	compiler description language
CDMA	code division multiple access
CDP	corporate document production
CDPD	cellular digital packet data
CDPF	composed document printing facility
CDS	control data set
CDTM	compressed time division multiplex
CDTP	colour diffusion transfer paper
CDTV	Commodore dynamic total vision
CE	(1) correctable error
	(2) channel-end
	(3) concurrent engineering
CECP	country extended code page
CEGL	cause-effect graph language
CEL	corporation for entertainment and learning
CEN	Comité Européen de Normalisation
CENELEC	Comité Européen de Normalisation Electrotechnique
CENTREX	central exchange
CEPS	color electronic prepress system
CEPT	Conference European Post and Telecommunication
CERC	computer entry and readout control
CERT	Computer Emergency Response Team
CFB	call forwarding busy
CFNR	call forwarding no reply
CFU	call forwarding unconditional
CG	computer graphics
CGA	colour graphics adapter

CGB	convert gray to binary
CGI	computer graphics interface
CGM	computer graphic metafile
CGRP	compound file element group chunk
cgs	centimeter-gramme-second
CHIO	channel input/output
CI	(1) colour index
	(2) computer interconnect
	(3) component interface
CIA	computerized image analysis
cic	cicero
CICP	communication interrupt control program
CICS	customer information control system
CID	(1) communication identifier
	(2) connection identifier
CIE	Commission Internationale de l'Eclairage
CIF	common intermediate format
CIFA	communications interface
CIM	(1) computer-integrated manufacturing
	(2) computer input microfilm
CIOC	central input/output control
CIS	card information structure
CISC	complex instruction set computer
CIT	computer intergrated telephony
cl	centilitre
CLASP	connecting link for applications and source peripherals
CLB	communication services local block
CLI	(1) command line interpreter
	(2) compression labs inc.
	(3) calling line identification
CLIP	calling line identification presentation
CLIR	calling line identification restriction
CLS	clear screen
CLUT	colour look-up table
CLV	constant linear velocity
cm	centimeter
CMC	common mails calls
CMIP	common management information protocol
CMM	colour matching methods
CMOS	complementary metal-oxide semiconductor
CMS	conversational monitor system
CMYK	cyan, magenta, yellow and black
COA	certificate of authencity

COAX	coaxial cable
CODEC	compressor/decompressor
CODEC	coding and decoding
COLP	connected line identification presentation
COLR	connected line identification restriction
COM	(1) computer output management
	(2) computer output microfilm
	(3) common object model
Comdex	computer dealer expo
COMSEC	communications security
CONF	add-on conference call
CONTU	Commission on New Technological Uses of Copyrighted Works
CORBA	common object request broker architecture
CORDIS	COmmunity R&D Information Service
COS	consumer operating system
COSE	common open software environment
CPF	cold pressure fusing
cph	characters per hour
cpi	characters per inch
cpl	characters per line
cpm	characters per minute
cpp	characters per pica
CPQN	clocks per quarter note (equivalent to PPQN)
cps	(1) characters per second
	(2) cycles per second
CPT	color picture tube
CPU	central processing unit
CR	carriage return
CRADA	Cooperative Research and Development Agreement
CRC	(1) cyclic redundancy check(ing)
	(2) carriage return character
	(3) camera-ready copy
CREOL	Center for Research in Electro-Optics and Lasers
CRISC	complex/reduced instruction set computer
CRL	Communication Research Laboratory
CRLF	carriage return linefeed
CRP	(1) channel request priority
	(2) configuration report program
CRT	cathode ray tube
CS	(1) communication services
	(2) current state
CSCW	computer-supported cooperative work

CSIRO	Commonwealth Scientific and Industrial Research Organisation
CSMA/CD	carrier sense multiple access/collision detection
CSS	communications service satellite
CSTA	computer supported telephony applications
CSU	(1) customer setup
	(2) channel service unit
CT	(1) continuous tone
	(2) call transfer
	(3) cordless telephone
CTC	channel-to-channel
CTCA	channel-to-channel adapter
CTF	consumer transaction facility
CTI	(1) color transient improvement
	(2) computer telephone integration
CTOC	(1) compound file table of contents
	(2) Convergent technologies operating system
Ctrl	control
CTS	(1) computer typesetting system
	(2) cartridge tape subsystem
CU	close up
cu ft	cubic foot
cu in	cubic inch
cu yd	cubic yard
CUA	common user access
CUG	closed user group
CVBS	color video blanking synchronisation
CVO	commercial vehicle operations systems
CW	call waiting
D/A	digital to analog
D/T	disk/tape
D2B	domestic digital bus
DA	distribution amplifier
da	deca
DAA	data access arrangement
DAB	digital audio broadcasting
DAC	digital-to-analog converter
dal	decaliter
dam	decameter
DARPA	Defense Advanced Research Projects Agency
DASD	direct access storage device
DAT	digital audio tape

DATV	digital assisted television
dB	decibel
DBC	decimal-to-binary conversion
DBMS	database management system
DBP	deutsche Bundespost
DBS	direct broadcast satellite
DCC	(1) data communications channel
	(2) digital compact cassette
DCC	digital cross connect
DCE	(1) distributed computing environment
	(2) data communications equipment
	(3) data country code
DCF	data communication function
DCI	display control interface
DCP	digital contour processor
DCS	(1) desktop color separation
	(2) digital camera system
DCT	(1) discrete cosine transform
	(2) digital component technology
DCT-SQ	discrete cosine transform-scalar quantization
DD	(1) data dictionary
	(2) device driver
DDA	digital differential analyzer
DDBMS	distributed database management system
DDD	(1) direct distance dialing
	(2) digital digital digital
DDE	dynamic data exchange
DDES	(1) digital data exchange specifications
	(2) digital data exchange standard
DDI	direct dialing in
DDK	driver development kit
DDL	data description language
DDLC	Data Description Language Committee
DDP	distributed data processing
DDPP	direct digital printing plate
DDS	(1) digital data storage
	(2) data description specifications
DDX	digital data exchange
DEC	Digital Equipment Corporation
DECT	digital European cordless telephone
DEL	delete (character)
DELTA	Developing of European Learning through Technological Advance

DES	(1) digital editing system
	(2) data encryption standard
DesCAF	design-controlled automated fabrication
DESRA	Defense Supercomputing Research Alliance
DFB-laser	distributed-feedback laser
DFC	(1) data flow chart
	(2) data flow control
DFD	data flow diagram
DFP	design for profitability
dg	decigramme
DGIS	direct graphics interface specification
DIA	document interchange architecture
DIANE	direct information access network for Europe
DICT	dictionary
DID	direct inward dialing
DIF	(1) data interchange format
	(2) document interchange format
	(3) document interchange facility
Digicipher	digital television compression and transmission system
DIN	(1) Deutsches Institut für Normalization
	(2) Deutsche Industrie Norm
DIP	dual in-line package
DIS	document information system
DISC	disconnect
DISW	data link switching
dl	deciliter
DLA	(1) data link adapter
	(2) direct line attachment
DLC	data link control
DLL	(1) dynamic link library
	(2) data link layer
DM	(1) desktop manufacturing
	(2) delay modulation
dm	decimeter
DM-M	delay modulation, mark
DM-S	delay modulation, space
DMA	direct memory access
DMD	deformable mirror device
DME	(1) distributed computing environment
	(2) distributed management environment
DMI	desktop management interface
DMN	Digital multimedia network
DMOS	double-diffused metal-oxide semiconductor

DMSD	digital multistandard decoding
DMUX	demultiplexer
DMX	demultiplexing
DN-1	Datanet 1
DNA	Digital network architecture
DNIC	data network identification code
DNS	(1) dynamic noise suppresion
	(2) domain name system
DOC	documentation
DoC	Department of Commerce
DOD	drop on demand
DoD	Departent of Defense
DoE	Department of Energy
DOS	disk operating system
DP	data processing
DPCM	differential pulse-code modulation
dpi	dots per inch
dpl	dots per line
dpm	documents per minute
DPMI	DOS protected mode interface
DPMS	DOS protected mode services
DPMS	display-power management system
DPNSS	digital private network signaling system
DPR	digital player recorder
dpt	dioptre
DPU	display processing unit
DQDB	distributed queue dual bus
DR	(1) density ratio
	(2) data rate
DR DOS	Digital Research disk operating system
DRAM	dynamic random access memory
DRAW	direct read after write
DRC	data recording control
DRD	data recording device
DS	distant shot
DSAP	destination service access point
DS/DD	double sided/double density
DS/ED	double sided/enhanced density
DS/HD	double sided/high density
DS/ND	double sided/normal density
DSD	(1) data set definition
	(2) data structure diagram
DSI	digital speech interpolation

DSP	(1) digital signal processor
	(2) digital sound processor
	(3) display system protocol
DSPU	downstream physical unit
DSR	(1) digital satellite radio
	(2) data set ready
DSS	digital signature standard
DSSI	digital storage system interconnect
DSSSL	document style semantics and specification language
DST	(1) digital storage technology
	(2) data services task
	(3) dedicated service tools
DSV	digital sum variation
DT	(1) diffusion transfer
	(2) dynamic tracking
DTC	dynamic tape tension control
DTE	data terminal equipment
DTF	document type definition
DTI	desktop imaging
DTM	digital terrain model
DTMF	dual tone multiple frequency
DTP	desktop publishing
DTR	data transfer rate
DTV	desktop video
DVC	digital video cartridge
DVD	direct view display
DVE	digital video effects
DVI	digital video interactive
DVR	digital video recording
DVTR	digital videotape recorder
DVX	digital voice exchange
DXC	digital cross connect
DXF	(1) data exchange format
	(2) drawing interchange format
E	emulsion
E to E	electronics to electronics
e-mail	electronic mail
E-NRZ	enhanced nonreturn to zero
E-to-B	emulsion-to-base
E-to-E	emulsion-to-emulsion
EAN	European article numbering
EAPROM	electrically alterable programmable read-only memory

EARN	European academic research network
EAROM	electrically alterable read-only memory
EAU	erase all unprotected
EAV	end of active video
EAX	electronic automatic exchange
EBCDIC	extended binary coded decimal interchange code
Ebeam	electron beam
EBR	electronic beam recorder
EBU	European Broadcast Union
EC	European Commission
ECB	(1) event control block
	(2) electronic codebook
ECC	(1) error checking and correcting
	(2) error correction code
ECD	error correction decoder
ECHO	European Community Host Organization
ECIS	European Centre for Infrastructure
ECITC	European Committee for IT&T Testing and Certfication
ECL	emitter-coupled logic
ECMA	European Computer Manufacturers Association
ECQAC	Electronic Components Quality Assurance Committee
ECS	European communications satellite
ECSA	Exchange Carriers Standards Association
ECT	explicit call transfer
ECU	extreme close up
EDAC	error detection and correction
EDC	error detection code
EDH	error detection and handling
EDI	electronic data interchange
EDIF	electronic design interchange format
EDIFACT	electronic data interchange for administration commerce and transport
EDL	edit decision list
EDP	electronic data processing
EEMS	enhanced expanded memory specification
EEPROM	electrically erasable programmable read-only memory
EFI	Electronics For Imaging
EFP	electronic field production
EFT	electronic funds transfer
EGA	enhanced graphic adapter
EGCS	extended graphic character set
EHF	extremely high frequency
EHT	extremely high tension

EI	external interrupt
EIS	executive information system
EISA	extended industrial standard architecture
EIUF	European ISDN users' forum
ELD	electro-luminescent display
ELF	extremely low-frequency
ELS	enterprise library services
EMC	eye movement camera
EMI	electro-magnetic interference
EMM	expanded memory manager
EMS	expanded memory specification
ENG	electronic news gathering
ENIAC	electronic numerical integrator and calculator
ENS	European nervous system
eod	every other day
EOF	end of file
EOL	end of line
EOP	end of page
EOT	(1) the end-of-transmission character
	(2) end-of-tape marker
EPA	Environmental Protection Agency
EPBX	electronic private branch exchange
EPC	electronic page composition
EPLD	erasable programmable read only memory
EPM	electronic photocomposing machine
EPOS	European PTT open learning service
EPRI	Electric Power Research Institute
EPROM	erasable programmable read-only memory
EPS	encapsulated PostScript
EPSCOR	Experimental Program to Stimulate Competitive Research
EPSS	electronic performance support system
EQ	equalization
ER	error recovery (procedures)
ERMES	European radio messaging system
ERTI	European Round Table of Industrialists
ESA	European Space Agency
ESC	escape character
ESD	electrostatic discharge
ESDI	enhanced small device interface
ESP	electronic still picture
ESPRIT	European Strategic Program for Research in Information Technology

ESRI	European Systems Research Institute
ESS	electronic still store
EST	Eastern standard time
ET	exchange termination
etc	etcetera
ETL	electrotechnical laboratory
ETNO	European Telecom Network Operators
ETR	European technical report
ETS	(1) European telecommunication system
	(2) European telecommunications standard
ETSI	European Telecommunications Standards Institute
EUTELSAT	European Telecommunication Satellite Organisation
EVE	European videotelephony experiment
EXCA	exchangable card architecture
EXE	executable
EXP	expand
F	Fahrenheit
FACE	framed access command environment
FAMT	fully automatic machine translation
FAT	file allocation table
FAX	facsimile
FAX4	facsimile group 4
FC	full color
FCB	file control block
FCC	(1) Federal Communications Commission
	(2) function class code
	(3) fiber channel standard
FCC	Federal Communications Council
FCCSET	Federal Coordinating Council for Science, Engineering and Technology
fci	flux changes per inch
fcl	flux change length
FCS	(1) frame check sequence
	(2) function control sequence
	(3) fiber channel standard
FD	(1) floppy disk
	(2) full duplex
FDC	floppy disk controller
FDD	floppy disk drive
FDDI	fiber distributed data interface
FDM	frequency division multiplexor
FDP	field-developed program

FDX	full duplex
FED	(1) field emission display
	(2) Research and Development Association for Future Electron Devices
FEP	front-end-processor
FET	field effect transistor
FF	(1) form feed
	(2) fast forward
FFS	(1) flash file system
	(2) floating foil security
FFT	fast Fourier transform
FHWA	Federal Highway Administration
FIF	fractal image format
FIFO	first in, first out
FILO	first in, last out
FITS	functional interpolating transformational systems
FLC	ferro-electric liquid crystal
flexo	flexography
FLOPS	floating-point operations per second
FM	(1) frequency modulation
	(2) facility management
	(3) frequency multiplexing
FMV	full-motion video
FP	floating point
FPH	freephone supplementary service
fpi	frames per inch
FPLMTS	future public land mobile telephone services
fpm	feet per minute
FPO	for position only
fps	frames per second
FPU	floating point unit
fri	flux reversals per inch
FSK	frequency shift keying
FSN	full service network
FSS	fixed satellite service
FST	flat square tube
FT	(1) flow time
	(2) file transfer
ft.	foot, or feet
FT2	fixed thermal transfer
FTAM	file transfer, access and management
FTC	fractal transform compression
FTD	fluorescent tube display

FTP	(1) folded, trimmed and packed (books)
	(2) file transfer program
	(3) file transfer protocol
FTS	favourite track selection
FTSA	fault tolerant systems architecture
FTTH	fiber-to-the-home
FTTO	fiber-to-the-office
FTTZ	fiber-to-the-zone
FX	effects
FYI	for your information
G	(1) giga
	(2) gauss
GASP	graphic application subroutine package
GATER	guide to acquisition in technology and emerging research
GATT	General Agreement on Tariffs and Trade
GB	gigabyte(s)
Gb	gigabit
Gb/s	gigabit per second
GBU	graphics business unit
GC	graphics context
GCR	gray component removal or replacement
GCR	group-coded recording
GDDM	graphical data display manager
GDF	graphics data file
GDI	graphics device interface
GDP	graphic draw primitives
GDS	graphic design system
GDU	graphical display unit
GDV	graphic deflection vector
GEM	graphical environment manager
GHz	gigahertz
GIF	graphic interchange format
GIP	graphic interactive processing
gips	giga instructions per seconds
GIS	geographic information system
GM	general MIDI
GML	generalized markup language
GND	ground
GOCA	graphic object content architecture
GOCO	government-owned, contractor-operated
GOGO	government-owned, government operated
GP	graphics processor

GPF	general protection fault
GPG	graphics program generator
GPGS	general purpose graphic system
GPI	(1) graphics programming interface
	(2) general purpose interface
GPIB	general purpose internal bus
GPO	U.S. government printing office
GPS	(1) graphic programming services
	(2) global positioning system
GRASP	graphic system for online plotting
GS	general synthesizer
GSM	groupe speciale mobile
GSS	graphics symbol set
GTF	generalized trace facility
GUI	graphical user interface
H	hue
h	hecto
H&J	hyphenation and justification
H-sync	horizontal synchronization signal
ha	hectare
HAMT	human aided machine translation
HAR	highway advisory radio
HD	(1) high density
	(2) half duplex
	(3) hard disk
HD-MAC	high definition-multiplexed analog components
HDCD	high density compact disc
HDDR	high density digital recording
HDLC	high-level data link control
HDTR	high density tape recorder
HDTV	high definition television
HEX	hexadecimal
HF	high frequency
HFT	host file transfer
hg	hectogramme
HGC	Hercules graphics card
Hi8	high-band 8 mm
HIFI	high fidelity
HIT	human interface technology
hl	hectoliter
HLS	(1) hue, luminance and saturation
	(2) hue, lightness and saturation

hm	hectometer
HMA	high memory area
HMD	head mounted display
HMS	hours, minutes and seconds
HOLD	call on hold
HPCCP	high performance computing and communication program
HPCN	high performance computing and networking
HPCS	high performance computing systems
HPFS	high performance file system
HPGL	Hewlett-Packard graphics language
HPPCL	Hewlett-Packard printer control language
HPPI	high performance parallel interface
HQ	high quality
hr.	hour
HSA	high speed adapter
HSAC	high speed analog computer
HSB	hue, saturation and brightness
HSDL	high speed data line
HSG	High Sierra Group
HSI	hue saturation intensity
HSL	hue, saturation and luminance
HSM	hierarchical storage management
HSP	high speed printer
HSV	hue, saturation and value
HT	(1) halftone
	(2) half total
HYP	hyphen
Hz	hertz
I-TIME	instruction time
I-way	information highway
i.e.	id est (that is)
I/O	input/output
IA	integrated adapter
IAB	Internet Activities Board
IAL	international algebraic language
IAS	immediate access storage
IAYF	information at your fingertips
ib.	ibidem (in the same place)
IBC	inside back cover
IBCN	integrated broadband communications network
IC	integrated circuit

ICA	(1) International Communication Association
	(2) integrated communications adapter
ICDA	integrated cached disk array
ICG	interactive computer graphics
ICOMP	Intel comparative microprocessor performance index
ICON	image converter
ICOT	Institute for New Generation Computer Technology
ICR	intelligent character recognition
ICU	(1) image converter unit
	(2) interactive chart utility
IDA	integrated digital access
IDAPI	independent database application programming interface
IDF	interactive data facility
IDL	intruder detection/lockout
IDN	integrated digital network
IDN1	integrated digital network 1*64 kbit/s
IDN30	integrated digital network 30*64 kbit/s
IDOS	image display operating system
IDPIA	integrated document production architecture
IDS	image distribution system
IDTV	improved definition television
IEC	International Electrotechnical Commission
IEEE	Institute of Electrical and Electronics Engineers (USA)
IEN	individualized electronic newspaper
IERE	Institute of Electrical and Radio Engineers (UK)
IETF	Internet engineering task force
IFEN	intercompany file exchange network.
IFIP	International Federation for Information Processing
ifr	inches per flux reversal
IFS	(1) interactive filesharing
	(2) installable file system
IFT	ink film thickness
IGDS	interactive graphic design system
IGES	initial graphics exchange specifications
IGS	(1) interactive graphics software
	(2) interactive graphics system
IHF	image handling facility
IIPRC	International Intellectual Property Rights Committee
IM	(1) imaging model
	(2) intermodulation
IMA	(1) International Multimedia Association
	(2) Interactive Multimedia Association
	(3) International MIDI Association

IMC	integrated multiplexer channel
IMD	intermodulation distortion
IMM	integrated memory module
IMPACT	Information Market Policy Actions
IMS	(1) intelligent manufacturing system
	(2) interactive multimedia services
IN	intelligent network
INGRES	interactive graphics and retrieval system
INMARSAT	International Maritime Satellite organization
INS	insert
INT	interrupt(ion)
IOC	input/output channel
IOCTL	input/output control
IOS	input/output system
IP	(1) image processor
	(2) intelligent peripheral
IPA	international phonetic alphabet
IPC	interprocess communication
IPCS	interactive problem control system
IPF	(1) image processing format
	(2) image processing facility
IPG	interactive presentation graphics
iph	impressions per hour
IPLS	instant program location system
IPMS	interpersonal messaging system
IPng	Internet Protocol new generation
IPP	in-plant printing
IPR	intellectual property rights
IPS	image processing system
ips	inches per second
IPSS	instant program search system
IPX	internetwork packet exchange
IR	infrared
IRD	information resource dictionary
IRDA	infrared data association
IRI	Industrial Research Institute
IRIG	Inter-Range Instrumentation Group
IRM	(1) inhereted right masks
	(2) information resource management
IRQ	interrupt request (signal)
IRS	interrecord-separator character
IRTF	Internet Research Task Force
IS	information system

ISA	industrial standard architecture
ISAM	indexed sequential access method
ISBD	International Standard for Bibliographic Description
ISBN	International Standard Book Number
ISCC	Inter-Society Colour Council
ISDN	Integrated Services Digital Network
ISDN-UP	isdn-user part
ISDN2	isdn-connection 2b+d
ISDN30	isdn-connection 30b+d
ISO	International Standards Organization
ISPF	interactive system productivity facility
ISR	image storage and retrieval
ISS	image symbol set
ISSN	international standard serial number
ISV	independent software vendor
IT	(1) image technology
	(2) information technology
ITSC	International Technical Support Center
ITSEC	information technology security evaluation criteria
ITU	International Telecommunications Union
ITV	interactive television
IV	interactive video
IVD	interactive videodisc
IVHS	intelligent vehicle-highway systems
IVR	interactive voice response
IVS	interactive videodisc system
IWF	inter working function
IWPS	infowindow presentation system
JCL	job control language
JCMA	Japan Construction Mechanisation Association
JEIDA	Japan Electronic Industries Development Association
JES	Japanese Engineering Standards
JESSI	Joint European Submicron Silicon Initiative
JFIF	JPEG interchange file format
JICST	Japan Information Center for Science and Technology
JIPDEC	Japan Information Processing Development Center
JIT	just in time
JMSC	Japan Midi Standards Council
JPEG	Joint Photographic Experts Group
JPS	Japan Society for the Promotion of Science
JSIMM	Japan Society of Industrial Machinery Manufacturers
JSMR	Japan shared mobile radio
JTAG	Joint Test Action Group

JTEC	Japanese Technology Evaluation Center
JTM	job transfer and manipulation
K	(1) kilo
	(2) Kelvin
KB	kilobyte(s)
Kb	kilobit
Kb/i	kilobits per inch
Kb/s	kilobit per second
KCMS	Kodak color management system
Kfr/cm	Kilo flux reversals per centimeter
kg	kilogram
KHz	kilohertz
km	kilometer
KRI	Kansai Research Institute
Kt/i	Kilotransitions per inch
kV	kilovolt
kW	kilowatt
kWh	kilowatt-hour
l.c.	loco citato (in the place cited)
LADDR	layered device driver architecture
LAN	local area network
LANC	local application numerical control
LAP	link acces protocol
LAPB	link access protocol-balanced
LAPB	link access protocol b-channel
LAPD	link access protocol d-channel
LASER	light amplification by stimulated emission of radiation
LAST	liquid archival sound treatment
LBE	(1) lower band edge
	(2) location based entertainment
LC	lower case
LCA	lowercase alphabet
LCD	liquid crystal display
LDCS	linear direct conversion system
LDR	(1) light dependent resistance
	(2) light dependent resistor
LED	light emitting diode
LEO	(1) laser and opto electronics
	(2) low-earth orbit satellites
LF	(1) line feed
	(2) low frequency

LFO	low frequency oscillator
LI	lead in
LIA	limited intelligence agent
LIC	(1) last-in-chain
	(2) licensed internal code
	(3) line interface coupler
LIFO	last in, first out
LILO	last in, last out
LIM	Lotus/Intel/Microsoft
Linasec	a line a second
LIPS	laser image processing scanner
LLC	logical link control
lm	lumen
LNA	low noise amplifier
LNC	low noise block down converter
LO	lead out
LP	long play
Lp	sound pressure level
lpc	lines per centimeter
lph	lines per hour
lpi	lines per inch
lpm	lines per minute
lps	lines per second
LQ	letter quality
LRC	longitudinal redundancy check
LS	(1) lectori salutem
	(2) locus sigilli (in the place of the seal)
	(3) link status
	(4) long shot
LSA	Lan security architecture
LSB	least significant bit
LSC	linear sequential circuit
LSI	large scale integration
LSL	link support layer
LSR	linear shift register
LT	line termination
LTC	longitudinal time code
LUFO	least used, first out
LUT	look-up table
LVDT	linear variable differential transformer
lx	lux
LZW	Lempel Ziv Welch

m	(1) meter
	(2) micron
M	(1) magenta
	(2) mega
M/MC	man-machine communication
mA	milliampere
MAC	(1) medium access control
	(2) multiplexed analog components
MAHT	machine aided human translation
MAN	metropolitan area network
MAPI	(1) mail application programming interface
	(2) messaging application jprogramming interface
MASH	multistage noise shaping
MASM	Microsoft assembler
MAU	multistation access unit
MAX	maximum
Mb	megabit
MB	megabyte(s)
MB/s	megabytes per second
Mb/s	megabits per second
MC	machine coated
mc	megacycle
MCA	(1) micro channel architecture
	(2) multi channel access
MCB	memory control block
MCC	(1) multichannel communication
	(2) Micro electronics and Computing Technology Consortium
MCD	(1) master copy distribution
	(2) multimedia cartridge drive
MCGA	multi color graphics adapter
MCI	media control interface
MCID	malicious call identification
MCM	multichip module technologies
MCT	manufacturer's center line tape
MCU	(1) multipoint control unit
	(2) medium close up
MD	minidisc
MD ROM	minidisc read only memory
MDA	monochrome display adapter
MDI	multiple document interface
MDK	multimedia development kit
MEM	memory

MEMO	memorandum
MESI	modified, exclusive, shared, invalid
MF	(1) medium frequency
	(2) mediation function
MFLOPS	million floating-point operations per second
MFM	modified frequency modulation
MFP	multi-frequency pulsing
MFS	(1) modified filing system
	(2) multiple file systems
mg	milligramme
MGC	manual gain control
MH	(1) message handler
	(2) MAC header
MHS	message handling system
MHz	megahertz
MIAS	multipoint interactive audiovisual system
MIB	management information base
MIDI	(1) musical instrumental digital interface
	(2) medium independent digital image
MIF	management information format
MIG	metal in gap
MIM	metal-insulator-metal
MIME	multipurpose internet mail extension
MIN	minimum
mips	million instructions per second
MIS	management information system
MISC	miscellaneous
MIT	Massachusetts Institute of Technology
MITI	Ministry of International Trade and Industry
mks	meter-kilogramme-second
ml	milliliter
MLID	multi-link interface driver
mm	millimeter(s)
MM	multimedia
MMA	MIDI Manufacturers Association
MMC	Multimedia Marketing Council
MMC	meet-me conference
MME	multimedia extensions
MMI	man-machine interface
MMPM	Multimedia presentation manager
MNP	(1) Microcom networking protocol
	(2) multiple network protocols
MO	magnetical optical disc

MODEM	modulator/demodulator
MOL	maximum output level
mops	million operations per second
MOS	(1) metal-oxide semiconductor
	(2) modem operating system
MOTIS/MHS	message oriented text interchange system/message handling system
MOU	memorandum of understanding
MP	multiprocessor
MPC	multimedia personal computer
MPDN	materials properties data network
MPEG	Motion Pictures Experts Group
MPG	multimedia presentation generator
MPL	multimedia presentation language
MPS	multimedia presentation system
MPT	Ministry of Post and Telecommunication
MPU	main power unit
MPX	multiplexer
MRCF	Microsoft real-time compression format
MRCI	Microsoft real-time compression interface
MRE	(Japan-US) Manufacturing Research Exchange
MRM	maximum right mask
MRS	(1) music reading software
	(2) Materials Research Society
MS	(1) mobile station
	(2) medium shot
ms	millisecond(s)
MS-DOS	Microsoft disk operating system
MSB	most significant bit
MSC	(1) MIDI show control
	(2) mobile service switching station
MSCDEX	Microsoft compact disc extensions
MSF	minutes, seconds and frames
MSI	medium-scale integration
MSN	multiple subscriber number
MSS	mass storage system
MT	machine translation
MTBF	mean time between failures
MTC	MIDI time code
MTF	modulation transfer function
MTP	message transfer part
MTS	(1) multichannel television sound
	(2) message transfer system

MTTR	(1) magnetic tape recorder/reproducer
	(2) mean time to repair
MTU	magnetic tape unit
MUMPS	Massachusetts utility multiprogramming system
mupi	mobilier urbain pour publicité et information
MUPS	multiprocessing system
MUSE	multiple sub-Nyquist sampling encoding
MUX	multiplexer
MVS	multiple virtual storage
MX	multiplexing
n	nano
NA	(1) not available
	(2) not assigned
NAB	National Association of Broadcasters
NADS	National Advanced Driving Simulator
NAFPD	North American flat panel display
NAFTA	North American Free Trade Agreement
NAMM	National Association of Music Merchants
NAP	National Academy Press
NAPLPS	North American presentation level protocol syntax
NAS	(1) network application support
	(2) National Academy of Sciences
	(3) network applications services
NASA	National AeroSpace Administration
NB	narrow band
NBC	National Broadcast Corporation
NC	(1) numerical control
	(2) network control
NCB	nickel cadmium battery
NCC	new common carrier
NCL	network control language
NCP	network control protocol
NCSA	National Center for Supercomputing Applications
NDDE	networking enabled dynamic data exchange
NDDK	network device driver kit
NDIS	network driver interface specification
NDK	network development kit
NDS	Netware directory service
NDSU	North Dakota State University
NEDO	New Energy and Industrial Technology Development Organization
NEF	network element function

NET	Norme Européenne de Télécommunications
NetBIOS	network basic input output system
NFS	network file system
NG	no good
NHTSA	National Highway Traffic Safety Administration
Ni-Zn	nickel-zinc
NIB	nickel iron battery
NIC	network interface card
NICAM	near instantaneously companded audio multiplex
NICE	network information and control exchange
NIFTP	network independent file transfer protocol
NIP	non-impact printer
NIST	National Institute of Standards and Technology
NISTEP	National Institute of Science and Technology Policy
NIU	(1) North American ISDN users' forum
	(2) network interface unit
NLM	network loadable module
NLQ	near letter quality
nm	nanometer
NMDA	New Media Development Association
NMI	non-maskable interrupt
NMO	network management option
NMOS	negative channel metal-oxide semiconductor
NN	network node
NNI	network node interface
NOS	network operating system
NPA	Network Printer Alliance
NPEL	noise power emission level
NPU	numeric processing unit
NR	noise reduction
NRC	National Research Council
NREN	National Research and Education Network
NRZ	non-return to zero
NRZI	non return to zero inverse
ns	nanosecond(s)
NSERC	Natural Sciences and Engineering Research Council of Canada
NSF	National Science Foundation
NSP	native signal processing
NT	New Technology
NT1	network termination 1
NT2	network termination 2
NTAS	New Technology advanced server

NTF	no trouble found
NTFS	New Technology file system
NTIS	National Technical Information Service
NTSC	National Television Standards Committee
NTT	Nippon Telegraph and Telephone
NURBS	non-uniform rational B-spline
NVP	nominal velocity of propagation
NVRAM	nonvolatile random access memory
O&M	(1) organization and methods
	(2) operation and maintenance
OASIS	open architecture system integration strategy
OB	outside broadcast
OBC	outside back cover
OCE	open collaborative environment
OCR	(1) optical character recognition
	(2) optical character reader
OCT	octal
ODA/ODIF	open document architecture/open document interchange format
ODBC	open database connectivity
ODD	optical data digitizer
ODI	open datalink interface
ODR	optical document reader
OE-PFF	Optoelectronics Prototype Fabrication Facility
OEM	original equipment manufacturer
OFC	outside front cover
OFR	optical form reading
OIC	optimized image compression
OIS	office information system
OK	okay
OLDT	on-line data transmission
OLE	(1) object linking and embedding
	(2) on-line equipment
OLFREFL	outline font reflection
OLFSHAD	outline font shadow
OLIR	on-line information retrieval
OLTP	on-line transactional processing
OMEGA	open-ended modular electronic graphic arts
OMG	Object Management Group
OMI	open messaging interface
OMR	optical mark reader
OMS	office mail system

ONA	open network architecture
OOS	(1) out of sync
	(2) object oriented software
op.cit.	opere citato (in the work quoted)
OPC	odd parity check
OPI	open prepress interface
opm	operations per minute
OR	(1) optical reader
	(2) orientation ratio
ORNL	Oak Ridge National Laboratory
ORPC	object remote procedure call
ORTA	Office of Research and Technology Application
ortho	orthochromatic
OS	operating system
OS/2	Operating System/2
OSA	(1) open system architecture
	(2) open scripting architecture
OSD	on screen display
OSEP	Office of Special Education Programs
OSF	(1) Open Software Foundation
	(2) operations system function
OSI	(1) Open System Interconnections
	(2) open systems integration
OSTC	Open System Test Consortium
OSTP	Office for Science and Technology
OTA	Office of Technology Assessment
OTP	one time programmable
OTR	one touch timer recording
OTT	Office of Technology Transfer (NIH)
OVPC	odd vertical parity check
oz	ounce
P-P	peak to peak
p.t.o.	please turn over
PABX	private automatic branch exchange
PAC	paging area controller
PAD	packet assembler/disassembler
PADU	package assembling/disassembling unit
PAL	phase alternated line
PALE	Phase alternating line encoding
PAM	pulse amplitude modulation
par.	paragraaf
PARC	Palo Alto Research Center

PAS	performance animation system
PASC	precision adaptive sub-band coding
pat.	patented
PATH	Program on Advanced Technology for the Highway
PAX	private automatic exchange
PBX	private branch exchange
PC	(1) personal computer
	(2) parity check
PCB	printed circuit board
PCC	personal communication computer
PCI	(1) peripheral component interconnect
	(2) personal computer interconnect
	(3) protocol control information
PCL	printer control language
PCM	pulse code modulation
PCMCIA	Personal Computer Memory Card International Organization
PCMS	precision color management system
PCN	personal communication network
PCR	polychromatic color removal
PCS	(1) personal communication system
	(2) personal communication services
PCSA	personal computing systems architecture
PDA	personal digital assistant
PDC	primary domain controller
PDF	portable document file
PDH	plesiochronous digital hierarchy
PDI	product data interchange
PDL	page description language
PDLC	polymer dispersed liquid crystal
PDM	pulse duration modulation
PDS	processor direct slot
PDU	(1) power distribution unit
	(2) protocol data unit
PE	(1) personal electronics
	(2) phase encoding
PEL	picture element
PF	page footing
PFL	pre fade listening
PFM	(1) printer font metrics
	(2) pulse frequency modulation
PGA	professional graphics adapter
PGF	presentation graphics feature

PGR	presentation graphics routines
PH	(1) page heading
	(2) packet handler
PHIGS	programmer's hierarchical interactive graphics standard
PHP	personal handy phone
PI	(1) program identification
	(2) performance index
PIC	personal intelligent communicator
PICT	picture
PIECE	productivity, information, education, creativity, entertainment
PIF	(1) programmable interface
	(2) program information file
PIL	(1) publishing interchange language
	(2) precision in-line
PIM	parallel inference machine
PIMOS	PIM operating system
PIN	personal identification number
PIP	(1) page image processor
	(2) peripheral interchange program
	(3) picture in picture
PISC	parallel instruction set computing
PIXEL	picture element
PJL	printer job language
PLD	programmable logical device
PLL	phase-locked loop
PLMN	public land mobile network
PLV	production level video
PM	(1) photomultiplier
	(2) Presentation Manager
PMA	program memory area
PME	privileged mode extensions
PMH	production per man hour
PMMU	paged memory management unit
PMS	Pantone matching system
PMT	photomechanical transfer
PNC	paging network controller
POD	printing-on-demand
POF	(1) program operator interface
	(2) point of failure
POH	power on hours
POI	point of information
POS	point of sale

POSIX	portable operating system interface
POST	power-on self test
POT	potentiometer
POV	point of view
pp	pages
PPC	(1) portable personal computer
	(2) program-to-program communications
ppH	prints per hour
PPISC	Professional Publishers Interchange Specification
	Committee
ppm	pages per minute
PPM	pulse position modulation
PPP	point to point protocol
PPQN	pulses per quarter note
PPS	page printing system
PQFP	plastic quad flat pack
PR	pseudorandom
PRA	primary rate access
PRBS	pseudorandom binary sequence
PREP	PowerPC reference platform
PREV	previous
PRI	primary rate interface
PRM	protocol reference model
PRMD	private managed domain
PRML	partial-respones maximum likehood
PRN	pseudorandom noise
PROC	procedure
PROLOG	PROgramming in LOGic
PROM	programmable read only memory
PRT	printer
ps	picosecond
PS	(1) presentation services
	(2) programmed symbols
	(3) programmed symbol set
	(4) PostScript
PSDN	packet switched data network
PSE	paper surface efficiency
PSIT	platform stimulering ISDN
PSN	packet switching network
PSPDN	packet switched public data network
PSTN	public switched telephone network
PT	pitch
pt.	point

PTM	pulse time modulation
PU	physical unit
PUS	performance upgrade socket
PWI	public Windows interface
PWM	pulse-width modulation
PWR	power
QA	(1) Q-adapter
	(2) quality analysis
	(3) quality assurance
QAM	quadrature amplitude modulation
QBE	query by example
QC	quality control
QCIF	quarter common intermediate format
QIC	quarter inch cartridge
QL	query language
QOS	quality of service
QPSK	quadrate phase shift keying
QRC	quick reference card
QRG	quick reference guide
QSAM	queued sequential access method
qt.	quart
R	red
R&D	research and development
R-DAT	rotary digital audio tape
R-NRZ-L	randomized nonreturn to zero, level
R/W	read/write
RA	random access
RACE	Research and development Advanced Communication in Europe
RAID	(1) redundant array of inexpensive disks
	(2) retrieval and information database
RAM	random access memory
RB	return to bias
RBOC	regional Bell operating company
RC	(1) rewritable consumer
	(2) remote concentrator
RCC	Range Commanders Council
RCR	Research and development Center for Radio systems
RCV	receive(r)
RDB	relational database
RDBMS	relational database management system

REF	reference
REJ	reject
REM	remark
REP	(1) repeat
	(2) resolution enhancement procedure
REPROM	reprogrammable read only memory
REQ	request
RES	reserve
RET	(1) resolution enhancement technology
	(2) return
RETMA	Radio Electronics and Television Manufacturers Association
REV	reverse
REW	rewind
REXX	restructured extended executor
RFA	remote file access
RFP	request for proposal
RGB	red, green, blue
RH	relative humidity
RIC	radio identity code
RIFF	resource interchange file format
RIP	(1) raster image processor
	(2) remote imaging protocol
RIS	ruimtelijk informatie systeem
RISC	reduced instruction set computer
RIT	raad voor informatie technologie
RITE	Research Institute for Innovative Technology for the Earth
RLE	run-length encoded
RLL	run length limited
RMI	resource manager interface
RMS	root mean square
RMT	remote
RMV	remove
RO	read only
ROD	rewritable optical disc
ROM	read only memory
ROP	run of press
ROS	real-time operating system
RP	rapid prototyping
RPC	remote procedure call
rpm	(1) revolutions per minute
	(2) rotations per minute

RPROM	reprogrammable read only memory
RPS	rapid prototyping system
rps	revolutions per second
RSU	remote switching unit
RTF	rich text format
RTMP	routing table maintenance protocol
RTOS	real time operating system
RTS	request to send
RTV	real-time video
RVA	recorded voice announcement
RW	read-write
RWC	(1) read write calibration
	(2) real world computing
RWD	rewind
RWW	read-while-writing
RZ	return to zero
S-VGA	super video graphics array
S-VHS	super video home system
S/F	store and forward
S/N	signal-to-noise ratio
S/O	send only
S/PDIF	Sony/Philips digital interface
s/s	same size
SA	selective availability
SAA	systems application architecture
SAE	Society of Automotive Engineers
SANE	standard Apple numeric extension
SAS	statistical analysis system
SAV	start of active video
SAW	surface acoustic wave
SBDC	Small Business Development Center
sc	single column
SCANDI	surveillance, control and driver information system
SCART	Syndicat des Constructeurs d'Appareils, Radiorécepteurs et Téléviseurs
SCCP	signalling connection control part
SCI VIS	scientific visualization
SCMS	serial copy master system
SCP	service control point
SCSI	small computer system interface
SDA	(1) screen design aid
	(2) sense data included

SDF	(1) screen definition facility
	(2) serial data field
SDH	synchronous digital hierarchy
SDI	serial digital interface
SDK	software development kit
SDLC	synchronous data link control
SDM	system development methodology
SDP	structured data processing
SDU	service data unit
SDVN	switched digital video network
SEC	second(s)
SECAM	Séquentiel Couleur à Memoire
SECT	sector
SEG	(1) segment
	(2) special effects generator
SEL	select
SEM	(1) scanning electronic microscopy
	(2) semiconductor manufacturing, testing and materials
SEP	separate
SER	satellite equipment room
SES	Société Européenne des Satellites
SFBI	shared frame buffer interconnect
SFD	switching field distribution
SFT	system fault tolerant
SFX	(1) sound effects
	(2) special effects
SGML	Standard Generalized Markup Language
SHD	super high definition
SHF	super high frequency
SI	(1) Système International d'Unités
	(2) system information
	(3) the shift-in character
Si	silicium
SIA	Semiconductor Industry Association
SID	symbolic instruction debugger
SIDF	system independent data format
SIG	(1) signal
	(2) special interest group
SIMM	single inline memory module
SIMNET	simulation network
SIP	single inline package
SIU	system input unit
SL	service layer

SLSI	super large scale integration
SMAE	systems management application entity
SMAP	systems management application process
SMB	(1) service message block
	(2) storage module drive
SMC	sheet molding compound
SMDS	multimegabit data service
SME	Society of Manufacturing Engineers
SMF	standard MIDI file
SMM	system management mode
SMP	symmetrical multiprocessing
SMPTE	Society of Motion Picture and Television Engineers
SMS	(1) storage management services
	(2) service management system
SMT	surface mounting technologies
SMTP	simple mail transfer protocol
SNA	systems networks architecture
SNMP	simple network management protocol
SNOS	super network operating system
SNR	signal-to-noise ratio
SOA	semiconductor optical amplifier
SOF	sound on film
SOHO	small office home office
SOM	(1) start of message
	(2) system object model
SONET	synchronous optical network
SOT	sound on tape
SP	standard play
SPA	Software Publishers Association
SPEC	specification
SPG	sync pulse generator
SPIE	Society of Photo-Optical Instrumentation Engineers
SPL	sound pressure level
Spool	simultaneous peripheral operation on line
SPP	song position pointer
SPX	sequenced packet exchange
sq.	square
SQA	software quality assurance
SQL	structured query language
SRAM	static random-access memory
SRI	Stanford Research Institute
SS/DD	single sided/double density
SS/ND	single sided/normal density

SSD	solid state disk
SSDL	storage structure definition language
SSI	small scale integration
SSP	service switching point
STA	Science and Technology Agency
STAIRS	storage and information retrieval system
START	system for analysis, research and training
STL	stereo lithography
STM	(1) scanning tunneling microscopy
	(2) synchronous transfer mode
	(3) synchronous transport module
STN	super twisted nematic
STP	(1) shielded twisted pair
	(2) signal transfer point
STRICOM	simulation, training and instrumentation command
SUB	subaddressing
SUBST	substitute
SVD	simultaneous voice/data
SWDT	synchronization word detect time
SWIFT	Society for Worldwide Interbank Financial Transactions
SYNC	synchronous
sync	synchronization
SYS	system
SysEx	system exclusive
SYSGEN	system generation
T	tera (1000,000,000)
TA	terminal adaptor
TAA	track average amplitude
TAB	tabulate
TalAE	Taligent application environment
TalDE	Taligent development environment
TalOS	Taligent object services
TAPI	telephone application programming interface
TASI	time assignment speech interpolation
TB	terabyte
Tb	terabit
TBC	time base corrector
TBE	time base error
TBF	time between failure
TC	(1) telecommunication
	(2) Technical Committee
	(3) transaction capabilities

TCal	thermal calibration
TCC	transmission control character
TCP	terminal control program
TCP/IP	transmission control protocol/internet protocol
tcysitcyg	the-color-you-see-is-the-color-you-get
TDM	time division multiplex
TDMA	time division multiple access
TDP	transactional data processing
TDR	time-domain reflectometer
TDT	telephonic data transmission
TE	terminal equipment
TE1	terminal equipment 1 ISDN
TE2	terminal equipment 2 non ISDN
TELEX	teletype exchange
TEMP	(1) temperature
	(2) temporary
TEPCO	Tokyo Electric Power Company
TFT	(1) thin film technology
	(2) thin film transistor
TFTP	trivial file transfer protocol
TGA	truevision Targa
THD	total harmonic distortion
THIC	Tape Head Interface Committee
TI	tone index
TIA	Telecommunications Industry Association
TIFF	tagged image file format
TIGA	Texas Instruments graphics architecture
TIGER	topologically integrated geographic coding and referencing
TIRIS	Texas Instruments Registration and Identification System
TLA	three letter acronym
TM	Turing machine
TMN	telecommunications management network
TMSF	times, minutes, seconds and frames
TOC	table of content
TOHO	tiny office home office
TOP	technical and office protocol
TOS	(1) tape operating system
	(2) Tramiel operating system
TP	(1) teleprocessing
	(2) terminal portability
TPA	transient program area

TPC	text processing center
TPD	tape packing density
tpi	tracks per inch
TPM	third party maintenance
TPS	tape program search
TQC	total quality control
TQM	(1) task queue management
	(2) total quality management
TRN	token ring-network
TRS	time reference signal
TSAPI	telephony service application interface
Tsapi	telephony services applications programming interface
TSCL	time sharing command language
TSO	time sharing option
TSR	terminate and stay resident
TSS	time sharing system
TSTN	triple super twisted nematic
TTE	transient tape errors
TTFN	ta-ta-for-now (goodbye)
TTL	(1) trough the lens
	(2) transistor-transistor logic
TTP	tape-to-printer
TTS	teletypesetter
TU	tape unit
TUP	telephone user part
TWA	terminal working area
TWAIN	technology without an important name
TXT	text
U&LC	upper case and lower case
UAE	unrecoverable application error
UART	universal asynchronous receiver/transmitter
UBE	upper band edge
UC	upper case
UCA	under color addition
UCC	universal classification system
UCR	under color removal
UCS	(1) universal character set
	(2) uniform chromaticness scale
UD	ultra density
UDC	universal decimal classification
UDP	user datagram protocol
UDTV	ultra high definition television

UHF	ultra high frequency
ULSI	ultra large scale integration
UMA	upper memory area
UMB	upper memory block
UNA	universal network architecture
UNC	University of North Carolina
UND	University of North Dakota
UNI	user-network interface
UNIX	uniform executive
UNO	universal network object
UPC	universal product code
UPD	update
UPS	uninterruptable power supply
URN	universal resource name
USC	United States Code
USCEA	US Council for Energy Awareness
USDC	US display consortium
USERID	user indentification
USITC	US International Trade Commission
USL	Unix System Laboratories
USM	unsharp masking
USPTO	US Patent and Trademark Office
UTC	universal teletex controller
UTIL	utility
UTP	unshielded twisted pair
UTS	ultimedia tools series
UUCP	Unix-to-Unix copy program
UUS	user-to-user signaling
UV	ultraviolet
UVPROM	ultraviolet programmable read-only memory
V	(1) version
	(2) volt
VA	(1) voltampere
	(2) video amplifier
VAFC	VESA advanced feature connector
VAN	(1) value added network
	(2) vehicle area network
VANS	value added network services
VAP	(1) value added proces
	(2) video access point
VAR	value added reseller
VAT	value added tax

VBR	variable area network
VBR	variable bit rate
VC	(1) video conferencing
	(2) virtual container
VCA	video capture adapter
VCE	visual color efficiency
VCO	voltage-controlled oscillator
VCPI	virtual control program interface
VCR	video cassette recorder
VCS	virtual computing system
VDD	virtual device driver
VDE	vertical doping engineering
VDI	video display interface
VDS	video direct slot
VDT	video display terminal
VDU	video display unit
VE	virtual environment
VEMM	virtual expanded memory manager
VER	version
VESA	Video Electronics Standard Association
VFN	vendor feature node
VfW	video for Windows
VGA	(1) video graphics array
	(2) visual graphics adaptor
VHD	very high density
VHF	very high frequency
VHS	video home system
VICS	vehicle information communication system
VIEWS	virtual environment workstation
VIM	vendor independent messaging
VIP	visual image processor
VIR	vertical interval reference
VIS	(1) video information system
	(2) voice identification system
VISCA	video system control architecture
VITC	vertical interval time code
VITS	vertical interval test signal
VKC	verkeerscentrale
VI&P	visual, intelligent & personal
VLF	very low frequency
VLMF	very low magnetic field
VLP	video long play
VLS	very long shot

VLSI	very large scale integration
VLT	video lookup table
VM	(1) virtual machine
	(2) virtual memory
VMC	VESA media channel
VMEC	Voice Messaging Education Committee
VMS	(1) virtual memory system
	(2) voice message system
VO	vedi originale (see copy)
VOGAD	voice-operated gain-adjusting device
VOL	volume
vol.	volume
VPC	voice processing computer
VPN	virtual private network
VR	virtual reality
VRAM	video random access memory
VRC	vertical redundancy check
VRS	virtual retinal scanning
VRT	voice response terminal
VRU	voice response unit
VS/OS	virtual storage operating system
VSAM	virtual storage access method
VSAT	very small aperture terminal
VSDT	very small device technology
VT2	variable thermal transfer
VTAM	virtual telecommunications access method
VTP	virtual terminal program
VTR	video tape recorder
VU	volume unit
VUE	visual user environment
VxDS	virtual device drivers
W	Watt
W3C	World Wide Web Consortium
WABI	Windows applications binary interface
WAN	wide area network
WAPI	Windows application programming interfaces
WBC	wide band channel
WFW	Windows for workgroups
Wh	watt hour
WIMP	windows, icons, mouse and pulldown menus
WIN	wireless inner network
WIPO	World Intellectual Property Organization

WMF	Windows meta file
WMRM	write multiple, read multiple
WOM	write only memory
WON	wireless outer network
WORM	write once, read many
WOSA	Windows open services architecture
wpm	words per minute
WPMA	Windows and Presentation Manager Association
WSF	workstation function
WVP	wireless voice platform
WWR	write while read
WWW	world wide web
WYNIWYG	what you need is what you get
WYSIWYG	what you see is what you get
WYSYHYG	what you see you hope you get
X-OFF	transmitter off
X-ON	transmitter on
XA	extended architecture
XAPIA	X.400 api association
XGA	extended Graphics Adapter
XIP	execute in place
XIS	Xerox imaging system
XMS	extended memory specification
XPG	X/open portability guide
XSMD	extended storage module drive interface
Y	yellow
yd	yard
YMC	yellow, magenta and cyan
YMCK	yellow, magenta, cyan and black
YUV	intensity, hue and value
ZAB	zinc air battery